ELITES AND DEMOCRACY

Elites and Democracy

HUGO DROCHON

PRINCETON UNIVERSITY PRESS
PRINCETON & OXFORD

Published by Princeton University Press
41 William Street, Princeton, New Jersey 08540
99 Banbury Road, Oxford OX2 6JX

press.princeton.edu

GPSR Authorized Representative: Easy Access System Europe - Mustamäe tee 50, 10621 Tallinn, Estonia, gpsr.requests@easproject.com

All Rights Reserved

ISBN 978-0-691-18155-4
ISBN (e-book) 978-0-691-27983-1

Library of Congress Control Number: 2025942394

British Library Cataloging-in-Publication Data is available

Editorial: Ben Tate and Josh Drake
Production Editorial: Jenny Wolkowicki
Jacket design: Chris Ferrante
Production: Danielle Amatucci
Publicity: James Schneider and Kathryn Stevens
Copyeditor: Bhisham Bherwani

This book has been composed in Arno

Printed in the United States of America

10 9 8 7 6 5 4 3 2 1

Ever tried. Ever failed. No matter. Try again. Fail again. Fail better.

—SAMUEL BECKETT, 'WORSTWARD HO'

CONTENTS

This is, undeniably, a scholarly work. Yet the notion of democracy as a perpetual struggle, never to be achieved, is something that can be universally grasped. The aim of this book is to offer a systematic account of that intuition.

ACKNOWLEDGEMENTS

MY FIRST encounter with the 'elite' theorists of democracy was during a final year undergraduate course, 'Contemporary Political Theories', with James 'Eddie' Hyland at Trinity College, Dublin, 2002–2003 (I take this opportunity to thank my friends from this period, James Brady, Ian Carroll, Nigel Clarke, Mark Jones, Sarah Lewis and Ruadhán Mac Cormaic). If the meeting with Nietzsche a couple of years earlier had set off intellectual fireworks, reading Mosca, Pareto and Michels had the effect of a cold shower: democracy, so it seemed, could never live up to its ideal of people-rule. Instead, the elites (always) rule. My second 'cold shower' came when confronted with John Dunn's *Western Political Theory in the Face of the Future* during my doctoral studies at Cambridge. Instead of abstract ideals we comfort ourselves with, what, indeed, can political theory teach us about the world we live in? On Dunn's account, characteristically, not much.

This book is an attempt to address both these challenges. It has two central questions. One: what can democracy be if the elites always rule? And two: what can political theory teach us about democracy? The answer to the second question is found in the first: to start to give a useful account of democracy we must start with the reality of elite rule. In this I am encouraged by the fact that Dunn, in the meanderings of a conversation, agreed that it was the right place to start. The answer to the first question is one I have tried to develop under the rubric of 'dynamic democracy': that if elites always rule, then democracy must be understood as the perpetual challenge to that rule.

In this endeavour, I have been singularly privileged to have had a number of superlative mentors. First in the list must be David Runciman, to whom I owe the possibility of an academic career at all. It is thanks to his guidance that I was recruited on the 'Conspiracy and Democracy' research project at CRASSH, Cambridge, and I was particularly encouraged when, after my having presented Michels' metaphor of democracy as a buried treasure in the field in one of our infamous Wednesday morning discussion groups, he turned to me to say that was his concept of democracy too. Unending thanks must also go to Richard Evans, for admitting he had worked on 'he who shall not be named' after all, and John Naughton, who precipitated my journalistic writing. My fellow postdocs should be thanked too, Tanya Filer, Rolf Fredheim, Rachel Hoffman and Hugo Leal, and especially those of the 'terrible four' quartet, of which I had the honour of being a member, Nayanika Mathur, Andrew McKenzie-McHarg and Alfred Moore.

Since 2018 I've been teaching politics at the University of Nottingham, first as an Assistant, now as an Associate Professor of Political Theory; to it I am eternally indebted for having offered me the chance of a permanent career in academia. The School of Politics has been a welcoming home in an increasingly managerial environment, with wonderful colleagues including Caitlin Milazzo, Andreas Bieler, Rory Cormac, David Gill, Paul Heywood, Jan-Hinrik Meyer-Sahling, Bettina Renz, Tony Burns, Cees van der Eijk, Fernando Casal Bertoa, Pauline Eadie, Andreas Fulda, Catherine Gegout, Gulshan Khan, Chun-Yi Lee, Helen McCabe, Scott Moser, Carole Spary, Jonathan Sullivan, Neema Begum, Louise Kettle and Matthew Rendall. Katharine Adeney, Mathew Humphrey, Todd Landman and David Stevens all served on my selection committee, so my sincerest gratitude to them for placing their faith in me; Andrew Mumford cheerfully chaperoned me around during the interview and Wyn Rees kindly welcomed me as Head of School. The most important mention, however, must go to notorious 'Pie Night' group, first and foremost its founders Steven Fielding and Ben Holland, who were my first friends at Nottingham, and its stalwarts Will Daniel, Simon Toubeau, Siim Trumm, Eloise Bertrand, Michaela Collard, Kevin Fahey, Carl Gibson, Jason Klocek, Adam Lindsay, Dan Lomas, Stephen Meek and Ellen Watts. Steve is now happily retired, but Ben and his husband Gary have kindly hosted me over the last few years, and our early-morning coffee chats with Ben are some of my happiest times at Nottingham. Recently, a new cohort of political theorists—Blake Ewing, Sean Fleming and Diana Popescu—has joined us, and we are thrilled to welcome their new ideas and energy.

I've had the great fortune that numerous venues and people have given their time to discuss this project. Chief amongst them was the book manuscript workshop organised by the History of Political Thought Project at the University Center for Human Values at Princeton University on the 9 December 2022. Special thanks must go first and foremost to Jan-Werner Müller for hosting the workshop, and indeed much else beside. My deepest gratitude goes to the discussants Joshua Cherniss, Gregory Conti, Lisa Disch, Melissa Lane, John

Medearis, Pratap Mehta, Nadia Urbinati, David Ragazzoni and Lucia Rubine-lli, who helped put the manuscript on the final tracks.

The workshop occurred during a Visiting Fellowship at the Remarque Institute at NYU, where my special thanks go to Stefanos Geroulanos for being such a congenial host. I also had the great fortune of spending a term at the EUI in 2021 as a Visiting Fellow thanks to Nicolas Guilhot, with whom I look forward to conspiring on future projects. In 2018 I spent a wonderful term at the MacMillan Center at Yale, and am thankful for the great conversations there with Bryan Garsten, Helene Landemore, Mordechai Levy-Eichel, Karuna Mantena, Giulia Oskian, Andrew Sabl, Ian Shapiro, Steven Smith and Joy Wang. Finally, I was able to spend time at the Centre Raymond Aron at the EHESS back in the spring of 2015, where I was able to deepen my knowledge of Aron and his legacy thanks to Marcel Gauchet, Pierre Manent, the late Bernard Manin, Sophie Marcotte Chénard and Giulio di Ligio.

Various papers relating to the project, at different stages of elaboration, were presented at APSA, MANCEPT, Columbia, Georgetown, NYU, Cambridge, Sheffield, New Delhi and Lisbon, and I am thankful to all the organisers and participants at those venues. They saved me from a number of mistakes; as is customary to say, those that remain are my own. As is also customary to say, I have obviously not been able to name individually everyone who should be thanked, but I hope they find themselves in these acknowledgements nevertheless.

Ben Tate at Princeton University Press, alongside his assistant Josh Drake, has been a model of the benevolent editor, in league with his US counterpart Rob Tempio, to whom I send all my warmest affections. The manuscript reader's report were the dream combination of encouragement and suggestions, fundamentally grasping what was at stake, and I am deeply grateful to them both: John Medearis and, again, Nadia Urbinati, to whom I am doubly indebted. The broader PUP team must be thanked here too: Jenny Wolkowicki for masterfully steering the manuscript through to production, Bhisham Bherwani for the elegant copy-editing, Chris Ferrante for the striking jacket design, Danielle Amatucci for the production, and James Schneider and Kathryn Stevens for the publicity.

I would like to thank Bernard Blistene, Marie-Laure Verroust and Lily Blistene, my *belle famille*. Deepest thanks, of course, go to my family: my parents Tommy and Annie, my sister Maud, her husband Chris, my nephews and niece Scott, Thomas and Lara, and my aunt Annie-Marie Wagnon. No amount of words can record my debt to them.

Most importantly, my greatest debt goes to my life-partner Pauline Blistene and to our very own dancing star Oscar, who graced us with his presence last year. He is *a new beginning, a game, a self-rolling wheel, a first movement*. This book is dedicated to him.

Chapter 3 appeared in a modified version as 'Robert Michels, the Iron Law of Oligarchy and Dynamic Democracy', *Constellations*, Vol. 27, No. 2, 2020, pp. 185–198 and chapter 6 as 'Raymond Aron's "Machiavellian" Liberalism', *Journal of the History of Ideas*, Vol. 80, No. 4, 2019, pp. 621–642.

Introduction

ON 23 JUNE 2016 the United Kingdom voted to leave the European Union. According to leading Brexiteer Michael Gove, the people had 'had enough of experts'.[1] At the October Conservative Party conference, the then Prime Minister Theresa May denounced the 'rootless cosmopolitan' international elite. Later that year, on 8 November, Donald Trump was elected president of the United States, having promised to take on the 'DC establishment' to chants of 'drain the swamp'. 2017 saw a wave of populist politicians in Europe, from the far-left to the far-right (think of France's Marine Le Pen or Jean-Luc Mélenchon, the Italian Five Star Movement, the German AFD), denounce the EU's 'Eurocratic elite': Viktor Orbàn, the original Hungarian anti-EU provocateur, had already been elected to office in a landslide election in 2010.[2] The Covid-19 pandemic was blamed on Bill Gates, the founder of Microsoft, who (allegedly) wanted to implant us all with microchips, and the financier George Soros, in a return to classic antisemitism.[3] And all this before we even look at the rise of Narendra Modi in India in 2014, Rodrigo Duterte's success in the Philippines in 2016, Jair Bolsonaro's—the 'Trump of the Tropics'—election in Brazil in 2019 and Javier 'El Loco' Milei's taking the Argentinian presidency in 2023. Today Trump is in his second term at the White House, Modi is still in power, Le Pen is preparing her third tilt at the French Presidency, Georgia Meloni is

---

1. Henry Mance, 'Britain Has Had Enough of Experts, Says Gove', *Financial Times*, 3 June 2016 (https://www.ft.com/content/3be49734-29cb-11e6-83e4-abc22d5d108c accessed on 4 March 2024).

2. Hugo Drochon, 'Between the Lions and the Foxes', *New Statesman*, 13 January 2017.

3. Hugo Drochon, 'The Conspiratorial Style in Pandemic Politics', *Project Syndicate*, 1 May 2020.

Prime Minister of Italy, and Brexit continues to upturn British society, economics and politics. We live in the age of the revolt against the elites.[4]

Populism has been the main lens through which this phenomenon has been interpreted.[5] It has brought many insights to light: how populists claim to speak for the 100% or the 'real' people; the structuring of politics into an 'us versus them' of a 'pure people' against a 'corrupt elite'; the highly-charged and conspiratorial nature of political discourse. Yet, whilst populists all reject the 'elite', they are often themselves elites. Indeed, most theories of populism emphasise the visceral link followers have with their populist leaders. If Trump in 2016 was no doubt a political outsider, he is also part of the 1%—the economic elite— and a media personality through his show *The Apprentice*. Nigel Farage, leader of the Brexit Party (now Reform UK), is a wealthy former stockbroker and was a Member of the European Parliament (MEP), ironically at that time elected to the institution he wanted to leave. Boris Johnson, whose rallying to the Leave cause got it over the line, is a quintessential product of the British establishment (Eton, Oxford). Le Pen junior is the daughter of Le Pen senior, the founder of the *Front National*, and whatever Meloni claims about being an 'outsider', she has been a member of the Italian political class since 2006, and even served in Silvio Berlusconi's 2008 government as the Minister for Youth. Similar things might be said of Modi, Duterte and Bolsonaro.

Populist politics, then, is the process of replacing one elite with another. Mainstream politicians like Barack Obama and David Cameron have been replaced by populist leaders like Trump and Johnson. There seems to be a paradox here, as populism and elitism are often thought to be opposites: populism pitting a 'pure people' against a 'corrupt elite'; elitism setting an enlightened elite against the squabbling masses.[6] Yet here they go hand in hand:

---

4. For a work that anticipates such a revolt, see the—aptly inversely titled—Christopher Lasch, *The Revolt of the Elites and the Betrayal of Democracy*, New York, W. W. Norton, 1996. See also, from a different perspective, José Ortega y Gasset, *The Revolt of the Masses*, New York, W. W. Norton, 1993.

5. Jan-Werner Müller, *What Is Populism?*, Philadelphia, University of Pennsylvania Press, 2016; Cas Mudde and Cristóbal Rovira Kaltwasser, *Populism: A Very Short Introduction*, Oxford, Oxford University Press, 2017; Federico Finchelstein, *From Fascism to Populism in History*, Berkeley, University of California Press, 2017. For the most original—and positive—theory of populism, see Ernesto Laclau, *On Populist Reason*, London, Verso, 2005.

6. Marte Mangset, Fredrik Engelstad, Mari Teigen and Trygve Gulbrandsen, 'The Populist Elite Paradox: Using Elite Theory to Elucidate the Shapes and Stakes of Populist Elite Critiques', *Comparative Social Research*, Vol. 34, 2019, pp. 203–222.

they are mirror images of one another. And the political end-result is the same: in both cases one elite replaces another.

If populism is a form of (non-pluralistic) democracy, then the same might be said of elitism. After all, aren't elections—the key democratic institution—simply one way of replacing one elite with another? In democratic theory, theorists such as Joseph Schumpeter and Robert Dahl, who both focus on elections, retain an undeniable elitist hue: it is either 'elite competition' or 'polyarchy'—i.e. 'control of elites'—respectively.[7] So neither in theory nor in practice do democracy and elitism appear to be in tension. Quite the contrary.

If the relationship elites entertain with democracy is no doubt a burning issue, it has been raised before. How can the fact that a small number of people wield disproportionate power in economic, social or political spheres be reconciled with democracy understood as political equality? At the turn of the twentieth century three key thinkers—Gaetano Mosca (1858–1941), Vilfredo Pareto (1848–1923) and Robert Michels (1876–1936)—were the first to grapple with the problem of democratic elites in a specifically modern setting, one characterised by the spread of universal suffrage and the rise of the mass, centralised, bureaucratic party to organise it. That context—universal suffrage and political parties—is still the context we operate in today, so that although much has undeniably changed, in many ways that setting, and its problems, remain our own. Indeed, many of the terms they coined—'ruling class' (Mosca), 'circulation of elites' (Pareto) and the 'iron law of oligarchy' (Michels)—is still the language we use to try to articulate our contemporary politics.

These theorists were the first to posit that modern democracy is in fact a façade behind which elites rule. Whilst Marxists had been theorising the state as the 'executive arm of the bourgeoisie' since the mid-nineteenth century, what marked these thinkers out was their rejection of the belief that democracy—in the sense of the people *actually* ruling—could ever be achieved, even after a proletarian revolution: we could never pass, as Friedrich Engels (borrowing from Saint-Simon) put it, from the 'government of people' to the 'administration of things'. As such, they were explicitly anti-Marxist thinkers, especially Mosca and Pareto, although Michels' relation to Marxism is more complicated, as we shall see.[8]

---

7. Joseph Schumpeter, *Capitalism, Socialism and Democracy*, London, Routledge, 2010; Robert Dahl, *Democracy and Its Critics*, New Haven, Yale University Press, 1989.

8. Geraint Parry, *Political Elites*, Colchester, ECPR Press, 2005, pp. 24–27.

Mosca was the *primo uomo* of the group: he developed an historical and political theory of elite rule in *The Ruling Class* (1896), which claimed that all but the most primitive societies are ruled by a governing minority. Hot on his heels—they were to have a *prima donna* debate over who first came up with the notion—Pareto sketched his theory of the 'circulation of elites' in *Les systèmes socialistes* (1902), which he more fully worked out in his 1-million-word and 3,000-page behemoth *Trattato di sociologia generale* (1916), in which he tried to lay the foundations for an all-encompassing psycho-scientific account of the world. Indeed, it is to Pareto that we owe the term 'elite' as we use it today.[9] And although Pareto was ten years Mosca's senior, priority here is given to the latter because *The Ruling Class* predates Pareto's *Systèmes socialistes*.

After Mosca and Pareto, the task of applying the concept of elite rule to a new phenomenon of modern politics, namely the highly centralised, bureaucratic and disciplined mass party, was left to Michels, which he (maintaining a friendship with both the theorists, a feat in itself) completed by theorising the 'iron law of oligarchy' in his masterpiece *Political Parties* (1911).[10] Together, the three are known as the 'elite theorists of democracy', although they have gone by other appellations too: 'Machiavellians', 'sociological pessimists', the 'Italian School' and 'theorists of minority domination'.[11]

I: Elite theory

The aim of this book is threefold. The first—what might be described as the history of political thought claim—is to recover the thinking of the three theorists within their historical contexts to see what resources they might offer us to conceptualise the relation elites entertain with democracy today. There is a tendency in the literature, from Dahl to more recently Nadia Urbinati, Jeffrey Winters and Jeffrey Green, to lump all three into a 'Mosca, Pareto and Michels'

9. Tom Bottomore, *Élites and Society*, London, Routledge, 1993, p. 1.

10. If the terms 'ruling class', 'elite' and 'oligarchy' are used here interchangeably as forms of minority domination, it is because the point of this study is to explore the different functions and senses of each theory in its own right.

11. S. M. Lipset, 'Introduction' to Robert Michels, *Political Parties: A Sociological Study of the Oligarchic Tendencies of Modern Democracy*, New York, The Free Press, 1962, p. 33; James Burnham, *The Machiavellians, Defenders of Freedom*, New York, John Day, 1943; Juan Linz, *Robert Michels, Political Sociology, and the Future of Democracy*, New Brunswick, Transaction Publishers, 2006; Ettore Albertoni, *Mosca and the Theory of Elitism*, Oxford, Basil Blackwell, 1987; Dahl, *Democracy and Its Critics*.

triumvirate.[12] Yet each had their own, individual, emphases: Mosca developed a narrower historical and political theory of the *classe politica*,[13] whereas Pareto offered an all-encompassing system of human society and activity through his notion of the 'circulation of elites'.[14] Neither, however, offered a systematic account of the modern political party—it is revealing that in his long review of Michels' *Political Parties*, Mosca just saw it as the confirmation of his own thesis, rather than a novel application to an institution he had overlooked[15]— which Michels did through his notion of the 'iron law of oligarchy'. If for Mosca history was the reference point, for Pareto it was economics and for Michels social classes.

Their contexts were different too. Mosca was a Sicilian politician, journalist and political theorist who made the best of the opportunities Italian Unification offered him, whereas Pareto was a Franco-Italian heir to a Genoese Marquis, best known for his economic theories such as 'Pareto efficiency' or 'Pareto distribution'. Michels was German, close to Max Weber, whose context was Imperial Germany and the rise of the German socialist party, the SPD, which he analysed. Both Pareto and Michels were influenced by Sorel.[16] If Mosca and Pareto were liberals—Mosca a 'conservative-liberal' and Pareto a 'free-market' liberal but with social tendencies—Michels was a committed socialist, at least at the time of writing his masterpiece, on the anarcho-syndicalist wing of the movement. This coloured Michels' critique of the SPD, and he would later switch to supporting Mussolini after his move to Italy, believing 'charisma' to be the only way to overcome the 'iron law'.[17] Yet in the

12. Dahl, *Democracy and Its Critics*; Nadia Urbinati, *Democracy Disfigured: Opinion, Truth, and the People*, Cambridge (MA), Harvard University Press, 2014; Jeffrey Winters, *Oligarchy*, Cambridge, Cambridge University Press, 2011; Jeffrey Green, *The Eyes of the People: Democracy in the Age of Spectatorship*, Oxford, Oxford University Press.

13. H. Stuart Hughes, 'Gaetano Mosca and the Political Lessons of History' in James Meisel, ed., *Pareto and Mosca*, Englewood Cliffs, Prentice-Hall, p. 151.

14. Charles Powers, 'Introduction' in Vilfredo Pareto, *The Transformation of Democracy*, New Brunswick, Transaction Publishers, 2009, p. 1.

15. Gaetano Mosca, 'La sociologia del partito politico nella democrazia moderna', *Partiti e Sindacati nella crisi del regime parlamentare*, Bari Laterza, 1949, pp. 26–36.

16. For Pareto, see Norberto Bobbio, 'Introduction to Pareto's Sociology' in *On Mosca and Pareto*, Geneva, Droz, 1972, pp. 68–69; for Michels, see Andrew Bonnell, *Robert Michels, Socialism and Modernity*, Oxford, Oxford University Press, 2023, pp. 6–9.

17. Francesca Antonini, 'Between Weber and Mussolini: The Issue of Political Leadership in the Thought of the Late Michels', *Intellectual History Review*, Vol. 34, No. 4, 2024, pp. 773–790.

conclusion of his 1911 edition of *Political Parties*, he defended a view of democracy that could be saved from within.

They also differed in temperament. Mosca was a moderate, and the image we have of him is of a moustached, world-weary paterfamilias, who nevertheless retained an 'ebullient Mediterranean good humour'.[18] Pareto, on the other hand, started his life as an aristocratic, liberal firebrand, to finish it as a recluse in the Swiss mountains surrounded by his cats. Michels was the quintessential '*Gesinnungsethiker*' who would serve as his friend Weber's model for the 'ethic of conviction'. Whilst all three can be styled as 'acerbic' and 'sophisticated', 'cool' is not exactly how one might describe Michels or the young Pareto, as Albert Hirschman famously depicted those who propounded the 'futility thesis' in *The Rhetoric of Reaction*.[19]

Although the 'elitist' epithet has been ascribed to them, it would be a mistake to understand them as somehow defending the status quo. In reality all three were highly critical of the elites of their day. Longing for a return of the Historical Right, Mosca deplored the corruption of the new Left leaders of the day, and made his last speech before the Italian Senate denouncing Mussolini, after which he promptly retired: his ideal was for a new, expert, cultivated and financially independent 'middle class'—of which he was a representative—to take over Italian politics. Pareto condemned 1920s Italy as a 'demagogic plutocracy' and wished to see a new elite rise up to challenge it, whilst Michels rejected the leaders of the German Social Democratic Party, the SPD, at the time the richest, most numerous and most powerful socialist party in the world, as being insufficiently revolutionary. All three defended ideas that today can be understood as democratic: Mosca the representative system grounded in a liberal and pluralist notion of 'juridical defence'; Pareto an 'open elite', regularly replenished by the best elements rising from below; and Michels how 'democracy' offered two 'palliatives' against the 'iron law of oligarchy', namely that it honed the intellectual abilities of the masses so that they might better hold their political rulers to account, and that the development of competing elites in other fields would effectively hold the different elites in check.

---

18. James Meisel, *The Myth of the Ruling Class: Gaetano Mosca and the Elite*, Ann Arbor, University of Michigan Press, 1962, p. 19 and H. Stuart Hughes, 'Gaetano Mosca and the Political Lessons of History', p. 144. On the liberal temperament, see Joshua Cherniss, *Liberalism in Dark Times: The Liberal Ethos in the Twentieth Century*, Princeton, Princeton University Press, 2021.

19. Albert Hirschman, *The Rhetoric of Reaction: Perversity, Futility, Jeopardy*, Cambridge (MA), Harvard University Press, 1991, pp. 43, 51.

Natasha Piano has recently argued that instead of 'elite theorists of democracy', Mosca, Pareto and Michels might best be understood, in a happy turn of phrase, as 'democratic theorists of elitism'.[20] Following in the footsteps of McCormick's 'populist' reading of Machiavelli, which places him squarely on the side of the plebs in their struggles against the patricians,[21] this reading of the 'Machiavellians' is reminiscent of Rousseau's footnote about Machiavelli's *Prince* in *The Social Contract*: that Machiavelli's 'mirror of princes' should not be understood as a handbook for rulers but instead reveals to the population the dark arts of rulership so that the people might better resist their overlords or indeed overthrow them.[22]

This is not the position adopted here. First of all, the reading of Machiavelli one gets from someone like Raymond Aron, whom we shall be exploring, is rather on the 'liberal' side of the interpretation, seeing liberty as emerging from the struggle—the 'tumult'—between the plebs and the patricians, a position he will attribute to Mosca. Although she is critical of elections, Piano nevertheless wants to retain them but to supplement them 'beyond the ballot'. Mosca, Pareto and Michels certainly doubted elections produced anything other than another form of elite rule, were interested in democracy 'beyond the ballot', and, as we have just seen, rejected the 'demagogic plutocratic' elites of their day. But the key difference is that they still affirmed the existence of elites, and selectively endorsed some of them. So the question for them was rather: what could—and *should*—democracy mean in this setting of elite rule? Whatever that was meant to be, it had to start with the empirical 'fact' of the existence of elites, and take it from there.

II: Democratic Theory

The second claim—one in intellectual history—is that we cannot understand the development of the twentieth century, in Europe and America, without reference to these 'elite' thinkers. This is valid for both democratic theory and the social sciences more generally. Schumpeter, for instance, who

20. Natasha Piano, *Democratic Elitism: The Founding Myth of American Political Science*, Cambridge (MA), Harvard University Press, 2025.

21. John McCormick, *Machiavellian Democracy*, Cambridge, Cambridge University Press, 2011; John McCormick, *Reading Machiavelli: Scandalous Books, Suspect Engagements, and the Virtue of Populist Politics*, Princeton, Princeton University Press, 2018.

22. Jean-Jacques Rousseau, *The Social Contract and Other Later Political Writings*, Cambridge, Cambridge University Press, 2019, p. 98.

straddled Europe and America, would not have been able to articulate his 'new' theory of democracy as 'competition for political leadership'—which remains one of the most powerful paradigms within democratic theory today—without recourse to Pareto's theory of the 'circulation of elites'. The 1956 'elitism v. pluralism' debate between C. Wright Mills and Dahl, foundational to the development of American social science, explicitly refers back to Mosca, Pareto and Michels, which both thinkers used to develop their competing theories of the 'power elite' and 'polyarchy': part of the story this book wants to tell is of the translation of these thinkers and themes into other settings, and the link 'elite theory' entertains with the rise of the social sciences post-war.[23]

In France Aron construed his Cold War theory of democracy on the basis of the 'fact of oligarchy', and in Italy Norberto Bobbio and Giovanni Sartori's work is in direct dialogue with the 'Neo-Machiavellians'. Taking Aron as his cue, Martin Conway, in *Western Europe's Democratic Age 1945–1968*, has reminded us that the re-establishment of democracy in post-war Europe was anything but a given. Indeed, Western European democracy, which has become a reference point for democracy worldwide, was explicitly top-down, with little thought given to wider political participation: popular sovereignty, with what had happened in previous years firmly on everyone's mind, was looked upon with suspicion. This was an elite-led process: mass participation was not on the cards.[24] As Jan-Werner Müller has also reminded us in *Contesting Democracy: Political Ideas in Twentieth-Century Europe*, post-war European democracy borrowed much from the regimes that preceded it, something that has often not been recognised or admitted.[25]

Seen against this backdrop, democratic theory reveals itself to be fundamentally elitist. None of the thinkers denied the existence of elites within the political system: the question was rather whether they were more likely to compete or cooperate. If they compete, then democracy can be saved, with

23. H. Stuart Hughes, *The Sea Change: The Migration of Social Thought, 1930–1965*, New York, Harper & Row, 1975. On the link between the social sciences and anti-Marxism, see Hirschman, *The Rhetoric of Reaction*, p. 73: 'to construct a social science with laws as solid as those that were then believed to rule the physical universe . . . ideally suited to do battle with the rising tide of Marxism and the scientific pretensions of that movement'.

24. Martin Conway, *Western Europe's Democratic Age 1945–1968*, Princeton, Princeton University Press, 2020.

25. Jan-Werner Müller, *Contesting Democracy: Political Ideas in Twentieth-Century Europe*, New Haven, Yale University Press, 2011.

various degree of participation or control by the population at large: Schumpeter and Dahl disagreed on how much elections act as a check on elites, Dahl being more sympathetic to participation. If they cooperate then we have a 'power elite'. This is the main dividing line between Mills and Dahl or Schumpeter: the former believed elites tend to cooperate, the latter two, to compete. Aron was open to the fact that there can be a 'divided' or a 'united' elite, whilst nevertheless preferring the former, and his analysis focused on whether elites were trapped in the same institution or were independent of one another. From a broader historical perspective, however, these debates appear to be two sides of the same (elite) coin.[26]

If the Cold War represents a second moment of elite discussion and recovery of Mosca, Pareto and Michels, we seem to be entering a third phase today, with the theme, and indeed Mosca, Pareto and Michels, all featuring prominently in recent work by McCormick, Green, Urbinati and Winters, amongst others.[27] This makes a full recovery of the original debate, in all its richness, urgent, to ensure that we build on this discussion, rather than simply repeat its arguments. As Istvan Hont has written: 'good history can unmask theoretical and practical impasses and eliminate repetitive patterns of controversy about them'.[28] By lumping Mosca, Pareto and Michels together, we close ourselves off to seeing the different emphases each had, and the individual elements of their theories. Because of this someone like Dahl, for instance, failed to see how his advocacy of increased competition within the political system was precisely what Michels had been arguing all along, or that Mills' demand for 'educated publics' overlooked Michels' view of democracy's educative function. Schumpeter's 'minimalist' democracy consciously restricted the larger range of the original elite thinkers, leaving us less well-equipped to

26. For a critique of 'democratic elitism' and a call for greater public participation, see Peter Bachrach, *The Theory of Democratic Elitism: A Critique*, Lanham, University Press of America, 1980 and Bottomore, *Élites and Society*. For an overview, see Parry, *Political Elites*, pp. 124–138.

27. McCormick, *Machiavellian Democracy*; McCormick, *Reading Machiavelli*; Green, *The Eyes of the People*; Jeffrey Green, *The Shadow of Unfairness: A Plebeian Theory of Liberal Democracy*, Oxford, Oxford University Press, 2016; Urbinati, *Democracy Disfigured*; Winters, *Oligarchy*; Pierre Rosanvallon, *The Society of Equals*, Cambridge [MA], Harvard University Press, 2016; Luke Mayville, *John Adams and the Fear of American Oligarchy*, Princeton, Princeton University Press, 2016; Gordon Arlen, 'Aristotle and the Problem of Oligarchic Harm: Insights for Democracy', *European Journal of Political Theory*, Vol. 18, No. 3, 2019, pp. 393–414.

28. Istvan Hont, *Jealousy of Trade: International Competition and the Nation-State in Historical Perspective*, Cambridge [MA], Harvard University Press, 2005, p. 156.

understand the world in which we live: have the lions replaced the foxes? Only a full retrieval of this first moment can ensure that we do not fall back onto familiar patterns of controversy.

One distinctive feature of today's debate about elites is its focus on wealth. This marks a departure from the mid-century debate between Schumpeter, Dahl, Mills and Aron, who were more concerned with the oligarchic nature of modern institutions, especially parties. In *The Power Elite*, to take but one example, Mills wrote that 'wealth also is acquired and held in and through institutions', and not the other way round (i.e. that it is wealth that leads to control over institutions).[29] Indeed, Jeffrey Winters has accused the elite theorists, Pareto and Michels in particular, of having obscured 'the central role of material power in their studies'.[30] That may not be fair, as we shall see, but it is certainly the case that today's theorists, in contrast, see wealth—the recent *Zeitgeist* best captured by the unexpected success of Thomas Piketty's *Capital in the Twenty-First Century*[31]—as the main force behind the influence of policy-making. Perhaps this is due to the decline of the mass modern political party, as Michels theorised.

One of the big questions facing this literature, as Winters has pointed out, is that if greater participation within politics has undeniably brought many benefits, notably by bringing formerly marginalised groups into the political system, it is unclear whether it fundamentally challenges the oligarchic nature of wealth.[32] As such it might be worth returning to Pareto's theory of 'demagogic plutocracy', where the rich rule behind the façade of democracy, to see what light it might shed on our current predicament.[33] It is Pareto who, after all—*pace* Winters—first coined the 80/20 rule: that 80% of the wealth of the country always belongs to 20% of the population. There is a strong—if intensified—echo of that notion in the slogan of the 99% v. 1%.

Tracing this history is also important in that it allows us to tell a different story about twentieth-century democracy, and what we might do about it in the twenty-first. Mosca, Pareto and Michels were the first to identify the gap

---

29. C. Wright Mills, *The Power Elite*, Oxford, Oxford University Press, 2000, p. 9.

30. Winters, *Oligarchy*, p. 8.

31. Thomas Piketty, *Capital in the Twenty-First Century*, Cambridge (MA), Harvard University Press, 2014.

32. Jeffrey Winters, *Domination through Democracy: Why Oligarchs Win*, Penguin Random House, forthcoming.

33. Joseph Femia, *The Machiavellian Legacy: Essays in Italian Political Thought*, Basingstoke, Macmillan, 1998, pp. 145–166.

between the ideal of democracy as rule by the people and the reality of the continuation of elite rule within a modern setting.[34] Nazism, fascism and communism all tried to close that gap by claiming that the 'true' people—the Aryans, the Italians or the working class—could directly rule through a symbiotic link with a 'leader' or a 'vanguard'. Here Michels is the most instructive figure in that he moved from radical syndicalism to fascism, in a classic move Zeev Sternhell had identified in his seminal study *Neither Right nor Left*.[35] What is meant by this is that if we mean to avoid the pitfalls of fascism or today's populism, which also claims to close the gap by 'incarnating' the 'true people', we must take seriously the 'fact of oligarchy' and start thinking about what democracy might mean from there.

Mosca, as we've seen, denounced Mussolini in his final senatorial speech, but Pareto's relation to fascism is more complicated, although this book will argue that prediction is not the same as endorsement, and that Pareto remained a high liberal, detached from the fray in his Villa Céligny in Switzerland, surrounded by his cats, until his death.[36] Schumpeter, as we shall explore, thought up his 'minimalist' democracy precisely to counter the broader claims of socialism, and Dahl and Aron defended the 'polyarchic' or 'Constitutional-Pluralist' regime against Soviet Russia or 'Party Monopolism'. Even Mills, who remained the most sympathetic to the socialist cause—famously visiting Castro in Cuba as part of his 'bad boy' routine—at least in *The Power Elite* took his inspiration from John Dewey to advocate for active 'educated publics', which were—revealingly—to be led by intellectual elites like himself.

III: Dynamic Democracy

The third claim—in political theory—is that the early elite thinkers, Mosca, Pareto and Michels, lay the groundwork for the elaboration of a *dynamic* theory of democracy. If elites always rule, what does democracy mean in this context? It can mean neither 'sovereignty of the people' nor 'majoritarian rule' in any true sense of the word. As Michels put it, the people can only be made

34. See Norberto Bobbio, *The Future of Democracy: A Defence of the Rules of the Game*, Cambridge, Polity, 1987, for the 'six broken promises of democracy'.

35. Zeev Sternhell, *Neither Right nor Left: Fascist Ideology in France*, Berkeley, University of California Press, 1986.

36. John Tomasi, *Free Market Fairness*, Princeton, Princeton University Press, 2012.

to rule '*in abstracto*', but not in reality.[37] For Mosca and Pareto, the notion of 'sovereignty of the people' can, respectively, only be part of the 'political formula' the ruling class use to justify their rule, or a post-facto rationalisation ('derivation') of an action that has already taken place. The same might be said of the notion of 'constituent power', which in this formulation can only be the *a posteriori* legitimisation of an existing power relation, upon which, nevertheless, it may have an impact.[38]

Instead, dynamic democracy starts with the reality of power and the 'fact of oligarchy': the existence of an elite who control the levers of power, namely the state.[39] In this sense it is Weberian, in that it sees politics as the struggle for control over the state.[40] 'Elite theory', after all, was developed within the historical context of the creation of the Italian nation-state, where the state was made before Italians themselves were 'made'. Indeed, most remained disenfranchised: a point worth remembering when thinking about 'elite theory'.

Movement

Perhaps the best metaphor for dynamic democracy is Aesop's fable, as used by Michels, of the old peasant on his death-bed telling his sons there is a buried treasure in the field. Michels writes:

> After the old man's death the sons dig everywhere in order to discover the treasure. They do not find it. But their indefatigable labour improves the soil and secures for them a comparative well-being. The treasure in the fable may well symbolise democracy. Democracy is a treasure that no one will ever discover by deliberate search. But in continuing our search, in labouring indefatigably to discover the undiscoverable, we shall perform a work which will have fertile results in the democratic sense.[41]

---

37. Michels, *Political Parties*, p. 366.

38. Lucia Rubinelli, *Constituent Power: A History*, Cambridge, Cambridge University Press, 2020 and Adam Lindsay, '"Pretenders of a Vile and Unmanly Disposition": Thomas Hobbes on the Fiction of Constituent Power', *Political Theory*, Vol. 47, No. 4, 2019, pp. 475–499.

39. Note how the state returned as a strong theme in post-war thought (see Ira Katznelson, 'A Seminar on the State' in *Desolation and Enlightenment: Political Knowledge after Total War, Totalitarianism, and the Holocaust*, New York, Columbia University Press, 2003, pp. 107–151).

40. Max Weber, 'Politics as Vocation' in *Political Writings*, Cambridge, Cambridge University Press, 1994.

41. Ibid., p. 368.

True democracy will never be found, but striving towards it will help reap democratic rewards.

This book argues that democracy must be understood as the continual challenge to elite rule: that it is in the moment of challenge to the established elite by a new elite that change may occur—for better or for worse, one hastens to add. This is the meaning of *dynamic democracy*. Democracy's true location is therefore not to be found where it is usually thought to lie: it is to be found neither in institutions nor in principles. Institutions like elections are insufficient to determine whether a regime is democratic or not: witness autocratic regimes with electoral scores of 88%,[42] or even, as Schumpeter conceded, free and fair elections but with a highly constrained franchise (women before the vote, disenfranchised African-Americans). But even in fully-fledged democracies like the US, where democratic rules appear to have been adhered to, democracy nevertheless appears imperilled. This is because certain democratic 'norms' have been flouted, yet norms on their own a democracy do not make.[43]

For democratic theory this is one of the biggest challenges facing Schumpeter's emphasis on elections: that elections are no guarantee of democracy. In response to this, Dahl offered several criteria and institutions which, should a regime match them, can be considered as representing a 'polyarchy', if not a democracy.[44] Yet this rather static view of democracy fails to identify where change might occur within the political system: after all, governments may change, but policies remain the same. Margaret Thatcher, a Conservative leader, famously claimed that her biggest success was Tony Blair: that although 'New Labour' had come to power, her neo-liberal economic policies remained intact.[45]

Instead, democracy must be found in the movement of challenge itself. In this, social movements have a crucial role to play: *democracy is to be located in the interaction between social movements and elites, mediated through institutions*. Historically these institutions, at least over the course of the nineteenth and

42. Pjotr Sauer and Andrew Roth, 'Vladimir Putin Claims Landslide Russian Election Victory', *The Guardian*, 18 March 2024 (https://www.theguardian.com/world/2024/mar/17/kremlin-vladimir-putin-claim-landslide-russian-election-victory accessed on 4 April 2024).

43. Jedediah Purdy, 'Normcore', *Dissent*, Vol. 65, 2018, pp. 120–128.

44. Dahl, *Democracy and Its Critics*.

45. Tony Blair, 'My job was to build on some Thatcher policies', *BBC*, 8 April 2013. On a possible link between the 'Italian tradition' and neo-liberalism, via James Buchanan, see Sean Irving, 'Power, Plutocracy and Public Finance: James M. Buchanan and the "Italian Tradition"', *Global Intellectual History*, Vol. 6, No. 6, 2021, pp. 956–976.

early twentieth centuries, were political parties, although the waning or 'hollowing out' of the latter has led to a populism that ties movements directly to a leader (think of MAGA-Trump), or the creation of 'people-parties', like Emmanuel Macron's *En Marche*, which reproduced his initials.[46]

Studies of social movements show that they have a political impact—they lead to political change—when a section of the political elite breaks with the established order and rallies to their cause.[47] Together they challenge the established elite and effect political change. Without one or the other—without either a rallying of a section of the elite or a social movement—change does not occur: the political elite remains the same, the same policies are continued. In the context of dynamic democracy, this is the expression of how a rising elite, leading a social movement, challenges the established elite. Whether the rising elite effects political change is dependent on whether a section of the established elite rallies to their cause to challenge the rest of the elite that remains in place.

This looks very much like Pareto's circulation of elites, whose metaphor is a river: the rising elite slowly merging with the established elite. Of course, sometimes there are dams that stop the river from flowing: the notion that the established elite doesn't split and take on the new cause. But as Pareto also pointed out, sometimes the river floods and breaks its banks: there is a revolt or a revolution, and the established elite is completely overthrown. What the work on social movements identifies is change within a regulated democratic system. But sometimes the democratic system is overthrown, or we are trying to account for elite circulation within a non-democratic context.

There is much to be learnt from these studies of social movements, not least that non-violent movements, because they bring in more people to their cause, are twice as likely to achieve their aims than violent ones (53% v. 26%), because violence alienates people (although note that success is only just over 50%). Indeed, they offer the figure of 3.5% as a way of measuring whether social movements will be successful: if 3.5% of the population gets behind the cause, it will succeed, although this figure has also been challenged.[48]

46. Peter Mair, *Ruling the Void: The Hollowing of Western Democracy*, London, Verso, 2013.

47. Daniel Schlozman, *When Movements Anchor Parties: Electoral Alignments in American History*, Princeton, Princeton University Press, 2015; Edwin Amenta, Neal Caren, Elizabeth Chiarello and Yang Su, 'The Political Consequences of Social Movements', *Annual Review of Sociology*, Vol. 36, 2010, pp. 287–307.

48. Erica Chenoweth and Maria Stephan, *Why Civil Resistance Works: The Strategic Logic of Nonviolent Conflict*, New York, Columbia University Press, 2011. For a critique, see Kyle Matthews, 'Social movements and the (mis)use of research: Extinction Rebellion and the 3.5% rule',

Another key element is that movements need to be organised. This brings us back to Mosca, Pareto and Michels, as organisation was Mosca's fundamental reason as to why elites rule: minorities are organised, majorities are not. In fact, much of what has been articulated above can be re-described through the theories Mosca, Pareto and Michels propagated: 'social movements', for instance, is another way of talking about Mosca's 'social forces', which are the drivers of historical change in his account. Pareto's theory of the 'circulation of elites' was based on an A-B-C diagram: B, the rising elite, would ally itself with C, the people, to challenge A, the established elite. Should B succeed, a new elite—D—will arise and play the same role with B as B did with A. And so on and so forth: the one continuum is that C, the people, will never rule, because the elite always rules. Michels, as we've seen previously, offers us the formulation of dynamic democracy grounded in movement, and organisation was for him the necessary reason for the emergence of the iron law of oligarchy: 'who says organisation, says oligarchy'.[49] His reflections, moreover, centred on political parties, the institution that plays the key role in articulating the interaction between movements and elites; the location of democracy.

Steven Klein and Cheol-Sung Lee have recently offered a dynamic theory of civil society, based on a forward and a backward infiltration between civil society, the state and the economy, which chimes with the approach taken here.[50] Infiltration can either be through influence (discursive), substitution (functional replacement) or occupation (institutional takeover). Respectively, these map well onto what, for instance, Michels says about intellectually keeping the elites in check, Mosca's 'social forces' that create their own sphere and, of course, elite-replacement. As argued above, the forward and the backward movements of infiltration are key as it is only when a section of the established elite breaks off to join the rising forces from below that true change occurs, which is why the more specific emphasis here is on how social movements lead to change in the political system by applying pressure to the institutions that mediate the two, namely, to parties.

Interface: A Journal for and about Social Movements, Vol. 12, No. 1, 2020, pp. 591–615. Note that Chenoweth has admitted that the 3.5% rule has been broken twice—Brunei in 1962 (4% mobilised) and Bahrain in 2011–2014 (6% mobilised)—both times failing. See https://www .directactioneverywhere.com/dxe-in-the-news/chenoweth-blog (consulted on 4 March 2024).

49. Michels, *Political Parties*, p. 365.

50. Steven Klein and Cheol-Sung Lee, 'Towards a Dynamic Theory of Civil Society: The Politics of Forward and Backward Infiltration', *Sociological Theory*, Vol. 37, No. 1, 2019, pp. 62–88.

Indeed, Mosca and Pareto also offer a *dynamic* theory of democracy. For Mosca, society's evolution depends on the development of ever-new 'social forces' that arise because of new technological, social, economic, legal and military phenomena. These come to challenge the established ruling class, which can either adapt to best integrate them within its bosom or be overthrown. Society's level of 'civilisation' depends on how many of the social forces it can integrate within a harmonious whole, and Mosca thought that the system he called 'juridical defence'—the parliamentary regime of the rule of law and checks-and-balances—is best equipped to do the orchestrating. It is the *movement* of social forces that drives political change in this account.

Pareto's 'circulation of elites' seems to speak for itself, and indeed in the original French formulation of *Les systèmes socialistes* the phrase used is 'the movement of the circulation of elites'.[51] As Sartori writes, 'as for Pareto, there is nothing inherently undemocratic in his law of the "circulation of elites"'.[52] For sure, the vision of the 'best' competing for power might still be our ideal of what democracy should be: Pareto defended an 'open' elite that would be continually renewed from below. For Pareto, history is the swing from one type of elite to another: the 'lions' and the 'foxes', borrowing Machiavelli's terminology,[53] who represent different types of rule: 'lions' rule through force and are more conservative, emphasising unity, homogeneity, faith and centralisation (centripetal forces), whereas 'foxes' are characterised by *combinazioni*: deceit, cunning, manipulation and co-optation, and theirs is a decentralised, plural and sceptical rule, uneasy with the use of force (centrifugal).

This displacement means democracy is not an end-point, but a continuous striving: the never-ending challenge to elite rule which, even though it never fully achieves its aim, nevertheless may bring about certain democratic benefits. It is not the by-product of this struggle, but the struggle itself: it is the democratic benefits that are the by-products. In many ways, as we shall explore, this is how one might read the German SPD that Michels studied: although it never succeeded in achieving its own ideology of democratic revolution, nevertheless, in striving towards it, it achieved real welfare benefits for its members.

51. Vilfredo Pareto, *Les systèmes socialistes*, Genève, Droz, 1978, p. 9.

52. Giovanni Sartori, *The Theory of Democracy Revisited. Part One: The Contemporary Debate*, Chatham, Chatham House Publishers, 1987, p. 47.

53. On how the 'elite theorists' inherited Machiavelli's legacy of anti-metaphysics, the empirical method and political realism, see Femia, *The Machiavellian Legacy*, pp. 1–63.

French political theory and history has often, notably through the work of François Goguel, opposed the forces of 'movement' with those of 'order'.[54] This distinction is sometimes proposed instead of the more common one of the left and the right: note how Blair's left-wing 'New Labour' continued the right-wing politics of Thatcher, as discussed above.[55] Indeed, it is the strength of the *dynamic* conception of democracy to see beyond the usual left/right divide to identify not simply continuities but also deeper structural change: change that can happen within the respective left or right parties themselves.[56] 'New Labour' was a change from what came before it on the left, but the Conservative Party has also changed significantly since Brexit, from the liberal government of David Cameron to that of the hard-liner Theresa May or indeed of the populist Boris Johnson, back to a libertarian one under Liz Truss followed by Rishi Sunak. Perhaps one way of conceptualising that change, which we'll return to in conclusion, is from foxes to lions.

Yet the approach formulated here is more in line with the one developed by Georges Burdeau, who, in a seminal article of 1968, 'The dialectic of order and movement', articulated a conception of politics as the dynamic interaction between the forces of order that aim to conserve society and those of movement that want to transform it: politics being the always-temporary equilibrium that results from the interaction between the two (Pareto's theory is also based on an ever-shifting equilibrium).[57] That never-static equilibrium, because it comes from a dialectic between the two forces, is not simply an addition of the two forces, but forms instead a new synthesis. Politics, in this account, is the 'art of making order from movement'.[58]

Dynamism

It is important to underline here that dynamic democracy puts the emphasis on *force* and not simply on *motion*. On its own, motion can simply mean the reproduction of the same, static, system, with the parts repeatedly circulating

54. François Goguel, *La politique des partis sous la III République*, Paris, Seuil, 1958.

55. On New Labour's 'Third Way', see Anthony Giddens, *Beyond Left and Right: The Future of Radical Politics*, Cambridge, Polity, 1994 and Anthony Giddens, *The Third Way: The Renewal of Social Democracy*, Cambridge, Polity, 1998.

56. Maurice Finocchiaro, *Beyond Right and Left: Democratic Elitism in Mosca and Gramsci*, New Haven, Yale University Press, 1999.

57. Georges Burdeau, 'La dialectique de l'ordre et du mouvement', *Revue français de science politique*, Vol. 18, No. 1, 1968, pp. 5–19.

58. Burdeau, 'La dialectique de l'ordre et du mouvement', p. 6.

along the same route. Here, instead, the focus is on the *movement of forces*, because those forces impose change within the system: the passage, for instance, of the lions to the foxes. This is why Pareto puts so much emphasis on force—as opposed to violence, a sign of weakness by embattled elites to his mind—either to preserve the system or to change it. If there is a pure circulation of elites, then new elites simply replace the old ones, but the paradigm of either foxes or lions remains the same. It is when different elites arise, those with the sentiment either of the 'instinct for combination' or of the 'preservation of aggregates', that a challenge occurs: that rising elites apply *force* to the established elites, to either change the system if successful, or not.

It is true that for Pareto there are certain immutable features, such as the 80/20 rule that sees eighty percent of the land belonging to twenty percent of the population. In other words: the elite always rules. And when he comes to describing the social system,[59] Pareto has it as a closed one, where there is circulation within it: i.e. there is always the same percentage of rich and poor people, but who might be rich and who might be poor changes. Indeed, that Pareto sees that it matters whether the lions or the foxes are in power—or the rentiers or the speculators in the economic sphere—and that society is determined by who is in control, means that even though the system is a closed one, it does indeed change. It is not always the same thing. To that end we can add Mosca, who underlined the role *social forces* play in determining the level of civilisation: the social system might expand or retract, depending on the number of social forces accommodated within 'juridical defence'.

This, then, is why the theory is a *dynamic* theory of democracy, in the philosophical sense of the word: 'a theory that all phenomena (such as matter or motion) can be explained as manifestations of force', where force is understood as 'an agency or influence that if applied to a free body results chiefly in an acceleration of the body and sometimes in elastic deformation and other effects'.[60] Here, by 'movement' is meant not (repetitive) motion but rather the application of force to produce change, change understood as the acceleration of the object to which it is applied. Translated to politics: dynamic democracy is democracy understood as the application of force by social movements onto a political system to speed up the circulation of elites, from lions to foxes or

---

59. Talcott Parsons famously developed the concept of the 'social system', drawing directly from Pareto, in his 1951 *The Social System* (Talcott Parsons, *The Social System*, London, Routledge, 1991). See, further, Powers, 'Introduction', p. 11.

60. 'Dynamic', 'Force', *Merriam-Webster*.

vice versa, and to make the 'iron law of oligarchy' more pliable (i.e. incentivise more participation). Force is applied via political institutions such as parties, and whether change occurs depends on the openness of those political institutions to change (the rallying of elites).

In a 1961 article entitled '"Static" and "Dynamic" as Sociological Categories', Theodor Adorno defended a 'dynamic' conception of society that, if left unimpeded, would be liberating and diversifying.[61] This contrasted with a 'static' vision that he thought exploitative: to try to stabilise society was to entrench the power structures of the day and ward off the challenges from below. The 'static' conception of society Adorno traced back to August Comte, the founder of sociology, who was concerned with stabilising the liberal bourgeois order that had arisen from the French Revolution against the more radical socialist and working-class demands that had started to appear over the course of the nineteenth century. In his later 1968 *Introduction to Sociology*, the final lectures Adorno gave, he opposed this 'static' vision of Comte to his predecessor Saint-Simon, who, according to Adorno, had been on the side of 'dynamism'.[62]

He wasn't the only one: Adorno listed Nietzsche and Pareto as being on the side of 'dynamism'.[63] Both, according to Adorno, because of their openness to violence: they were willing to let the forces of the irrational loose, and we can presume that Adorno thought a degree of violence was the only way to challenge the static bourgeois order. Indeed, in the lectures Adorno lauds Pareto as being one of the first to integrate dynamism into a social system.[64] And yet Pareto, according to Adorno, ultimately was a conservative figure because he sought a social equilibrium, one that was inherently static. This was compounded by the fact that Pareto was one of those 'knowing winkers' who claimed that there are no revolutions or classes, only social interests.[65] This put him in the reactionary camp, one opposed to socialist revolution, all too easily put in the service of 'Signore Mussolini'.[66] It should come as no surprise that Aron's first piece on Pareto, whom he described as a reactionary thinker

61. Theodor Adorno, '"Static" and "Dynamic" as Sociological Categories', *Diogenes*, Vol. 9, No. 33, 1961, pp. 28–49.

62. Theodor Adorno, *Introduction to Sociology*, Stanford, Stanford University Press, 2000, p. 12.

63. Adorno, *Introduction to Sociology*, pp. 14; Adorno, '"Static" and "Dynamic" as Sociological Categories', p. 48.

64. Adorno, *Introduction to Sociology*, p. 14.

65. Ibid., p. 11.

66. Ibid., p. 14.

for having given the bourgeoisie an anti-revolutionary theory of class circulation—even if there is a proletarian revolution, a ruling class will always rule, and there are no 'classless societies'—was published in Adorno's long-time collaborator Max Horkheimer's *Zeitschrift für Sozialforschung*.[67]

Aron, however, as we shall see in chapter 6, later changed his mind, seeing Pareto as a 'Machiavellian' defender of liberty, following James Burnham.[68] And whilst Adorno is right to say that Pareto was interested in irrational action—or what Pareto would call the 'non-logical'—that is not to say that Pareto thought all action was simply post-hoc justification of irrational impulses: that everything should be irrational. Instead, he believed that much of human action was indeed rational, if rooted ultimately in different 'residues'—that if 'sentiments' were irrational, actions that sprung from them could indeed be rational—and belonged to the realm of political economy. Pareto had originally planned his *Treatise on Sociology* to have five parts, the last two focused on 'applied economics', which, as S. E. Finer has pointed out in his excellent overview of Pareto's work, 'would have put the logical actions . . . on an equal footing with the non-logical ones'.[69] Moreover, although Pareto did see an important role for violence in the maintaining or circulating of elite rule, he was careful to distinguish force, which could either maintain or change the system, from violence, which he thought was the weapon of the weak, and signalled the disintegration of the system in place.

It is important not to confuse circulation with repetition: yes, Pareto did search for equilibrium within his system, but the movement between the different parts has real consequences for the system as a whole, notably on whether the lions or the foxes are on top. This is why Pareto's system, and indeed those of the rest of the 'elitists', is a dynamic system, not one simply based on motion. In fact, the same might be said of Nietzsche's eternal return, to which the 'circulation of elites' carries certain affinities: as George Simmel has pointed out, if a system has the same amount of force but an unlimited amount of time, then no point of power distribution will ever recur.[70] One question is whether Pareto's system can expand or not: whether it can or not, Mosca's

67. Raymond Aron, 'La sociologie de Pareto' in *Zeitschrift für Sozialforschung*, Vol. 6, No. 3, 1937, pp. 489–521.

68. Burnham, *The Machiavellians*.

69. S. E. Finer, 'Introduction' to Vilfredo Pareto, *Sociological Writings*, London, Pall Mall Press, 1966, p. 48.

70. George Simmel, *Nietzsche and Schopenhauer*, Champaign, University of Illinois Press, 1991.

theory of different levels of 'civilisation', determined by the number of social forces brought within the harmonious bosom of 'juridical defence', certainly allows for the system to expand.

Yet Adorno leaves us with two key points. The first is that a 'static' system, because it is by essence exploitative, will by necessity bring about forces to challenge it from below: in a word, movement. The second is that, with his Frankfurt School hat on, Adorno was aware that dynamism itself can also become oppressive, in the way rationality had become in modernity, as dissected in *Dialectic of Enlightenment*:[71] a thought that can be linked to Mosca's view that rising social forces can become tyrannical if they impose themselves on other forces without giving them their own space, such as socialism, in Mosca's account, or fascism.[72] In the end, Adorno, in a Hegelian dialectical vein, wanted a new synthesis to arise from this clash between static and dynamic forces, where two forces collided not for one to dominate the other, but for a new—third—force to appear.[73]

Much of contemporary democratic theory can be described through this static/dynamic dichotomy. Although John Rawls was not a democratic theorist per se, his 'two principles of justice' are meant to provide the theoretical basis for a 'well-ordered' society.[74] Indeed, in *Justice as Fairness* Rawls explicitly presents political philosophy as offering an Hegelian reconciliation with the world we live in—we are to 'accept and affirm our social world positively, not merely to be resigned to it'[75]—quite reminiscent of Comte's desire to stabilise the post-Revolutionary liberal bourgeois order. The same might be said of Dahl. In his self-declared masterpiece *Democracy and Its Critics*, Dahl listed seven conditions for a country to be recognised as a polyarchy.[76] These conditions are static; they don't change: it is on how well the different political systems match these seven criteria that they are to be judged. Again, this can be viewed as an attempt to stabilise the political system.

Chapter 4 will argue that Schumpeter's aim with his 'minimalist' conception of democracy was also to render democracy static, or at least to slow it down. The point was to limit 'movement' to the competition between

71. Theodor Adorno and Max Horkheimer, *Dialectic of Enlightenment*, London, Verso, 1997.

72. Adorno, '"Static" and "Dynamic" as Sociological Categories', p. 47.

73. Ibid., p. 38.

74. John Rawls, *A Theory of Justice*, Cambridge (MA), Harvard University Press, 1999.

75. John Rawls, *Justice as Fairness: A Restatement*, Cambridge (MA), Harvard University Press, 2001, p. 3.

76. Dahl, *Democracy and Its Critics*, p. 233.

politicians for votes. The rest of the political system, in particular the bureau-cracy and the military, was to remain static: it was not to change. This was because, as John Medearis has persuasively argued, Schumpeter was worried about the more 'transformative' demands that democracy, understood here as socialism, had on the political system, demands he had experienced first-hand in his native Austro-Hungary.[77] To counter this, and the possibility of a social-ist take-over of the economy in the form of 'corporatism', which he thought possible, Schumpeter posited instead his 'procedural' democracy focused on a narrow field that could persist even within a socialised economy.[78]

Medearis, a critic of Schumpeter, develops his own theory of 'oppositional' democracy with which the theory of dynamic democracy offered here shares a number of affinities.[79] For one, Medearis also singles out certain democratic theories as being static: he explains how deliberative democracy, for instance, 'builds [a] wall' to isolate itself from the tumult of real politics. It becomes a 'refuge' from the reality of politics.[80] Indeed, whilst throughout his life Jurgen Habermas showed an interest in and support for political movements, the 'siege model' of democracy he developed in *Theory of Communicative Action* is rather static too: a 'siege' is a blockage or defensive position in contrast to waves constantly breaking against the shoal, as in dynamic democracy (later, in *Between Facts and Norms*, Habermas moved towards a more procedural 'sluice' model).[81] Moreover, dynamic and oppositional democracy both see democracy as a never-ending struggle, as an 'intervention' in a specific histori-cal context, and share a focus on the state.

But there are differences. Whilst Medearis sees Mosca, Pareto and Michels as part of Schumpeter's attempt to render democracy static—elite theory 'quarantines' itself from the people[82]—dynamic democracy sees the early elit-ists as being in reality the foundation of the dynamic conception of democracy (oppositional democracy takes its inspiration instead from Marx and

77. John Medearis, *Joseph Schumpeter's Two Theories of Democracy*, Cambridge (MA), Har-vard University Press, 2001.

78. Schumpeter, *Capitalism, Socialism and Democracy*.

79. John Medearis, *Why Democracy Is Oppositional*, Cambridge (MA), Harvard University Press, 2015.

80. Ibid., pp. 17 and 40.

81. Jurgen Habermas, *The Theory of Communicative Action: Reason and Rationalisation of Society*, Cambridge, Polity, 1986; Jurgen Habermas, *Between Facts and Norms*, Cambridge, Polity, 1997.

82. Medearis, *Why Democracy Is Oppositional*, p. 149.

Dewey[83]). Their understanding of social movements is different too: Medearis is interested in the role of movements *within* democracy and democratic theory, whereas dynamic democracy thinks democracy *is* the movement of challenge to elites. As its link to 'elite' theory suggests, dynamic democracy remains sceptical, in contrast to oppositional democracy, that the people can in fact rule. Ultimately, oppositional democracy is quite defensive, resisting the same oppressive economic, bureaucratic and political forces, whereas dynamic democracy has a more active conception of politics as a continual process—and possibility—of change.

There are also affinities between dynamic democracy and agonistic theories of democracy as developed by Chantal Mouffe, Bonnie Honig and William Connolly, notably in their shared emphasis on conflict, pluralism and a Nietzschean tragic worldview.[84] But there are differences too: dynamic democracy does not look to transform antagonism into a more democratic and respectful agonism. Or, to put it another way, from the perspective of dynamic democracy, agonism seems to be the circulation of the same elite, whereas antagonism its possible replacement. Moreover, dynamic democracy reveals the fundamentally elitist basis of agonistic democracy: the amount of time, energy and work demanded by agonistic democracy can only realistically be undertaken by a very select group of people.[85] The people—'C' in Pareto's account—even if they don't ever come to power, seem absent from this conceptualisation. Nevertheless, perhaps Honig's view of politics as a dialectic between order and movement remains the closest to the account articulated here.

Sheldon Wolin has theorised 'fugitive democracy' as a way of escaping from the 'inverted totalitarianism' of corporate economic domination and the authoritarian 'managed democracy' the US has morphed into following 9/11 and the War on Terror.[86] Again, although there is a shared criticism of certain

83. Ibid., p. 5

84. Chantal Mouffe, *On the Political*, Abingdon, Routledge, 2005; Bonnie Honig, *Political theory and the Displacement of Politics*, Ithaca, Cornell University Press, 1993; William Connolly, *Identity/Difference: Democratic Negotiations of Political Paradox*, Minneapolis, University of Minnesota Press, 2002.

85. See Hugo Drochon, 'Nietzsche and Politics', *Nietzsche-Studien*, Vol. 39, 2010, pp. 663–677.

86. Sheldon Wolin, *Democracy Incorporated: Managed Democracy and the Specter of Inverted Totalitarianism*, Princeton, Princeton University Press, 2008 and Sheldon Wolin, *Fugitive Democracy and Other Essays*, Princeton, Princeton University Press, 2016.

aspects of elitism, 'fugitive democracy' seems more like a (momentary) escape from state structures to create more participatory forms of politics instead of a direct engagement with the regime of power as in dynamic democracy, which has a focus on the state. Ian Shapiro has defended 'nondomination' as the form politics should take.[87] It is not the position of this book that that pursuit is in vain—that it is futile—although it admits, as Shapiro does, that some form of (elite) domination is inevitable. The focus, rather, is on how changes in elites allows for, if not the replacement, then at least a change in the form of domination, with its attenuation as its attendant hope. More recently, Samuel Bagg has argued democracy must be understood as resisting state capture.[88] Dynamic democracy shares the view of democracy not being understood as collective self-rule, not looking beyond formal procedures, and not being invested in maintaining inter-group competition, but it is focused on the process of elite change as leading to a change in politics, even a redistributive one: that change being indeed the capture of a part of the state, but one that is ever-renewed and ever-changing.

It is true that these theories have more specific concerns—whether it be markets, neoliberal ideology, runaway technologies and their effect on political culture and social relations, ethnic and racial conflict, archaic institutions and laws, flawed constitutions, war, militaries and militarism, state capture or something else[89]—than those of dynamic democracy. Yet it is also true that all these challenges ultimately resolve into a more general, permanent phenomenon of elite dominance, even if the elites are quite different from each other. There is a difference here in the level of abstraction: dynamic democracy posits the permanence of elites at the structural level, but the question of which elite dominates at a given point in time is an empirical question to be determined historically. It depends, in Mosca's language, on which 'social force' is dominant at the time. Dynamic democracy offers an account of elite domination, going so far as to distinguish between foxes and lions, but specifying which elite is dominating at any given point is a discrete exercise—an *analytical* one—drawn from the overall theory, of which the Conclusion will offer illustrations.

87. Ian Shapiro, *Politics against Domination*, Cambridge (MA), Harvard University Press, 2016.

88. Samuel Bagg, *The Dispersion of Power: A Critical Realist Theory of Democracy*, Oxford, Oxford University Press, 2024.

89. See, further, K. Sabeel Rahman, *Democracy against Domination*, Oxford, Oxford University Press, 2016.

A final kindred spirit must be found in E. E. Schattschneider. By advocating in *The Semisovereign People*[90] the expansion of the realm of social conflict as a means of increasing political participation, he also proposed a 'dynamic' theory of democracy. Schattschneider was, of course, one of the fiercest critics of Dahl's pluralism: 'The flaw in the pluralist heaven is that the heavenly chorus sings with a strong upper-class accent'.[91] One difference, however, is that it is the 'losers' of economic competition, for Schattschneider, who call for governmental intervention,[92] whereas dynamic democracy sees the challenge to established politics coming from ascending forces.

Regimes

'Elite theory' rejects the usual tripartite of political regimes inherited from Aristotle—monarchy, aristocracy and polity, alongside their corrupted forms tyranny, oligarchy and democracy—although when Aristotle himself turned to analysing Greek constitutions he departed from his own schemata to explain the dynamics of ancient politics as the struggle between oligarchy, understood as the rule of the rich, and democracy, understood as the rule of the poor.[93] In many ways that latter vision is closer to the elite one, which sees politics as the struggle between the elite and the 'masses'. Dynamic democracy, therefore, sees democracy as a continuum between more and less oligarchic rule: full democracy understood as the rule of the people will never be achieved. Indeed, democracy, based on this understanding, is when pressure is applied to the 'iron law of oligarchy', to reprise Michels' formulation. The distinction here between democratic, oligarchic and monarchic regimes is void. As Rousseau himself conceded in *The Social Contract*, and Michels reports in the epigraph to the 'Final Considerations' of his *Political Parties*: 'to take the term in its fully rigorous meaning, there has never existed a true democracy and one will never exist. It is against the natural order of things that the great number governs and that the small number be governed'.[94]

90. E. E. Schattschneider, *The Semisovereign People: A Realist's View of Democracy in America*, Boston, Wadsworth, 1975.

91. Ibid., p. 34.

92. Ibid., p. 39.

93. Aristotle, *The Politics* and *The Constitution of Athens*, Cambridge, Cambridge University Press, 1996.

94. Michels, *Political Parties*, pp. 73, 364.

Instead, dynamic democracy offers a way of thinking about how a regime might be more or less authoritarian, or, in this paradigm, more or less democratic, in the sense of whether elite rule is tighter or laxer, allowing a greater number to participate. It is a continuum. In some ways, dynamic democracy collapses the distinction between democracy and democratisation: democracy, as an abstract ideal, will never be achieved, however much we strive towards it, so instead we are always in a process of democratisation; a process that might go forward or indeed backwards (backsliding). Whether a regime is democratising or not is an empirical question to be measured over time: one always starts with a certain historical moment along the continuum; there is no abstract ideal point outside of time. *What the theory of dynamic democracy offers is a way of conceptualising that change—for instance, between lions and foxes–and an indication of where to look to identify that change, namely in the interaction between social movements (social forces) and political institutions such as parties.* The uncertainty about whether a moment of democratic challenge will lead to greater democratic participation or not—both Brexit and the election of Trump have led to increased authoritarianism—is part and parcel of what democracy is: a regime of uncertainty.[95]

In his *Mass and Elite in Democratic Athens*, Josiah Ober challenged the view that, in an Athenian context, an 'iron law of oligarchy' always obtained and that all democracies are in fact disguised oligarchies. The reason is that the ideological discourse of democracy from the 'masses' kept the 'elite' politicians of Athens, according to Ober, in check.[96] In this he followed Moses Finley, who in his *Democracy Ancient and Modern* first contested the 'elitist' reading of democracy:

> Athens therefore provides a valuable case-study of how political leadership and popular participation succeeded in coexisting, over a long period of time, without either the apathy and ignorance exposed by public opinion experts, or the extremist nightmares that haunt elitist theorists.[97]

---

95. Jan-Werner Müller, *Democracy Rules: Liberty, Equality, Uncertainty*, New York, Farrar, Straus and Giroux, 2021.

96. Josiah Ober, *Mass and Elite in Democratic Athens: Rhetoric, Ideology, and the Power of the People*, Princeton, Princeton University Press, 1989, pp. 11, 15–16, 33–34, 327–333. Thanks to Mordechai Levy-Eichel for insisting on this point.

97. Moses Finley, *Democracy Ancient and Modern*, New Brunswick, Rutgers University Press, 1985, p. 33. For a Marxist take on class conflict in ancient Greece, see G. E. M. de Ste. Croix, *The Class Struggle in the Ancient Greek World*, London, Duckworth, 1981.

But Ober's understanding of Michels is based on an historical anachronism:[98] Michels' theory was a specifically *modern* one, intimately linked to the rise of the modern, bureaucratic, state.[99] As such, the law was never meant to be applied to an ancient setting. Nevertheless, Michels thought that there was an inverse proportionality between democracy and the number of participants: the greater the number, the lesser the democracy (or the more the oligarchy). As we shall see in chapter 3, C. W. Cassinelli estimated that with under 1,000 participants, some degree of 'democracy' could be maintained: a figure that doesn't seem too far from the number who actively participated in the agora at any point in time.[100] In this sense a degree of Athenian 'democracy' could still be possible within Michels' law. Moreover, the type of discursive ideological check that Ober posits as a way of reining-in elite power is precisely the second 'palliative' Michels proposed to counter the iron law. Finally, it is worth noting that Ober still uses the terms 'elite' and 'masses', and sees the politics of ancient Athens as the struggle between the two: exactly as the elite theorists themselves saw modern politics. So, in the end, the overall 'elitist' framework, if not the 'iron law' as such, is validated in an ancient context.

Building on Ober's work—and Michels' iron law of oligarchy—Matthew Simonton has recently argued in *Classical Greek Oligarchy* that ancient oligarchy was not the most common form of constitution of the Greek polis, but rather emerged in reaction to the development of democracy in the ancient world.[101] He sees ancient oligarchy as a form of authoritarianism, and the challenges those oligarchies faced—of coordination and keeping the masses at bay—echo the themes of elite organisation versus mass disorganisation that is fundamental to the 'elite' thinkers.[102] Yet faced with naming minority rule before the emergence of the term 'oligarchy', Simonton tries to resolve the conundrum by calling Archaic regimes 'elite-led', for 'lack of a better term', as he confesses.[103] Whilst using a term coined in 1902 to describe an ancient regime presents certain difficulties—*eunomia* is the term most used during this

98. Quentin Skinner, 'Meaning and Understanding in the History of Ideas', in *Visions of Politics, Volume I: Regarding Method*, Cambridge, Cambridge University Press, 2002, pp. 57–89.

99. Bonnell, *Robert Michels, Socialism, and Modernity*.

100. C. W. Cassinelli, 'The Law of Oligarchy', *The American Political Science Review*, vol. 47, no. 3, 1953, p. 782; Ober, *Mass and Elite in Democratic Athens*, p. 337.

101. Matthew Simonton, *Classical Greek Oligarchy: A Political History*, Princeton, Princeton University Press, 2017. See pp. 3–4 for Michels' iron law.

102. Ibid., pp. 71–73.

103. Ibid., p. 8, n. 22.

period[104]—Simonton's account of the rise of democracy shares many points of contact with dynamic democracy.

He writes:

> *Dēmokratia* was not simply a spontaneous movement by the newly awakened masses, nor was it a gift from elite to demos. Instead, it had (at least) three necessary conditions: 1) times had to be bad enough to give the demos good reason to risk uniting for political change; 2) certain members of the elite had to be alienated from the status quo enough to ally with the demos against their peers; and, crucially, 3) the members of the demos had to form a mass movements powerful enough that renegade members of the elite in question felt they had no choice but to offer power to the common people.[105]

Or, in short: democracy is achieved when a social movement places enough pressure on the established elite that a faction of it joins with the rising elite to overthrow the old elite. In other words: dynamic democracy.

But if it is the few who rule, then there are still many questions to be answered: Who are the few? How do they rule? From which principles? Who can be part of them? How do they relate to other elite groups? How do they relate to the people?

Pessimism

In his *The Rhetoric of Reaction*, Hirschman famously depicted Mosca, Pareto and Michels, alongside Tocqueville, as proponents of the 'futility thesis', where 'attempts at social transformation will be unavailing, that they will simply fail to "make a dent"'.[106] The futility thesis is captured by the popular saying '*plus ça change*', or again Tancredi's famous line in *The Leopard*: 'everything must change for everything to remain the same'.[107] As Hirschman more fully elaborates: 'the attempt at change is abortive, that in one way or another any alleged change is, was, or will be largely surface, façade, cosmetic, hence illusory, as the "deep" structures of society remain wholly untouched'.[108]

104. Ibid.
105. Ibid., p. 20.
106. Hirschman, *The Rhetoric of Reaction*, p. 7.
107. Ibid., pp. 43–44.
108. Ibid., p. 43.

Interestingly, Hirschman casts this discussion through the metaphor of movement, where Mosca, Pareto and Michels are meant to be the defenders of the 'law of no-motion' against those who advocate change, the 'law of motion'.[109] Hirschman's charge against the futility thesis is that it is either self-fulfilling or self-refuting: it is self-fulfilling if 'the assertions about the meaninglessness of intended changes and reforms weaken resistance to their further emasculation and outright abandonment'—in this, in pouring 'ridicule and discredit on the country's fledging democratic institutions', the 'elitists' are guilty of having contributed to the rise of fascism—and it is self-refuting if 'the very tension set up by the futility claim makes for new, more determined, and better informed efforts at achieving real change'.[110]

Certainly, Hirschman is right to say that for the elite thinkers—and, by extension, dynamic democracy—the 'deep' structures of society are unalterable if by 'unalterable' is meant the inevitability of elite rule.[111] Yet that in no way means that actions do not have consequences: most simply put, the passage from lions to foxes. Contra Hirschman, there is allowance for 'social learning or for incremental, corrective policy-making':[112] note the role the SPD had in improving the lot of workers, discussed above, even if it did not achieve its revolutionary aim of proletarian revolution.

At the end of *Political Parties*, Michels offered us a second metaphor for dynamic democracy, that of successive waves breaking against the shoal:

> The democratic currents of history resemble successive waves. They break ever on the same shoal. They are ever renewed. This enduring spectacle is simultaneously encouraging and depressing. When democracies have gained a certain stage of development, they undergo a gradual transformation, adopting the aristocratic spirit, and in many cases also the aristocratic forms, against which at the outset they struggled so fiercely. Now new accusers arise to denounce the traitors; after an era of glorious combats and of inglorious power, they end by fusing with the old dominant class; whereupon once more they are in their turn attacked by fresh opponents who appeal to the name of democracy. It is probable that this cruel game will continue without end.[113]

109. Ibid., p. 44.
110. Ibid., p. 78.
111. See also ibid., p. 72.
112. Ibid., p. 78.
113. Michels, *Political Parties*, p. 371.

This seems to capture precisely Hirschman's 'self-fulfilling' claim that the tension built up against the established elite will necessarily lead to new, more determined and better-informed efforts to challenge the status quo.

In his Inaugural Address at the University of Turin, Mosca explicitly rejected the thesis of the 'futile labour of Sisyphus', explaining that if there is always a political class, the question remained open as to how good that political class could be, and that 'some minorities have the necessary attitudes to direct the social corpus beneficially'.[114] So although democracy as 'rule of the people' will never be achieved—the few will always rule—striving towards it need not be in vain, and may indeed bring about some positive results. Democracy is not a sham, but a species of elite rule.

In his *Against the Masses*, Joseph Femia, discussing Hirschman's futility thesis, actually concedes the point when he mentions—he is one of the few to do so—both Aesop's fable and Michels' 'palliatives' against democracy, requesting that these reflections be deepened. He concludes: 'pursuit of the unattainable is not always a waste of time; the futility thesis, correctly understood, need not be a counsel of despair'.[115] In truth, the futility thesis—that if democracy is not *impossible* it is at least *imperilled*—is one of 'the most profound contributions to democratic theory'.[116]

Dynamic democracy, therefore, need not be a 'counsel of despair'. It is, certainly, a pessimistic account of democracy: the 'people' will never rule in any true sense. Yet that pessimism need not be disheartening.[117] It can be, to borrow Nietzsche's phrase, a 'pessimism of strength', where the fact of 'elite rule' need not be the end-point of the democratic discussion but instead its start: the *affirmation* of elite rule can open up new ways of thinking and acting upon democracy.[118] That is the 'profound' contribution to democratic theory. Indeed, there is an undeniable Nietzschean hue to this work, whether it be the circulation of elites as a form of 'eternal return', the ranking of elites or the iron law of oligarchy as 'beyond good and evil', Schumpeter's 'entrepreneur' as a value-creating *Übermensch*, the masses considered to be the 'much too many'

114. Beetham, 'From Socialism to Fascism II', p. 162.

115. Ibid., p. 109.

116. Ibid., p. 15.

117. Joshua Dienstag, *Pessimism: Philosophy, Ethic, Spirit*, Princeton, Princeton University Press, 2006.

118. For a critique of the 'elite theorists' as 'precluded them from understanding the main alternatives of political life', see Giulio De Ligio, 'The Iron Law of Elites and the Standards of Political Judgment', *Perspectives on Political Science*, Vol. 50, No. 4, 2021, pp. 262–277.

and participating in a 'downward levelling',[119] or, finally, democracy as always being 'in becoming'.

It is, moreover, a *liberal* theory of democracy, one invested in defending the institutions of liberal-democracy: representative democracy, the rule of law, political parties. Political parties, we can note, were born with liberalism and are intimately linked to it.[120] It is when political parties start to die that illiberal populist forces take over: populists fill the vacuum left by political parties by appealing directly to the 'people', whereas parties served both a socialisation and mediating function. Indeed, liberalism and elitism, because of a shared suspicion of the 'masses', as Alan Kahan has reminded us, often go hand in hand.[121] Conversely, liberalism and democracy are not synonymous: liberalism focuses on rights whereas democracy focuses on participation. The two can come into conflict.

In his classic work *The Principles of Representative Government*, Bernard Manin argued that representative government as first thought-up over the course of the eighteenth and nineteenth centuries—the period with Mosca, Pareto and Michels that concerns us here—was not understood as being synonymous with democracy as it is today, but was expressly considered to be a different—if not altogether opposed—political system. In fact, for Madison and Siéyès, it was considered eminently *superior*. As such, when Mosca defends representative government, it is through this prism that it must be understood.[122]

Things have, of course, changed since the nineteenth century, not least the advent of universal suffrage.[123] But Manin is adamant that today's elections have both a democratic and an oligarchic dimension: oligarchic in that elections still 'select' the best representatives, who often, if they are professional politicians, start with an unfair advantage, unlike lot (democratic in that 'all citizens [have] an equal power to designate and dismiss their rulers'). 'Election inevitably selects elites', Manin concludes, 'but it is for ordinary citizens to

119. Sartori, *The Theory of Democracy Revisited*, p. 167.

120. Moisei Ostrogorski, *La democratic et les partis politiques*, Paris, Seuil, 1979.

121. Alan Kahan, *Aristocratic Liberalism: The Social and Political Thought of Jacob Burckhardt, John Stuart Mill, and Alexis De Tocqueville*, New Brunswick, Transaction Publishers, 2001. See also Olivia Leboyer, *Élite et libéralisme*, Paris, CNRS Editions, 2012.

122. Bernard Manin, *The Principles of Representative Government*, Cambridge, Cambridge University Press, 1997, pp. 1–3.

123. See Hirschman, *The Rhetoric of Reaction*, p. 50, who discusses Mosca, Pareto and Michels explicitly in the context of universal suffrage and the extension of the franchise.

define what constitutes an elite and who belongs to it'.[124] When dynamic democracy defends representative government, it is through the duality—oligarchic/democratic, elite/mass—Manin has exposed.

Manin criticises Schumpeter for being a 'demystifier' of democracy, who set out to prove—incorrectly for Manin—that the 'power of the people' in democracy was a 'mere myth': our current system has an essentially democratic element to it, so his study showed. In reality the core disagreement between the two is whether the people are to be captured, as in Schumpeter's account we will explore further in chapter 4, or whether they do, through a process of repetition, anticipation and retrospective judgement, emit a verdict on their representatives the latter need to take account of.[125] Both aspects are undeniably at play in our democracies, yet if Schattschneider is correct, then the role politicians play is precisely to *politicise* conflict already in existence in society.[126] As such, perhaps 'capturing' is closer to the truth, especially in more transformational moments. Manin actually comes close to conceding the point in his discussion of Schumpeter's notion of the 'manufactured will' when he writes that 'representatives are persons who take the initiative in proposing a line of division. They seek to identify cleavages within the electorate, and to bring some of them to the public stage'.[127] Or, in other words, to capture the public.

If dynamic democracy is a liberal theory of democracy, it remains on the progressive side of liberalism.[128] This is for two reasons. The first, because of its emphasis on institutions: liberal theories that focus on a certain 'ethos', where the project is reforming character, tend to be more conservative in their orientation.[129] There the interest is on individuals and society, whereas here the attention is on society and politics (i.e. structures). The second is because of movement: standing still means inevitably going backwards, whilst dynamism is forward-facing.[130] In this left-liberal form, dynamic democracy shares certain features with

124. Ibid., p. 238.

125. Ibid., pp. 175–179, 192.

126. Schattschneider, *The Semisovereign People*, p. 138.

127. Manin, *Principles*, p. 226.

128. For elite theory's influence on R. G. Collingwood's 'Continental' liberalism, which opposed laissez-faire economics, see Christopher Fear, 'Collingwood's New Leviathan and Classical Elite Theory', *History of European Ideas*, Vol. 45, No. 7, 2019, pp. 1029–1044.

129. Cherniss, *Liberalism in Dark Times*. See, further, Michael Oakeshott, 'On Being Conservative' in *Rationalism in Politics and Other Essays*, London, Methuen,1962, pp. 168–96.

130. Lawrence Silverman, 'The Ideological Mediation of Party-Political Responses to Social Change', *European Journal of Political Research*, Vol. 13, No. 1, 1985, pp. 69–93.

theories of (neo-republicanism), not least its convergence on the state.[131] But 'non-domination' on this account can never be achieved due to persistence of elite-rule, which *de facto*, if not *de jure*, means some form of coercion will exist, even if the aim of dynamic democracy is precisely to challenge that, as with republicanism. Finally, if dynamic democracy is a liberal theory, it is also a theory of *democracy*, which it affirms in its dynamic and representative iteration.

Elite theory has often been decried as what Bobbio, in his deeply reflective piece on Mosca's theory of the ruling class, has described as 'ideology masquerading as a scientific theory'.[132] Moreover, in Mosca's case this theory is 'incorrigibl[y] conservative'.[133] Quentin Skinner made a similar point in his 1973 *Political Theory* article 'The Empirical Theorists of Democracy and Their Critics', where he declared a Mercutian 'plague on both their houses'.[134] Focusing on Dahl's *Preface to Democratic Theory*, Skinner argued that Dahl's 'speechact' of associating 'polyarchy' with democracy brought about a positive valuation of polyarchy through the back door: this is done by associating polyarchy with the 'rule of the people' even if their participation is no longer a necessary condition for the attainment of democracy. Skinner concludes:

> It is in this way that the application of the term democracy to the type of political system Dahl describes constitutes an act of political conservatism: it serves to commend the recently prevailing values and practices of a political system like that of the United States, and it constitutes a form of argument against those who have sought to question the democratic character of those values and practices.[135]

More pointedly, Skinner showed how Dahl and the other 'empirical theorists' had in effect obscured the elitist and oligarchic nature of their theories

131. Quentin Skinner, *Liberty before Liberalism*, Cambridge, Cambridge University Press, 1997 and Philip Pettit, *Republicanism: A Theory of Freedom and Government*, Oxford, Oxford University Press, 1999. On the state, see Philip Pettit, *The State*, Princeton, Princeton University Press, 2023. On elitism and republicanism, see Camila Vergara, 'Republican Constitutional Thought: Elitist and Plebian Interpretations of the Mixed Constitution', *History of Political Thought*, Vol. 43, No. 5, 2022, pp. 28–55.

132. Norberto Bobbio, 'Gaetano Mosca and the Theory of the Ruling Class' in *On Mosca and Pareto*, Genève, Librarie Droz, 1972, p. 21. See also Parry, *Political Elites*, pp. 19–24.

133. Ibid. See also Hirschman, *The Rhetoric of Reaction*, p. 79.

134. Quentin Skinner, 'The Empirical Theorists of Democracy and Their Critics: A Plague on Both Their Houses', *Political Theory*, Vol. 1, No. 3, 1973, pp. 287–306.

135. Ibid., pp. 303–304.

and US democracy.[136] The aim of this book is precisely to bring these elements to light: chapter 5 will reveal the fundamentally elitist foundation of Dahl's polyarchy, and the oligarchic nature of modern democracy is the essential theme that traverses the work. Based on that 'fact', what is proposed here, if perhaps a little too crudely for Skinner's taste, is a new theory of democracy: dynamic democracy.[137]

Bobbio, moreover, was quick to point out two things. The first is that, to get going, political science, at least in Italy, needed a realistic starting point from which to build—one not drawn from a priori principles—and the theory of the ruling class provided that. According to Bobbio, the theory of the ruling class 'was accepted as a useful tool for historical analysis and doctrinal adjustments'.[138] Indeed for Bobbio, writing in 1962,[139] although the theory had shown its intellectual 'fertility' and had been confirmed by 'authoritative writers',[140] the question was whether the theory had been tested empirically.[141]

Today, with the publication of Martin Gilens and Benjamin Page's seminal study 'Testing Theories of American Politics: Elites, Interest Groups, and Average Citizens' in *Perspectives on Politics* in 2014, we can say that it has been. And the results are unequivocal: between theories of the median voter, economic elite domination, general interest groups and business lobbies, it is economic elites and business lobbies that get their way.[142] In other words, as the BBC reported, American democracy is not a democracy, but an oligarchy.[143] There is no reason to believe Europe is any different.

The second point is that although Mosca gave a conservative rendering of his theory of the ruling class, one need not read it in that way. Bobbio explains:

136. Ibid., p. 302.

137. See ibid., p. 296, for the 'crudest possible ideological move' of moving the definition of democracy away from 'people rule'.

138. Ibid., p. 22.

139. Norberto Bobbio, 'Foreword' in *On Mosca and Pareto*, p. 9.

140. Bobbio, 'Gaetano Mosca and the Theory of the Ruling Class', p. 30.

141. Ibid., p. 28.

142. Martin Gilens and Benjamin Page, 'Testing Theories of American Politics: Elites, Interest Groups, and Average Citizens', *Perspectives on Politics*, Vol. 12, No. 3, 2014, pp. 564–581.

143. 'Study: US Is an Oligarchy, Not a Democracy', *BBC*, 17 April 2014, https://www.bbc.co.uk/news/blogs-echochambers-27074746 (consulted on 30 December 2023).

The difference between a conservative attitude and a progressive one does not consist in the acceptance or rejection of the concept of the ruling class, but in the different way of solving the problems regarding the four points to which we have reduced the analysis of Mosca's thought, that is, the composition, extension, replacement and organisation of the ruling class.[144]

So, if Mosca, according to Bobbio, emphasised a theory of the ruling class that is hereditary, restricted, slow to be renewed and claiming power from above (divine right of kings, traditional powers)—and we'll have occasion to challenge such a conservative reading in chapter 2, arguing instead that Mosca favoured a 'mixed' regime—a progressive account of the ruling class can be offered too. 'To be democratic', Bobbio writes, 'it is not necessary to disavow the theory of the ruling class'.

A democratic reading would comprise the following elements. The first element, in terms of the 'composition' of the ruling class, is to admit that it can be formed by 'other than hereditary means', through education or culture, for example, something Bobbio will recognise was in reality Mosca's end-goal.[145] The second element, in terms of the 'extension' of the ruling class, is, Bobbio writes, that 'a democratic society is distinguished from an aristocratic one by the greater number of the people forming the ruling class'.[146] For replacement, Bobbio notes that Mosca offered two tendencies: that of 'seal[ing] itself off' or 'open[ing] its doors and hence initiat[ing] a process of renovation'.[147] The first tendency was aristocratic and the second democratic, and we shall see that Mosca offered the ideal of a moderately 'open elite', drawn from the idealised English gentry, which would bring in the best elements from below without being completely overwhelmed by them. Finally, in terms of the 'political formula', there is the option of justifying its power from either above (divine right of kings) or below (Bobbio offers 'contractual theories' as an example), the latter necessarily being more democratic.[148] Here we have a democratic theory of the ruling class.

144. Ibid., p. 23.
145. Ibid. For culture, see p. 15: 'he expressed a longing for a society in which culture would prevail'.
146. Ibid.
147. Ibid.
148. Ibid., p. 24.

A final point: if dynamic democracy is indeed a *liberal* theory, then it's ultimate aim, as a liberal theory, is the preservation of liberty, understood as defending the rights of different groups. The touchstone for this notion, given its Neo-Machiavellian provenance, is Machiavelli himself, specifically how, in the *Discourses*, it is the *tumult* between the plebs and the patricians that guarantees not simply the liberty of the two groups—they do not oppress one another[149]—but the regime itself: it is through conflict that liberty emerges. The *Discourses* have often been read through a republican lens, but as stated above the reading offered here is a much more liberal, read through both Aron and Mosca. So, translated to a modern context: it is the conflict, democratised into competition, between the elites and the masses that secures their liberty and the liberty of the whole.[150]

IV: Book Structure

There will be six chapters in what follows, on Mosca, Pareto, Michels, Schumpeter, Dahl and Mills, and Aron, respectively. In many ways the book can be divided into two: the first part, consisting of the first three chapters, presents a recovery of Mosca, Pareto and Michels' thought in their own context (the history of political thought claim). The second part, the chapters on Schumpeter, Dahl and Mills, and Aron, is an attempt to show how we cannot understand post-war democratic theory, and indeed the social sciences more broadly, without reference to the earlier 'elitists' (the intellectual history claim). Through this, the aim is to build a *dynamic* theory of democracy (the democratic theory claim). And although part of what will be argued is that the thought of Mosca, Pareto and Michels is richer than we have recently seen, and indeed what the mid-twentieth century saw, nevertheless Schumpeter, Dahl, Mills and Aron offer us additional insights and building blocks—Aron's *personnel politique*, for example—towards this theory.

A word, to conclude, on what this book will not do. First, although Weber (in Michels' chapter) and Moisei Ostrogorski (in Aron's chapter) will be

149. To pick up the provocative question whether we should worry whether the masses have liberty: articulated through Machiavelli the masses simply don't want to be oppressed, whereas the elites want to oppress, so for the former limiting oppression is a form of liberty in itself.

150. The conflict between two 'spheres' is perhaps the final link back to Nietzsche; see Marshal Zeringue, 'Hugo Drochon's "Nietzsche's Great Politics", the Page 99 Test', 23 July 2016 (https://page99test.blogspot.com/2016/07/hugo-drochons-nietzsches-great-politics.html accessed on 4 October 2024).

discussed, a systematic account of the latter, especially, will not be offered. Yet there is reason to believe that Ostrogorski also proposes a dynamic theory of democracy, with his suggestion to replace stultifying omnibus parties that follow the 'party line' with more temporary 'leagues' that would come together to defend one interest before disbanding: 'down with the party and up with the league!'. This is why Ostrogorski is often considered the father of 'Single-Issue' parties.[151] Second, the story of the second half of the twentieth century is by necessity a partial one, especially when it comes to the question of the birth of the social sciences, which has been covered by others, as we shall see in chapter 5. A complete account would require a study of its own, which is beyond the scope of this book.

That being said, it is worth noting that the first reception of the elite theorists in the US was during the 1930s as a way of trying to make sense of the rise of fascism.[152] Indeed, the two periods considered here—the turn of the twentieth century and the Cold War—share a common matrix: distrust or scepticism of democracy, not simply direct democracy but also electoral democracy. And although post-war it is America that reigns supreme, in reality it is European democracy, as Conway has argued, that provides the ideological structure for post-war democracy, in its dualism between 'totalitarian' and 'liberal' democracy and its fear of popular participation. The theory of the 'elitists' is the bedrock upon which that democracy was built.

The line, therefore, followed here is one that starts with Mosca, Pareto and Michels and goes forward from there, with an emphasis on democratic theory. This means that linked thematic debates, such as that between Walter Lippmann and John Dewey,[153] for instance, will not feature, as the classic 'elitists' were not their touchstone. Nor, it should be added, will there be a specific chapter on Italian thinkers such as Bobbio and Sartori, who will be more utilised as interpreters and commentators of Mosca and Pareto; nor on Antonio Gramsci, where an excellent study on Mosca and Gramsci's 'democratic elitism', according to which 'authority flows from the masses to the elites', has

151. Ostrogorski, *La democratie et les partis politiques*. See, further, Philipp Erbentraut, 'Moisei Ostrogorski, Political Parties, and the Dawn of Realist Theories of Political Elites', presented at the Mancept Workshop 2019, University of Manchester, 9–11 September 2019, who places Ostrogorski within the Mugwumps' nineteenth-century liberal reform movement in America.

152. Giorgio Volpe, *Italian Elitism and the Reshaping of Democracy in the United States*, Abingdon, Routledge, 2021.

153. Note that Lippmann does cite Michels in his *Phantom Public* (Walter Lippmann, *The Phantom Public*, New York, Harcourt, Brace, 1925, pp. 19–23).

been penned by Maurice Finocchiaro.[154] All these will be the subject of future work.

As such, the story is meant to be illustrative rather than comprehensive, but should others wish to complete the canvas, they're very welcome to do so. Nevertheless, if the borders of the tableau remain somewhat impressionistic, the hope is that its main figures, and themes, will be sufficiently sharply drawn.

154. Maurice Finocchiaro, *Beyond Right and Left: Democratic Elitism in Mosca and Gramsci*, New Haven, Yale University Press, 1999, p. viii.

1

Mosca and the Ruling Class

ON 19 DECEMBER 1925, an elderly senator stood up in the Italian Senate to make a speech. He did so with a 'certain trepidation': in the same manner as when a deputy dies it falls on their successor, even if the successor is a political rival, to give the funeral oration, here the speaker was about to give the funeral oration of the parliamentary regime.[1] The irony that the responsibility should fall to him, one who had been so critical of the regime, was not lost on the speaker, who reminded his audience, to some applause, that he believed the regime had made two mistakes—one before the war and one directly after, namely, universal suffrage and proportional representation—that had led to the degeneration of a system that between 1919 and 1922 had worked quite well.[2]

And yet, for all its faults, the speaker was forced to concede, with a certain emotion, that he would lament the regime's departure. 'One may say in all sincerity', the senator explained, that compared to the regime that was called to replace it—the senator was speaking against Mussolini's motion that would make the Prime Minister's power absolute—'the parliamentary regime was better'.[3] Although the senator had previously made a number of suggestions to strengthen the executive power in relation to parliament, here the Chamber,

---

1. Gaetano Mosca, 'Prerogative del capo del governo' in *Partiti e Sindacati nella crisi del regime parlamentare*, Bari, Laterza, 1949, pp. 277, 282. See, further, James Meisel, *The Myth of the Ruling Class: Gaetano Mosca and the Elite*, Ann Arbor, University of Michigan Press, 1962, pp. 225–7, who mistakenly dates the speech to 25 December, and David Ragazzoni and Nadia Urbinati, 'Theories of Representative Government and Parliamentarism in Italy from the 1840s to the 1920s' in Pasi Ihalainen, Cornelia Ilie and Kari Palonen, eds., *Parliament and Parliamentarism: A Comparative History of a European Concept*, New York, Berghahn, 2016, p. 258.

2. Ibid., pp. 282–3. See, further, Fritz Morstein Marx, 'The Bureaucratic State: Some Remarks on Mosca's Ruling Class', *The Review of Politics*, Vol. 1, No. 4, 1939, p. 465.

3. Ibid., p. 283.

having lost its right to initiate legislation, would lose all power altogether.[4] He would therefore be voting against the motion (more applause). Having finished his speech, the senator promptly sat down and resigned from public life the following year. His name was Gaetano Mosca.

What had changed? Well-known for his critique of parliamentarism through his works *Sulla teorica dei governi e sul governo parlamentare* (*Theory of Governments and Parliamentary Government*), first published in 1884 (second edition 1925), and *Elementi di scienza politica* (translated into English as *The Ruling Class*), published in 1896 (second edition 1923),[5] Mosca, as he reminded his audience during his speech to the Senate, had vehemently argued against universal suffrage and the extension of the franchise, defending a constitutional monarchy with a limited vote. Indeed, one of the reasons Mosca gave against the motion was that the 'Capo del Governo' (Head of Government) would no longer need the confidence of the King to rule, thereby vitiating the latter's role in the institutional set-up.[6] This placed him in the liberal-conservative camp, much like his French predecessor François Guizot,[7] although, as we shall see, that intellectual positioning can be *nuanced*, and moreover strict disciplined political parties as we know them today were not yet fully established in Italy—at least not before the rise of the fascists—meaning that prime ministers accepted support from where they could find it, often composing rather heteroclite alliances.[8] As Richard Bellamy writes: 'although the Italian parliament contained two broad groupings of deputies, the 'Right'

4. Ibid., p. 280. See also Meisel, *The Myth of the Ruling Class*, p. 225. In *The Ruling Class*, Mosca had shown some sympathy to a more 'presidential' system extant in the US. See Gaetano Mosca, *The Ruling Class: Elementi di Scienza Politica*, ed., Arthur Livingston, trans. Hannah Kahn, New York, McGraw-Hill, 1939, pp. 150 ('as an organ of juridical defence the American presidency is far superior to the cabinets in the parliamentary countries of Europe, since European cabinets have less authority than the American president and more need of kowtowing to assemblymen and politicians than he') and 263.

5. Mosca, *The Ruling Class*.

6. Mosca, 'Prerogative del capo del governo', pp. 278–9; Meisel, *The Myth of the Ruling Class*, p. 225.

7. Pierre Rosanvallon, *Le moment Guizot*, Paris, Gallimard, 1985. See further Alan Kahan, *Aristocratic Liberalism: The Social and Political Thought of Jacob Burckhardt, John Stuart Mill, and Alexis De Tocqueville*, London, Routledge, 2017.

8. Ragazzoni and Urbinati, 'Theories of Representative Government and Parliamentarism in Italy from the 1840s to the 1920s', pp. 243–261.

and the 'Left', neither constituted real parties with the ideological and bureau-cratic structures we expect today'.[9]

Yet by the turn of the century Mosca seemed to have changed his mind. Although critical of the parliamentary regime, he had signed the 'Manifesto of the Anti-Fascist Intellectuals' penned by Benedetto Croco, which appeared simultaneously in the liberal newspaper *Il Mondo* and the Catholic newspaper *Il Popolo* on 1 May 1925. This was in response to Giovanni Gentile's 'Manifesto of Fascist Intellectuals' that had appeared a few days earlier, on 21 April 1925. The symbolism of the dates was that 21 April was the day of celebration of the founding of Rome, whereas 1 May was Worker's Day, which had, in fact, origi-nally been celebrated on 21 April, before being changed by royal decree that same year.

One answer can be found in the difference between the first edition of the *Elementi*, published in 1895, and the second, in 1923—twenty-seven years later—in which Mosca added six new chapters to the original ten: they were, in many ways, two separate books. The 1895 edition concluded with a critique of 'collectivism' (split into two chapters—10 and 11—in the English transla-tion), namely Mosca's concern that democracy meant the extension of the 'rule of the people' into all aspects of life: not just in parliament, but also the bureaucracy, the army, economics, law etc.[10] At this point in his life, this is what Mosca understood democracy to mean—a form of direct Rousseauian democracy[11]—a view, it must be said, widely shared. And like many of his time, Mosca thought the logical end-point of democracy was a form of (social-ist) collectivism, where everything would be decided through a form of direct democracy: 'it seems evident to us that socialism is a necessary consequence

9. Richard Bellamy, *Modern Italian Social Theory*, Cambridge, Polity Press, p. 5. On Mosca and the right and left, see Maurice Finocchiaro, *Beyond Right and Left: Democratic Elitism in Mosca and Gramsci*, New Haven, Yale University Press, 1999. Finocchiaro makes the good point that for a liberal like Mosca, opposing state intervention in the market but favouring state in-tervention in religious education are compatible, as we will also see with Pareto, because both aimed to break up monopolies (the Catholic Church in the latter instance) to restore a sense of balance (Finocchiaro, *Beyond Left and Right*, p. 170).

10. Mosca, *The Ruling Class*, pp. 271ff. On the dangers of bureaucratisation for Mosca, see Marx, 'The Bureaucratic State: Some Remarks on Mosca's Ruling Class', pp. 457–472. On col-lectivism, see John Tashjean, 'Mosca Revisited: Exegesis of an Elitist Argument', *Revue europée-nne des sciences sociales*, Vol. 10, No. 217, 1972, pp. 123–126.

11. Ibid., pp. 271–274.

of pure democracy'.[12] As a good liberal, Mosca feared the arrival of the masses into politics.[13]

The second, revised, edition of *Elementi* of 1923, published a few weeks after Mussolini came to power, however ended with a defence of the liberal parliamentary regime.[14] Had he changed his mind? Certainly his thinking on certain subjects had evolved, or perhaps gotten clearer: now Mosca distinguished more clearly the institutions of parliamentary government from 'parliamentarism', a form of ideology he still took to be synonymous with collectivism.[15] As Arthur Livingston, his English-language editor, writes:

> But the most significant portions of the 'second part' are a clarification, and first of all in Mosca's own mind, of the import of the criticism of democracy that he had made in the past and his impassioned appeal for a restoration of the representative system in Europe.[16]

Yet already in the first edition of the *Elementi* there were a number of different elements—juridical defence, social forces—that would intellectually predispose Mosca to reject the Fascist regime and defend the institutions of what we would now call constitutional liberal-democracy. To those others were added in the second edition not least the notion of liberal legitimacy, though the foundations for this were already there in the original. Indeed, in the first edition Mosca had opened with the view that, anticipating Churchill, representative government may be regarded as the 'least imperfect form of government', going so far as to warn in conclusion that the 'sound criterion' for judging political systems is to 'compare them with others', forestalling what he would say in his Senate speech, and that, if judged by that standard,

> the defects of parliamentary assemblies, and the evil consequences which their control of power and their participation in power produce in all representative systems, are merest trifles as compared with the harm that would inevitably result from abolishing them or stripping them of their influence.[17]

---

12. Ibid., p. 276. Marx, 'The Bureaucratic State: Some Remarks on Mosca's Ruling Class', p. 464.

13. Bellamy, *Modern Italian Social Theory*, p. 52.

14. Mosca, *The Ruling Class*, pp. 465ff; Bellamy, *Modern Italian Social Theory*, p. 49.

15. Mosca, *The Ruling Class*, p. 255; Ragazzoni and Urbinati, 'Theories of Representative Government and Parliamentarism in Italy from the 1840s to the 1920s', pp. 255–6.

16. Arthur Livingston, 'Introduction' in Mosca, *The Ruling Class*, p. xxxiii.

17. Mosca, *The Ruling Class*, pp. 13 and 256.

The aim of this chapter is to articulate Mosca's critique of democracy, distinguishing between his rejection of parliamentarism and his defence of the liberal, constitutional parliamentary regime. In contrast to his self-presentation in his speech to the senate, it will argue that Mosca held consistent views throughout his intellectual and political life, namely, a defence of a liberal-parliamentary form of constitutional monarchy, based on the English model,[18] which he defended against two 'extremes': socialism on the one hand, and, from the 1920s onward, fascism on the other.[19] This maps itself well onto Mosca's own thinking, which might best be described as 'in becoming': seizing a subject at an early stage, to develop and deepen it over time.[20] As has often been said, Mosca was a 'monomaniac' who 'wrote three versions of the same book'; yet that does not mean that his thesis did not expand over time.[21] The notion of the 'ruling class', for instance, first appeared in his *Teorica*,[22] which was on parliamentary democracy, but deepened in *Elementi* both I and II, to find its final formulation—at least according to both Norberto Bobbio and James Meisel, the latter adding it as a supplement to his *The Myth of the Ruling Class*[23]—in the ultimate chapter of his 1937 *Storia delle dottrine politiche* (*History of Political Doctrines*), which was based on lectures he gave at the University of Rome.[24] Note that this book came out at the height of the Fascist regime, meaning Mosca maintained the views he had defended in the revised edition of the *Elementi*.[25]

18. Ibid., pp. 254, 262, 326.

19. Cook, 'Gaetano Mosca's "The Ruling Class"', p. 442. On 'extremes', see Hugo Drochon, 'From Dusk till Dawn: Bobbio on the Left/Right Dichotomy', *Journal of Political Ideologies*, Vol. 27, No. 3, 2022, pp. 330–346.

20. On the notion of Mosca's thought being 'in becoming', borrowed from the literature on Nietzsche, see Hugo Drochon, *Nietzsche's Great Politics*, Princeton, Princeton University Press, 2016, pp. 8–9.

21. Bellamy, *Modern Italian Social Theory*, pp. 3–4. See also Meisel, *The Myth of the Ruling Class*, p. 18.

22. On the *Teorica* see Bellamy, *Modern Italian Social Theory*, pp. 35–44.

23. Gaetano Mosca, 'The Final Version of the Theory of the Ruling Class' in Meisel, *The Myth of the Ruling Class*, pp. 382ff.

24. Bobbio, 'Gaetano Mosca and the Theory of the Ruling Class', pp. 11–12. For Bellamy the three books are *Teorica*, *Elementi I* and *Elementi II* (Bellamy, *Modern Italian Social Theory*, p. 36). In this Bellamy follows Piane, who was the first to offer such a divide (Mario delle Piane, *Gaetano Mosca: Classe Politica e Liberalismo*, Naples, Edizioni Scientifiche Italiane, 1952).

25. This book was first published in French as Gaetano Mosca and Gaston Bouthoul, *Histoire des doctrine politiques*, Paris, Payot, 1965). Mosca wrote the first part, up to 1914, with Bouthoul

The chapter will first turn to Mosca's life, to show how his academic and political career oriented him to develop a more restricted *political* theory of the ruling class, in opposition to the work of Vilfredo Pareto, who would elaborate a more all-encompassing model of elite rule.[26] Indeed, it is important to underline that Mosca's theory of the 'ruling class' emanated from his critique of majority rule, whereas Pareto's concept of the elite arose from his study of (economic) inequality. As Livingston puts it:

> There is no dialectical or historical connection between Pareto's theory of the élite and Mosca's theory of the ruling class. On the dialectical side, Mosca's theory of the ruling class derives from a criticism of the doctrine of majority rule. . . . Pareto's theory of the élite derives from a study of the relations of distribution of wealth to class differentiations in society.[27]

Second, this chapter will explore the historical context within which Mosca operated, marked by the first years of Italian unification, which led him to defend the 'middle-class' as the worthy inheritors of the liberal nobles who had forged the nation.[28] Third, it will analyse Mosca's key concept of the 'classe politica' or 'classe dirigente'—the 'political class' or 'ruling class'[29]—which, simply put, claims that in all except small, early communities, the organised few always rule over the disorganised many. As Livingston notes: 'Mosca's "ruling class", therefore, covers a narrower field than Pareto's élite (the sum of outstanding talents) or the Marxian "ruling class" (the employer or property-holding class and its appendages, political or social)'.[30] Adding to this, fourth, it will bring to light a number of different notions present in Mosca's thought that are often overlooked: juridical defence, civilisation, social forces, justice, legitimacy. Finally, it will ask in what ways Mosca's ideas are related to the model of dynamic democracy, underlining how the continual rise and fall of new social forces lays the basis for a theory of democracy founded in movement.

---

writing the second part, from 1914 onwards. See, further, Ettore Albertoni, *Mosca and the Theory of Elitism*, Oxford, Basil Blackwell, 1987, p. 10.

26. Bellamy, *Modern Italian Social Theory*, p. 39.

27. Livingston, 'Introduction', p. xxxvi.

28. Cook, 'Gaetano Mosca's "The Ruling Class"', p. 445.

29. Albertoni, *Mosca and the Theory of Elitism*, p. 16 explains that in the *Teorica*, Mosca uses 'classe politica', but he uses 'classe dirigente' in the *Elementi*. Renzo Sereno, *The Rulers*, New York, Praeger, 1962 suggests using simply 'rulers', but the aim of this chapter is to show how rich Mosca's theory is.

30. Ibid.

I: Sicily

Mosca was born in Palermo on 1 April 1858. He was Sicilian.[31] By that is not meant that Mosca was an Italian who happened to be born in Sicily, like one might have been born in Tuscany, but he was born in the Sicily of the Kingdom of the Two Sicilies, comprising of the Kingdom of Naples and the Kingdom of Sicily—the region of Southern Italy still known today as the Mezzogiorno—both under Spanish Bourbon rule. The Risorgimento—the unification of Italy—came to Sicily when Giuseppe Garibaldi landed at Marsala on the western coast on 11 May 1860 with his 'Expedition of the Thousand' and overthrew King Francesco II, after which the people of Sicily and Naples voted in a plebiscite to join the Savoyard Kingdom of Sardinia: the last territorial conquest before the creation of the Kingdom of Italy on 17 March 1861. The period of transition is perhaps best captured by two of Sicily's most famous books: Federico de Roberto's *Viceré* (The Viceroys) and Giuseppe Tomasi di Lampedusa *Il Gattopardo*, famously mistranslated as *The Leopard* into English: a 'gattopardo' is in fact a serval, a small wildcat native of Africa that can sometimes be found on the island of Lampedusa.[32]

That Mosca was Sicilian is important.[33] After all, he wrote one of the first studies of the Mafia—*Che cose è la Mafia*—in 1900.[34] In *What Is the Mafia*, he

---

31. Note that his parents were from the north of Italy (Novara): his father was secretary general of the city-hall. See Alberto Puppo, 'Gaetano Mosca et la théorie de la classe politique: une pensée antidémocratique au service de la liberté', *Revue Française d'Histoire des Idées Politiques*, Vol. 2, No. 22, 2005, pp. 17–31.

32. See Federico De Roberto, *The Viceroys*, London, Verso, 2015 and Giuseppe Tomasi di Lampedusa, *The Leopard*, London, Vintage, 2007. On Lampedusa, see Steven Smith, 'The Political Teaching of Lampedusa's *The Leopard*' in *Modernity and Its Discontents: Making and Unmaking the Bourgeois from Machiavelli to Bellow*, New Haven, Yale University Press, 2016, pp. 313–329. On whether the famous line 'everything must change for everything to remain the same' is in fact drawn from Machiavelli's *Discourses on Livy*, Book I, Chapter 25, see Carlo Ginzburg, 'Lire entre les lignes: Notule sur *Le Guépard*' in *Néanmois: Machiavel, Pascal*, Lagrasse, Verdier, 2018, pp. 257–266.

33. Massimo Ganci, 'La Sicile en tant que milieu culturel et politique dans les premières œuvres de Gaetano Mosca' in Ettore Albertoni, ed., *Études sur la pensée politique de Gaetano Mosca: Classe politique et gouvernement*, Milan, Giuffrè Editore, 1984, pp. 101–114.

34. Gaetano Mosca, 'Che cose è la Mafia' in *Partiti e Sindacati nella crisi del regime parlamentare*, pp. 214–256. An English online translation exists under the title *What Is Mafia*, trans. Marco Lazzarotti, with a preface by David O'Kane, M&J Publishing House, 2014. For another great book on the Mafia, which echoes a number of the points Mosca makes in this piece, see

explains that the Mafia is in fact two things. First, it is a certain mindset or conduct whose biggest concern is to be respected, and that personal slights have to be handled individually: appealing to the authorities meant accepting one was weaker, and was therefore considered shameful.[35] This personal aspect meant revenge took the form of a vendetta, and keeping one's honour by not going, or indeed speaking, to the authorities sustained a form of omerta (silence),[36] all words that have passed into our everyday language (note, however, that the Sicilian Mafia never referred to itself as such, but rather as the 'cosa nostra', 'our thing'). Although Mosca was quick to point that this mindset is not restricted to Sicily—one can find in the upper echelons of Italian society in the North a form of 'bravado' that goes under the name of 'duelling'[37]—nevertheless there was a Sicilian specificity to it that had to do with its history of colonial rule, lastly by the Bourbons, which had led to the creation of an alternative system of justice. So there was nothing 'genetic' about the Sicilian Mafia, and indeed a Sicilian who left a mafiosi context—more prevalent in the poorer western part of Sicily beyond Palermo, and non-existent in the richer east—would come to renounce this way of life: themes that were important to Mosca we'll have occasion to return to.

Second, if the Mafia were indeed criminal groups—Mosca in chapter 6 gives a colourful account of how a local small landowner becomes prey to a Mafia clan, or 'cosche' as he calls them[38]—they were not a highly centralised and all-encompassing one as mythology might make them out to be, but were, at best, federations.[39] And yet these had been able to infiltrate the new Italian Republic, notably by forging links with certain Deputies.[40] Building on the fact that local Sicilian lords often took the defence of local clans during the Bourbon period,[41] this tradition of finding compromises with the Mafia had continued under the new regime for reasons of political expediency. The political system itself was in part responsible by bringing these clans into politics through the extension of the franchise, which in turn brought many

---

Leonardo Sciascia, *The Day of the Owl*, London, Granta, 2013. On Mosca and the Mafia, see Puppo, 'Gaetano Mosca et la théorie de la classe politique', p. 244.

35. Mosca, 'Che cose è la Mafia', pp. 215.
36. Ibid., p. 217.
37. Ibid., pp. 219–220.
38. Ibid., pp. 233–8.
39. Ibid., pp. 248–9. See Dwight Smith, *The Mafia Mystique*, New York, Basic Books, 1975.
40. Ibid., p. 244.
41. Ibid., pp. 241–4.

ordinary voters, under the influence of the Mafia, into the political system, even if the representative system—says Mosca—had much to commend it.[42] As Bellamy writes: 'unification had simply legalised the local oppression of the peasants by landowners and mafia bosses, and extended their ominous influence into national politics into the bargain.'[43]

Moreover, Mosca took the opportunity to denounce the corruption the new regime had fallen into, with public officials conferred a status of 'semi-impunity':[44] the occasion for the discussion was the murder of Emanuele Notarbartolo, former mayor of Palermo and director of the Bank of Sicily.[45] As a good liberal, Mosca wished for the extension of the rule of law throughout the new kingdom, and recommended that if the state stuck seriously to the task, notably by enforcing the ban on firearms and house arrest, it would see off the Mafia, a project that besides had the support of the people, Mosca giving the hard sentences handed out by popular juries to mafiosi as proof of that.[46]

But Mosca was a Sicilian who *left* Sicily: he gave his lecture on the Mafia in Milan in 1900. After completing his degree in law and political theory at the University of Palermo in 1881, he became an unsalaried lecturer there till 1886. In 1887 he moved to Rome to become the editor of the *Proceedings of the Chamber of Deputies*, continuing his unsalaried lecturing at the University of Rome. The position of editor was a bureaucratic position that maintained him during his unpaid lectureship at the University: academic precarity, it seems, isn't new. He obtained the post through the patronage of the Sicilian politician Antonio Di Rudini, who served as prime minister of Italy from 1891 to 1896.[47] Di Rudini, who led the right of the liberal party, was a rival to that other famous Sicilian politician Francesco Crispi, whom he criticised for his failed Abyssinia adventures and financial scandals. He also opposed the socialists on the one hand and the Catholics on the other—a position Mosca was to repeat—thereby finding himself with few friends, and during his time in power proposed a moderate conservative reform of balancing universal suffrage with

---

42. Ibid., p. 243
43. Bellamy, *Modern Italian Social Theory*, p. 5.
44. Ibid., p. 254.
45. Ibid., p. 249.
46. Ibid., pp. 241, 245.
47. On Mosca and Di Rudini, see Richard Bach Jensen, 'Was Mosca the Marquis Di Rudini's *Eminence Grise*?' in Ettore Albertoni, ed., *Studies on the Political Thought of Gaetano Mosca*, Milan, Giuffrè editore, 1982, pp. 125–136. The answer is 'no'.

decentralisation, something Mosca had proposed in *Teorica* and repeated in *Elementi*.[48]

From Rome he pursued an academic, political and journalistic career. In academia he finally received recognition when he was invited to become the chair of constitutional law at the University of Turin in 1896, holding that position until 1924, when he became chair of public law and political theories at the University of Rome. Politically, he was elected to the Chamber of Deputies in 1909, representing Palermo, sitting with the Destra storica—the Historical Right—as a liberal conservative. He held that seat until 1919, when he was nominated life senator of the Kingdom of Italy, from which he resigned in 1926, after his final speech. During his time as deputy he served as undersecretary for the colonies from 1914 till 1916 in the conservative Salandra cabinet, which was responsible for bringing Italy into the war on the side of the Triple Entente (England, France and Russia).[49] During his political career he also wrote for the Milanese *Corriere della Sera* from 1901, the most-read Italian newspaper of the day,[50] known for its opposition to socialism and prime minister Giovanni Giolitti—to whom we shall return—and also the *Tribuna* of Rome, from 1911 to 1921, which was more sympathetic to the latter.[51] He died in Rome on 8 November 1941 at the age of 83, a few years before Mussolini's death.

48. Mosca, *The Ruling Class*, p. 265; Bellamy, *Modern Italian Social Theory*, p. 44. Albertoni describes Mosca as 'undoubtedly conservative, but also openly reformist' (Albertoni, *Mosca and the Theory of Elitism*, p. 6). For 'moderate', see Bellamy, *Modern Italian Social Theory*, p. 34, and on 'moderation', see Aurelian Craiutu, *A Virtue for Courageous Minds: Moderation in French Political Thought, 1748–1830*, Princeton, Princeton University Press, 2012 and Aurelian Craiutu. *Faces of Moderation: The Art of Balance in an Age of Extremes*, Philadelphia, University of Pennsylvania Press, 2017. For a critique of moderation, see Hugo Drochon, 'Aurelian Craiutu, *A Virtue for Courageous Minds* and *Faces of Moderation*', *Journal of Modern History*, Vol. 90, No. 4, 2018, pp. 918–921. For an alternative view, which places Mosca in the social-welfare camp, see Thomas Cook, 'Gaetano Mosca's "The Ruling Class"', *Political Science Quarterly*, Vol. 54, No. 3, 1939, pp. 442–447. Bobbio sees Mosca decidedly in the 'incorrigibly' conservative camp (Norberto Bobbio, 'Gaetano Mosca and the Theory of the Ruling Class' in *On Mosca and Pareto*, Genève, Librairie Droz, 1972, pp. 21, 24).

49. Albertoni, *Mosca and the Theory of Elitism*, pp. 65–78.

50. On how the *Corriere della Sera* moved from being the journal of the Milanese bourgeoisie to becoming a national newspaper, see Adrian Lyttelton, 'Introduction' in Adrian Lyttelton, ed., *Liberal and Fascist Italy*, Oxford, Oxford University Press, 2002, pp. 2–4.

51. See Livingston, 'Introduction', pp. xii–xiv and Meisel, *The Myth of the Ruling Class*, pp. 19–20.

Livingston has this to say about Mosca's political career:

Not all Sicilians are politicians, but when a Sicilian is a politician he is a good one. The Sicilian takes to politics as a duck to water. North Italians, too, of course, have been seen in Italian public life. But they make a great to-do about it. They shout and wave their arms from soap-boxes, they fill the newspapers with their publicities, their polemics, their marches on Rome, they fight libel suits and duels; and finally they get into the government, only to be upset, as likely as not, at the next turn of the wheel. The Sicilian, instead, simply takes the train and goes to Rome, where a coach-in-four is waiting to drive him to what Carducci called 'the summit of the Capitol'.[52]

But *leaving* Sicily remains key: in the famous scene of *Il Gattopardo* when the Prince of Salina refuses a seat in the Senate of the new realm—a position Mosca himself would take up in 1919—Don Fabrizio explains that Sicily has been a 'colony' of other civilisations for a very long time, echoing what Mosca had said in his lecture on the Mafia, which made it feel very old and desirous of 'sleep'. Yet some Sicilians remain 'half-awake': Crispi is cited as an example, although the Prince warns that as an old man he'll 'fall back into our voluptuous torpor; they all do'.[53] He was right: Crispi, a companion of Mazzini and Garibaldi during the Risorgimento, was a Sicilian politician who served as prime minister of Italy from 1887 to 1891 and 1893 to 1896. At first a liberal, as an admirer of Bismarck he became increasingly bellicose, populist and authoritarian during his rule, and his career ended in controversy and failure: he was involved in a banking scandal and Italy's colonial ambitions in Ethiopia were thwarted at the Battle of Adwa.

'I don't deny that a few Sicilians', Fabrizio concludes, 'may succeed in breaking the spell once off the island; they would have to leave it very young; by twenty it's too late; the crust is formed; they will remain convinced that their country is basely calumniated like all other countries, that the civilised norm is here, the oddities elsewhere'.[54] Mosca might not have been twenty by the time he left for Rome (he was twenty-nine), but he left nonetheless.

As Meisel puts it, 'his migrations encompassed the very poles of the Italian geographical and national character'. 'The Sicilian became a Piedmontese'

52. Livingston, 'Introduction', p. xiv.
53. Lampedusa, *The Leopard*, pp. 136–7.
54. Ibid., pp. 138–9.

when he took up his position at Turin, 'and married a young lady of that region, which was to the rest of Italy what Prussia had been to the German Reich':[55] the Kingdom of Sardinia, which had conquered Sicily through Garibaldi, was after all also the Kingdom of Piedmont, and Garibaldi had set sail from Genoa. Turin had been the capital of Italy till 1865, moving first to Florence and then to Rome in 1871, and remained a powerful hub. In short, Mosca took the opportunities a united Italy offered him. This is why Meisel describes Mosca's theory of the ruling class as a 'defensive' middle-class one: like a Tory grammar schoolboy, Mosca had risen to his position—not without some difficulty—by working through the system as it presented itself to him.[56] He was therefore naturally wont to defend it. Whether that meant Mosca had created a 'myth' that the middle-class must rule from the 'fact' that a minority always does, as Meisel accuses elite theory of doing more broadly, remains to be seen.[57]

Mosca's trajectory as a politician, journalist and scholar helps explain why his theory of the 'ruling class' remained a more narrowly focused political one, in contrast to Pareto's all-encompassing theory of the 'circulation of elites' that attempted an explanation of everything.[58] There is no need to be detained here

55. Meisel, *The Myth of the Ruling Class*, p. 19.

56. Ibid., p. 10. See p. 20 for Mosca's difficulties: 'It had not been all smooth sailing. . . . It seems that invidious colleagues managed to block the path of the young instructor for a considerable time. Not being able to denigrate his splendid gifts, they made much of the fact that he, whose speciality was constitutional law, had dared to write and publish a book on contemporary politics'.

57. Ibid., pp. 6–7. Meisel is an interesting character, originally from Berlin and doing a doctorate at Heidelberg in 1922. He emigrated to the US in 1934 (he was Jewish): somewhere across the Atlantic 'Hans' became the 'H.' of 'James H. Meisel'. He served at first as Thomas Mann's secretary in Princeton, before getting a position at the University of Michigan in 1945, where he would remain for the rest of his academic life (he retired in 1971). His literary background—he wrote a number of plays in his native Germany—is present in his *The Myth of the Ruling Class* book, which often gives the impression of his enjoying too much his own writing. He died in 1991. See *The New York Times*, 'James H. Meisel, 90, Political Scientist, Dies', 12 March 1999 (https://www.nytimes.com/1991/03/12/obituaries/james-h-meisel-90-political-scientist-dies .html, accessed on 13 April 2023) and Albertoni, *Mosca and the Theory of Elitism*, p. 126. On myth in Sorel and Mosca, see Giovanna Cavallari, '"Myth" et "réalisme" dans les doctrines politiques de Mosca et Sorel' in Albertoni, ed., *Études sur la pensée politique de Gaetano Mosca*, pp. 167–178.

58. Livingston, 'Introduction', pp. xxxvi–xxxix; Meisel, *The Myth of the Ruling Class*, pp. 14–18; Bellamy, *Modern Italian Social Theory*, p. 34.

long over the 'small polemic'[59] between the two to know who was the *prima donna* who first came up with the idea that a minority always rules—in terms of publication history, Mosca's *Teorica* (1884) predates Pareto's *Les systems socialistes* (1902), where the term of the 'circulation of elites' first appears, by 18 years, although Pareto seems to have arrived at his own theory independently[60]—but it is worth noting that Mosca's case wasn't helped by the fact that the translation in the English language of Pareto's magnum opus, *The Treatise on General Sociology* (1935), was published as *Mind and Society* four years before Mosca's *Ruling Class* (1939). As H. Stuart Hughes writes: 'there was no doubt that Mosca was the injured party'.[61]

This wasn't what the editor of both books, Livingston, had originally planned.[62] But events, *dear boy*, got in the way: Livingston originally wanted to publish *The Ruling Class* in 1923, the first in a series that was to allow the 'monuments of Italian Machiavellian thought available to English-speaking scholars', but the Wall Street crash of 1929 struck.[63] Yet the 'unrecognised'[64] priority of Pareto has continued: even Bellamy, in his seminal *Modern Italian Social Theory*, puts him first,[65] although he is quick to point out that Mosca was anything but Pareto's 'shadow', and indeed his chapter on Mosca, alongside Livingston's introduction and, of course, Bobbio's work, remains one of the best written to this day.[66] This has led to Mosca often being considered, certainly in the English-speaking world, as something of a 'second-class Pareto', as Hughes puts it. 'Pareto looms as the larger figure', Hughes writes, 'his range is wider, his books are longer, his "scientific" apparatus is more

---

59. Gaetano Mosca, 'Piccola Polemica' in *Partiti e Sindacati nella crisi del regime parlamentare*, pp. 116–120. On the 'feud', see Meisel, *The Myth of the Ruling Class*, pp. 169–183.

60. Livingston, 'Introduction', pp. xxxvi–xxxvii. Livingston points out that Pareto's *Cours d'économie politique* of 1896 contains his theory of the elite in a nutshell, a point echoed by Meisel (*The Myth of the Ruling Class*, p. 177), but that is still after Mosca's *Teorica* and also doesn't yet see the appearance of the term 'elite': Pareto still uses 'aristocracy'.

61. H. Stuart Hughes, 'Gaetano Mosca and the Political Lessons of History' in James Meisel, ed., *Pareto and Mosca*, Englewood Cliffs, Prentice-Hall, p. 142.

62. Livingston, 'Introduction', p. xxxvi.

63. Ibid.

64. Ibid.

65. As noted in the Introduction, it is the case that Pareto (1848–1923) was senior to Mosca (1858–1941) by ten years, but the claim here is about intellectual precedence.

66. Bellamy, *Modern Italian Social Theory*, p. 34.

impressive, and his criticism cuts deeper'. All Mosca had going for him was that 'he wrote more gracefully than Pareto and his views were more moderate'.[67]

Pareto's wider theory naturally appealed to a post-war US academia interested in building new research methods,[68] but outside that milieu the interest in Mosca was on par with—in some instances even surpassing (Mills, Aron)—that in Pareto.[69] Mosca himself reflected on why the term 'elite' ended up overtaking his own 'political class' as the dominant term to designate minority rule—something reproduced in this book—namely, that Pareto was a world-famous economist (his was a slightly more parochial background), and that French was a more widely used language than Italian.[70] This hurt Mosca no end, but the point of this chapter is to underline the richness of Mosca's theory, and the attention it deserves in its own right.

II: Making Italians

The Risorgimento had been led by liberal nobles of the North, those of Pareto's father's ilk. They were the 'Historical Right', whom Mosca defended. But after unification, these nobles, considered to be disinterested and independent rulers, and generally supportive of the Savoy monarchy, collapsed at the general election of 1876, to be replaced by 'professional' men often trained as lawyers.[71] This was the Left—the *Sinistra storica* (Historical Left)—that came to dominate Italian politics during the turn of the century. If the Right was an alliance between the Northern aristocrats and Southern landowners, who wanted—not without some inconsistencies—free trade, a centralised government and balanced budgets, the Left was the party of the Northern middle-class, and favoured decentralisation and local politics.[72] As Bellamy writes:

---

67. Hughes, 'Gaetano Mosca and the Political Lessons of History', p. 141.

68. Joel Isaac, *Working Knowledge: Making the Human Sciences from Parsons to Kuhn*, Cambridge (MA), Harvard University Press, 2012, pp. 63–91 and Joseph La Palombara, 'The Study of Gaetano Mosca in the United States' in Albertoni, ed., *Studies on the Political Thought of Gaetano Mosca*, pp. 153–164.

69. Robertino Ghiringhelli, 'Gaetano Mosca et la culture politique française des années 1920 et 1930' in Albertoni, ed., *Études sur la pensée politique de Gaetano Mosca*, pp. 145–166.

70. Meisel, *The Myth of the Ruling Class*, pp. 176, 185. See further Renzo Sereno, 'The Anti-Aristotelianism of Gaetano Mosca and Its Fate', *Ethics*, Vol. 48, No. 4, 1938, pp. 509–518.

71. Hughes, 'Gaetano Mosca and the Political Lessons of History', pp. 150–151.

72. Bellamy, *Modern Italian Social Theory*, p. 5.

Lawyers rather than landowners, the Left's foremost concerns were local and personal. . . . They devised schemes which, by channelling central funds through to their friends in the municipalities, increased their local power base. Given the lack of party organisation and the relations between national and local politics, the descent into clientelism seemed inevitable.[73]

Instead of disinterested service to the community the Right was associated with, the Left quickly came to be seen as 'unscrupulous manipulators and common fixers, with no personal convictions and no dignity'.[74] This came to a head first with Agostino Depretis, who served three times as prime minister between 1876 and 1887, and subsequently Giovanni Giolitti, who served five times between 1892 and 1921—both of the 'Historical Left'—who developed the system of *trasformismo*, a form of political wheeling-and-dealing to keep heteroclite alliances drawn from the left and the right together, oiled through bribery. 'The policy of *trasformismo*', as Bellamy explains, is that of 'transforming an erstwhile opponent into a supporter by bribery and corruption'.[75] 'In Rome the parliamentary chambers', Hughes writes, 'had become the scene of an unabashed trading of votes against local favours'.[76]

With the rise of socialism in the industrial north-west (Turin, Milan) and the Emilia-Romagna region around Bologna, and the Catholic movement growing in the Venice region and the north-east, liberals quickly found themselves without an organisational basis and reliant on southern politicians and their local clientele, as Mosca had indicated in his speech on the Mafia: it is telling that after the World War II it is the better organised Socialist and Catholic movements that dominated Italian politics.[77]

Politically the peasantry were in the pockets of the landowners, who traded their votes to the northern businessmen to maintain their respective power bases. As long as this system remained mutually beneficial, democratic procedures were little more than a façade behind which the dominant groups exploited the mass of the population.[78]

73. Ibid.
74. Ibid.
75. Ibid. See also Hughes, 'Gaetano Mosca and the Political Lessons of History', p. 151.
76. Hughes, 'Gaetano Mosca and the Political Lessons of History', p. 151.
77. Lyttelton, 'Introduction', pp. 4–5.
78. Bellamy, *Modern Italian Social Theory*, p. 5.

The system widened the gap between the ruling class and the people, between the 'legal' and the 'real' country, between theory and practice.[79] And the new regime had a mountain of challenges to face: unemployment, rural overpopulation and poverty, especially in the South, which came to be known as the 'Southern question', still largely resolved through immigration.[80] 'Economically, the rural south', Bellamy writes, 'provided a cheap source of materials and labour, and a market for the industrialised north.'[81] In 1861 75% of the population was illiterate, with only 8% able to speak the national language, i.e. Tuscan. Only 418,696 citizens had the right to vote, namely 1.9% of the population, and of those who could, just 57.2% did in what were essentially rigged elections controlled by factory owners in the north and landowners in the south.[82] This wasn't aided by the fact that the Catholic Church, which the vast majority of the population remained faithful to, did not recognise united Italy till after World War I, and generally forbade participation in elections.[83] As Massimo d'Azeglio famously put it: 'We have made Italy. Now we must make Italians.'[84]

In this, aside from some marginal improvements, the liberals mostly failed. They were faced with the tension between what Bellamy calls the 'Machiavellian issues of "force" and "consent"':

> The Italian state's lack of 'force' was manifested in its inability either to defend and promote itself externally or to uphold law and order internally. The absence of 'consent' allegedly arose from a failure to 'make Italians', with the result that few people identified strongly with the new states.[85]

The effect of this was twofold: on the one hand the rising support for 'anti-system' parties, in this instance the socialists and the Catholics, and we are still feeling the effects of support for 'anti-system' parties today (think Five Start Movement, the League);[86] on the other hand the tendency to reject the

---

79. Ibid., pp. 1–2; Richard Bellamy, 'Social and Political Thought, 1890–1945' in Lyttelton (ed.), *Liberal and Fascist Italy*, p. 233.

80. Bellamy, *Modern Italian Social Theory*, p. 2.

81. Ibid., p. 6.

82. Bellamy, *Modern Italian Social Theory*, p. 5.

83. Ibid., p. 6.

84. Ibid., pp. 6–7.

85. Bellamy, 'Social and political thought, 1890–1945', p. 233.

86. Lyttelton, 'Introduction', p. 13. On 'anti-system' parties, see Giovanni Sartori, *Parties and Party Systems: A Framework for Analysis*, Colchester, ECPR Press, 2005.

parliamentary regime in toto: 'the view that Giolittian Italy had failed to either act sufficiently forcefully or promote a suitably strong consensus had a tendency to shade into a critique of liberalism and democracy *tout court*'.[87]

At the start of his intellectual career this had been Mosca's position too: subsuming his rejection of parliamentary democracy as a rejection of the functioning of Italian democracy more broadly. As Livingston explains:

> One may therefore explain the antidemocratic intonation of Mosca's earlier works as partly a matter of fashion and partly a matter of youth. . . . Democracy was unpopular, especially in south Italy. One was therefore swimming with the current in overstressing the corruption and inefficiency of parliamentary politicians and in waving the menace of socialism in the face of those who were eager to strengthen popular education and extend the suffrage.[88]

Indeed, 'if one were deliberately to choose a time and a place that would display parliamentary institutions to their maximum discredit', Hughes explains, 'it would be hard to find a more telling example than southern Italy in the 1880s'.[89]

But over the course of his life, and especially with the second edition of *Elementi* in 1925, Mosca came to separate the two, seeing how parliamentary democracy, well-constituted, could indeed be a viable system. We have already seen that in his Senate speech Mosca defended the regime as it was from 1919 to 1922: i.e. in its infancy and before universal suffrage and proportional representation. This was the moment when the original Risorgimento nobles of the 'Historical Right' dominated, but these were being replaced by professional politicians only interested in feathering their own nests.

The challenge for Mosca was then to define a class that would continue the work of the 'Historical Right' by independently pursuing the common good. His solution was to be found in a 'middling class of independent proprietors, who were free from the influence of quasi-feudal landlords', and also factory-owners, whom Mosca put in the class of dominant 'grand electors' who made those dependent on them for their livelihood vote according to

---

87. Bellamy, 'Social and political thought, 1890–1945', p. 234. See also Sereno, 'The Anti-Aristotelianism of Gaetano Mosca and Its Fate', p. 516 and Piane, *Gaetano Mosca*, pp. 9–46.

88. Livingston, 'Introduction', p. xxxv.

89. Hughes, 'Gaetano Mosca and the Political Lessons of History', p. 150.

their wishes.[90] It is these men of 'moderate means', unbeholden to private interest—thereby reproducing the disinterested service of the 'Historical Right' nobles—who could continue to work for the common good.[91] This educated, cultured class—made up of lawyers, scientists and technicians—should be appointed to the top echelons of the civil service, and named in the Senate and as ministers by royal decree: Mosca maintaining his commitment to constitutional monarchy, with a role for the king.[92]

In the context of trying to 'make Italians', modernising the country and resolving the Southern 'social question', it should come as no surprise that a form of 'cultural politics'—the 'ethical transformation of society on the part of an intellectual elite'—should play a role in Mosca's theory on how society and politics should be re-organised.[93] It was the 'cultural class', which he belonged to, that would lead the charge.[94] This quality marked the new ruling class out from previous ones, based on martial ability, wealth or membership of the priesthood. Culture prevailed 'only in a very advanced stage of civilisation'.[95]

What Mosca wanted to do was to create alternative sources of power within government to counter-balance that which was conferred by election to the Deputies of the Chamber, which threatened to become tyrannical: the legitimacy conferred by elections would swamp all other forms of legitimacy.[96] He wanted to bring non-economic forces into the ruling class—although this middle-class needed to be financially independent, it drew its legitimacy more from its expertise—and indeed Mosca advocated that government intervention was warranted to reduce growing inequalities.[97]

Like all good liberals, Mosca's ideal for this middle-class was the English gentry.[98] But it is important to note that this ideal of the middle-class's role in politics he held consistently from *Teorica* onwards.[99] Later, in *Elementi*,

90. Mosca, *The Ruling Class*, pp. 270, 301; Bellamy, *Modern Italian Social Theory*, pp. 35, 40.

91. Bellamy, *Modern Italian Social Theory*, p. 38.

92. Ibid., pp. 42, 47.

93. Bellamy, *Modern Italian Social Theory*, p. 8.

94. Hughes, 'Gaetano Mosca and the Political Lessons of History', p. 152.

95. Bobbio, 'Gaetano Mosca and the Theory of the Ruling Class', p. 15.

96. Mosca, *The Ruling Class*, pp. 259, 270.

97. Mosca, *The Ruling Class*, p. 141; Bellamy, *Modern Italian Social Theory*, p. 43.

98. Mosca, *The Ruling Class*, p. 268; Bellamy, *Modern Italian Social Theory*, pp. 38, 42, 48.

99. Bellamy, *Modern Italian Social Theory*, p. 35ff.

building on his separation of economic and political power,[100] he would add that the different functions of government should be autonomous: that the bureaucracy, judiciary and army should not be beholden to elected representatives, and he lauded the development of the freedom of the press.[101] Continuing the anti-clericalism of his mentor Di Rudini, Mosca also wanted to see the Church separated from the state.[102] Although the term did not yet exist, Mosca's insistence of the separation of powers and the need to diversify the ruling class moved him towards advocating a form of pluralism. As Bellamy writes: 'he re-conceptualised democratic theory away from the notion of popular majority rule and towards modern-day doctrines of pluralism'.[103]

So yes, Mosca defended a form of middle-class rule—a middle class, one should hasten to add, that has always been the backbone of modern democracy[104]—although that he did so through construing a 'myth', which combines the three 'Cs' of 'group consciousness, coherence and conspiracy',[105] seems a little unpersuasive. Indeed, that Mosca should immediately recognise that it could be something other than the type of middle-class he was advocating that would come to power—either the 'Historical Left' or, increasingly, the Fascists—is precisely what led him to defend the 'cultured' class he belonged to: he had seen, and experienced, different types of ruling classes. That Mosca developed his theory of the ruling class—a historical fact, according to him—is separate from the fact that he believed the middle-class should be the ruling class, and indeed previously Mosca had celebrated the rule of the liberal nobles of the 'Historical Right'. But to get a better sense of that, we must get a better sense of his theory of the ruling class.

---

100. In the *Storia*, Mosca explains: 'the state control of the means of production would leave the administrators of the state—who are sure to be a minority—in a position where they should be able to combine all economic and political power in their hands and to appropriate the largest share in such a manner as would advance the career of their own sons and protégés' (Mosca, 'The Final Version of the Theory of the Ruling Class', p. 389), a warning indeed.

101. Mosca, *The Ruling Class*, pp. 145, 147, 235, 258, 261; Bellamy, *Modern Italian Social Theory*, p. 47.

102. Mosca, *The Ruling Class*, p. 139; Bellamy, *Modern Italian Social Theory*, p. 45.

103. Bellamy, *Modern Italian Social Theory*, p. 42. See, further, Finocchiaro, *Beyond Right and Left*, pp. 42–51 for the notion of 'balanced pluralism' and Suzanne Keller, *Beyond the Ruling Class: Strategic Elites in Modern Society*, New Brunswick, Transaction Publishers, 2014 for the difference between 'monolithic' and 'pluralism'

104. Lyttelton, 'Introduction', p. 9.

105. Meisel, *The Myth of the Ruling Class*, pp. 4, 16.

III: The Ruling Class I

'In all societies', Mosca writes, 'two classes of people appear—a class that rules and a class that is ruled'.[106] This is Mosca's theory of the ruling class. And it is valid from societies that are 'very meagrely developed and have barely attained the dawnings of civilisation, down to the most advanced and powerful societies'.[107] 'The first class', Mosca continues,

> always the less numerous, performs all political functions, monopolises power and enjoys the advantages that power brings, whereas the second, the more numerous class, is directed and controlled by the first, in a manner that is now more or less legal, now more or less arbitrary and violent, and supplies the first, in appearance at least, with the material means of subsistence and with the instrumentalities that are essential to the vitality of the political organism.[108]

The fundamental reason for this division is division: the minority is organised, the majority are not. A hundred men acting in concert with a mutual understanding will triumph over a thousand, to use Mosca's example, who are not.[109] In fact, there is an inverse proportionality between the size of the minority and that of the majority: 'the larger the political community, the smaller will the proportion of the governing minority to the governed majority be, and the more difficult will it be for the majority to organise for reaction against the minority'.[110] If the three 'C's, as Meisel himself recognises, are not to be found in Mosca's theory, then we have here Meisel's real objection to Mosca: that the majority cannot organise—which Meisel thinks it can, and should— and that saying it can't organise is the 'myth' created to keep it docile.[111] Moreover, Meisel is suspicious of the claim that the 'elite' are indeed the best,[112] although Mosca too, in part, shares that view: 'members of the ruling minority regularly have some attribute, *real or apparent*, which is highly esteemed and very influential in the society in which they live'.[113] As Bobbio noted: 'the

106. Mosca, *The Ruling Class*, p. 50.
107. Ibid.
108. Ibid.
109. Ibid., p. 53.
110. Ibid.
111. Meisel, *The Myth of the Ruling Class*, p. xi.
112. Ibid., p. vi.
113. Mosca, *The Ruling Class*, p. 53, emphasis added.

expression "ruling class", as Mosca himself rightly observed . . . , has the advantage over "élite" that it does not imply a positive judgment on the members of that class'.[114] As we have just seen, Mosca had little time for the 'Historical Left', and instead wanted the 'cultured' middle-class to take over.

As is suggested by the 'reaction' in the quote above, it is not Mosca's view either that the majority are simply 'lorded over',[115] to borrow Meisel's term, by the minority. Quite the contrary: 'whatever the type of political organisation, pressures arising from the discontent of the masses who are governed . . . exert a certain amount of influence on the policies of the ruling, the political, class'.[116] Indeed, Mosca is willing to concede that 'even in absolute governments the ruling classes are obliged to take account of mass sentiments'.[117] Moreover, should the masses succeed in revolting against the established ruling class, this would not mean the abolishment of the ruling class as such— this is an anti-Marxist point[118]—but, rather, an organised minority from within the masses would arise to discharge the functions of rule: 'granting that the discontent of the masses might succeed in deposing a ruling class, inevitably . . . there would have to be another organised minority within the masses themselves to discharge the functions of a ruling class'.[119] 'Within the lower classes another ruling class, or directing minority, necessarily forms', Mosca later explains, and these will have 'their own hierarchies of officials, their own leaders, their own recognised institutions'.[120]

This means there are always rising forces, led by competing organised minorities, that are there to challenge the established ones: Mosca immediately recognises the fact of leadership that takes the 'helm' of political organisation.[121] Additionally, as Bellamy notes, that challenge might come from a section of the ruling class itself: 'the split could even occur within the ruling class itself, and that the difference sections of the minority would appeal to the masses for support'.[122] As Mosca explains in his 'final' version of the theory of

114. Bobbio, 'Gaetano Mosca and the Theory of the Ruling Class', p. 13.

115. Meisel, The Myth of the Ruling Class, p. xi.

116. Mosca, The Ruling Class, p. 51.

117. Ibid., p. 156.

118. Marx, 'The Bureaucratic State: Some Remarks on Mosca's Ruling Class', p. 459.

119. Mosca, The Ruling Class, p. 51. See further Sereno, 'The Anti-Aristotelianism of Gaetano Mosca and Its Fate', p. 510.

120. Ibid., pp. 116–117.

121. Ibid., pp. 50–51.

122. Bellamy, Modern Italian Social Theory, p. 45.

the ruling class as presented in the *Storia delle dottrine politiche*, the convulsions of the social order in his time are mostly due to 'internal factors', that is to say, they are 'revolutions', where the ruling class, attacked from below, disintegrates, whereas in the past changes in the ruling classes had more to do with outside conquests: 'instead of invasions, we have today revolutions'.[123] The revolutions Mosca has in mind are the French and Russian revolutions. And yet: 'almost invariably some elements, more or less numerous, of the old ruling class will enter the ranks of the new'.[124] Indeed, when Mosca talks about elections in the *Storia*, although he reprises his line about choosing between a 'small number of candidates presented by those minorities', it is noticeable that Mosca renders minority rule in the plural—'organised minorities controlling the disorganised majority'—indicating plurality within the ruling class itself.[125]

Here we see the possibility of a section of the ruling class allying itself with the ruled class to overthrow another section of the ruling class, meaning Mosca was open to the possibility the ruling class might be divided within itself: quite far for the 'coherence' Meisel was postulating. In the *Storia*, Mosca writes that in the 'liberal' regime, which we'll have occasion to return to, one in which 'power is transmitted from the bottom to the top' and where 'functionaries are elected by the citizens who subsequently are expected to obey them', as opposed to the opposite autocratic regime, where 'the supreme chief appoints his immediate aides who in turn appoint the lower officials',[126]

> the necessity to make a bid for the allegiance of the vast, unorganised majority obliges each of those groups to adapt itself, if only in appearance, to the thoughts and sentiments prevailing among the masses. The necessity sometimes enables liberal regimes to display an amazing vigour, but it has also the effect of forcing the ruling class to play up to the great majority of people who are less aware of the true interests of the society.[127]

So Mosca does see a degree of accountability of the ruling classes to the people, however much it is in 'appearance'. Note, too, that this reciprocity leads to an 'amazing vigour' of the liberal regime. But we also get to the reason here

---

123. Mosca, 'The Final Version of the Theory of the Ruling Class', p. 390.
124. Ibid.
125. Ibid., p. 388.
126. Ibid., p. 387.
127. Ibid., p. 388

why Mosca opposed the extension of the franchise: it would bring too many of the 'uncultured' strata of the populations into politics, forcing the ruling class to take too much into account their interests and therefore overwhelming the 'true interests' of society they are usually privy to. To domesticate the 'base instincts which so often are joint to the will to power', there is needed a 'great deal of education' of the masses, which is always a 'slow process'.[128]

Beyond a residual liberal fear of the masses, this concern expressed by Mosca admits that the ruling classes do need to be responsive, at least in some capacity, to those below them.[129] As Mosca writes:

> The great majority of voters are passive, it is true, in the sense that they have not so much freedom to choose their representatives as a limited right to exercise an option among a number of candidates. Nevertheless, limited as it may be, that capacity has the effect of obliging candidates to try to win a weight of votes that will serve to tip the scales in their direction, so that they make every effort to flatter, wheedle and obtain the good will of the voters. In this way certain sentiments and passions of the 'common herd' come to have their influence on the mental attitudes of the representatives themselves, and echoes of a widely disseminated opinion, or any serious discontent, easily come to be heard in the highest spheres of government.[130]

Indeed, that there should be feedback in the political system is precisely exemplified by Mosca's fear not only of the masses being integrated into politics, but also of the consequences of the Historical Left replacing the Historical Right. The ruling class does change.

What Bobbio accuses Mosca of having missed is opposition within the ruling class itself: 'he did not concern himself with the other aspect of the problem, that is, the division of the ruling class into two parts—one in power

---

128. Ibid., p. 391.

129. Giovanni Sartori, *The Theory of Democracy Revisited. Part One: The Contemporary Debate*, Chatham, Chatham House Publishers, 1987, p. 170 makes an important distinction between responsible *to* and responsible *for*: 'a government that simply yields to demands, that simply gives in, turns out to be a highly irresponsible government, a government that does not live up to its responsibilities. . . . This is the same as saying that representation intrinsically consists of two ingredients: responsiveness *and* independent responsibility. And the more governments become responsive *to* at the detriment of being responsible *for*, the more we are likely to be misgoverned and/or ungoverned'.

130. Mosca, *The Ruling Class*, p. 155.

and one in opposition'.[131] Perhaps Bobbio had Pareto's 'circulation of elites' in mind here, which might offer a more systematic account of change within the ruling class itself, and it is true that when Mosca talks about divisions within the ruling class, he seems to think more about the opposition between, say, parliament and the bureaucracy. Yet it seems strange for someone who was actively engaged in parliamentary politics for much of his life, as a deputy, under-secretary and senator, some of it in power but most of it in opposition, not to have thought about divisions with the ruling class, understood as the political class here. Perhaps because of his experience with *trasformismo*, which specifically aimed at reducing division between politicians of supposedly different persuasions, this was not at the foremost of his reflections.

Returning to the *Ruling Class*, in a passage that is worth quoting at length, because it presents many of the themes we are interested in in this overall study, Mosca explains:

> the whole history of civilised mankind comes down to a conflict between the tendency of dominant elements to monopolise political power and transmit possession of it by inheritance, and the tendency toward a dislocation of old forces and an insurgence of new forces; and this conflict produces an unending ferment of endosmosis and exosmosis between the upper classes and certain portions of the lower.[132]

The view that history is the struggle between established minorities and rising ones that challenge them, sometimes with the aid of or co-optation by a part of the ruling class itself, will be repeated over the works of Pareto and Robert Michels, and indeed forms the basis of the notion of 'dynamic democracy'.

That dynamic is often couched through the metaphor of water: Mosca speaks of 'crystallised' societies, in which the ruling class has become closed and stationary—in a word, conservative—but also of how ruling classes are 'infiltrated' by new elements.[133] This is the natural and continuous process of the 'renovation' of the ruling class, which if it is very rapid might instead take the form of a 'revolution'.[134] Mosca describes these two tendencies as producing 'now calm, now wind and storm',[135] and the river metaphor

131. Bobbio, 'Gaetano Mosca and the Theory of the Ruling Class', p. 25.
132. Mosca, *The Ruling Class*, p. 65.
133. Ibid., pp. 66–68.
134. Ibid.
135. Ibid., p. 66.

Pareto is so fond of also appears in a discussion of Taine, where Mosca warns that people believe that 'since social life has flowed blandly and smoothly on for centuries, like an impetuous river confined with sturdy dikes, the dikes have become superfluous and can readily be dispensed with, now that the river has learnt its lesson'.[136] The image of the river and dikes brings us all the way back to Machiavelli and his discussion of Fortuna in Chapter 25 of *The Prince*—hence the appellation 'Machiavellians' as bestowed by James Burnham[137]—where Fortuna is described through the metaphor of a 'dangerous river' against which one must build 'dykes and dams',[138] although it is important to note that Mosca himself rejected Machiavelli in favour of his friend and rival Guicciardini, whom he associates with his liberal 'juridical defence'.[139]

Whilst Mosca had yet to serve as under-secretary for the colonies, he notes that 'rapid restocking of the ruling classes is a frequent and very striking phenomenon in countries that have recently been colonised'.[140] When different 'currents' start to impose themselves, they can be voluntarily integrated into the established ruling class, but in other instances—revolution—they are completely overthrown: it is always 'at bottom a question of one clique, more or less numerous, superseding another clique in the management of the commonwealth'.[141] In fact, Mosca writes that the more 'closed' the ruling class is to rising elements, the more likely it is to be violently overthrown.[142] Whether this replacement is by a new rising minority or a faction of the ruling class itself, the new ruling class will always seek the 'support of the lower classes' in its struggle against the established order, and it is in these instances that the latter might claim some concessions.[143] This continued process of the 'renovation' of the ruling class, through either gradual 'infiltration' or stormy overthrow, occurs because of the 'decline in energy in the upper classes, which grow poorer and poorer in bold and aggressive characters and richer and richer

---

136. Ibid., p. 118.

137. James Burnham, *The Machiavellians: Defenders of Freedom*, New York, John Day, 1943.

138. *Machiavelli: The Prince*, Cambridge, Cambridge University Press, 2019, p. 85.

139. Mosca, *The Ruling Class*, pp. 1, 43, 130, 202–3. Albertoni, *Mosca and the Theory of Elitism*, p. 64 argues that Mosca's liberalism turned him away from Machiavelli, but what made him really 'Machiavellian' was his realism.

140. Ibid., p. 68.

141. Ibid., p. 199.

142. Ibid., p. 119.

143. Ibid., p. 117.

in "soft", remissive individuals'[144] on the one hand, and because of the development of new 'social forces' on the other.

As Livingston explains in his introduction to his edition of *The Ruling Class*, a 'social force' is 'any human activity or perquisite that has a social significance— money, land, military prowess, religion, education, manual labour, science— anything'.[145] These social forces appear and develop in response to changes in economics, society, ideas—whatever they might be. For Mosca, different civilisations are judged by the number of social forces that exist within their bosom: the higher the number of social forces, the higher the civilisation. 'As civilisation grows', Mosca writes, 'the number of the moral and material influences that are capable of becoming social forces increases'.[146] The ruling classes here retain the leading role—'the varying structure of the ruling classes has a preponderant importance in determining the political type, and also the level of civilisation, of the different peoples'[147]—but these forces need to be kept in harmony with one another so as to keep each other in check and not allow one of them to become tyrannical: 'different powers will harmonise with each other and check each other effectively enough to prevent absolute control'.[148] The ruling class is pluralist. This is achieved through what Mosca names 'juridical defence'.

Inspired both by Guicciardini's emphasis on integrity and justice as the truly liberal regime and Montesquieu's study of the English constitution, 'juridical defence' consists in two elements: government by law—i.e. 'due process', we should do well to remember Mosca's training as a lawyer[149]—and the separation of power.[150] It is 'juridical defence' that establishes the 'character of the relations between the governing class and the governed and between the various levels and various sections of the ruling class'.[151] It is, in short, the organisational system of a well-run political regime. Its role is to balance and curb the other social forces within a harmonious whole, under the guises of

144. Ibid.
145. Livingston, 'Introduction', p. xix.
146. Mosca, *The Ruling Class*, p. 144.
147. Ibid., p. 51.
148. Ibid., p. 139.
149. Bellamy, *Modern Italian Social Theory*, p. 47.
150. Mosca, *The Ruling Class*, pp. 126, 130, 138.
151. Ibid., p. 130.

the ruling class.[152] For that it needs the various forces to be able to transform themselves into political forces: 'if one political institution is to be an effective curb upon the activity of another it must represent a political force—it must, that is, be the organised expression of a social influence and a social authority that has some standing in the community, as against the forces that are expressed in the political institution that is to be controlled.[153]

Each social or political force has its own 'directing' class,[154] but Mosca's biggest fear is for one political force to come to dominate all others. Not only does that mean the various social forces cannot express and counter-balance themselves, leading to a decrease of the overall level of civilisation,[155] but, moreover, 'the absolute preponderance of a singly political force, the predominance of any over-simplified concept in the organisation of the state, the strictly logical application of any single principle in all public law are the essential elements in any type of despotism.[156] In his own time, Mosca thought the biggest threat came from the legitimacy elections conferred, meaning the social forces upon which deputies stood would come to overwhelm all the others, whether they came from expertise in the bureaucracy or the court system, the 'culture' of the intellectuals, or the economic nous in the commercial realm. Mosca held this view consistently throughout his career: during *Elementi I* he thought it was democratic socialism that threatened to overwhelm the state, society and the economy through a form of 'collectivism'. But when fascism later threatened to do the same, he mounted the same critiques, as his final senatorial speech demonstrates.

In response to this, Mosca lauds, in the concluding chapter of his *Elementi I*, 'the highest grade of juridical defence, the greatest respect for law and morals on the part of those in power, can be obtained only through the participation of many different political forces in government and through their balancing one another.[157] So there needs to be balance in the system. Indeed, when it

---

152. Ibid., pp. 106, 145.

153. Ibid., p. 138.

154. Ibid., p. 106.

155. 'When a system of political organisation is based upon a single absolute principle, so that the whole political class is organised after a single pattern, it is difficult for all social forces to participate in public life, and more difficult still for any one force to counterbalance another' (ibid., p. 147).

156. Ibid., p. 134.

157. Ibid., p. 244.

came to political reform, Mosca always counselled a slow, instead of radical, pace of change. This is not without recalling the difference Mosca makes between absolute justice, which, following Rousseau, demands that all political institutions should have as their basis the same notion of justice, and relative justice, which stipulates that every institution can have its own—a form of juridical defence—in his conclusion to *Elementi I*.[158] In *Elementi II*, Mosca elaborates on his thinking:

> But even if there is never to be an absolute justice in this world until humanity comes really to be moulded to the image and likeness of God, there has been, there is and there will always be a relative justice in societies that are fairly well organised. There will always be, in other words, a sum of laws, habits, norms, all varying according to times and peoples, which are laid down and enforced by public opinion, and in accordance with which what we have called the struggle for pre-eminence—the effort of every individual to better and to conserve his own social positions—will be regulated.[159]

As Meisel puts it:

> Mosca's 'ideal state' would be one in which the 'balance of the social forces' would make possible 'juridical defence': a government of law dispensing 'relative justice'. *Relative* justice as the result of a power equilibrium between competing groups—all absolutism is alien to the mind of Gaetano Mosca.[160]

A final stone must be added to Mosca's theoretical edifice: the 'political formula'. This is the 'legal and moral basis, or principle, on which the power of the political class rests'.[161] Mosca is quick to concede that this need not be entirely rational, nor indeed is something approaching a 'scientific truth'—the 'formula normally contains a large amount of nonsense mixed in with a certain small of amount of verifiable truth', as Livingston puts it[162]—yet he posits that humankind has a real social need that needs to be fulfilled, such that 'one is

---

158. Ibid., p. 273.
159. Ibid., p. 456.
160. Meisel, *The Myth of the Ruling Class*, p. 12.
161. Ibid., p. 70.
162. Livingston, 'Introduction', p. xxx.

governed not on the basis of mere material or intellectual force, but on the basis of a moral principle', and that "great superstitions" are still needed as social forces to powerfully 'consolidate political organisations and unify peoples or even whole civilisations'.[163]

As Livingston explains:

Mosca was on safe ground in asserting that great human masses can be organised and utilised for the attainment of specific purposes only by uniting them around some formula that will contain a large measure of illusion. He was also right in asserting that one element in that fact is the further fact that human beings more readily defer to abstract principles that seem to have an abiding validity than to the will of individual persons.[164]

These formulae include the 'divine right of kings', the 'sovereignty of the people', the 'dictatorship of the proletariat'.[165] For Mosca, the 'great superstition' of his age was the 'divine right of elected assemblies'.[166]

It is important to note that all social groups have their own 'beliefs, sentiments and habits', but that the political formula must be based upon the 'strongest sentiment' of the ruling class.[167] Indeed, for Mosca the answer to the question of 'force' and 'consent' discussed above is to be found, given that all political organisations are 'both voluntary and coercive at one and the same time', in the strength with which the ruling class makes the ruled believe in their formula.[168] 'The amount of consent', writes Mosca, 'depends upon the extent to which, and the ardour with which, the class that is ruled believes in the political formula by which the ruling class justifies its rule'.[169] This is why the ruling class cannot fall into sentimentalism and humanitarianism—lose its 'virility',[170] a theme dear to Pareto—but must assert its belief in the strongest possible manner.[171]

---

163. Mosca, *The Ruling Class*, p. 71.
164. Livingston, 'Introduction', p. xxxiii.
165. Ibid.
166. Mosca, *The Ruling Class*, p. 71.
167. Ibid., p. 71–72.
168. Ibid., p. 96.
169. Ibid., p. 97.
170. Sereno, 'The Anti-Aristotelianism of Gaetano Mosca and Its Fate', p. 511.
171. Ibid., p. 118.

Yet were the political formula to change, so would the nature of the ruling class. As Livingston puts it: 'does the type create the formula or the formula the type?'[172] For him, there is interdependence:

> The type partly creates the formula in that the latter is usually a dogma put forward by some seer or prophet—now Mahomet, now Rousseau, now Marx—in response to certain 'demands' of the given era. Once the formula exists and is accepted, it helps powerfully in moulding the type by formulating maxims and precepts to which individuals more or less necessarily and successfully conform.[173]

If one way in which change occurs is by a change in the elements that compose the ruling class, another is by a change in the political formula, which will have an impact on the type of ruling class. Note, too, that this is always made within a certain context—the 'demands' of a given era—which arises from a change in the social forces.

In the *Storia*, Mosca elaborates on this thinking, explaining that the reason the French Revolution came about is because 'the great majority of Frenchmen ceased to believe in the divine rights of kings'.[174] The same might be said of the Russian Revolution, where the 'whole intelligentsia, and perhaps also the majority of the Russian workers and peasants', had stopped believing the Tsar had received the right to rule Russian from God directly.[175]

> Any indication that a political formula has become 'dated', that the faith in its principles has become shaky, that the ardent sentiments which once inspired it have begun to cool down is a sign that serious transformations of the ruling class are imminent.[176]

And yet at the same time, should the political formula be 'in harmony' with the prevailing sentiments and mentality of the time, the formula's utility is 'undeniable'.[177] Indeed, in such circumstances it 'often serves as a check on the

---

172. Livingston, 'Introduction', p. xxx.
173. Ibid.
174. Mosca, 'The Final Version of the Theory of the Ruling Class', p. 384.
175. Ibid.
176. Ibid.
177. Ibid.

power of the ruler and ennobles somewhat the subjection of the ruled, making it appear less the result of merely brute coercion'.[178]

IV: The Ruling Class II

The ruling class determines the political type, and the level of civilisation, of the respective society. But it is always the political class—i.e. the organised minority—that rules. This means a move away from the classic tripartite division—monarchy, aristocracy, polity, and their respective negatives—one gets of politics from Aristotle.[179] Instead Mosca was drawn to thinkers who divided society into two, such as Comte, Spencer and Saint-Simon.[180] For Livingston, the inspiration for the young Mosca during his studies at Palermo was Taine's study of the *Ancien régime*, from which he concluded that beyond the usual appellation of monarchy, tyranny or republic, one always found a small group that dominated—in this instance, the French aristocracy—and that gave society at large its dominant traits.[181]

Mosca based his conclusion on 'historical facts'.[182] As a 'positivist', his claim was that humankind had garnered sufficient data from history to draw out certain 'laws' of political science—remember, the title of the book is *Elements of Political Science*—of which the main one was the existence of a ruling class.[183] It is this 'fact' of the ruling class that allowed political science, according to Bobbio, to be born in Italy: 'the theory of the ruling class represents the beginning, or, if one prefers, the first outline, of modern political science conceived of as objective research into political phenomena'.[184] It was this 'constant' that provided the 'basis for scientific research' upon which political science could build, one not 'deduced from *a priori* principles' but instead based on a 'realist' 'unprejudiced and ruthless observation of the facts', leading to the first chapter of a scientific study of politics.[185]

178. Ibid.

179. Mosca, *The Ruling Class*, p. 1.

180. Ibid., pp. 95–96. See, further, Meisel, *The Myth of the Ruling Class*, p. vii.

181. Livingston, 'Introduction', pp. ix–x.

182. Mosca, *The Ruling Class*, p. 41.

183. Bellamy, *Modern Italian Social Theory*, pp. 7, 37; Meisel, *The Myth of the Ruling Class*, pp. 11–12; Bellamy, 'Social and Political Thought', pp. 234–5.

184. Bobbio, 'Gaetano Mosca and the Theory of the Ruling Class', p. 21.

185. Ibid., p. 22. See also Joseph Femia, 'Mosca Revisited' in Joseph Femia, *The Machiavellian Legacy: Essays in Italian Political Thought*, Basingstoke, Macmillan, 1998, pp. 126–144, who

Mosca rejected many popular theories of his day, whether they concerned the effects of climate, race, the Darwinian 'struggle for existence', or indeed the view that society is an 'organism'.[186] In his lecture on the Mafia, Mosca had argued that a Sicilian taken out of his context would lose his mafiosi ways, thereby vitiating the 'climate' argument, and in *The Ruling Class* he had already pointed out that climate played no role in the development of great societies over time, which could be found in all sorts of different places, whether hot or cold, lush or arid.[187] He rejected Gobineau's and Gumplowicz' racial theories as 'mere pretexts' to awaken antipathies between different groups,[188] pointing out how supposedly different 'races' had no difficulty mastering other languages—the surest proof of rationality—anticipating what Noam Chomsky would later argue.[189] Finally, he rejected the view of the 'struggle for existence' and posited instead, in a somewhat Nietzschean vein, the 'struggle for pre-eminence'.[190]

This rather liberal account was continued in his view of history, which had if not teleological then certainly progressive elements to it. For even though Mosca held the ancient civilisations of Athens and Rome in high regard, writing of the latter that 'republican Rome was the one in which juridical defence was most solidly established, and in which civil strife was, therefore, least bloody and least frequent'[191]—high praise indeed!—he also concluded that the 'cultivated modern nations' of the eighteenth and nineteenth had overtaken them, notably in their ability to harmonise numerous social forces, which in Mosca's account appear to continually grow over time.[192]

Added to this somewhat progressive view of history[193] is a critique of popular sovereignty: 'we deem it sufficient for our purposes here to

---

describes Mosca as a 'pioneer' of modern political science, if an unfashionable one, embodying *spregiudicatezza* (i.e. looking at things without prejudice) and Machiavelli's *verità effettuale* ('effective truth').

186. Mosca, *The Ruling Class*, pp. 7–34. See, further, Cook, 'Gaetano Mosca's "The Ruling Class"', p. 442, who describe these attacks as 'mordant'.

187. Ibid., pp. 7–13.

188. Ibid., p. 72.

189. Ibid., pp. 20–28. See Noam Chomsky, *Syntactic Structures*, Berlin, De Gruyter 2020.

190. Ibid., p. 29. The reference here is to Nietzsche's notion of the 'will to power', which aims to overcome itself, instead of to a Hobbesian self-preservation. See Drochon, *Nietzsche's Great Politics*, p. 59.

191. Ibid., p. 204.

192. Ibid., p. 253.

193. See ibid., p. 139: 'if a political organism is to progress in the direction of attaining greater and greater improvement in juridical defence'.

demonstrate that the assumption that the elected official is the mouthpiece of the majority of his electors is a rule not consistent with the facts,' because even in the representative system, as it is with all forms of government, the 'organised minority imposes its will on the disorganised majority'.[194] This is something that happens 'to perfection' under elections, anticipating some of what he will later say in his lecture on the Mafia: 'mass democracy in many ways extended rather than constrained the possibilities for élites to govern'.[195] Here we come to one of Mosca's most famous passages:

> When we say that the voters 'chose' their representatives, we are using a language that is very inexact. The truth is that the representative *has himself been elected* by the voters, and, if that phrase should seem too inflexible and too harsh to fit some cases, we might qualify it by saying that *his friends have had him elected*.[196]

Move aside Schumpeter: your 'minimalist' theory of democracy as 'rule by politicians' was already articulated over thirty years before![197]

And yet, as he has done throughout the book, Mosca also offers a qualified defence of the representative system, writing that 'the real juridical safeguard in representative governments lie in the public discussion that takes place within representative assemblies', and also that 'the referendum is in some respects a fairly effective instrument'.[198] His concern remains, as always, that the parliament would come to dominate everything, and that 'all the prestige and power of legitimate authority' would be vested in assemblies, such that 'the whole administration and judiciary machine' would fall prey to the 'irresponsible and anonymous tyranny of those who win in the elections and speak in the name of the people'.[199]

What Mosca feared most was that juridical defence would be obviated and a single social force would come to rule over everything, something he repeated throughout the book, that 'one single crushing, all-embracing,

194. Ibid., p. 154.

195. Bellamy, 'Social and Political Thought', pp. 237–8.

196. Mosca, *The Ruling Class*, p. 154.

197. Femia, 'Mosca Revisited', p. 136: 'Schumpeter, without mentioning Mosca, substantially endorses his assessment of what actually happens in parliamentary systems'.

198. Ibid., p. 157.

199. Ibid.

all-engrossing tyranny will weigh upon all'.[200] This is why already at the end of *Elementi I* Mosca defended the type of pluralism we associate with juridical defence that could exist within the representative system, where 'it cannot be denied that the representative system provides a way for many different social forces to participate in the political system and, therefore, to balance and limit the influence of other social forces'.[201] So representative democracy well-understood, defined by juridical defence, is a form of the 'least-worst' type of government possible, if it can ensure that the social forces that come to dominate the assembly are constrained within that role, and do not extend to the rest of the political institutions.

Here we return to Mosca's denunciation of fascism. Although when he was writing *Elementi I* in 1896 it was a Rousseauian-inspired form of direct-democracy socialist collectivism he was most concerned would become the single tyrannical force that would come to dominate everything, it is easy to see how such a concern could be moved to fascism when it appeared, which claimed the same thing. At the high point of his speech, Mosca asked what would happen to the prime minister if the social forces that brought him to power were to desert him: on what basis could he claim to rule? And what of the other social forces: would they still be represented? That is to say: what would happen to the other social forces under fascism: would they just be suppressed, disbanding juridical defence and therefore leading to a decrease in civilisation?[202]

The ruling class. Social forces. Juridical defence. Civilisation. The political formula. From the perspective of a political theory, one might be tempted to say: 'tout y est'.[203] So what might be the difference between *Elementi I* and *Elementi II*? Much that was in *I* is repeated in *II*, notably the lauding of Rome, the English Constitution, Montesquieu, the middle-class, and the critique of Marx, socialism and collectivism transformed here into syndicalism.[204] And

200. Ibid., p. 285.

201. Ibid., p. 138.

202. Mosca, 'Prerogative del capo del governo', p. 281.

203. This is in contract to Bobbio's view, which regards Mosca's theory as 'unfinished' or not systematic, because it didn't sufficiently discuss 'the *recruitment* of the ruling class . . . and its *organisation*', although Bobbio will admit Mosca starts to do so in the final chapter of *Storia* (Bobbio, 'Gaetano Mosca and the Theory of the Ruling Class', pp. 12–13). As I aim to show with the notion of the 'two strata' below, Mosca can be said to have at least started to address those questions.

204. See Mosca, *The Ruling Class*, pp. 347, 381, 386, 391, 443 and 481.

Mosca is quick to present his predecessors in developing the theory of the ruling class, citing Saint-Simon, Comte and Taine.[205] This was in response to the 'Piccola Polemica' Mosca had had with Pareto over who was the first to come up with the theory of the ruling class, to which Mosca's answer was to list all those who had preceded him, but also those who came after, not least Pareto, whose Les Systèmes socialistes of 1902 he explicitly put after his own Teorica of 1884. This passage—the opening of Elementi II—is important because it is where Michels makes his first appearance in the Ruling Class.[206]

But here also, for the first time—and this is the first point of difference between Elementi I and II—Mosca labels his theory of the ruling class a 'political doctrine'.

> A doctrine is a thread by which those who are examining a given body of facts try to guide themselves in the maze which the facts seem to present at first glance; and a doctrine becomes the more useful in practice the more it facilitates and simplifies the understanding and analysis of the facts.[207]

A political doctrine, therefore, is a theory that simplifies yet captures something essential about the subject at hand—in this case, politics—so that the notion of 'ruling class' both captures and simplifies something about political societies, namely that a minority will always rule over a majority. This is why Mosca again rejects Aristotle's tripartite division of governments into monarchies, aristocracies and democracies, adding this time Montesquieu's despotic, monarchical and republican governments[208]—although he'll return to praise both thinkers soon in other instances. Note, too, that Mosca's subsequent and final book will be his 1936 Storia delle dottrine politiche—History of Political Doctrines—where he will give an exposition of the 'political doctrines' of the great thinkers from Plato to 1914, concluding with his own theory of the ruling class.[209]

205. Ibid., pp. 329–330.

206. Ibid., pp. 331–332. Mosca had previously written, in 1912, a review-essay on Michels' Political Parties (see Gaetano Mosca, 'La sociologia del partito politico nella democrazia moderna' in Partiti e Sindacati, pp. 26–36).

207. Ibid., p. 336.

208. Ibid., p. 336.

209. Mosca, 'The Final Version of the Theory of the Ruling Class', pp. 382–4. There Mosca writes (p. 383): 'today, a whole new method of political analysis attempts to draw attention to that very fact; its major purpose is to study the formation and organisation of that ruling stratum

The 'ruling class' as a political doctrine was in fact a further way to answer Pareto. As Livingston writes: 'I believe Croce has said it somewhere: the originality of thinkers lies not always in their seeing things that nobody else has even seen, but often in the stress they give now to this commonplace and now to that'.[210] In listing all the different thinkers who had thought about the idea that 'the few' always rule, Mosca inserted himself into a longer tradition of political thought, or political doctrines, as he would put it. But what marked Mosca out from that tradition was the fact that he was the first to explicitly theorise it. That was his 'genius'.[211]

Livingston also writes that 'the maxim that there is nothing new under the sun is a very true maxim; that is to say, it covers about half the truth, which is a great deal of truth for a maxim to cover'.[212] Mosca's theory of the ruling class is one such maxim, covering half the truth of politics (the few always rule). But in *Elementi II* Mosca is aware that he has only covered half the truth, that 'merely to assert that in all forms of government the real and actual power resides in a ruling minority is to dismiss the old guides without supplying new ones'.[213] This is why 'the comprehensive and generic demonstration that a ruling class necessarily exists has to be supplemented, therefore, with an analytical study'.[214] And that, again aided by a 'great store of data' furnished by 'history, statistics and economics', is the existence of an 'intermediary strata'—this is the second difference—upon which so much depends:

> If this new perception of the importance of the ruling class is to gain a hold, we must, without denying the great importance of what has been done at the vertex and at the base of the pyramid, show that, except for the influences of the intermediate social strata, neither of the others could have accomplished very much of any significance and permanence, since the type to which a political organism belongs and the efficacy of its action depend primarily upon the manner in which the intermediate strata are formed and function.[215]

---

which in Italy is by now generally known by the name of *ruling class*—an expression which together with the term *elite*, used by Pareto, begins to find international acceptance'.

210. Livingston, 'Introduction', p. x.

211. Ibid., p. xi.

212. Ibid., p. x.

213. Mosca, *The Ruling Class*, p. 336.

214. Ibid.

215. Ibid., p. 337.

Both autocratic and liberal systems have intermediary strata. In autocratic systems, one based on military rule, the higher stratum corresponds to the 'general and staff', the second stratum to the 'officers who personally lead the soldiers under fire': the second stratum is always more numerous and 'comprises all the capacities for leadership in the country'.[216] In 'liberal' systems, i.e. those based on consent, representation and the law, there are also two strata.[217] Note that this 'consent' can be direct or indirect:

> One may say that in such systems the law is based upon the consent of the majority of citizens, though only a small fraction of the inhabitants may be citizens; and then that the officials who apply the law are named directly or indirectly by their subordinates, that their posts are temporary and that they are personally responsible for the lawfulness of their acts.[218]

The first group, the smallest, is what we might describe as the politicians proper, drawn from the elective structure, who may—this is important—be in competition with one another, in the same way that court cliques are in autocracies.[219] Below them are what we might call party officials, those who organise political meetings, give speeches, publish newspaper articles and opinion-leaders, as 'the chief task of the various party organisations into which the ruling class is divided is to win the votes of the more numerous classes'.[220] Mosca has recast the middle class he so vehemently defended into this meritocratic second stratum, which, to his mind, forms the 'backbone' of all great political organisations, which is why they need to be the 'best' morally.[221] As Bellamy puts it, Mosca believed that 'ideally the élite should be . . . the most capable'.[222]

---

216. Ibid., pp. 404–405.

217. Ibid., p. 409.

218. Ibid. On consent see further Finocchiaro, *Beyond Right and Left*, pp. 57, 145.

219. Ibid., p. 410.

220. Ibid., pp. 410–411. See, further, Puppo, 'Gaetan Mosca et la théorie de la classe politique', p. 249, where he explains: 'au sein de la minorité gouvernante il y a deux niveaux: le premier, la classe politique, ne compte que quelques douzaines d'hommes; l'autre, la classe dirigeante, dont les membres sont sensiblement plus nombreux, constitue l'élément politico-administratif sans lequel toute organisation deviendrait impossible'. This anticipates Aron's later distinction between 'le personnel politique' and the 'catégories dirigeantes'.

221. Ibid., pp. 408, 413, 450. On meritocracy, see, further, Finocchiaro, *Beyond Right and Left*, pp. 51–56.

222. Bellamy, 'Social and Political Thought', p. 239.

Building on this, Mosca adds two new ideas, and whilst the above points about political doctrines and the intermediary stratum were about refining and deepening ideas, this conceptual pair are Mosca's true innovations in *Elementi II*. The first is that 'in any form of political organisation, authority is either transmitted from above downward in the political or social scale, or from below upward', the former known as 'autocratic', more suited to great political regimes likes Mesopotamia, Persia, China, Turkey and Russia, the latter as 'liberal', as found in modern nations such as England and the United States.[223] Indeed, as Bobbio points out, the modern parliamentary state was born in seventeenth-century England and then transplanted with varying success to the Continent.[224] Needless to say, when the liberal principle dominates, these are 'exceptional periods', where the 'noblest faculties of man are able to show themselves in their intensity and energy', which leads to 'considerable increases in political power and economic prosperity'.[225] On the other hand, autocracies are characterised by 'a long sleep'.[226]

To this set of principles Mosca adds another, namely dividing societies into those dominated by the 'democratic' or the 'aristocratic' tendency.[227] This has to do with how rapidly the ruling class is replenished by elements derived from the lower classes: the faster it is, the more 'democratic' it is; the slower, the more 'aristocratic', when power becomes more stable and hereditary.[228] Although one might be tempted to marry the autocratic principle with the aristocratic tendency, and indeed the liberal with the democratic, Mosca is quick to point out that that need not be the case: the Chinese Empire was both autocratic and democratic (power from above but quick replacement); Venice, liberal but aristocratic (power from below but slow replacement).[229] There are therefore four ideal types: aristocratic-autocratic, aristocratic-liberal, democratic-autocratic, democratic-liberal.[230]

223. Mosca, *The Ruling Class*, pp. 394–398.

224. Bobbio, 'Gaetano Mosca and the Theory of the Ruling Class', p. 20.

225. Mosca, *The Ruling Class*, p. 398. On liberal/autocratic and democratic/aristocratic, see Claudio Martinelli, 'Gaetano Mosca's Political Theories: A Key to Interpret the Dynamics of Power', *Italian Journal of Public Law*, Vol 1, 2009, pp. 10–11.

226. Ibid.

227. Ibid., p. 395.

228. Ibid.

229. Ibid., pp. 395–396.

230. Bobbio, 'Gaetano Mosca and the Theory of the Ruling Class', p. 20.

The democratic tendency, for Mosca, is constantly at work in all societies, with greater or lesser intensity.[231] Here we find again the language of 'infiltration' and 'revolution' Mosca had used previously, although Mosca adds that if infiltration occurs slowly, this has a conservative force, as new elements brought in won't want to overthrow the system they have profited from and that revolutions are more likely to occur in periods of turmoil.[232] And if Mosca praises the democratic tendency for allowing individuals from the lower echelons of society to fully develop all their qualities—meritocracy—he nevertheless also sees the use of having a degree of stability, therefore recommending a *'juste milieu'* or 'golden mean' between the two tendencies.[233] As Bellamy writes:

The ideal was a mixture of both tendencies and both principles, so that the political class did not atrophy, nor become unstable through a lack of continuity, and the efficacy of government was combined with a certain accountability to the interests of the people as a whole.[234]

Mosca writes that all the great thinkers, whether Plato, Aristotle or Montesquieu, in reality advocated a 'fusing' of both the principles and tendencies developed here—a form of 'mixed regime'[235]—and concluded that representative government was best able to do so.[236] In the *Storia*, Mosca writes:

The best regimes, that is, those lasting a long time and able to avoid the violent convulsions which have plunged mankind back into barbarism, are the mixed regimes. We call them mixed because in them neither the autocratic nor the liberal principle rules supreme, and the aristocratic tendency is tempered by a gradual but continuous renewal of the ruling class, enabling it thus to absorb the better elements into its ranks.[237]

---

231. Mosca, *The Ruling Class*, p. 413.

232. Ibid., pp. 414–416.

233. Ibid., pp. 422–429. In his final Senate speech, Mosca had counselled a slow pace of change when it came to political reform, something that seems to have been anticipated here (Mosca, 'Prerogative del capo del governo', p. 282).

234. Bellamy, *Modern Italian Social Theory*, p. 51.

235. Mosca, *The Ruling Class*, p. 137. On the 'mixed regime', see, further, Norberto Bobbio, 'Mosca e il governo misto' in Norberto Bobbio, *Saggi dulla scienza politica in Italia*, Bari, Laterza, pp. 201–220. Mosca distinguishes between feudal and bureaucratic states (Mosca, *The Ruling Class*, pp. 70–102). See, further, Albertoni, *Mosca and the Theory of Elitism*, p, 54.

236. Ibid., pp. 394, 427–428.

237. Mosca, 'The Final Version of the Theory of the Ruling Class', p. 390.

With these notions of autocratic/liberal and aristocratic/democratic, Mosca's masterpiece is complete.

Conclusion: Dynamic Democracy

At the end of *The Ruling Class* (*Elementi II*), in a touchingly personal passage, Mosca writes:

> Fifty years ago the author of this volume opened his career as a writer with a book which was a book of his youth but which he still does not disown.[238] In it he sought to lay bare some of the untruths that lie imbedded in certain assumptions of the representative system, and some of the defects of parliamentarism. Today advancing years have made him more cautious in judgement and, he might venture to say, more balanced. His conclusions at any rate are deeply pondered. As he looks closely and dispassionately at the conditions that prevail in many European nations and especially in his own country, Italy, he feels impelled to urge the rising generation to restore and conserve the political system which it inherited from its fathers.[239]

That political system was representative democracy. Finishing with a call for a certain form of European union and the defence of the middle class,[240] Mosca at the end of *Elementi II* had certainly made his desire to 'restore' representative democracy more explicit than he had at the end of *Elementi I*, where it was more qualified. Maintaining that universal suffrage had been a mistake, a criticism he had made all his life, Mosca conceded that going back on it would be committing a 'second mistake', and even if the representative system can be improved, nevertheless one is bound to see 'the great superiority of the representative system'.[241] In part this was helped by distinguishing between representative governments that take their inspiration from Rousseau, which he continued to decry as wanting to tyrannically impose one social force through the electoral system that would dominate all others, and those that take their inspiration from Montesquieu, who guaranteed political liberty through a separation of power, or, as Mosca would call it, juridical

---

238. I.e. the *Teorica*.

239. Mosca, *The Ruling Class*, p. 491. As Hughes puts it: 'on balance, he concluded, his theory had stood up well' (Hughes, 'Gaetano Mosca and the Political Lessons of History', p. 146).

240. Ibid.

241. Ibid., pp. 475, 490, 492.

defence.[242] Mosca and Montesquieu, according to Hughes, share a common aversion to all forms of despotism.[243]

What guarantees the superiority of representative government is its ability to balance competing demands:

> the participation of the elective element is very important in the modern state, and the great superiority and the main strength of modern political systems like in the ingenious balancing that they admit of between the liberal principle and the autocratic principle, the former represented by parliaments and local councils, the latter by permanent bureaucracies.[244]

Although the term did not yet exist, what Mosca is defending here, through his notion of juridical defence, is a form of pluralism, where numerous different interests compete and curb one another to ensure one does not become tyrannical, the 'assumption that only the opposition—one might almost say only *the competition*—of these contrary principles and tendencies can prevent an overaccentuation of the vices that are congenial to each of them'.[245] Yet, away from contemporary theories of interest group 'veto powers',[246] with his concept of civilisation Mosca is advocating the growth and harmony of as many social forces as possible within the larger political whole, and the ability of the ruling class is its ability to do so: 'that high level of civilisation made it possible to create in the political field the great modern representative state, which, as we have seen, is of all political organisms the one that has succeeded in coordinating the largest sum of individual energies and activities and applying them to purposes that are related to the collective interest'.[247]

Whilst we can readily recognise Mosca's defence of representative government as a defence of our modern democracies, his theory of the ruling class also puts dynamic democracy—the understanding of democracy as the continual challenge of elite rule—on a firm footing. That is because Mosca recognised that all ruling classes naturally decay and need to be 'infiltrated'—a terms he used at least from *Elementi I* onwards—by rising elements of the lower:

242. Ibid., p. 333.

243. Hughes, 'Gaetano Mosca and the Political Lessons of History', p. 154.

244. Mosca, *The Ruling Class*, p. 487.

245. Ibid., pp. 428–429, emphasis added.

246. Marx, 'The Bureaucratic State: Some Remarks on Mosca's Ruling Class', p. 437; Meisel, *The Myth of the Ruling Class*, p. viii.

247. Mosca, *The Ruling Class*, p. 416.

'nations die when their ruling classes are incapable of reorganising in such a way as to meet the needs of changing times by drawing from the lower and deeper strata of society new elements that serve to give them new blood and new life'.[248] Indeed, Mosca recognises that the 'struggle between those who are at the top and those who are born at the bottom but aspire to climb' determines the degree of civilisation that can be achieved.[249]

Added to this view of a ruling class that needs to remain 'open'[250] to talent from below, there are a number of elements in Mosca's theory that captures the 'movement' associated with dynamic democracy, not least the metaphor of 'infiltration' he uses to discuss the constant renewal of the ruling class.[251] And not just movement but also force, a key element of 'dynamism', as the force of the river reshapes the landscape it passes through, sometimes violently so. The extension to social movements—applying force to the political system—is clear.

Another is the notion of 'social forces' itself, which are constantly emerging, growing, evolving.[252] It is they, and the emerging minorities that lead them, who challenge the established forces and participate in the balancing of the political system Mosca terms juridical defence. Perhaps most importantly is the concept of the 'democratic tendency' Mosca uses in Elementi II, one of the great theoretical innovations there, to describe this constant renewal of the ruling class. Done within 'moderate limits', Mosca in fact praises such a tendency as 'indispensable to what is called "progress" in human societies'.[253] Indeed, Mosca will write that the democratic tendency has 'greater powers of self-preservation than other systems'—note that for Machiavelli the best test of a political regime is its 'duration'[254]—not simply because everyone today must pay lip service to it, which has an effect in itself,[255] but also because if the ruling class closes itself off completely, then it is doomed to failure through either decay of usurpation.[256]

248. Ibid., p. 460.

249. Ibid., p. 415.

250. Hughes, 'Gaetano Mosca and the Political Lessons of History', p. 144.

251. Mosca, The Ruling Class, p. 474.

252. In the past Mosca named military valour, wealth, birth or individual merit as different means of accessing the ruling class (Albertoni, Mosca and the Theory of Elitism, p. 22).

253. Mosca, The Ruling Class, p. 415.

254. Machiavelli, The Prince, p. 71.

255. Jan-Werner Mueller, Contesting Democracy: Political Ideas in Twentieth-Century Europe, New Haven, Yale University Press, 2011.

256. Ibid., pp. 333–334.

Mosca sees that this 'democratic' replacement is not simply good for the ruling class itself, but also for the lower classes. Already in the conclusion to *Elementi I* he had written that 'one cannot fail to see' how 'the rise of new elements to social influence comes to improve the relations between the rulers and ruled and render them more equitable'.[257] In *Elementi II*, he went one step further. Explaining, in rather Machiavellian tones, that the lowest classes want first and foremost 'to be governed as little as possible', he adds that their second desire 'is to profit by government in order to better their economic situation', something that has arisen directly through the exercise of the suffrage.[258] What Mosca is saying here is that the new social forces that have come to the fore through the representative system have materially benefitted the worst-off: that the continual conflict that is the essence of the democratic tendency, once it is not carried too far and becomes tyrannical through the Rousseauian syndicalist tendency, or becomes corrupted through the system of *trasformismo*, affords benefits for the lower classes. Bellamy writes:

> He saw electoral competition between élites and an openness to demands and recruitment from the lower strata as mechanisms for reducing rather than exacerbating corruption. For they ensured that rulers could further their own interests in governing only by taking account of the interests of the ruled in good government.[259]

'The best and the most welcome of all these concessions was a rapid raising of wages', Mosca writes.[260] In the *Storia*, having already complemented the 'liberal' regime for its 'vigour', Mosca explains that those 'delicate' regimes only exist within certain conditions, namely, 'periods of economic prosperity and of great intellectual flowering'.[261] These 'highly civilised' communities must be led by 'men of cultural and technical accomplishment'.[262] Reform liberalism is still the way forward.

257. Ibid., p. 299.

258. Ibid., p. 411. On the people not wanting to be oppressed, see Machiavelli, *The Prince*, p. 34.

259. Bellamy, 'Social and Political Thought', p. 239. On how 'public opinion', through the representative system, finds an echo in the 'highest spheres of government', see Hughes, 'Gaetano Mosca and the Political Lessons of History', p. 154.

260. Mosca, *The Ruling Class*, p. 472.

261. Mosca, 'The Final Version of the Theory of the Ruling Class', p. 388.

262. Ibid., p. 391.

2

Pareto and the Circulation of Elites

IT IS to Vilfredo Pareto that we owe the term 'elite' as we know it today. In his 1902 *Les systèmes socialistes* (*The Socialist Systems*), he writes: 'these classes represent an élite, an *aristocracy* (in the etymological sense: ἄριστος = the best)'.[1] For Pareto, society can be divided into different strata (*souches*) according to their respective abilities (intelligence; mathematical prowess; musical, literary or poetic talent; moral character), which may be good or bad: Pareto is happy to talk about an 'elite of brigands' as much as an 'elite of saints'.[2] What he does seem to hold constant, however, coming from his training as an economist, is that those with the most political and social power will also be the richest (note the difference with Mosca, who instead defended the middle class).[3] Yet these aristocracies never last. They degenerate. Here, too, there is a difference with Mosca: as H. Stuart Hughes writes, there is no 'inexorable law of degeneration and fall from power' in Mosca's theory of the ruling class.[4] This might, for Pareto, be because of wars which disproportionally affect their numbers, but even in times of peace there is a loss in the number of births and the decomposition of their elements. There is, in short, a continual 'movement of the circulation of elites'.[5]

---

1. Vilfredo Pareto, *Les systèmes socialistes*, Genève, Droz, 1978, p. 8. Translation mine. Note that the book came out in two volumes: the first in 1902, the second in 1903 (see Giovanni Busino, 'Avertissement' in ibid.). I concentrate here on the first one. Thanks to Stefanos Geroulanos for helping to track down the original old Greek spelling of *aristos*.

2. Ibid., pp. 7–8, 56.

3. Ibid., p. 8.

4. H. Stuart Hughes, 'Gaetano Mosca and the Political Lessons of History' in James Meisel, ed., *Pareto and Mosca*, Englewood Cliffs, Prentice-Hall, p. 144.

5. Ibid., p. 9. Note that in his discussion of the circulation of elites in the *Trattato di Sociologia generale*, Pareto also refers to Taine's *Ancien régime*, much as Mosca does, to explain that the

Paired with the term 'elite', Pareto's theory of the 'circulation of elites' is his greatest conceptual innovation. He explains it as 'the movement of circulation that carries the elites, born of the lower classes, to the summit, and that makes the elites in power descend and disappear'.[6] To illustrate his theory, Pareto gives the example of A-B-C: A is the elite in place, B the elite that wishes to challenge A, and C the rest of the population. A and B are the leaders, C does not have any, yet: it is an 'army without generals'.[7] Both A and B will appeal to C: B, not being in power, can have the easier time of it by making promises it won't be able to keep. If B slowly takes A's place, then C is without leaders and there is no generalised revolt. Pareto uses the term 'infiltration' to talk about this slow circulation, the same term Mosca uses.[8] Indeed, both share an interest in Rome, a rejection of sentimentalism, racism and theories about the 'climate', the recognition for the need to use force, the praise of rural classes as containing the best elements of the nation, and the defence of an 'open elite'.[9] But if A resists, then battle will be joined and B will call upon C. Were B to succeed, a new elite—D—will arise and play the same role with B as B did with A. And so on and so forth: the incessant movement of the circulation of elites is one of the main features of human history.[10] It is a historical 'fact'.[11]

B can come from inside society or outside it: the circulation can be a conquest or a revolution. Either way, for Pareto, society must find a new equilibrium.[12] When things might change is hard to predict, as the movement of circulation is an undulating curve. When the curve is about to change, often it is not a diminishing of intensity that one sees, but rather its intensification.[13] The telltale sign for Pareto that a decadent elite is losing its way is in its descent into a form of 'humanitarian' sentimentalism, no longer able to defend its

French Revolution should be understood as a 'religious' revolution, where 'popular faith overwhelms the scepticism of the higher classes' (Vilfredo Pareto, *The Mind and Society*, New York, Harcourt, Brace, 1935, Vol. III, #2049, n. 5).

6. Ibid., p. 34.

7. Ibid., p. 35.

8. Ibid.

9. Ibid., pp. 12, 37, 38 and 47. See, further, S. E. Finer, 'Introduction' to Vilfredo Pareto, *Sociological Writings*, London, Pall Mall Press, 1966, pp. 17, 32. This is in contract to Robert Michels, who did think about race, and had a more linear conception of time, which he associated with progress (see chapter 3).

10. Ibid., pp. 15 and 35.

11. Ibid., p. 41.

12. Ibid., p. 11.

13. Ibid., p. 31.

position.[14] The willingness to use force is key to maintaining its position, although Pareto is quick to distinguish between indiscriminate violence, which is a sign of weakness, and necessary force.[15] When B comes to power, this is often followed by an era of great prosperity, the decadence of A having been swept away.[16] But it is important to underline that C will never rule as such: it might produce new leaders (D), but on its own it is incapable of ruling. 'Ochlocracies have only ended in disaster'.[17]

Les systèmes socialites, as its name indicates, was written in response to the rising tide of socialism throughout Europe.[18] The period from 1900 to 1902, when Les systèmes was composed, witnessed an unprecedented number of strikes: 1,034 in 1901 and 801 in 1902.[19] Adding to this, there were various popular uprisings in 1894, 1898, 1904 and 1914.[20] In the book, Pareto addressed directly the 'materialist theory of history'. He conceded that it has a 'true' starting-point, namely that economics has an impact on social institutions and doctrines, but explained that there are other facts that need to be taken into account that cannot be reduced to pure questions of the economy, a point Mosca made too.[21] And although he agreed that class struggle was indeed a motivating force in history,[22] he rejected as an illusion the *Communist Manifesto*'s claim that the socialist movement can be the movement of the majority instead of a minority: the elite will always rule.[23] This is why, for Pareto, the 1900s was a period of growing religious sentiment, because socialism, and its belief in a happy future, was a form of 'secular religion'.[24]

14. Ibid., p. 37

15. Ibid.

16. Ibid., p. 36.

17. Ibid.

18. Ibid., p. 3.

19. Richard Bellamy, 'Vilfredo Pareto' in *Modern Italian Social Theory*, Cambridge, Polity Press, 1987, p. 21.

20. Finer, 'Introduction', p. 3.

21. Ibid., p. 26.

22. Bellamy, 'Vilfredo Pareto', p. 19: 'Pareto agreed that "class struggle . . . is the great dominant fact in history", but argued that it took two forms. In the first, beneficial form, it was equivalent to economic competition and produced maximum ophelimity. Usually, though, it took the second, harmful form, "whereby each class endeavours to get control of the government so as to make it an instrument for spoilation".'

23. Ibid., p. 61.

24. Ibid., p. 33. See Bellamy, 'Vilfredo Pareto', pp. 22–23 for Sorel's influence on Pareto's comparison between socialism and religion. On Sorel and 'myth', see, further, Finer,

This rejection of the Marxist ideal—that an elite will always rule, and that a proletarian revolution will simply mean the coming to power of a new elite, not the abolition of class altogether—has led to Pareto, and to a lesser degree Mosca, being labelled the 'Marx of the bourgeoisie'. Indeed, Pareto's ambition had been to 'turn Marx on his head', much as Marx had turned Hegel.[25] As Norberto Bobbio puts it, the 'daring nature' of his political views, the 'discovery of the irrational forces that make history' and the 'necessity to meet violence with violence' resulted in Pareto being described as 'another Machiavelli, the Nietzsche of sociology or the Marx of the middle classes (or of fascism)'.[26] As Hughes well explains:

> Redefined in this fashion, the class interpretation of history is transformed from a revolutionary into a conservative doctrine. It becomes a vehicle for restoring the self-confidence of the European ruling classes, whose will to govern has been sapped by the Rousseauist dogmas of democracy and social equality.[27]

Yet Pareto, much like Mosca, was anything but a defender of the status quo.[28] Again, like Mosca, he harked back to the founding liberal nobles of the

---

'Introduction', pp. 22, 46, 53, and also Hughes, *Consciousness and Society*, p. 250 for Pareto considering Sorel's theory of myth as being one particular case of his theory of residues. See, further, Norberto Bobbio, 'Introduction to Pareto's Sociology' in Norberto Bobbio, *On Mosca and Pareto*, Geneve, Droz, 1972, p. 68 and Joseph Femia, 'Pareto's Concept of Demagogic Plutocracy' in Joseph Femia, *The Machiavellian Legacy: Essays in Italian Political Thought*, Basingstoke, Macmillan, 1998, p. 150 for myth as a form of 'social poetry, providing the proletariat with one of those great social myths which have incited men to action through the ages'.

25. H. Stuart Hughes, *Consciousness and Society: The Reorientation of European Social Thought 1890–1930*, New York, Vintage, 1961, pp. 79, 81.

26. Bobbio, 'Introduction to Pareto's Sociology', p. 72.

27. Hughes, 'Gaetano Mosca and the Political Lessons of History', p. 148. Raymond Aron makes a similar point at first, as we shall see in chapter 6. For Finer ('Introduction', p. 77–78), although the *Treatise* is a 'gargantuan retort to Marx', Pareto's strategy is not of 'confrontation but envelopment': 'he constructs social concepts and categories so broad as to reduce Marxist propositions to the status of more mere special cases of a much more general theory', i.e. Marxism itself is an ideology, class rule becomes elite rule, and class exploitation, 'spoliation'.

28. Charles Powers writes: 'the son of an exile and a member of a family that had a tradition of fighting against autocrats and autocratic rule. Pareto grew up finding it natural to pit himself against established power . . . [having] suspicions of elites and revulsion to political rhetoric. Pareto was not an apologist for the status quo.' (Charles Powers, 'Introduction' in Vilfredo Pareto, *The Transformation of Democracy*, New Brunswick, Transaction Publishers, 2009, p. 2).

'Historical Right', but he was an extreme—oftentimes even more extreme than Mosca—critic of his time, as we shall see.

If socialism's promise, according to Pareto, is untrue, that does not mean it hasn't brought some positive elements too, and on a couple of occasions Pareto lauds English Trade-Unionism.[29] First amongst these is the fact that belief in socialism had given workers the energy to defend their rights, which has morally lifted them.[30] Second, socialism has facilitated the organisation of the new elite that is rising from the lower classes, perhaps something like D in the previous schemata. Finally, socialism is the best instrument for the education of the lower classes.[31] Faced with the growing decadence of the elite in power, suffering from the '*manie sentimentale*', Pareto sees the possibility of an alliance between the new socialist elites, intellectuals drawn from the bourgeoisie, and members of the working class to further the latter's interest: 'no social class is homogenous, there are always rivalries, and one party can find support in the inferior classes. . . . Almost all revolutions have as their leaders dissident members of an elite'.[32] The future, it seems, belongs to a new socialist elite.[33]

The other important thing to note about *Les systèmes socialistes* is that it was written in French. Pareto was bilingual (French-Italian), born in France of a French mother and an Italian father, and at the time of writing the book was living in Geneva.[34] This is important because Pareto used the word *élite* in French, i.e. with the accent. Yet when in 1916 Pareto published his masterpiece, the three thousand pages and one million word behemoth that is the *Trattato di Sociologia generale* (*Treatise on General Sociology*), *in Italian*, he continued to use the French word *élite*.[35] This was the consecration of the term. It is only

29. See ibid., pp. 13 and 63.

30. Ibid., p. 63. Bellamy, 'Vilfredo Pareto', p. 17.

31. Ibid., p. 63.

32. Ibid., p. 71.

33. Bellamy, 'Vilfredo Pareto', p. 23 writes: '"bourgeois socialism" was being replaced by the new leaders of "popular socialism". . . . A direct clash would occur and the new elite of workers' leaders would take over. This would not inaugurate the communist utopia, but another era of oppressors and oppressed'.

34. The Franco-Italian context, alongside the links with Sorel, is key for both Pareto and Michels, who also came to sociology through socialism, whereas Mosca stood apart (Hughes, *Consciousness and Society*, p. 252).

35. Note that, for Hughes, *Les systèmes socialistes* was the superior book, a 'biting, spirited, witty book—a magnificent polemic' that gave Lenin many sleepless nights, whereas the *Trattato* consisted in a 'complicated methodology only tenuously connected with an entertaining catalogue of *faits divers*' (Hughes, *Consciousness and Society*, pp. 78).

later, notably with the publication of C. Wright Mills' *The Power Elite* in 1956, that the term became anglicised and lost its French accent (and, we might note, became more pejorative): one of the few publications that retains élite in English is *The New Yorker*, which says more about it than anything else.

Pareto was searching for a term that would capture his theory of minority rule. Previously, in his 1900 *Application of Theoretical Sociology*, where he first started developing his views, he used the term aristocracy, still present in *Les systèmes*. But too reminiscent of the *Ancien Régime*, it was no longer fitting in a modern democratic context. Nor did he want to use the Marxist 'class'—he preferred 'souche' (strata) in *Les systèmes*—or the more usual term used in Italian at the time: *classe dirigeante*. Nor, finally—although he was seemingly unaware of it at the time—did he want to use the *classe politica* (political or ruling class) of his great rival Mosca. So he settled on *élite*, a French word drawn from the Latin *eligere*, meaning the elect. It is thanks to French that Pareto was able to articulate his theory.[36]

The aim of this chapter is to recover Pareto's theory of the circulation of elites, first by recounting Pareto's biography that led him to the term 'elite', and the political context within which he was operating. Today, Pareto is best known as an economist, theorist of 'Pareto efficiency' or the '80/20 rule', but the first section will highlight the links Pareto's training as an engineer and as an economist had with his political theory, notably when it comes to the question of equilibrium. Second, it will turn to relating the different stages of the development of the theory of the circulation of elites, from the 1900 *Application* to the *Treatise*, determining where it meets, and where it differs from, Mosca's *Ruling Class*. Third, it will explore Pareto's final work, *The Transformation of Democracy*, where he applied his theory of the circulation of elites to his contemporary 1920s Italy, emphasising his notion of 'demagogic plutocracy'. There the thorny question of Pareto's relation to nascent fascism will be discussed, and the thesis of Pareto as a patrician 'high liberal',[37] staying above the fray in his Villa Angora in Switzerland, will be defended: there is a difference between seeing in fascism the confirmation of one's thesis and a full

36. Giovanni Sartori, *The Theory of Democracy Revisited. Part One: The Contemporary Debate*, Chatham, Chatham House Publishers, 1987, p. 143.

37. For a discussion of 'high liberalism', see John Tomasi, *Free Market Fairness*, Princeton, Princeton University Press, 2012, chapter 2, and Samuel Freeman, *Liberalism and Distributive Justice*, Oxford, Oxford University Press, 2018, chapter 1. Although Pareto defended many 'classical liberal' themes such as free trade, he also supported compulsory education and workers' rights to strike and unionise, placing him more in the 'social', 'left' or 'high' liberalism camp.

endorsement of it. Finally, the conclusion will ask what Pareto's theory brings to dynamic democracy, underlining its richness, and bringing to the fore the dual pairing of the 'lions' and the 'foxes', and also Pareto's concept of 'demagogic plutocracy'.

I: France, Italy

Vilfredo Pareto was born on 15 July 1848 in Paris, the year of revolutions. S. E. Finer, one of the finest commentators on Pareto, describes it as the *'annus mirabilis* of liberalism'.[38] The previous February, the July Monarchy of France had been overthrown, leading to the founding of the Second French Republic. This set off a wave of revolts throughout Europe, aiming to topple the old monarchical regimes and replacing them with independent republican nation-states. Key demands included widening democratic participation, freedom of the press and workers' rights. This was a liberal-democratic revolution, demanding individual rights, freedom of expression, free trade, the market economy, pacifism, humanitarianism and universal male suffrage, although the bourgeois-proletarian coalition that drove it quickly fell apart, and reaction set in.[39] In honour of the revolution taking place in Germany at the time, Pareto was first named Fritz Wilfried, although this was later latinised into Vilfredo Federico upon his return to Italy. Pareto's father was the Marquis Raffaello Pareto, forced into Parisian exile in 1835/6 from his native Genoa because of his Mazzinian sympathies (Mazzini was his contemporary).[40] Working there as a civil engineer, he met and married a French lady, Marie Métenier, who may have been a Calvinist,[41] with whom he had three children: two daughters and Vilfredo.[42]

38. Finer, 'Introduction', p. 3.

39. Ibid. Christopher Clark (*Revolutionary Spring: Fighting for a New World 1848–1849*, London, Penguin, 2023) argues that, instead of 'reaction', the following period saw the search for a new centre-ground.

40. Finer, 'Introduction', p. 9. Both Mazzini and Pareto senior were born in Genoa, in 1805 and 1812, respectively (Powers, 'Introduction', p. 2).

41. Powers, 'Introduction', p. 2. See further George-Henri Bousquet, 'A propos de Marie Metenier, mère de V. Pareto: Faits et réflexions', *Cahiers Vilfredo Pareto*, Vol. 6, No. 15, 1968, pp. 223–229.

42. Finer, 'Introduction', p. 9.

As such, Pareto's background, at least on his father's side, was radical:[43] the Marquis Pareto was part of the aristocratic liberal generation that 'made' Italy, participating in the Risorgimento and unifying Italy under Garibaldi's guide. It was Pareto's great-great-grandfather, Giovanni Lorenzo Pareto, who ennobled the family in 1719 by inscribing the Pareto name in the 'golden book' of the aristocracy in exchange for 100,000 lire, a substantial sum at the time.[44] It would seem that the family was rich—merchants and industrial wealth from inland, indeed a small hamlet still bears the 'Pareto' name, a relatively common name for the area—but considered of low standing: the request had been rejected twice before by the *Consiglietto*, the Republic's government, but in the end it needed the money.

This is something worth bearing in mind when considering Pareto's theory of the 'circulation of elites': every year in Genoa certain families would enter the aristocracy either by certain remarkable feats, whether intellectual, artistic, martial or otherwise, or by buying their way through. This meant that there was a continual 'renewal' of the Genoese aristocracy, with elements from the lower classes rising up, and those at the higher falling off: elite-circulation in action. Whatever its formal name, the Republic of Genoa was in reality an open form of aristocracy.

The Pareto family had a distinguished record of serving the republic as senators, members of the Legislative Council, mayors, ministers of finance and gonfaloniers during the Napoleonic era. Later, a number of them agitated for Mazzini, even serving jail sentences—Pareto told the story of an aunt, of Irish extraction, who 'hid Mazzini during a police search by sewing him into a mattress'—and upon Mazzini's return served as members of parliament, foreign ministers and presidents of the chamber of deputies.[45]

On return to Italy in 1855 after the general amnesty, Pareto senior entered the Piedmontese civil service, rising to high rank and honour.[46] Pareto junior followed in his father's footsteps, entering the Polytechnic University of Turin (then the Technical School of Engineers), to study engineering. He showed a

43. As Charles Powers writes: 'Pareto's grandfather and his grandfather's brother were ardent supporters of republicanism and assisted the French incursion during the Napoleonic Period' (Powers, 'Introduction', p. 1).

44. Finer dates this 1729 (Finer, 'Introduction', p. 9).

45. Powers, 'Introduction', p. 2. Thanks to Giovanni Damele for information concerning Pareto's background.

46. Finer, 'Introduction', p. 9.

certain proficiency in mathematics, which laid the foundation for this future success as an economist, and in 1869 he earned a doctorate with a dissertation entitled 'The Fundamental Principles of Equilibrium in Solid Bodies'.[47] The thesis attempted to 'describe equilibria in solids in terms of shifting balance among countervailing forces of expansion and contraction'.[48] This tension between change and equilibrium was to provide the foundation upon which Pareto would later develop his theory of the 'circulation of elites'. This equilibrium is 'dynamic', because society is in continual motion between movements and counter-movements, meaning the equilibrium itself is always a 'moving' one, adjusting itself to the respective forces.[49] From there he would take up a position of director of the Rome Railway Company (1870–1874) and in 1874 he became the managing director of the Società Ferriere d'Italia, which had its headquarters in Florence.[50]

His father died in 1882 and his mother in 1889, which seemed to have affected him deeply: he resigned his managing directorship, married a penniless Russian girl from Venice, Alessandrina 'Dina' Bakunina (no relation), and moved to the Villa Rosa on the hills outside Florence, Fiesole, which now houses the EUI (European Union Institute).[51] There he became a journalist and economist, defending a liberalism of free trade, republicanism, disarmament and universal suffrage.[52] As Richard Bellamy writes, Pareto was an admirer of Mill and Spencer, arguing for individual liberty.[53] Due to his rejection of state intervention in the economy, he has often been presented as a 'classical liberal'. Yet he had a social side to him too, bringing him into contact with T. H. Green's 'new liberalism': he argued in favour of compulsory education, which he renamed 'freedom of education', explaining it was indispensable for a full exercise of liberty.[54] As Bellamy writes: 'compulsory education

47. Ibid.

48. Powers, 'Introduction', p. 4.

49. Finer, 'Introduction', pp. 13, 32.

50. Finer, 'Introduction', p. 9. On Pareto's (not always successful time) in business, see Fiorenzo Mornati, *Vilfredo Pareto: An Intellectual Biography, Volume 1: From Science to Liberty (1848–1871)*, London, Palgrave Macmillan, 2018.

51. Ibid., p. 10. Power, 'Introduction', p. 5.

52. Bellamy, 'Vilfredo Pareto', p. 13.

53. Ibid., p. 14. For the influence of Spencer's concept of 'social differentiation' on Pareto's pluralism, see Finer, 'Introduction', pp. 16–17. On Pareto's knowledge of Spencer, see Bobbio, 'Introduction to Pareto's Sociology', p. 65.

54. Ibid., p. 15.

was therefore a prerequisite in a country where 78% of the people were illiterate, if universal suffrage was to become not just "an empty word, but a beneficial reality".[55] Indeed, Pareto posited that 'responsible government would only result when all, through elections, were involved in it'.[56] Pareto was therefore a 'classical' liberal when it comes to economics—for free trade, against state intervention, for international peace—but a 'social', 'left' or 'high' liberal, much like Weber came to be, when it came to social and political questions, defending universal education, universal suffrage, and trade unions.

He certainly showed sympathy to socialism. He defended workers' rights to strike and unionise, and argued that responsible government would only be achieved through elections when everyone was given the right to participate.[57] He was aware of and deplored the factory conditions of workers in the north, which his work had brought him into contact with, and also the poverty of the southern peasantry: it is worth remembering that the electorate only made up between 2% and 7% of the population, 78% of Italians were illiterate, and the country faced abysmal poverty.[58] Although from a well-to-do background and moving in aristocratic salons in Florence before his rupture with the business world, he despised the Italian aristocracy and accused it of 'sucking the blood' of the Italian poor.[59] There he professed 'extremist' views in support of democracy, republicanism, free trade, disarmament and peace, against the state protectionism the economic and political elites were using at the time to further their own personal interests.[60]

He started writing polemics against the Italian government: monthly 'chronache' for the *Giornale degli Economisti* from 1891 to 1897.[61] As Finer notes: 'between 1889 and 1893 he wrote 167 articles, many of them scholarly, but the vast majority anti-government polemics'.[62] He gave public lectures in working men's institutes, which were closed by the police, and ran as an opposition candidate twice, on a radical, anti-elitist and free-trade platform,[63] in 1880 and

55. Ibid.
56. Ibid.
57. Ibid., p. 14.
58. Ibid., p. 15; Finer, 'Introduction', p. 5.
59. Finer, 'Introduction', p. 10.
60. Ibid., p. 10; Powers, 'Introduction', p. 5.
61. Ibid., p. 11; Bellamy, 'Vilfredo Pareto', p. 16.
62. Ibid., p. 10.
63. Powers, 'Introduction', p. 5.

1882, refusing a third time in 1886 (he was never successful).[64] Later, when in Switzerland, he welcomed socialist refugees and become a Dreyfusard, declaring himself, in Nietzschean terms, an 'anti-antisemite'.[65] He became a marked man in governmental circles.

Pareto denounced the policy of *trasformismo* that characterised the politics of his day, namely a form of corrupt wheeling-and-dealing between left and right to stay in power. During the elections of 1876 the 'Historical Right' that had unified Italy fell from power, replaced by the 'Young Left'.[66] The 'Historical Right' had defended the type of free-trade, free-market and peace Pareto advocated. They had become obsessed with reducing the debts that had been incurred by the Risorgimento, making Italians the most taxed population in Europe.[67] The 'Historical Left' under their leader Agostino Depretis quickly abandoned these free-trade and free-market Mazzinian ideals to safeguard their position by maintaining a delicate balance between northern and southern interests through government patronage.[68] They reduced taxation and increased the electorate from 2% to 7% of the population.[69] Later, in the *Trattato*, Pareto made a distinction between 'compromising' and 'uncompromising' political parties, between those willing to participate, fox-like, in 'transformist' politics, and those, more intransigent, unwilling to do so, and who would rather overthrow the whole system.[70]

Although the post-Risorgimento age has often described as the 'Long Liberal Period', it was anything but, becoming increasing authoritarian, corrupt and incompetent. On his death in 1887, Depretis was replaced by Francesco Crispi, a Sicilian politician and follower of Garibaldi's expedition to the island, who became an admirer of Bismarck and pursued a disastrous colonial policy and fell from grace in 1896 after a series of personal and financial scandals.[71] He was replaced by Giovanni Giolitti, who continued the policy of *trasformismo*.[72] It is worth noting that Depretis served three terms (1876–1878, 1878–1879, 1881–1887), Crispi two (1887–1891, 1893–1896) and Giolitti five

64. Finer, 'Introduction', p. 10; Bellamy, 'Vilfredo Pareto', p. 16.
65. Ibid., p. 11.
66. Ibid., p. 10; Bellamy, 'Vilfredo Pareto', p. 14.
67. Bellamy, 'Vilfredo Pareto', p. 13.
68. Finer, 'Introduction', p. 10.
69. Bellamy, 'Vilfredo Pareto', p. 14.
70. Finer, 'Introduction', p. 67.
71. Bellamy, 'Vilfredo Pareto', p. 16.
72. Ibid., p. 21.

(1892–1893, 1903–1905, 1906–1909, 1911–1914, 1921–1921), with some overlap between the latter two. If one is looking for a historical representation of the circulation of elites, look no further.

During this period Pareto continued to defend his liberal views. As Bellamy writes: 'Pareto argued that if there were really uncorrupt elections and free competition then everyone's welfare would improve, because opinions and talents of the best would prevail to the advantage of the whole community'.[73] But to describe this period, Finer explains that

> in the name of liberalism, the wealthy and the cultivated had denounced state intervention, whether this manifested itself in progressive income tax, in protective tariffs, or in welfare legislation; but the socialists, in the name of democracy, demanded precisely these measures. The vector of the two contending forces, the path actually followed by the professedly liberal-democratic states, was collectivism. On the one hand, the employer received tariff protection and subsidies; on the other, the worker received social welfare benefits. The free-trading, free-enterprising economy was on its way out, and its defenders, the mid-century liberals, increasingly became anachronistic survivals.[74]

This is what Pareto became, an 'anachronistic survival'. He defended the type of liberalism that had been the centre-ground of the Historical Right at the foundation of the Kingdom of Italy. But that centre-ground had shifted towards a form of authoritarian, transformist, corrupt collectivism, which made his views professed in the Florentine salons 'extreme'.[75] This also explains why he rejected the '*consorteria*' of the left and the right, which pursued similar policies of a patron-client state with their own clienteles to satisfy.[76] As Bellamy puts it: 'his coruscating deconstruction of *Socialist Systems* in 1902 and

73. Ibid., pp. 15–16.

74. Finer, 'Introduction', p. 4. For Pareto's critique of protectionism as destroying national wealth, see *Mind and Society*, #2208. See, further, Bellamy, 'Vilfredo Pareto', p. 17. See, further, Femia, 'Pareto's Concept of Demagogic Plutocracy', pp. 155, 157: 'the cumulative effect of controlled markets and uncontrolled public expenditure is macro-economic distortion. Massive public debts accumulate and these are inevitably accompanied by higher prices and interest rates. . . . If we pursue this line of reasoning, we can grasp how demagogic plutocracy may maximise utility *for* the community even when destroying the utility *of* the community'.

75. On the centre-extremes dynamic, see Hugo Drochon, 'From Dusk till Dawn: Bobbio on the Left/Right Dichotomy', *Journal of Political Ideologies*, forthcoming.

76. Finer, 'Introduction', p. 79.

his later Fascist sympathies arose largely because he felt that from 1900 the balance had swung the other way'.[77] Finer's view that in 1900 Pareto's views underwent a 'total revolution' therefore seems a little off.[78] It is certainly the case that Pareto criticised socialism in *Les systèmes socialistes*—a socialism he had expressed sympathy for beforehand—but his criticism was consistent with what he had said before: namely, he rejected it as a doctrine that was in any way meant to be 'true'. But as we've already seen above he praised it for the energy it had furnished the working class, and anticipated that a new bourgeois-socialist elite might be the future.

As Bellamy writes: '*Les systèmes socialistes* did not signify the historical break between the young liberal and the future fascist. It sprang from the same liberal belief in the rights of the individual against all forms of authority'.[79] Finding himself outside the mainstream of Italian politics, he was happy to endorse either side that criticised what had become the new centre-ground. At first he had hoped that the rising socialists would signal a new form of politics, but quickly came to realise that it merely replaced bourgeois privileges with working-class privileges.[80] Yet that was consistent with his theory of the circulation of elites. This is worth bearing in mind when we return to the question of his—alleged—support of fascism.

II: Lausanne, Economics

Either way, an exit was on the cards, and he found it in academia.[81] Alongside his polemics, Pareto wrote a number of scholarly articles in the *Giornali*, defending free-market theories. That brought him into contact with the liberal economist Maffeo Pantaleoni, whose book *Pure Economics* (1889) he reviewed, and with whom he formed a life-long friendship.[82] Pantaleoni introduced Pareto to Leon Walras' mathematical economic theories, which Pareto soon

77. Richard Bellamy, 'Social and Political Thought, 1890–1945' in Adrian Lyttelton (ed.), *Liberal and Fascist Italy*, Oxford, Oxford University Press, 2002, p. 233.

78. Finer, 'Introduction', p. 11.

79. Bellamy, 'Vilfredo Pareto', p. 22.

80. Finer, 'Introduction', p. 11; Bellamy, 'Vilfredo Pareto', p. 17.

81. Bellamy, 'Vilfredo Pareto', p. 12: 'disappointment with Italian politics is indeed the key to his sociological thought'.

82. Powers, 'Introduction', p. 6. On Pareto and Pantaleoni, see Norberto Bobbio, 'Vilfredo Pareto's Sociology in his Letters to Maffeo Pantaleoni' in Bobbio, *On Mosca and Pareto*, pp. 33–53.

proved adept at, thanks to his former training. Walras was one of the pioneers of the 'marginalist revolution' in economics, centred around the notion of 'marginal utility'—namely the change in satisfaction one receives through the consumption of an additional unit of the good or service—and the general equilibrium theory, which stipulates that the laws of supply and demand will tend towards equilibrium.

Alongside the technical aspects of pure economics, Pareto was drawn towards equilibrium theory, which was consonant with his engineering thesis, and he developed these Walrasian ideas in the *Giornali*, bringing him to international notoriety. In 1893, with the help of Pantaleoni, Pareto succeeded Walras as the Chair of Political Economy at Lausanne, and together they are known as the Lausanne School of Economics, with a special emphasis on equilibrium within markets.[83]

In 1896, Pareto published his *Cours d'économie politique*, based on the lectures at Lausanne. Alongside his later *Manual of Political Economy* (1906 Italian, 1909 French), this made his name as an economist.[84] There he developed his famous theories in the field of econometrics: Pareto efficiency, Pareto distribution, Pareto principle.[85] The latter, otherwise known as the 80–20 rule, he developed from his study of land distribution in Southern Italy—he subsequently expanded it to include most of Europe and Latin America—where he concluded that twenty percent of the population always owns eighty percent of the land, and that this was an immutable universal historical law. He also observed that twenty percent of the pea pods in his garden produced eighty percent the peas. If that social distribution cannot be changed, nevertheless poverty could be reduced by increasing productivity. As Charles Powers puts it: 'if the pie is always going to be sliced unevenly, then the best way to help the poor is by enlarging the pie.'[86]

In the chapter on 'Social Physiology' in the *Cours*, Pareto put forward an important theory, that of 'spoliation', something that will be repeated in *Les systèmes*.[87] As Finer explains: 'this is the idea that in all societies at all times there exists a class of persons who seize on the goods of others, sometimes by legal and sometimes by illegal means'.[88] For example, when the 'governing

---

83. Finer 'Introduction', p. 10; Bellamy, 'Vilfredo Pareto', pp. 16–18.
84. Ibid., p. 10; Bellamy, 'Vilfredo Pareto', pp. 18–19.
85. Hans Zetterberg, 'Introduction' in Pareto, *The Rise and Fall of Elites*, p. 1.
86. Powers, 'Introduction', p. 7.
87. Finer, 'Introduction', p. 22.
88. Ibid., p. 16.

class' imposes protective tariffs it is, according to Pareto, engaging in legal spoliation—a critique of the politics of the day. For Finer, Pareto thought Marx's theory of class struggle important because it had brought the theory of spoliation to light, and it would play a later role in Pareto's theorisation of 'demagogic plutocracy'.[89] As Albert Hirschman explains in *Rhetoric of Reaction*: 'Pareto distances himself from Marxism by using the term "spoliation" rather than "exploitation" or "surplus" and by making it clear that spoliation is due to the dominant class's obtaining control of the state, which is called a machine for spoliation'.[90]

A caesura between Pareto the classical liberal economist and Pareto the anti-democratic political theorist is sometimes posited,[91] but there is an evident continuity here between the 80/20 rule and his theory of elites. In fact, in *Les systèmes socialistes* Pareto explicitly linked his theory of elite rule to his previous *Cours d'économie politique*, saying that he is building on what he had written earlier on 'social physiology'.[92] The link is to the 'curve' of the distribution of wealth (Pareto uses *'toupie'*, a 'spinning top')—i.e. the 80/20 rule— explaining that the social pyramid is reproduced in other spheres of activities, whether mathematics, music, poetry, literature, morals, etc., as we had seen in opening, although those who are on top political and socially will also be on top in terms of prosperity.[93] This distribution is in part explainable through the theories of 'pure economics', namely rational choices, but also through the physiological and psychological characteristics of men: the qualities of a St Francis are not the same as Krupp's, the manufacturer.[94] But both are at the top of their sphere of activity. And although the shape of the curve never changes, there is circulation within the body politic—much like there is circulation of blood in an animal—between its respective parts: people get rich,

89. Ibid.

90. Albert Hirschman, *The Rhetoric of Reaction: Perversity, Futility, Jeopardy*, Cambridge (MA), Harvard University Press, 1991, p. 55.

91. See Bellamy, 'Vilfredo Pareto', p. 12, who attributes this view even to Joseph Schumpeter in his *Ten Great Economists: From Marx to Keynes* (ibid., p. 176, n. 1). Bellamy, it should be stressed, does not share this view, writing that he wishes to demonstrate the 'continuity between the supposed two Paretos', that the 'principles of his economic liberalism governed those of his sociology', and that he used 'the insights of the *Trattato* to describe political developments from the First World War to his death in 1923'.

92. Pareto, *Les systèmes socialistes*, p. 6; Bellamy, 'Vilfredo Pareto', p. 19

93. Ibid., pp. 7–8.

94. Ibid., p. 8.

others become poor.[95] 'The molecules that make up the social aggregate do not remain at rest', Pareto explains, 'certain individuals become richer, other poorer. Fairly extensive movements therefore agitate the interior of the living organism'.[96] 'The fact of utmost importance for social physiology is that aristocracies don't last'.[97]

In his contemporaneous *Application of Theoretical Sociology*, to which we shall now turn, Pareto pursued the link between his economic and his sociological theories. Again referencing his *Cours d'économie politique*, he drew a link between the circulation of elites (here aristocracy) and the business cycle, which share a 'psychological rhythm': 'there is a rhythm of sentiment that we can observe in ethics, in religion and in politics as waves resembling the business cycle'.[98] But as Hans Zetterberg points out, there is also a link between the theory of elites and utility: '"elite" should be treated as a value-free term meaning those who score highest on scales measuring any social value or commodity ("utility"), such as power, riches, knowledge'.[99] We can go even further than that. Remember that the theory of 'marginal utility' is the greater *marginal* satisfaction of a product or service. Yet the same can be said of men. As Pareto explains, drawing from his own background expertise:

> to drive a locomotive . . . one needs a man of judgement and intelligence. Should he be but a little deficient in these qualities, the situation could not be remedied by putting two engineers into the locomotive instead of one; two, three or even four mediocre engineers cannot achieve the output of one capable and intelligent engineer.[100]

The 'marginal' utility of the good engineer is higher than that of the two, three or even four mediocre ones: the locomotive is always better driven by him. He can therefore ask for a higher 'price', or in this case a salary. This is how you get to the elite: so we have here a very potent force incessantly at work, which divides labour into various strata, assigning great advantages to the

95. Ibid., p. 7.
96. Ibid.
97. Ibid., p. 9.
98. Vilfredo Pareto, *The Rise and Fall of Elites: An Application of Theoretical Sociology*, New Brunswick, Transaction Publishers, 1991, pp. 30–31. Pareto repeats this point in *Les systèmes socialistes*, p. 30: 'the religious and moral movement is rhythmic alongside the economic one'.
99. Zetterberg, 'Introduction', p. 8.
100. Pareto, *Rise and Fall*, p. 76.

superior ones. This is a principal factor in the formation of a new elite.[101] Later in the *Trattato*, Pareto will make the distinction between utility *of* and utility *for* the community. The former is the satisfaction that individuals draw, from their consumption, for example, of goods, shelter and clothing. The latter is the utility of the community as a whole. The former, needless to say, may come at the detriment or the latter, and vice versa.[102]

In 1898, his uncle, who had inherited the marquis, died, leaving him a substantial sum that in effect made him a man of independent means.[103] With his health deteriorating, he moved to his Villa Angora at Céligny and resigned from his chair at Lausanne in 1907, although he continued to lecture there till 1916. It was time to write his masterpiece.

III: The Application

In 1901, Pareto published a long article in the *Rivista Italiana di Sociologia* (*Italian Sociological Review*) entitled '*Un applicazione di teorie sociologiche*' ('An Application of Theoretical Sociology'). It was the first time he wrote in the field of sociology, instead of economics, and it was his first attempt to lay out what was to become his theory of the circulation of elites. As Zetterberg writes, the article 'provides the shortest and most readable introduction to his theory of the circulation of elites'.[104] Finer presents it as 'a notable work: it foreshadows all the positions Pareto was to take up later',[105] namely in *Les systèmes socialistes*, *Manuale di economia politica* and the *Trattato di sociologia generale*.[106] Although it may have been written, as Finer speculates, after the opening chapter of *Les systèmes*, from which it draws, the *Application* is notable for not using the word 'élite', preferring to use 'aristocracy'—*aristocrazia* in Italian—instead:[107] this may have to do with the fact that it was written in Italian, and not in French. As such, the English translation of the text, which follows in the tradition of imposing on the English translation a different title than that of the original Italian or German—Mosca's *Ruling Class* instead of *Elementi di scienza politica*; Pareto's *Mind and Society* instead of *Trattato di sociologia*

---

101. Ibid.
102. Finer, 'Introduction', p. 45.
103. Ibid., p. 11; Powers, 'Introduction', p. 7.
104. Zetterberg, 'Introduction', p. 4.
105. Finer, 'Introduction', p. 20.
106. Zetterberg, 'Introduction', p. 4.
107. See Pareto, *The Rise and Fall*, p. 36, where *aristocrazia* is translated as 'elite' into English.

generale; Michels' *Political Parties* instead of *Zur Soziologie des Parteiwesens in der modernen Demokratie*—mistakenly renders the title as *The Rise and Fall of Elites: An Application of Theoretical Sociology*, again, as in Michels' case, changing the title to the subtitle: the word 'elite', though, is nowhere to be seen. If Pareto is indeed trying to articulate his theory of the circulation of elites, the term never appears there.

That being said, the *Application* does set out one of the clearest formulations of elite circulation, as both Zetterberg and Finer had indicated. It is as follows:

> Except during short intervals of time, peoples are always governed by an aristocracy. I use the word aristocracy in its etymological sense, meaning the strongest, the most energetic and most capable—for good as for evil. However, due to an important physiological law, aristocracies do not last. Hence—the history of man is the history of the continuous replacement of certain aristocracies: as one ascends, another declines.[108]

Here we have aristocracy as the best, for good or for (Nietzschean) evil;[109] the physiological law of the decline of aristocracies; history as the replacement of one aristocracy by another. To this he adds that the new aristocracy takes on the 'leadership of all the oppressed'—what Pareto will describe as B-C in *Les systèmes*—going to battle with the old aristocracy for the rights of all and not just itself, seeking either to 'supersede' the old aristocracy (A in *Les systèmes*) or merely 'share in its power and honour'. Once victory is achieved, its allies (C) are subjugated again (they will never in reality rule)—here Pareto uses the term 'lean' on the people, the 'poor and humble'[110]—or they are offered 'formal concessions': later Pareto writes that they 'let them keep certain earnings'.[111] This is what happened with the *plebs* and *patres* in Rome, with the bourgeoisie and the nobility during the French Revolution, and was then happening with the socialists (D), whom Pareto, unlike his friend Pantaleoni, thought were bound to win.[112]

---

108. Ibid.

109. As Femia points out, 'as Robert Michels once remarked, the "iron law of oligarchy" is "beyond Good and Evil"' (Joseph Femia, 'Mosca Revisited' in Femia, *The Machiavellian Legacy*, p. 132).

110. Ibid., pp. 72, 87.

111. Ibid., p. 88.

112. Ibid., p. 36.

But that is not all. Anticipating what he will develop in *Les systèmes*, Pareto in the *Application* also presents socialism as a form of religion, explaining that heightened periods of religious feeling presage a period of crisis, much as Tocqueville had observed in the French Revolution, and the 'materialist interpretation of history' is criticised for being solely focused on economic conditions, whereas other elements prevail.[113] He denounced the increasing humanitarian sentiment of the established elite, which will lead to its decline, signalling the rise of a new elite that will vindicate the humble and the weak against the powerful and the strong.[114] Indeed, even if the old elite is becoming weaker, unable or unwilling to use force to defend its position,[115] nevertheless its rapacity has not decreased, such that 'on one hand it makes the yoke heavier, and on the other it has less strength to maintain it', meaning an increase in violence, the weapon of the weak.[116] 'There must be a certain equilibrium between the power a social class possesses', writes Pareto, 'and the force at its disposal to defend it. Domination without that force cannot last'.[117]

Dismissing the notion that the people could ever rule, Pareto measures how if until recently socialist leaders were bourgeois, increasingly they come from the working class itself, especially its trade unions.[118] Pareto comes out in favour of an open elite, warning that if it becomes too rigid and exclusive, this could lead to a generalised revolution—note the similarity with Mosca's view that a slow replacement of the elite was in reality a 'conservative' force, as otherwise this would lead to a generalised revolt—and the imposition of a 'military dictatorship on some European nation'.[119] Zetterberg explains: 'an imbalance between innovation and consolidation can most easily be avoided by open recruitment into the elite';[120] or again as Finer nicely puts it: 'the open elite fends away revolution by creaming off the potential leaders of the counter-elite into its own ranks'.[121] Elites are most likely to survive if they are both 'open' and willing to use 'force' to maintain their position.[122] Finally, Pareto

113. Ibid., pp. 32–42.
114. Ibid., p. 41.
115. Zetterberg, 'Introduction', p. 10.
116. Pareto, *The Rise and Fall*, pp. 59, 71.
117. Ibid., p. 60.
118. Ibid., pp. 72–8.
119. Ibid., pp. 86, 101.
120. Zetterberg, 'Introduction', p. 10.
121. Finer, 'Introduction', p. 23.
122. Ibid., pp. 23–24.

starts to develop something that will become the key innovation of the *Treatise* in terms of what came before it,[123] namely the idea that 'the greater part of human actions have their origin not in logical reasoning but in sentiment', and that man 'likes to tie his actions logically to certain principles; he therefore invents these *a posteriori* in order to justify his actions'.[124]

IV: The Treatise

Pareto worked on the *Trattato* from 1907 to 1912, although it was published only in 1916, an inauspicious time. Another infelicity, beyond its sometimes ironical and invective style, is that its 'vast' and 'monstrous' million words do not amount to a systematic treatise, but instead to a 'great, sprawling, untidy torso', or, again, to a 'compendium of awkward terms'.[125] As Finer puts it

arguments peter out, to be renewed at another place. Minor points received vast and meticulous attention, whereas major points are often dismissed with short shrift. Footnotes of vast length—minor essays of great literary and argumentory artistry—are thrust into the text at unexpected places.[126]

Yet it is here that we get Pareto's full theory of the elite. And it is the French word *élite* that Pareto uses, even if the work is in Italian: it is here that the term gets its full consecration. Pareto himself makes the point explicitly. He writes: 'the term "circulation of elites" has been applied—in French *circulation des élites*'.[127]

123. See Bobbio, 'Vilfredo Pareto's Sociology in his Letters to Maffeo Pantaleoni', pp. 41–42: 'the first chapter of the *Systèmes*, which is devoted to the clarification of these problems, contains the whole *Treatise* in a nutshell, and may well be regarded as the first draft, however rough, imperfect and incomplete, of the future work on sociology'.

124. Pareto, *The Rise and Fall*, p. 27. See also Pareto, *Les systèmes socialistes*, pp. 2, 21–22. Bobbio, 'Introduction to Pareto's Sociology', p. 62 explains: 'the term logical actions is applied to actions which have the dual characteristic of establishing a link which is objectively adequate for the purpose, and of being achieved with the awareness of this adequacy'.

125. Finer, 'Introduction, pp. 8, 30; Bellamy, 'Vilfredo Pareto', p. 25; Powers, 'Introduction', p. 17; Norberto Bobbio, 'Introduction to Pareto's Sociology' in Bobbio, *On Mosca and Pareto*, p. 55.

126. Ibid., p. 29.

127. Pareto, *Mind and Society*, #2042. The English-language translator and editor Arthur Livingston writes that the Italian 'circulation of the elite' is a 'cumbersome phrase and not very exact', preferring 'class-circulation' (ibid. #2026, no. 1). On the first point he might be

In his section on 'social elites and their circulation' in the *Treatise*, Pareto offers his definition of an elite. He suggests judging people within their given branch of activity and giving them a mark out of 10 depending on how successful they are, as one would for a school examination.[128] He gives the example of a lawyer:

> The highest type of lawyer, for instance, will be given 10. The man who does not get a client will be given 1—reserving zero for the man who is an out-and-out idiot. To the man who has made his millions—honestly or dishonestly as the case may be—we will give 10. To the man who has earned his thousands we will give 6; to such as just manage to keep out of the poor-house, 1, keeping zero for those who get in.[129]

A few points are worth noting here. The first is the link between elites and wealth ('lawyers with his millions'), which we've come across before. The second is that the judgement is beyond 'good or bad':[130] the lawyer who has made his millions honestly or dishonestly, and Pareto is willing to judge courtesans like Madame de Pompadour; the 'clever rascal who knows how to fool people and still keep clear of the penitentiary, we shall give 8, 9, or 10 according to the number of geese he has plucked and the amount of money he has been able to get out of them', whereas the 'sneak-thief who snatches a piece of silver from the restaurant table and runs away into the arms of a policeman' will get 1. A poet like Carducci will get 8 or 9 depending on one's taste, and a 'scribbler who puts people to rout with his sonnets', zero. Finally, chess-players are easier to rank because we can know the indices of how many matches they have won. 'And so on for all the branches of human activity'.[131] Third, the ranking is meant to be based on quantifiable facts, not potential: if one could learn a foreign language but chose not to, when it comes to judging the foreign language, the ranking will be low; likewise, if one could be an excellent thief but is disinclined to do so because one is a gentleman, to use Pareto's own example,

---

right—although *circulation des élites* is perfectly fine in French—but on the second he is wrong: 'class' has too much Marxist baggage, which Pareto was trying to move away from. There seems no reason to depart from the consecrated 'circulation of elites', or, if one prefers, as a concession to Livingston, 'elite circulation'.

128. Ibid., #2027. For the *Treatise* the convention of giving the paragraph number, instead of the page, is followed.

129. Ibid.

130. Ibid., #2026.

131. Ibid., #2027.

then one could be judged highly on one's character but low on one's success as a thief.[132] Fourth is that this ranking is not an exact science: 'in the concrete, there are no examinations whereby each person is assigned to his proper place in these various classes'.[133]

'So let us make a class of the people who have the highest indices in their branch of activity, and to that class give the name *élite*'.[134] Pareto gives another example, of Napoleon, and this is important because he divides the elite into two: 'a *governing élite*, comprising individuals who directly or indirectly play some considerable part in government, and a *non-governing élite*, comprising the rest'.[135] A chess champion, for example, is certainly a member of the chess-elite, but, unless one is Gary Kasparov, does not necessarily have political power. Napoleon, however,

> Whether [he] was a good or a bad man, he was certainly not an idiot, nor a man of little account, as millions of others are. He had exceptional qualities, and that is enough for us to give him a high ranking, though without prejudice of any sort to questions that might be raised as to the ethics of his qualities or their social utility.[136]

Society is thus divided into two strata: '(1) a lower stratum, the *non-élite*, with whose possible influence on government we are not just here concerned; then (2) a higher stratum, *the élite*, which is divided into two: (*a*) a governing *élite*; (*b*) a non-governing *élite*'.[137] Society is divided into rulers and the ruled.[138] It is the governing elite that particularly retains Pareto's attention.

Pareto is aware that he is dealing in 'labels', that the label '"lawyer" is affixed to a man who is supposed to know something about the law and often does, though sometimes he is an ignoramus'.[139] There are always exceptions. But when it comes to the governing elite, there are more exceptions than usual: 'such exceptions are much more numerous than the exceptions among lawyers, physicians, engineers, millionaires (who made their own money), artists of

132. Ibid., #2028.
133. Ibid., #2035.
134. Ibid., #2031.
135. Ibid., #2032.
136. Ibid., #2029.
137. Ibid., #2034.
138. Ibid., #2047.
139. Ibid., #2035.

distinction, and so on'.[140] There are many reasons for this, including family and social connections, but the most important is wealth, which is hereditary. As Pareto writes—a clear swipe at Italian *trasformismo*:

> an individual who has inherited a sizable patrimony can easily be named Senator in certain countries, or can get himself elected to the parliament by buying votes or, on occasion, by wheedling voters with assurances that he is a democrat of democrats, a Socialist, an Anarchist.[141]

As such the elite is not always the elite: the 'best' do not always rule. There is market distortion, or as Finer puts it: '"the governing elite = those best capable of governing" is true only in a condition of perfect social mobility'.[142]

Pareto is often presented as positing that his 'elites' are indeed the best[143]— that this is a moral claim[144]—in contrast to Mosca, who was very critical of the ruling class of his day and who defended his own, cultivated 'middle class' (Pareto thought the middle-class of his day had bought into protectionism and *trasformismo*).[145] But two points are worth retaining here. The first, not least, is that Pareto was also highly critical—one might say even *more* critical than Mosca—of the political class of his time. The second, perhaps more importantly, is that Pareto's elite are the best *in theory*, but not necessarily in practice: as Finer points out, they are the best only in conditions of perfect market

---

140. Ibid., #2036. Finer, 'Introduction', p. 52.

141. Ibid., #2036.

142. Finer, 'Introduction', p. 52.

143. Bellamy, 'Social and Political Thought', p. 239. Hughes, *Consciousness and Society*, p. 254, writes that Pareto discounted 'systematic training' and how some skills might guarantee 'success in one situation and bring catastrophe in another'. Yet Pareto does emphasise the need to actualise those skills, not simply posses them 'in theory', and his whole theory of the circulation of elites is to say certain values succeed in certain circumstances but not in others (and none ever fully succeed, which is why we have circulation).

144. Sartori, *The Theory of Democracy Revisited*, pp. 144, 166 is often presented as thinking that Pareto's 'elite' is the 'best', but he distinguished between 'capable', i.e. 'true', elites, and the elites in power: 'Pareto's ultimate winner always is, in history, the capable elites, not the elite in power'. Mosca's 'political class', in contrast—according to Sartori—is 'value free' (ibid., p. 168). Sartori's ideal is a 'polyarchy of merit' of competing elected minorities, decided upon by the demos, to and for which they are responsive: 'responsiveness *and* independent responsibility' (ibid., pp. 151–170).

145. Bellamy, 'Vilfredo Pareto', p. 32.

equilibrium.[146] But as we've just seen, Italy at that time was full of market distortions.

Aristocracies are a good example of this. If previously military, religious or commercial aristocracies were part of the governing elite—the 'victorious warrior, the prosperous merchant, the opulent plutocrat'—over time the 'capacity' no longer refers to the label, and these 'aristocrats', although retaining their name, in reality no longer form a part of the ruling elite.[147] As Pareto famously puts it: 'history is the graveyard of aristocracies'.[148] The Athenians, the Romans, the Franks, the English nobility have all disappeared.[149] They decay and degenerate not simply in numbers—they are more exposed to the vagaries of their time, in particular, a higher proportion of them are likely to be killed in wars, as we saw previously, and they reproduce less—but also because they lose their vigour.[150] Yet due to the fact that society, according to Pareto, must always be in equilibrium,[151] what goes down means that something must go up: 'the governing class is restored', Pareto writes, 'not only in numbers, but—and that is the more important thing—in quality, by families rising from the lower classes and bringing with them vigour and the proportions of residues necessary for keeping themselves in power', a form of *redorer le blason*.[152] Here we arrive at the theory of the circulation of elites.

Building on the water imagery he used in *Les systèmes* ('infiltration'), in the *Treatise* Pareto uses the metaphor of a river to describe this process:

> In virtue of the circulation of *élites*, the governing *élite* is always in a state of slow and continuous transformation. It flows on like a river, never becoming today what it was yesterday. From time-to-time sudden violent disturbances occur. There is a flood—the river overflows its banks. Afterwards, the new governing *élite* again resumes its slow transformation. The flood has subsided, the river is again flowing normally in its wonted bed.[153]

---

146. Finer, 'Introduction', p. 52.
147. Pareto, *Mind and Society*, #2052.
148. Ibid., #2053.
149. Ibid.
150. Zetterberg, 'Introduction', p. 9.
151. Pareto, *Mind and Society*, #2032.
152. Ibid., #2054.
153. Ibid., #2056.

The circulation of elites happens in a twofold manner: either the gradual and continual integration of the new elite into the old elite (the river flowing), or a revolutionary change where the old elite is completely ousted to be replaced by a new elite (the river flooding and breaking its banks), before again resuming its slow and gradual transformation. Sometimes there are revolutions, but most of the time the circulation of elites is characterised by gradual change.

There is an element of 'velocity' to be taken into account when considering circulation, related to the demand and supply of certain social elements.[154] Pareto gives the example of peace-time, where there might not be a great need of soldiers for the army, but where there is an overabundance of generals, whereas during war there is a great need of soldiers, whose production might not meet demand. It is often through war, as noted previously, that many aristocracies meet their demise.[155]

Revolutions occur when decadent elements in the higher strata accumulate such that the governing elite is no longer willing to use force to defend its position: they have fallen prey to 'humanitarian' beliefs.[156] This may occur because the ruling elite has closed itself off from integrating within its bosom the best elements rising from the lower strata—Pareto was in favour of an 'open' elite[157]—meanwhile those at the bottom in contrast become increasingly open to the use of force.[158] And whilst revolutions come from below, Pareto still thinks at first—a thought similarly expressed in the *Application* and *Les systèmes*—that these will be led by elements of the higher strata, who have retained in tactics what they have lost in combativeness, which the lower now provides.[159] Pareto expresses these qualities through the term 'residues', and the conceptual couple of 'residues' and 'derivations' is his greatest conceptual innovation in the *Treaty*.[160]

---

154. Zetterberg, 'Introduction', p. 3.
155. Pareto, *Mind and Society*, #2044.
156. Ibid., #2057.
157. Ibid., #2046.
158. Ibid., #2179.
159. Ibid., #2058.
160. For Bobbio, Pareto's innovation was to have asked new questions—on logical and non-logical action, logical-experimental theories, and residues and derivations—which were distinct from the philosophy of history that dominated sociology at the time (Bobbio, 'Vilfredo Pareto's Sociology in His Letters to Maffeo Pantaleoni', pp. 33, 50, 77).

Across both the *Application* and *Les systèmes* Pareto had suggested that not all human action derived from reason, but much also arose from 'sentiment'.[161] In the *Trattato*, this thought was developed fully, Pareto wishing to distinguish the 'objective' from the 'subjective' element in human behaviour through his use of his 'logico-experimental' scientific method, which was inductive— starting from the facts up—instead of deductive, which drew logical conclusions from first principles.[162] He concluded that there were both logical and non-logical actions, and that in fact the vast majority of human behaviour fell into the latter camp.[163] The constant element that drove human behaviour he dubbed 'residues' and the variable aspect—the *a posteriori* theoretical justification of it—he called 'derivations'.[164] 'The residues are the major motivations of human action', explains Zetterberg, 'and the derivations are the external elaboration of man's action'.[165] When used by the ruling class to justify their rule, 'derivations' play a similar role in Pareto's system to Mosca's 'political formula', and Pareto lists 'the will of the people', 'universal suffrage' and 'majority rule' as amongst these types of derivations.[166] As Bobbio puts it, derivations are 'simultaneously an interpretation and an extension of the Marxian critique of ideologies'.[167] Indeed, the 'true and proper monument of the *Trattato* is the theory and critique of ideologies'.[168]

Yet derivations, as Finer points out, are not unimportant. They have the power of making residues more or less intense.[169] They 'make people more conscious of the residue that is in play and give it emotional overtones'.[170] For instance, nationalist propaganda might make people more conscious of

161. Pareto, *The Rise and Fall*, pp. 25–27, 48, 91; Pareto, *Les systèmes socialistes*, pp. 2, 21.

162. Bobbio, 'Introduction to Pareto's Sociology', p. 61.

163. Pareto, *Mind and Society*, #146, 149–152, 161, 842–845, 2030, 2041, 2079; Pareto, *Les systèmes socialistes*, pp. 3, 17; Bellamy, 'Vilfredo Pareto', p. 26; Finer, 'Introduction', p. 20; Zetterberg, 'Introduction', p. 20; Pareto.

164. Pareto, *Mind and Society*, #850, 863, 868, 2205, 2048, 2050, 2079, 2178, 2181–3, 2201, 2209, 2221.

165. Zetterberg, 'Introduction', p. 6.

166. Ibid., #2182–2183. Finer, 'Introduction', p. 53. See, further, Richard Bellamy, *Modern Italian Social Theory*, Cambridge, Polity Press, 1988, p. 2: '[for] Pareto, the connection between ideology and political behaviour was purely instrumental, presenting an *ex post facto* justification of action performed for quite different, usually irrational, motives'.

167. Bobbio, 'Introduction to Pareto's Sociology', p. 68.

168. Ibid., p. 76.

169. Finer, 'Introduction', p. 44.

170. Ibid.

'group-solidarity'. Yet at the same time, residues have to be there in the first place, and ultimately conflicts arise out of different sentiments or residues, and not between the arguments of derivations themselves, understood here as different ideologies, which are manifestations of those residues, more or less intensified.[171]

Hughes thought Pareto's 'derivations' a deeper theory than Mosca's 'political formula' because the latter is simply 'one example of a more inclusive category of rationalisations'.[172] As such, out of the three 'Machiavellians', Pareto is the more important figure, even if Pareto himself is secondary to Freud and Weber (being on par with Durkheim): Hughes' ambition with *Consciousness and Society*, as the title of the book indicates, was to integrate psychoanalysis into intellectual history.[173] So although Hughes ranked Pareto's contribution as being superior to Mosca and Pareto's, it still did not attain the level of Freud's, the *dramatis personae* of the era, because it did not contain the requisite psychological depth (although residue VI, 'sex'—see below—came closest to it).[174]

Pareto's supposed superiority over Mosca and Michels should only be accepted, as Hughes was quick to point out, with 'the strongest reservations'.[175] Because of his political experience, Mosca was in fact the better empirical worker, married to his sunnier and more moderate disposition that never succumbed to the charms of fascism, and who, although he attempted less—he was not a 'systems-builder' like Pareto, confining himself to developing a *political* theory—succeeded better in what he set out to do.[176] Michels came closest to 'contemporary standards of scientific investigation'[177]. Indeed, for Hughes what has stood the test of time in Pareto's work is what most resembled Mosca's, namely the theory of the 'ruling class' or elite'.[178] Specifically, it was his notion of 'residues':

> 'Persistence of aggregates', however, is a subtler complex, grouping under one heading such diverse manifestations as conservative ideals,

171. Ibid., pp. 44–45.
172. Hughes, *Consciousness and Society*, p. 257.
173. Ibid., pp. 19, 250, 257.
174. Ibid., pp. 19, 262, 263.
175. Ibid., p. 257.
176. Ibid., pp. 257–258, 266.
177. Ibid., p. 258.
178. Ibid., pp. 258, 268.

revolutionary ardour and religious zeal. Its definition as an abiding element in human society is perhaps Pareto's single greatest contribution to contemporary political speculation.[179]

Pareto discovered fifty-two residues, which he organised into six classes.[180] They are: I: combination, II: preservation, III: expressiveness, IV: sociability, V: integrity, and VI: sex.[181] Thankfully (for us), it is the first two that account for, according to Pareto, most of society.[182]

Class I, the 'instinct of combination', is the innovative one, willing to see new combinations in otherwise unrelated things: the Italian term is *combinazioni*.[183] Class II, the 'preservation of aggregates', in contrast, is more conservative, emphasising stability.[184] In the political realm, the former are 'foxes', the latter 'lions', following Machiavellian terminology.[185] Foxes, the innovators, are happier with disaggregation (centrifugal forces), plurality and scepticism, placing the individual over the community. Their rule is characterised by deceit, cunning, patronage, co-optation, ideological manipulation, and control via large complex decentralised bureaucracies. They tend to be more mercantile and materialistic, and their periods of rule are associated with the propensity to spend and, at least according to Powers, sexual permissiveness.[186] They are less comfortable with the use of force.

Lions are more conservative, emphasising the maintenance of unity (centripetal forces), homogeneity, established ways and faith, and place the community's needs over those of the individual. They show a willingness to use force, and they rule through a small, centralised bureaucracy which is clearly hierarchical. Their rule is more suited to agricultural societies, and are characterised by a traditionalism and the propensity to save. Whichever elite is in

179. Ibid., p. 269.

180. Bellamy, 'Vilfredo Pareto', p. 27.

181. Pareto, *Mind and Society*, #852, 869; Zetterberg, 'Introduction', p. 7.

182. Ibid., #2206.

183. Finer, 'Introduction', p. 39.

184. Pareto, *Mind and Society*, #846–865; Bellamy, 'Vilfredo Pareto', p. 27; Zetterberg, 'Introduction', p. 7; Finer, 'Introduction', p. 14.

185. For Bobbio, it is this emphasis on ruler and ruled that makes Pareto a continuator of Machiavelli (Bobbio, 'Introduction to Pareto's Sociology', p. 57). Likewise for Hughes, who adds the 'role of force and fraud in government' and the 'inevitable degeneration of all political groups and institutions' (Hughes, *Consciousness and Society*, p. 253).

186. Power, 'Introduction', p. 14.

power will determine what the rest of society will look like.[187] As Pareto had written as far back as *Les systèmes*: 'the foundation is the movement of the circulation of elites, the form is that which dominates in the society where the movement takes place'.[188]

Following Machiavelli's precept, as put forward in *The Prince*, the ideal ruler would be both fox and lion: lion to scare off the wolves, fox to avoid the 'snares'.[189] In a word: force and persuasion.[190] 'A governing class can only maintain itself', Finer writes, 'if it is prepared to use both force and persuasion'.[191] The difficulty is that the class I and II residues are for Pareto mutually exclusive: one cannot be both fox and lion at the same time. This is why there is a circulation of elites: elites that are predominantly lions over time will not be sufficiently innovative enough to 'keep up with the times', and will be replaced with foxes who are. In turn, foxes will lose their ability or willingness to use the force necessary to keep them in power, and will be replaced by lions. And so on and so forth: history is the pendulum swinging from one to another. Sometimes the swing is slow, as when one elite gradually replaces the other, sometimes it speeds up, as in times of revolution.[192]

The lion/fox divide is reproduced in the economic sphere, with rentiers (R) and speculators (S) respectively.[193] The distinction is between those who live off fixed incomes (savings, rents, government bonds) and those who live off variable incomes (stock-exchange, loans—Pareto puts *entrepreneurs* generally in this category),[194] and they match their Class II and Class I residues: rentiers with their 'preservations of aggregates' and speculators with their 'instinct for combination'.[195] 'A person of pronounced capacity for economic combinations is not satisfied with a fixed income', Pareto writes.[196] Rentiers

187. Bellamy, 'Vilfredo Pareto', p. 28.

188. Pareto, *Les systèmes socialistes*, p. 55.

189. *Machiavelli: The Prince*, Cambridge, Cambridge University Press, 2019, p. 61.

190. Pareto, *Les systèmes socialistes*, pp. 39, 56; Pareto, *Mind and Society*, #2174, #2178, #2201; Bellamy, 'Vilfredo Pareto', pp. 27, 30; Zetterberg, 'Introduction', p. 9.

191. Finer, 'Introduction', p. 54.

192. Zetterberg describes this as a 'wheel': 'the wheel has completed a full turn. The new elite is now established and the process can start all over again' (Zetterberg, 'Introduction', p. 14).

193. Pareto, *Mind and Society*, #2235. See, further, Bellamy, 'Vilfredo Pareto', p. 28.

194. Zetterberg, 'Introduction', p. 7, adds: 'in the category of innovators fall also two other famous sociological types, Schumpeter's "entrepreneur" and Weber's "modern capitalist"'. On 'entrepreneurs', Finer ('Introduction', p. 60), agrees.

195. Pareto, *Mind and Society*, #2234.

196. Ibid., #2235.

focus more on long-term economic growth, whereas speculators want to make a quick buck.[197]

Interestingly, Pareto does not follow the line of dividing the population between capitalists and proletarians, to follow the Marxist terminology, but rather aligns the rentiers and speculators with those who depend on them. For rentiers he has 'farmers, working-people, clerks' and for speculators he has 'lawyers, engineers, politicians, working-people, clerks'.[198] If there is a bit of overlap between the two, what is important to understand is that these are professions and people who depend on either rent or speculative wealth—i.e. are employed in those sectors. R and S should not be confused with economic occupation: retails merchants are more likely to be Rs, according to Pareto, whereas wholesalers, Ss. And, of course, different occupations and industries might move from R to S at certain moments, or have a combination of both elements.[199] Later in the *Transformation*, as we shall soon see, Pareto clarifies his thought, aligning farmworkers and landowners with the rentiers, and wage-labourers with the speculators, because they are interested in increasing their wages (this is why they strike).

Rentiers (R) ensure the stability of society, whilst speculators (S) are responsible for change. A society dominated by R is stationary, 'crystallised', whereas a society dominated by S is unstable.[200] Yet it would be a mistake, Pareto warns, to associate R with conservatives and S with progressives, innovators or revolutionaries. There might overlap, but there is no identity.[201] Indeed Rs can show themselves to support revolutions, especially 'movements tending to restore to the ruling classes certain residues of group-persistence that had been banished by the Ss': Pareto gives the founding of the Roman Empire and the Reformation as examples of these.[202] Later, in the 1923 edition of the *Trattato*, Pareto gave examples of recent revolutions in Italy and Germany where the middle class had been 'despoiled' of their savings by inflation. He may have had fascism on his mind.[203]

Although Pareto's theory is generally seen as top-down—it is the type of elite, foxes or lions, that determine society's form—he also sees how a

197. Powers, 'Introduction', p. 9.
198. Pareto, *Mind and Society*, #2233–#2234.
199. Ibid., #2235.
200. Ibid.
201. Ibid. See also Finer, 'Introduction', p. 61
202. Ibid.
203. Finer, 'Introduction', p. 61

bottom-up revolution can occur if there is too much of a gap between the types of residues that dominate in the elite class compared to those in the lower one: should that gap be too pronounced, there will be a revolt from below.

> The differences in temperament between the governing class and the subject class become gradually accentuated, the combination-instincts tending to predominate in the ruling class, and instincts of group-persistence in the subject class. When that difference becomes sufficiently great, revolution occurs.[204]

This is why Pareto advocates for an open elite, able to skim off the best cream from the rising top, leaving the subject class leaderless and disorganised.[205] This may be inherently conservative, as a way of stemming any revolutionary tide, but it can be seen as reformist too, ensuring a slow and continual turn-over of the ruling class. Indeed, as Finer suggests, 'the greater the mobility, the better the "health" of the governing class'.[206] It is a middle course between a too-strong crystallisation that will lead to revolution—Pareto speaks of an elite becoming 'petrified'[207]—or indeed encourage a revolution, full stop. Yet Pareto had a left-liberal side to him, and noted that a changing of the elite-guard led to a new era of prosperity.[208] Indeed, average economic wealth for him was the surest mark of progress and civilisation.[209]

V: The Transformation of Democracy

In 1920, Pareto wrote a series of four articles in the *Rivista di Milano*: 'Generalisation', published on 5 May; 'The Crumbling of Central Authority', published in two parts, on 20 May and 5 June; 'The Plutocratic Cycle', on 5 July; and finally 'Sentiments', on 20 July.[210] In 1921, he collected the four essays and

---

204. Pareto, *Mind and Society*, #2179. See also Finer, 'Introduction', p. 27.

205. Ibid.

206. Finer, 'Introduction', p. 55.

207. Ibid., p. 57.

208. Ibid.,

209. Pareto, *Les systèmes socialistes*, p. 40. Note that Pareto disavows the notion of 'progress' in favour of 'historical movement as a wave-motion' (Bobbio, 'Introduction to Pareto's Sociology', p. 57). See also Hughes, *Consciousness and Society*, p. 270, who attributes this cyclical view of history to both Machiavelli and Vico.

210. Charles Powers, 'Introduction: The Life and Times of Vilfredo Pareto' in Vilfredo Pareto, *The Transformation of Democracy*, New Burnswick, Transaction Publishers, 1984, p. 18.

published them as a book, *Trasformazione della democrazia*[211] — *The Transfor-mation of Democracy*—adding an 'Appendix' at the end where he discussed the economic and social situation of Italy (the attempt to devalue the currency, the rising power of the trade unions, the recent killings of strikers and national guards), and Giolitti's response to them. Although he continued to write short pieces till his death on 19 August 1923, this was, in many ways, his last work.[212] He was pushed to write it because of his frustration with the reception of his *Treatise*, which he thought had been misunderstood.[213] He decided not just to summarise his main ideas in more accessible form, but to apply them more explicitly to the Italian politics of the time.[214]

His greatest innovation was the term 'demagogic plutocracy', which he used to characterise the Italy of his day. He explained that those who were profiting from the system were the speculators and the wage-earners. 'The growing power of wealth speculators might be viewed as a "plutocratic" tendency while the growing power of wage earners might be viewed as a "democratic" ten-dency', Pareto wrote—note the association between wage-earning and democracy—and these two classes have 'cooperatively united or formed a partial alloy' that gives rise to 'demagogic plutocracy'.[215]

This alliance Pareto had already drawn when he had made the distinction between 'speculators' and 'rentiers', classifying, in an anti-Marxist sense, those who depended on the two classes as being part of that group instead of sepa-rating out the capitalist class, comprised of both speculators and rentiers, and the proletariat. For the former, Pareto cites the 'tradesman, industrialists and managers of public works', whilst the latter includes 'farmworkers and land-owners'.[216] Explicitly referring back to the *Treatise*, Pareto links the former to the 'instinct of combination'—rule through deceit and cunning, manipulation through analytical reasoning and rationalised legitimisation—and the latter to the 'persistence of aggregates'—the stubborn adherence to established ways, whether religious sentiments, customs, prejudices.[217]

The study of history makes it clear that passage of time is invariably char-acterised by cyclical oscillations rather than uniform change in a single

211. Vilfredo Pareto, *Trasformazione della democrazia*, Rome, Lit, 2016.
212. Pareto, *Transformation*, pp. 73–85.
213. Powers, 'Introduction', pp. 17–18.
214. Pareto, *Transformation*, pp. 26, 37, 73.
215. Ibid., p. 55.
216. Ibid., p. 56.
217. Ibid.

direction. . . . We are regulated and governed by agents divided into two groups: one preferring to rule primarily through consensus and the other preferring to rule primarily through the use of force. The social order consequently fluctuates between these two poles.[218]

The term 'demagogic plutocrat' had appeared briefly in the *Treatise*, in a passage where Pareto explained that employers and employees are in fact part of the same class: they are both 'speculators' because they wish to increase their income, and in reality strikes are a manner for employees to do so.[219] There Pareto also broached a topic that was to be central to *Transformation*, and indeed was to give the title to the second chapter, namely the 'Crumbling of Central Authority': the state no longer has any power to enforce its decisions, and Italians of all sorts regularly flaunt their ability to break the law with impunity.[220] 'It does not really matter whether the central power is monarchical, oligarchic, or popular in form', Pareto writes, 'for "sovereignty" is a word that ceases to have much meaning as central power crumbles and covers the country with its debris'.[221] Anarchy, instead, is to be on the rise, with 'rivalries among loci of decentralised power grown as their fears of central power diminish'.[222] Not only will trade unions be in conflict with the rest of the population, but also amongst each other.[223] And yet, neither is 'government via unions' the solution, as a 'change in form of government does not provide the substance for a solution'.[224]

Lack of force; corruption; speculation: in short, the foxes, in league with the entrepreneurs, have taken over.[225] And modern parliaments, because they promote the 'instinct of combination', are an 'effective tool' of demagogic plutocracy: 'first in elections and later during deliberations, parliamentary procedures favour those who are skilled in manipulative dealings'.[226] 'In reality parliaments',

218. Ibid.

219. Pareto, *Treatise*, #2187. 'Plutocracy' also appeared in *Les systèmes socialistes*, p. 49.

220. Pareto, *Transformation*, pp. 45–6.

221. Ibid., p. 41. This sentence, which can be captured by the phase 'politics without sovereignty', in which sovereignty is reduced to state capacity, is key to understanding the 'elite' conception of politics, which sees it as fundamentally the elite control of the state. Any changes to that control or the state itself will lead to a change in politics.

222. Ibid.

223. Ibid., p. 46.

224. Ibid., p. 48.

225. Finer, 'Introduction', p. 69.

226. Pareto, *Transformation*, p. 56.

Pareto explains, 'represent only the dominant strata of society'.[227] Indeed, there is a broader sense in which Pareto links parliamentary democracy to the rule of the foxes, and more specifically plutocracy: 'parliamentary government follows, in part, the fate of plutocracy. It thrives and declines with plutocracy'.[228] As Finer explains, 'modern mass democracies' fall into the demagogic-fox category of political regimes, where the circulations of elites is high. Although these regimes can be economically very productive, they are expensive to run and face the challenge of continuing to increase production. Because the foxes are in power, they are afraid to use force and can be easily overthrown.[229]

Yet the democratic façade is kept up, and Pareto thinks this form of rule particularly insidious for two reasons: first, those in power are more interested in siphoning off wealth to their own personal ends rather than encouraging the production of new wealth, thus undermining national prosperity (remember Pareto's training as an economist). Second, as the demagogic elite govern through deceit and cunning, they are able to mask their rule for longer periods of time. As Charles Powers puts it: 'their power is maintained until they bankrupt the government, disrupt the economy, and offend the conservative inclinations of common people'.[230]

But these centrifugal forces, those who foster the erosion of power because of their scepticism and individualism, naturally call upon their countervailing centripetal forces, those who encourage the concentration of central power through the strength of traditional attachments.[231] This means the return to power of those who have been losing out during this period: the class of 'independent property owners who are wealthy or well-to-do but do not speculate, and the military class', who have lost power since the end of the World War I.[232] In Pareto's account of the circulation of elites, speculators must give way to rentiers; foxes to lions; demagogic plutocracy to 'military plutocracy'.[233] 'The decadence of Roman plutocracy', Pareto speculates, 'could really be, at least to some extent, the image of plutocracy which is our impending fate'.[234] Did Pareto predict the rise of Mussolini?

227. Ibid., p. 48.
228. Ibid., p. 56.
229. Finer, 'Introduction', pp. 58–59.
230. Powers, 'Introduction', p. 20.
231. Ibid., p. 37.
232. Ibid., p. 55.
233. Ibid., p. 57.
234. Ibid., p. 60.

VI: Fascism

The debate concerning Pareto's relation to fascism is a longstanding one. Certainly Mussolini claimed to have attended his lectures at Lausanne in 1904, and in 1923 invited him to be Senator of the Realm, although Pareto never returned the papers before his death at the age of 75 on 19 August 1923.[235] There is little doubt that some sections of fascist rule tried to appropriate his thought to legitimise their rule, describing themselves as the 'new elite' overthrowing the old one, yet when he died a 'journal founded by Mussolini took pains to point out that, regretfully, Pareto was not a fascist, but that he had contributed much to fascist thinking'.[236] In his private letters, Pareto seems to have welcomed the rise of Mussolini as a 'victory' for his theories and a personal victory too: he wrote to Lello Gangemi that 'the victory of fascism confirms splendidly the previsions of my *Sociology* and many of my articles. I can therefore rejoice both personally and as a scientist'.[237] He praised Mussolini as a 'statesman of the first' rank: he was his 'Machiavellian Prince' who would bring about the 're-surgence of Italy'.[238] But that his theory should have been borne out is not the same as endorsing that course of action. In the *Transformation*, Pareto is clear that a social science should have predictive powers—predictions he himself professes in terms of the rise of 'military plutocracy'—but he is also adamant that there is a difference between something that is 'good for science' and something that is 'good for society': i.e. there is a difference between a scientific and a normative claim.[239] 'It is one thing to reason about ideal ends and another thing to assess real patterns of change'.[240]

One of the more subtle theories of why Pareto ended up supporting Mussolini is offered by Bellamy, who proposes that Pareto argued himself into an intellectual dead-end by describing most of human action as 'non-logical', meaning he was left with a position that could only endorse the reality of power.[241] But as we've just seen above, Pareto separated out, like Weber, means

---

235. Finer, 'Introduction', pp. 12, 28.
236. Zetterberg, 'Introduction', p. 2.
237. Quoted in Bellamy, 'Vilfredo Pareto', p. 33.
238. Ibid.
239. Pareto, *Transformation*, p. 27.
240. Ibid., p. 31.
241. Bellamy, 'Vilfredo Pareto', pp. 13, 33.

from ends.[242] In the *Treatise*, Pareto wrote: 'there are actions that use means appropriate to ends and that logically link means with ends', strongly associating those actions to the realm of political economy: 'the actions dealt with in political economy also belong in very great part in the class of logical actions'.[243] Later he would add: 'the hypothesis that in satisfying their tastes human beings perform economic actions that may on the whole be considered logical is not too far removed from realities'.[244]

Even Bellamy recognises this, writing that 'for Pareto, reason corresponded to what Weber meant by *zweckrational*—that is, action to attain a given practical end by the most appropriate means'.[245] Moreover, as it was first construed, the *Treatise* in fact was meant to comprise of a second part that was to discuss logical action as pertaining to the field of political economy, underlining how, for Pareto, the two elements—logical and non-logical—were intrinsically linked. As Finer writes: 'such a work would have put the logical actions . . . on an equal footing with the non-logical ones'.[246] Indeed, if it is the case that most actions are non-logical—desires for something and post-facto rationalisations of them—that does not mean that the actions to achieve them cannot be rational, which Pareto strove to point out. As Zettterberg puts it:

> the inability to solve the problem of the role of reason in the circulation of elites is most obvious when the issue is phrased as reason *versus* sentiment. It is neither reason nor sentiment that should be maximised to insure the survival of an elite, but *efficiency*. And efficiency is produced through a delicately balanced mixture of reason and sentiment, working not against one another, but in harness'.[247]

It is certainly the case that Pareto thought force to be an indispensable means of maintaining power by elites: he berated Louis XVI for thinking he could 'halt the Revolution with his royal veto, for his was the illusion of a

---

242. See also Femia, 'Pareto's Concept of Demagogic Plutocracy', p. 147: 'Reason . . . can help us to get from A to B, but it cannot determine whether B is a desirable destination. The conflict between competing ethical systems is incapable of rational resolution. . . . [Pareto] saw himself as an heir of Machiavelli, separating morality from political analysis'.

243. Pareto, *Treatise*, #150, 152.

244. Ibid., #2079.

245. Bellamy, 'Vilfredo Pareto', p. 31.

246. Finer, 'Introduction', p. 48.

247. Zetterberg, 'Introduction', pp. 20–21.

spineless weakling who was soon to lose what little head he had'.[248] But we should remember that Pareto distinguished between violence, the weapon of the weak, and force, that of the strong, a distinction he feared the fascists were not able to make. He wrote to Pantaleoni that 'there are growing signs in Italy, very slight it is true, of a worse future than one ever could have imagined. The danger of using force is of slipping into abusing it'.[249] Yet through all this work, from his early dissertation, to his journalism and *Les systèmes socialistes*, up to and including the *Treatise* and *Transformation*, Pareto never deviated from his free-trade and free-market liberalism, rejecting government interventions, criticising corporatism (from where fascism would grow) and denouncing secular religions and ideologies.[250] If Pareto retired from private life after his journalistic years, he maintained the same political position throughout.

There are therefore strong continuities not simply between his economic and sociological work, as we have underlined above, but also his political thinking.[251] In his private correspondence, he expressed reservations about the new regime, and counselled it to follow liberal policies. Had he lived longer, there is no doubt he would have become an opponent of the regime as he had been of all regimes. In this he would have been much like Benedetto Croce, another liberal who cautiously welcomed the new regime—although Pareto seemed more critical from the start—but quickly turned against it. Hughes probably gets it right when he writes:

> The anti-humanitarian in him applauded Mussolini's hardness and realism. The liberal deplored the Fascist measures that curbed the citizen's freedom

248. Pareto, *Treatise*, # 2180. This is a claim Pareto also made in *The Rise and Fall*, p. 61.

249. Quoted in Bellamy, 'Vilfredo Pareto', p. 33.

250. Pareto, *Les sytèmes socialistes*, p. 41; Pareto, *Treatise*, #2188; Pareto, *Transformation*, pp. 68–71. On Pareto's rejection of 'nationalism, imperialism, racism, anti-semitism, and the like', see Finer, 'Introduction', p. 29. On Pareto's critique of ideologies, see Bobbio, 'Vilfredo Pareto's Sociology in his Letters to Maffeo Pantaleoni', p. 39 and Norberto Bobbio, 'Pareto e la critica delle ideologie' in Norberto Bobbio, *Saggi sulla scienza politica in Italia*, Bari, Laterza, 2005, pp. 65–94.

251. See Bellamy, 'Vilfredo Pareto', p. 12 on his different periods. Bellamy argues for the continuity of Pareto's thinking from the First World War to 1923, although claims that, in his last year, Pareto turned to fascism, which we dispute. Bellamy writes on p. 30, concerning the *Trattato* and Pareto's alleged move from liberalism to proto-fascism: 'the assumptions behind his sociology were clearly the same as those inspiring his earlier liberalism. The retained the atomistic model of society . . . committed to the belief that the best balance of forces was that which yielded the greatest social utility . . . and that this would be achieved in a libertarian free-market society'.

of expression. Hence it was psychologically appropriate that Pareto's last published statements should have been pleas for the preservation of liberty of the press and teaching.[252]

At the end of *Transformation* Pareto denounced Italy's colonialism, much as he had systematically done throughout his life. He explained that if colonialism might benefit 'successful' colonial power like England, the United States and France, it will not benefit Italy, which must 'be content with crumbs that fall from the table of those other greedy eaters'. He continued:

A policy like the one adopted at the end of the Roman Empire, which allows the demagogy to have its way within a country under the supposition that domestic prosperity can be maintained via the exploitation of foreign territories, will fail countries like Italy.[253]

He concluded with a question: how can the balance between successful colonial countries like England, France and the US and unsuccessful ones like Italy be kept? 'Will they ever come into direct conflict?' he asks. 'This might be one way in which the catastrophe could materialise. Afterward a new cycle would begin'.[254]

These are not the words of a fascist sympathiser. We would do well to remember Pareto's personal circumstances at the time too: in ill-health, with a worsening heart condition, living as a recluse in his Villa Angora overlooking Lake Geneva in Switzerland—a country whose democratic political system he approved of[255]—with his new wife Jane Régis, whom he married in 1923 after a lengthy divorce (Bakunina having run off in 1901 with the household goods and one of the socialist refugees Pareto had been sheltering) and eighteen cats.[256] The 'hermit of Céligny', following the famous sobriquet attributed to him, was not an active participant in Italian politics. He was a

252. Hughes, *Consciousness and Society*, p. 271.

253. Pareto, *Transformation*, p. 84.

254. Ibid.

255. '"The best government now in existence . . . is the government of Switzerland, especially in the forms it takes on in the small cantons—forms of direct democracy. It is a democratic government, but it has nothing in common with the governments also called democratic in such countries as France and the United States"', quoted in Finer, 'Introduction', p. 65.

256. Finer, 'Introduction', p. 12; Powers, 'Introduction', pp. 8–10, 17, 22. Cats appear throughout Pareto's work, see, for instance, Pareto, *Les systèmes socialistes*, pp. 13 and 65.

sceptic.[257] There remains with Pareto, even during his journalistic and *agitateur* period, a touch of the patrician remaining above the fray in of politics with 'Olympian detachment',[258] and he appears to have remained a high liberal to his death.[259]

Conclusion: Dynamic Democracy

What does Pareto bring to the concept of dynamic democracy? Most obviously the theory of the circulation of elites. And it is the idea of *movement* that is central to the circulation of elites: in *Les systèmes socialistes*, where Pareto first introduces the term, the full phrase is '*le movement de circulation des élites*'. Rejecting the conventional notions of monarchical, oligarchic or popular power, it is in the *movement* of the circulation of elites that regimes change, most famously from those of the lions to those of the foxes. These forms of rules also allow us to get a grasp of where the change is heading: towards a firmer, more centralised and faith-based system, or towards a more open, decentralised and sceptical one. It is certainly the case that Pareto broadly associates democracy with the rule of the foxes—the 'instinct of combination' is best adapted to the negotiation and compromise associated with parliamentary regimes—and that generally those values have dominated recent European history.[260]

This means that when the challenge from the lions come, it is often from outside the parliamentary regime itself, or at least from members not usually associated with it. There is also a link to capitalism here: the interdependence

257. Joseph Femia, 'The Sceptical Liberal' in Joseph Femia, *Pareto and Political Theory*, London, Routledge, 2011, pp. 124–141.

258. Hughes, *Consciousness and Society*, p. 260. Hughes describes Pareto as combining the 'aristocrat's distaste for the multitude and a technician's respect for the facts' (ibid., p. 78).

259. For a debate on whether Pareto was or not a fascist, see James Vander Zanden, 'Pareto and Fascism Reconsidered', in *American Journal of Economics and Sociology*, Vol. 19, No. 4, 1960, pp. 399–411 and Renato Cirillo, 'Was Vilfredo Pareto Really a "Precursor" of Fascism', *American Journal of Economics and Sociology*, Vol. 42, No. 2, 1983, pp. 235–245. We can note that Mosca himself never became a supporter of Mussolini; in fact, Mussolini's rise pushed him in the opposite direction, towards a more sympathetic view of representative government.

260. Finer, 'Introduction', pp. 47, 71: 'an elected parliament acts as the forum or market place for cementing alliances and concluding transactions between the various components of this ruling class, and at the same time as the platform from which the masses are persuaded to consent to these. Thus the governing class in a modern democracy is very widespread indeed, comprising the trade union bosses as well as employers, the captains of pressure groups as well as the party leaders, social democrats as well as conversatives'.

between the political and the economic cycles, even if they are not exactly the same. So, capitalism might in some instances—certainly as it was in Pareto's time—be dominated by speculators. Indeed, through his notion of 'demagogic plutocracy'—perhaps his greatest conceptual innovation alongside the circulation of elites—Pareto clearly saw how plutocracy and democracy can be combined: that behind the façade of parliamentary politics the wealthy still rule. This we can link to his 'power rule' of the 80/20 split: that 20% of the population will always own, even in a supposedly redistributive democratic regime, 80% of the wealth. There are anticipatory echoes here of the 1%.

Pareto's elite theory has sometimes been seen as too broad to be able to offer a more detailed analysis of elite rule, but as Finer points out, within the governing elite Pareto identified an 'inner government' as such. As we will see in chapter 6, this is something Raymond Aron will elaborate on further by distinguishing between the *catégories dirigeantes*—what we might term the *political classes* (the plural is key)—and the *personnel politique*, namely the more directly political class or politicians.[261] By emphasising the role non-logical sentiments play in politics, Pareto reminds us that economics do not always trump all other considerations, and what we call today 'identities' play an important role too. Finally, there is the question of force, rightly, precisely and proportionally applied, which Pareto almost gleefully brought back to our attention—although always distinguishing it from indiscriminate violence, the weapon of the weak—to sharpen our minds to the fact that politics is that delicate Machiavellian balance between persuasion and force.

Force is the ultimate stone Pareto brings to the edifice of 'dynamic democracy': it is not just movement that brings about political change—movement can just be circular and follow the given path—but the application of *force* to it that changes the political system. It is by force being brought to bear by rising elements or conflicts within the elite itself—often a combination of the two—that change occurs: in Pareto's theory a move from lions to foxes or vice versa.

261. Ibid., p. 69.

3

Michels and the Iron
Law of Oligarchy

'OLIGARCHY' COMES from the Greek 'oligarchēs', made up of 'olig' ('few')
and 'arches' ('ruler'), according to the *Merriam-Webster* dictionary. An oligarch
is a 'member or supporter of an oligarchy', and 'oligarchy' is 'a government in
which a small group exercises control especially for corrupt and selfish
purposes'.

The greatest theorist of modern oligarchy is Robert Michels (1876–1936).
It is he who, in his classic 1911 text *On the Sociology of the Party System in Modern Democracy*, coined the phrase the 'iron law of oligarchy'.[1] Paired with
Gaetano Mosca and Vilfredo Pareto, whom Michels both knew and was influenced by, the three are collectively known as the 'elite theorists of democracy',
although they have gone by other appellations too: 'Machiavellians', 'theorists
of minority domination' and, again, 'sociological pessimists'.[2] Writing at the
turn of the twentieth century, they were the first, in a modern context, to
grapple with the fact that although we live in a democracy, the few still rule. In
contrast to the ancient Greeks, these thinkers were addressing the question of
minority rule within a specifically modern setting, one marked by the spread
of universal suffrage and the rise of the modern, highly centralised and disciplined mass party to organise it—two novel developments at that time. If
Mosca and Pareto theorised elite rule, it was left to Michels to apply it to the

1. Robert Michels, *Political Parties: A Sociological Study of the Oligarchic Tendencies of Modern
Democracy*, trans. Eden and Cedar Paul, New York, The Free Press, 1962, p. 356.

2. S. M. Lipset, 'Introduction' to Michels, *Political Parties*, p. 33; James Burnham, *The Machiavellians, Defenders of Freedom*, New York, John Day, 1943; Juan Linz, *Robert Michels, Political
Sociology, and the Future of Democracy*, New Brunswick, Transaction Publishers, 2006; and Robert Dahl, *Democracy and Its Critics*, New Haven, Yale University Press, 1989.

modern political party. It is the aim of this chapter to make sense of that application.

The first section will offer an account of Michels' 'iron law' by placing it within the context of turn-of-the-century European socialism and syndicalism, paying particular attention to Michels' relationship with the German Social Democratic Party, the largest, richest and most powerful socialist party of the time, and syndicalism in Germany, France and Italy.[3] The second section will turn to evaluating the law itself—notably through the criticisms Max Weber, Michels' mentor, expressed in a letter of December 1910 thanking him for an advance copy of the book—suggesting that it is perhaps not as iron-clad as it might at first appear. The third section will address the thorny issue of Michels' subsequent conversion to fascism, and will posit that this must be understood within the context of Michels still trying to find a way to overcome the 'iron law'. Michels' under-explored *Lectures in Political Sociology* he gave in Rome in the 1920s will play a key role in this account.[4]

In contrast to his later period, and indeed the 1925 reedition of the book, the conclusion to the 1915 English translation of *Sociology of the Party* ended on a much cheerier note, with Michels articulating how democracy will naturally give rise to two 'palliatives'—an increase in education and competition between different oligarchies—something that has often been overlooked in the secondary literature. Moreover, there Michels begins to articulate, through two metaphors, what might be termed a 'dynamic' theory of democracy, one grounded in continually challenging elite rule. If it is always the few who rule, then democracy must be understood as the movement that repetitively challenges the extent of that rule. The conclusion will reflect on that notion and offer an evaluation of Michels' thinking for democracy today.

I: Germany, France, Italy

Michels is best remembered today—if at all—as the theorist of the 'iron law of oligarchy'. Born into a wealthy, Catholic and relatively cosmopolitan bourgeois-patrician textile manufacturing family in Cologne, he had French

---

3. On how *Sociology of the Party* is a continuation of Michels' syndicalist positions, see Peter LaVenia, 'Rethinking Robert Michels', *History of Political Thought*, Vol. 40, No. 1, 2019, pp. 120, 132.

4. Roberto Michels, *First Lectures in Political Sociology*, trans. Alfred de Grazia, Minneapolis, University of Minnesota Press, 1949.

(Huguenot, but converted to Catholicism), Belgian and Dutch German background on his mother's side; and on his father's side, which claimed some Italian roots, a number of relatives were involved in politics.[5] Born a Catholic in the midst of the *Kulturkampf* (Bismarck's anti-Catholic legislation), Michels grew up wary of the Imperial Germany. This led to a break with his father, who welcomed the new regime.[6] He studied throughout Europe—Germany (Munich, Leipzig, Halle), France (Sorbonne), England and Italy (Turin)—which made him a polyglot, and over the course of his life he would seamlessly switch from writing in German to French and Italian, often serving as a conduit between the respective countries and their traditions.[7] Later he would even write in English, and he spent a year (1927–1928) teaching both at Williams College and at the University of Chicago in the US.[8]

He became a protégé of Max Weber,[9] who admitted him into what he called the *salon des refusés* in Heidelberg,[10] and a close relationship between the two developed from at least 1906 onwards.[11] Weber saw in Michels the

---

5. H. Stuart Hughes, *Consciousness and Society: The Reorientation of European Social Thought 1890–1930*, New York, Vintage Books, 1961, p. 251; Juan Linz, *Robert Michels, Political Sociology, and the Future of Democracy*, New Brunswick, Transaction Publishers, 2006, pp. 5–7; Alfred de Grazia, 'Introduction' to Roberto Michels, *First Lectures in Political Sociology*, Minneapolis, University of Minnesota Press, 1949, p. 7.

6. Andrew Bonnell, *Robert Michels, Socialism, and Modernity*, Oxford, Oxford University Press, 2023, p. 15. Bonnell sees Michels as part of a generational revolt against the values of his father's generation, who had aligned themselves with the nationalistic, militaristic, and bourgeois-conformist values of the Bismarckian German upper and middle classes (ibid., p. 265).

7. Hughes, *Consciousness and Society*, p. 251; Wolfgang Mommsen, 'Robert Michels and Max Weber: Moral Conviction versus the Politics of Responsibility' in Wolfgang Mommsen and Jürgen Osterhammel, eds., *Max Weber and his Contemporaries*, London, Allen and Unwin, 1987, p. 121.

8. Roberto Michels, 'Some Reflections on the Sociological Character of Political Parties', *American Political Science Review*, vol. 21, no. 4, 1927, pp. 753–772, reprinted as chapter 7 of Michels, *Lectures in Political Sociology*, pp. 134–155. It is here that Michels first develops his theory of the 'accordion effect' of political parties: swelling to encompass as many members as possible but, having lost its coherence, expelling them again (pp. 153–4; see, further, Linz, *Robert Michels*, p. 58).

9. Wolfgang Mommsen, 'Max Weber and Roberto Michels: An Asymmetrical Partnership', *European Journal of Sociology*, vol. 22, no. 1, 1981, pp. 100–116; Lawrence Scaff, 'Max Weber and Robert Michels', *The American Journal of Sociology*, vol. 86, no. 6, 1981, pp. 1269–1286; Sandro Segre, 'Notes and Queries: On Weber's Reception of Michels', *Max Weber Studies*, vol. 2, no. 1, 2001, pp. 103–113.

10. Linz, *Robert Michels*, p. 11.

11. Mommsen, 'Robert Michels', p. 122.

quintessential 'Gesinnungsethiker' he would later famously theorise in his *Politics as Vocation* (1919),[12] leading Wolfgang Mommsen to argue that Weber recognised in Michels his 'ethics of conviction' alter ego against which he strove, although often starting from the same premise, to incarnate the 'ethics of responsibility'.[13] Through Michels, Weber sensed the opportunity to learn more about socialism, and he opened his *Archiv für Sozialwissenschaft und Sozialpolitik* to him in 1906—socialists were excluded from contributing before—eventually making him co-editor in 1913, not entirely to the pleasure of the other editors, Edgar Jaffé and Werner Sombart.[14]

If Weber was a liberal, Michels was, at least in his early days, a committed socialist, on the revolutionary anarcho-syndicalist far-left wing of the movement.[15] He first joined the socialist party at the age of 24 during his student years in Italy,[16] and would remain in close contact with the syndicalist leaders there, including Enrico Leone and Arturo Labriola, frequently contributing to their journal *Il Divenire Sociale*.[17] From his time in France, Michels also developed a close intellectual proximity to Georges Sorel and his followers, including Edouard Berth and Hubert Lagardelle, and he would write a number of articles in French on French syndicalism in their *Le Mouvement Socialiste* from 1904 to 1914.[18]

Following a brief sojourn in Italy, on his return to Germany to write his *Habilitation* in Marburg, where he also became a *Privat Dozent*—Michels, under the supervision of Gustav Droysen, son of the renowned historian

---

12. Mommsen, 'Max Weber and Roberto Michels', p. 103; Scaff, 'Weber and Michels', p. 1272; David Beetham, 'From Socialism to Fascism: The Relation between Theory and Practice in the World of Robert Michels. I. From Marxist Revolutionary to Political Sociologist', *Political Studies*, vol. XXV, no. 1, 1977, p. 20.

13. Mommsen, 'Robert Michels', pp. 122, 132.

14. Mommsen, 'Max Weber and Roberto Michels', p. 102.

15. Mommsen, 'Robert Michels', p. 121. Bonnell, *Robert Michels, Socialism, and Modernity*, p. 10 resists calling Michels a syndicalist because he saw the same oligarchic tendencies at work in trade unions as in political parties, and remained rather focused on the latter throughout his life. Yet the type of 'spontaneous mass strike' Michels was systematically in favour of chimes well with the type of syndicalism Georges Sorel advocated.

16. Ibid.

17. Beetham, 'From Socialism to Fascism I', pp. 5–11.

18. Robert Michels, *Critique de socialisme: Contribution aux débats du début de XX siècle*, Paris, Editions Kimé, 1992; Linz, *Robert Michels*, p. 9; Hughes, *Consciousness and Society*, p. 251–2. On the similarities between Michels' and Lagardelle's syndicalist critiques of socialism, see LaVenia, 'Rethinking Robert Michels', pp. 118, 134.

Johann Gustva Droysen, completed his PhD in 1900 in Halle on Louis XIV's 1680 incursion into Holland[19]—he joined the local branch of the SPD, where he was active from 1902 to 1907.[20] During this time he also taught at the *Université Nouvelle* in Brussels (1905–08), from which he commuted irregularly from Marburg, keeping in touch with the syndicalists there,[21] and the Collège libre des sciences sociales in Paris (1903–1905), what was to become Sciences Po after World War II.[22] At the numerous party congresses he attended (1903, 1904, 1905 and 1907, as an Italian delegate, after which he resigned)[23] he was known as an uncompromising critic of Eduard Bernstein and Jean Jaures' revisionism, and as a defender of local autonomy within the party, for which he was temporarily supported by August Bebel.[24] As per his syndicalism he advocated the revolutionary mass-strike, as propagated at the time by Karl Liebknecht and Rosa Luxembourg, denounced the quietist political strategy of the leadership, and was vehemently anti-militaristic, in part because of his own military experience (he had enlisted in 1895 as a young man in the Grand Duke of Saxony's Imperial German Army).[25] He sought to defend the syndicalist faction within the party, which he saw as its only hope for survival.[26]

Michels' socialism came at a great personal cost, leading to a break with his family and with Catholicism (he refused to have his children baptised). He was aggressively secular and had a real aversion to clerical influence in society and 'priest-rule'.[27] He often made a point of underlining these sacrifices in his writings, presenting himself as a purified intellectual who had thrown in his lot with the masses, much as Karl Marx, on his account, had done.[28] Indeed, Michels tended to interpret Marx as a revolutionary intellectual instead of

19. Bonnell, *Robert Michels, Socialism, and Modernity*, p. 16.

20. Andrew Bonnell, 'Oligarchy in Miniature? Robert Michels and the Marburg Branch of the German Social Democratic Party', *German History*, vol. 29, no. 1, 2011, pp. 23–35.

21. Philip Cook, 'Robert Michels's Political Parties in Perspective', *The Journal of Politics*, vol. 33, 1971, p. 777.

22. Jean-Christophe Angaut, 'Postface' in Robert Michels, *Sociologie du parti dans la démocratie moderne*, trans. Jean-Christophe Angaut, Paris, Gallimard, 2015, p. 555.

23. Ibid.

24. Scaff, 'Weber and Michels', p. 1271.

25. Mommsen, 'Robert Michels', pp. 124–7; Angaut, 'Postface', p. 554; Linz, *Robert Michels*, p. 7.

26. Beetham, 'From Socialism to Fascism I', p. 10.

27. Bonnell, *Robert Michels, Socialism, and Modernity*, pp. 261–264. As has often been pointed it, Michels sought in political activity the transcendentalism he had lost in religion.

28. Ibid., p. 265.

engaging profoundly with historical materialism, which was secondary for him: the most important, for Michels, was class struggle, which also had a cleansing effect.[29] His socialism, alongside his slightly unorthodox view (for the time) on marriage and sexual ethics—he supported gender equality[30]— also barred him from getting a job in Germany: Marburg refused to grant him his *Habilitation*, which he needed to be able to teach, and so did Jena in 1906 when he tried again a little later there. He would continue to strive to achieve an academic position throughout his life, as Andrew Bonnell puts it: 'some of the contradictions in his biography came from the conflicts arising between his search for personal and ethical fulfilment in radical political action and his desire for the dignity of a professorial chair.'[31]

Weber was furious, and he wrote an angry column in the *Frankfurter Zeitung* on 20 September 1908, 'On the so-called "academic freedom" at German universities', stating that 'the "freedom of scholarship"' exists in Germany only within the 'limits of political and ecclesiastical acceptability', and that excluding Michels was a 'disgrace and ignominy for a *Kulturnation*', in comparison not only to France and Italy but even with Russia.[32] Weber ultimately helped secure him a position in Turin as a *libero docente*,[33] and he completed his *Habilitation* there under the political economist Achille Loria.

At Turin Michels was a junior colleague of Mosca's, whom he frequented at the famous criminologist Cesare Lombroso's home and at Turin's Café Voigt (Fiorina). It is here that Michels, through Lombroso, came into contact with 'criminal anthropology', influencing his views on ethnicity and race.[34] Weber and Michels would later fall out over Italian participation in World War I— Michels wrote a violent opinion piece in the *Basler Zeitung* blaming Germany for the war and Italy's entry into it in the opposing camp, which many

29. Ibid., pp. 28, 123.

30. Robert Michels, *Sexual Ethics: A Study of Borderland Questions*, New Brunswick, Transaction Publishers, 2002. See, further, Bonnell, *Robert Michels, Socialism, and Modernity*, pp. 147–185.

31. Bonnell, *Robert Michels, Socialism, and Modernity*, p. 268.

32. Mommsen, 'Max Weber and Roberto Michels', p. 101; Linz, *Robert Michels*, p. 11; Mommsen, 'Robert Michels', p. 123; Hans Gerth and C. Wright Mills, 'Introduction' in *From Max Weber: Essays in Sociology*, Hans Gerth and C. Wright Mills, eds, Abingdon, Routledge, 2009, p. 19.

33. Linz, *Robert Michels*, p. 5

34. Bonnell, *Robert Michels, Socialism, and Modernity*, p. 229. Although Michels had a relatively subtle view of race and ethnicity, this seems to separate him out from Mosca and Pareto, who had no time for these types of theses.

considered to be a stab in the back—although Weber continued to defend Michels to the end, and their relationship endured, although without the same intimacy as before.[35] The forced move to Italy would ultimately lead Michels, somewhat ironically, into the arms of Mussolini, to which we shall return, but in his 1911 masterpiece *Zur Soziologie des Parteiwesens in der modernen Demokratie. Untersuchungen über die oligarchischen Tendenzen des Gruppenlebens* (*On the Sociology of the Party System in Modern Democracy: Investigations into the Oligarchic Tendencies of Group Life*), he came to a slightly different conclusion.

II: The Iron Law

The Sociology of the Party System was first translated into Italian in 1912 by Alfredo Polledro as *Sociologia del partito politico nella democrazia moderna: studi sulle tendenze oligarchiche degli aggregati politici*, and then from Italian into English in 1915 by the British Communist translating couple Eden and Cedar Paul as *Political Parties: A Sociological Study of the Oligarchy Tendencies of Modern Democracy*—the change of title, one might surmise, to give the book more visibility.[36] Its thesis can be found in the subtitle—the oligarchic tendencies of party life—and Michels presented the 'iron law of oligarchy' in conclusion to the book as follows: 'reduced to its most concise expression, the fundamental sociological law of political parties . . . may be formulated in the following terms: "It is organisation that gives birth to the domination of the elected over the electors, of the mandataries over the mandators, of the delegates over the delegators. Who says organisation, says oligarchy."'[37]

The specific political party Michels had in mind when he wrote the book was the German Social Democratic Party which, alongside the German Labour Union, was at that time the largest, richest, best organised and most powerful socialist party in the world.[38] By the time Michels published his *Sociology of the Party* in 1911, the SPD had three million members and in 1912 won one-third of all votes, thereby becoming the biggest German political party of the time.[39] From a Marxist perspective this meant that the SPD was the most

35. Ibid., p. 102.

36. On the problems with the English edition, especially concerning the excising of a number of Michels' footnotes, see LaVenia, 'Rethinking Robert Michels', pp. 114, 135.

37. Michels, *Political Parties*, p. 365.

38. Ibid., p. 357.

39. Angaut, 'Postface', p. 547.

advanced party *en route* to the forthcoming proletarian revolution, and thus represented the future development of the others, even if this overlooked developments within the other socialists parties in Europe.[40] The SPD claimed to be organised on a democratic basis, and that if it were to come to power it would rule the state in a democratic manner: the party was, in essence, a 'state in miniature'.[41] The problem was that although the SPD dominated the Reichstag, power was still in the hands of the Chancellor and the Junkers in large part due to the 'three-class franchise' in operation in Germany, and especially in Prussia.[42] The 'democratic party' (SPD) was meant to be in contrast to the older conservative parties, which were organised—and therefore ruled the state—in a highly oligarchic fashion. The SPD would bring a 'democratic revolution' to the state itself, transforming it into a 'democratic state'.[43]

What made Michels' critique so devastating was not solely that it came from one of its own officials and sympathisers—Peter LaVenia describes it as a 'polemic'[44]—but that he sought to demonstrate that in its internal ruling the SPD was no different from the older, oligarchic, parties it decried. The reasons the SPD was no better than the other parties were twofold. Influenced by Gustav Le Bon's psychology of crowds,[45] Michels posited two 'psychological' explanations for the iron law of oligarchy. The most important is the 'psychology of organisation itself, that is to say, the tactical and technical necessities which result from the consolidation of every disciplined political aggregate'.[46] This is not what we might immediately recognise today as a psychological reason, and indeed the emphasis on organisation clearly carried with it Weber's stamp. But Michels' desire to talk of psychology as a 'science' stemmed from his recent encounter with Pareto's *Les systèmes socialistes* (1902), in which

40. David Beetham, 'Michels and His Critics', *European Journal of Sociology*, vol. 22, no. 1, 1981, p. 91.

41. Ibid., pp. 160, 193. Gordon Hands, 'Roberto Michels and the Study of Political Parties', *British Journal of Political Science*, vol. 1, no. 2, 1971, p. 170.

42. Beetham. 'From Socialism to Fascism I', p. 6. Bonnell, *Robert Michels, Socialism, and Modernity*, p. 110, notes: 'Germany had universal (manhood) suffrage and a weak parliament, Italy had a very restricted franchise but a powerful parliament. Michels suggested that a general strike to expand the franchise in Italy could have a major impact'.

43. Michels, *Political Parties*, pp. 50, 335; Hands, 'Roberto Michels and the Study of Political Parties', p. 156; Joseph Femia, *Against the Masses: Varieties of Anti-Democratic Thought since the French Revolution*, Oxford, Oxford University Press, 2001, p. 97.

44. LaVenia, 'Rethinking Robert Michels', p. 114.

45. Michels, *Political Parties*, p. 205; Beetham, 'From Socialism to Fascism I', p. 14.

46. Michels, *Political Parties*, p. 365.

the latter attempted to found a new science of mankind based on the persistence of certain constant psychological traits, which he dubbed 'residues'.[47] Indeed, the 'iron law of oligarchy' was meant to be 'beyond good and evil',[48] to reprise a Nietzschean phrase; namely, it was meant to be scientifically 'neutral'. Of course, whether it was or not is a different matter.[49]

Following Le Bon and Pareto's lead, Michels viewed the mass as generally immobile and passive, in need of a leader to guide them whom they felt gratitude towards.[50] He seemed to have taken on Nietzsche's view of the masses as the 'much-too-many',[51] and believed that they needed to be educated and civilised before they were ready—had the political maturity—to take over.[52] It was for intellectuals like Michels, of course, to propose that educational and civilising mission.[53] Throughout the book Michels tried to show how in general the masses, even when organised within a party, were apathetic about the running of their own affairs—committees set up to organise the day-to-day running of the party were systematically unattended—nor indeed, to Michels' surprise, did they seem particularly interested in debating the finer points of revolutionary praxeology, preferring instead to go listen to their heroes speak.[54] He explained attempts to run referenda within the party as abject failures because of the 'incompetence of the masses and lack of time'.[55]

The principle of oligarchy in modern democratic parties arises, therefore, from the 'technical indispensability of leadership'.[56] As Michels puts it: 'at the outset, leaders arise *spontaneously*; their functions are *accessory* and *gratuitous*.

47. Beetham, 'From Socialism to Fascism I', p. 14.

48. Femia, *Against the Masses*, pp. 68, 101; Giovanni Sartori, *The Theory of Democracy Revisited. Part One: The Contemporary Debate*, Chatham, Chatham House Publishers, 1987, p. 149.

49. Femia (ibid., p. 163) writes: 'but the futility "school" is most vulnerable in this respect, for their predictions were apparently based on the erroneous assumption that the study of human behaviour could be modelled on the techniques of natural science. If this is not possible, if there are no inescapable laws of social existence, then democracy need not be dismissed as a forlorn hope. Still, it is hard to deny that the futility theorists uncovered definite "trends", if not "laws"'.

50. Michels, *Political Parties*, p. 364.

51. Bonnell, *Robert Michels, Socialism, and Modernity*, p. 195.

52. Ibid., pp. 127, 196.

53. Ibid., p. 100.

54. Michels, *Political Parties*, pp. 88, 105, 111; Hands 'Roberto Michels and the Study of Political Parties', p. 162.

55. Ibid., p. 309. Gerhard Lenski, 'In Praise of Mosca and Michels', *Mid-American Review of Sociology*, vo. 5, no. 2, 1980, p. 7; Linz, *Robert Michels*, p. 51.

56. Ibid., p. 364.

Soon, however, they become *professional* leaders, and in this second stage of development they are *stable* and *irremovable*.[57] In other words, every efficient organisation needs a hierarchical—and permanent—bureaucracy with a division of labour and a chain of command. This is both a technical—to ensure the smooth running of the party through a process of delegation—and a tactical necessity—democracy is too slow a decision-making process to react to political events. It is that bureaucracy that will form the ruling oligarchy, such that the end result is that there is an inverse proportion between the size of an organisation and democracy: the larger and more complex an organisation is, the less democratic it will be: 'Where organisation is stronger, we find that there is a lesser degree of applied democracy'.[58]

It should be clear that Michels has what he calls a 'Rousseauian' understanding of democracy, much like Mosca and Pareto, namely that the people, or in this case the members of the party, in some sense directly rule ('applied democracy').[59] The concept of representation was foreign to him, as S. M. Lipset correctly saw: Michels and the Machiavellians 'prove the impossibility of democracy within a larger polity by definition, by *seeing any separation* between leaders and followers as *ipso facto* a negation of democracy'.[60] Indeed, it was the representatives themselves who formed the 'oligarchy'.

The second reason for the iron law of oligarchy Michels attributes to what we would more easily recognise as a directly psychological phenomenon: 'oligarchy derives, that is to say, from the psychological transformations which the leading personalities in the parties undergo in the course of their lives'.[61] What Michels meant by this is that the growing professionalisation of the party/labour union leads to the creation of a distinct class of bureaucrats, leaders and politicians who are separated from the rest of the party members they represent. As they live different lives, their psychological make-up is different from that of the regular party members. These party officials are recruited, in the case of the German socialist party, from the proletariat itself, and, to a lesser degree, from the intellectual bourgeoisie. The end result is that both of these groups become *déclassé*, at least according to a conventional Marxist class analysis:

57. Ibid.
58. Ibid., p. 71.
59. Ibid., p. 73; Hands, 'Roberto Michels and the Study of Political Parties', p. 158; Mommsen, 'Robert Michels', p. 127.
60. Lipset, 'Introduction', p. 34.
61. Ibid., p. 365. Beetham, 'From Socialism to Fascism I', p. 13.

Michels likens the class of the party official to that of the petty bourgeois, leading to a certain embourgeoisement for the proletarians and a fall in class for the intellectuals.[62] As Bakunin put it, there can never be a 'workers' government, only a government of ex-workers'.[63] The case is accentuated in the children of these officials, who tend to have quite bourgeois upbringings, leading to a reproduction of elites that in effect creates a party 'caste'.[64]

The party officials henceforth no longer belong to the same class as their ancient colleagues they claim to represent, meaning their interests, according, at least, to Marxist lore, will differ. Most importantly, their loyalties will no longer be directly with their ancient comrades, but now lie with the party itself, which provides them with a living. They will come to believe, as Michels puts it paraphrasing Louis XIV, 'Le Parti, c'est moi',[65] and the party will become a 'state within the state'.[66] As such, for them the survival of the party will always come first, over and above any demands from the regular members of the party, whether economic or ideological. The simple reason, as anticipated above, is because the party is no longer a means but has become an ends in itself: without the party they are nothing.[67]

Michels discusses this in the context of World War I, explaining that the European socialist parties did not oppose the war, as their internationalist ideology would have suggested, because the parties were dependent upon the national framework for their own existence. He writes: 'the outcome of this regressive evolution is that the party is no longer regarded as a means for the attainment of an end, but gradually becomes an end-in-itself, and is therefore incapable of resisting the arbitrary exercise of power by the state when this power is inspired by a vigorous will'.[68] The raison d'être of the political party is to control the state; thus it cannot vote against a policy that would harm it.

There are three different resources that, according to Michels, ensure the leaders keep control of their party. These are: a) officials have superior knowledge, in that they are privy to much information that can be used to secure assent for their programme; b) they control the formal means of communication, because they dominate the organisation's press (parties still had their own

62. Hands, 'Roberto Michels and the Study of Political Parties', p. 161.
63. Beetham, 'From Socialism to Fascism I', p. 16; Beetham, 'Michels and His Critics', p. 85.
64. Ibid., pp. 279, 301, 338.
65. Lenski, 'In Praise of Mosca and Michels', p. 7.
66. Femia, *Against the Masses*, p. 195.
67. Ibid., p. 338.
68. Ibid., p. 358.

newspapers at the time), and as full-time salaried officials, they can travel from place to place presenting their case at the organisation's expense, where their position enables them to command an audience; and c) they have skill in the art of politics, in that they are far more adept than nonprofessionals in making speeches, writing articles, and organising group activities.[69]

An oligarchy thus rules the SPD. A 'small group exercises control', to return to our opening definition, because a party needs a permanent bureaucracy—intermediaries[70]—in order to function and that that bureaucracy becomes permanent and irreplaceable over time, and comes to dominate all proceedings. The oligarchy rules if not for corrupt—Michels is quite clear they rule with the best intentions,[71] but it is the logic of organisation itself that perverts their original intentions in what has become known as 'goal displacement'[72]—then for 'selfish purposes', in that they put the survival of the party, which provides them with their livelihood, above all other considerations, whether ideological or socio-economic. Their salaried dependence on the party turns them into *déclassé* petty bourgeois, removed from the (class) interests of their former working colleagues or more bourgeois intellectuals.

III: Michels and Weber

Although considered a classic of political sociology, Michels' *Sociology of the Party* has given rise to a number of criticisms.[73] A recent piece has looked at Marburg, where Michels was active as an organiser, speech-giver and agitator—to test the field, he even ran as the Social Democratic candidate in the neighbouring, highly rural, Lauterbach-Alsfeld, known in German as a *Zählkandidat* (he won 8.5% of the vote)—and concludes that the small membership there was dominated by small artisans and independent craftsmen.[74] This was thus a far cry from the type of significant industrial working class to be found in larger cities such as Berlin, meaning that Michels' first-hand

69. See Lipset, 'Introduction', p. 16 for a good summary. The second element identified by Lipset explains why, in his view, there is a strong link between the iron law of oligarchy and that of spokesmanship.

70. Michels, *Political Parties*, p. 278.

71. Linz, *Robert Michels*, p. 54.

72. Ibid., p. 40; Hands, 'Roberto Michels and the Study of Political Parties', p. 167.

73. Beetham, 'From Socialism to Fascism I', p. 4; Cook, 'Michels's Political Parties', p. 773; Hands, 'Roberto Michels and the Study of Political Parties', p. 155.

74. Bonnell, 'Oligarchy in Miniature?'.

experience of the labour movement and trade-union organisation was quite limited, and may help to explain why the 'spontaneity' of syndicalism was more appealing to him.[75] France and Italy, where syndicalism dominated, did not have much of an organised labour movement either—it was dominated by 'bourgeois intellectuals'[76]—and it is quite revealing that although Michels regularly contributed to the French and Italian syndicalist journals, he wrote quite infrequently for the German equivalent, *Einigkeit*.[77] Moreover, he seems to have grown quickly disenchanted with the 'slow boring through thick boards' as Weber later characterised political activity. The Marburg membership itself, which comprised a significant number of printing workers, had a natural deference to university-educated intellectuals, whom they relied upon to write the books they were to print, which the city industrial proletariat did not, and might have biased Michels' view in terms of the docility of the membership towards their officials, Michels included.

But already these types of criticisms had been picked up by Weber himself, who wrote a letter to Michels in December 1910 thanking him and praising him for the book, which had been dedicated to him, and offering a number of objections.[78] That letter and those objections—Michels' first—contain most of the criticisms levelled at Michels even today. Alongside the two points raised above—how there is a difference, as Weber puts it, between 'academic revisionists' (i.e. Michels) and 'syndicalist leaders', and how the industrial proletariat is more defiant in the big cities—three points stand out.

The first concerns the conservative basis of organisation, which had been one of Michels' conclusions: 'political organisation leads to power. But power is always conservative'.[79] To that Weber objected that the 'power of the Trust Directors has a revolutionary effect, the power of the Jacobins did too'.[80] Indeed, although Michels might have responded that neither of these were political parties in the modern sense, i.e. highly centralised and bureaucratised mass parties. *Sociology of the Party* was first published in 1911, but by the second German edition of 1925 an event Michels couldn't ignored had occurred,

75. Bonnell, *Robert Michels, Socialism, and Modernity*, p. 48.

76. Ibid., p. 90. In general, it seems that Michels felt more comfortable in these Italian and French circles.

77. Cook, 'Michels's Political Parties', p. 782.

78. Cf. Michels, *Sociologie du parti*, pp. 535–540.

79. Michels, *Political Parties*, p. 333.

80. Michels, *Sociologie du parti*, pp. 538–9; Scaff, 'Weber and Michels', p. 1281.

namely the Bolshevik take-over of Russia during the 1917 Revolution.[81] In the preface to the second edition, Michels tried to tackle that head-on, explaining that Bolshevism was not a democratic movement.[82] That, needless to say, is a point of contention, but one might conceive how Lenin's restricted card-carrying and unitary vanguard party, with its emphasis on a top-down 'democratic centralism' of a cadre of 'professional revolutionaries' leading the masses—the reason for their break with the Mensheviks, who favoured looser party discipline and a larger base—might still be interpreted through the lenses of the 'iron law of oligarchy'.[83]

Nevertheless, what Weber had put his finger on was the fact that the leadership of the party might be more revolutionary than the membership base. Which brings us to our second point, namely whether the interests, and specifically the *economic* interests, of the base and the leadership must align.[84] One needn't be a Marxist to see how the interests of the officials, who depended for their livelihood on the party, and were dominated by craftsmen-bourgeois types, might have diverged from that of the broader membership, composed of 54% unskilled factory workers, but did this imply an irreconcilable clash of interests?[85] Michels is at his best when pointing out the tension between the official revolutionary ideology the party propagated and its much more conservative rule; yet, and in the same manner, even though the party leadership like the Bolsheviks' might be more revolutionary than its base, it would be a mistake to think that the base must be more revolutionary than its leadership. Michels, as we have seen previously, had a very ethical understanding of socialism with a syndicalist focus on class struggle, led by intellectuals, which the party leadership was betraying by not fulfilling.[86] It lacked, according to Michels, sufficient *élan*.[87] But

81. Beetham, 'Michels and His Critics', p. 91.

82. Michels, *Sociologie du parti*, p. 32.

83. We can note that legend has it that Pareto's *Les Systèmes socialistes*, where he first exposed his theory of the 'circulation of elites' that influenced Michels, 'caused Lenin graver worry than any other anti-Marxist writing, and that he took more than one sleepless night to work out his own counter-refutation' (Hughes, *Consciousness and Society*, p. 78).

84. Ibid., p. 539; Segre, 'Weber's Reception of Michels', p. 110.

85. Cook, 'Michels's Political Parties', p. 791.

86. Beetham, 'From Socialism to Fascism I', p. 11; Bonnell, *Robert Michels, Socialism, and Modernity*, pp. 41, 127.

87. Bonnell, *Robert Michels, Socialism, and Modernity*, p. 69. Indeed, there is a sense, at least in his earlier work, that Michels would have been happy with the SPD party oligarchy if it were sufficiently revolutionary (ibid., p. 190).

if that was not their role, perhaps the leadership was in fact responsive to the more reformist demands of its membership.[88]

Michels actually concedes this point, when he explains that the leadership will resort to demagogy to keep the masses on its side, instead of pursuing the revolution its ideology demanded.[89] But it turns out that the move away from the revolutionary platform to focusing on improving living conditions was in reality in line with the desires of the rank and file.[90] Indeed, Michels fully recognises that organisation 'is the weapon of the weak in their struggle with the strong'.[91] There is a debate here of course between revolutionary versus reformist trade unionism, and whether the role of leaders is precisely to instil the revolutionary consciousness into the masses—a view Michels shared[92]—but the concession on the notion that the membership at large preferred reform rather than revolution has led to someone like Day to argue that Michels should in fact be understood as the theorist of party democratisation.[93]

Certainly this depends on where one starts from. If the starting point is a small equal organisation—C. W. Cassinelli estimates this as having to be lower than 1,000 members[94]—then the move to a much larger organisation will undoubtedly reduce the equal distribution of democratic power across the membership that Michels so well diagnosed. However, as Weber points out, democratic parties have been founded by intellectuals, that is to say, an 'aristocracy':[95] if the starting point is rather a charismatic leader trying to found a party around him—whether it is Lassalle, Liepknecht or Bebel, whom Michels himself acknowledges as charismatic[96]—then the bureaucratisation of the party might indeed integrate more people into the democratic process, and that membership might prove to be more socially plural than the original faithful.[97]

88. Linz, *Robert Michels*, pp. 49–51.

89. Michels, *Political Parties*, p. 173; John Day, 'Democracy, Organization, Michels', *The American Political Science Review*, vol. 59, no. 2, 1965, p. 427.

90. Cook, 'Michels's Political Parties', p. 793.

91. Michels, *Political Parties*, p. 61; Hands, 'Roberto Michels and the Study of Political Parties', p. 164.

92. Beetham, 'From Socialism to Fascism I', p. 17.

93. Day, 'Democracy, Organization, Michels'.

94. C. W. Cassinelli, 'The Law of Oligarchy', *The American Political Science Review*, vol. 47, no. 3, 1953, p. 782.

95. Michels, *Sociologie du parti*, p. 536.

96. Michels, *Political Parties*, pp. 93–5, 117.

97. Day, 'Democracy, Organization, Michels', p. 423.

In his *The Principles of Representative Government*, Bernard Manin—who explains that 'party democracy is the rule of the *activist* and the *party bureaucrat*'[98]—nicely explains that 'the analyses of Michels showed that mass parties were dominated by elites distinct from the rank and file, but it was reasonable to think that the distance between party bureaucrats and ordinary citizens was smaller than the one separating notables from the rest of the population.'[99]

Party democratisation was, thirdly, ultimately Weber's view too.[100] His main objection to Michels was that he had a too unequivocal view of 'domination' [*Herrschaft*], which he considered to be more ambiguous.[101] For Michels, the officials in the party dominated their members, but for Weber domination is extensible both ways. Anticipating what will become one of Michel Foucault's main themes, Weber explains that every human relationship has elements of domination, sometimes reciprocal ones. This time unconsciously channelling l'Abbé de Sieyès, he gives the example of the shoemaker: 'is the shoemaker that makes my boots necessarily my "master"[?]', he asks. 'In a sense *the shoemaker dominates me*, but in another *I dominate him*.'[102] So if party officials dominate members because of their superior technical expertise, in another—and perhaps lesser—sense, the members also dominate the officials, through elections. This explains the move from revolution to reform within the party, which is in response to the desires of the members.

Thus Weber, in contrast to Michels, welcomed the bureaucratisation of the SPD, which he thought would see it abandon its revolutionary phraseology to concentrate instead on trying to concretely advance the plight of the working class, which he supported. He also thought that it would lead to the integration of the party, and thereby also its members, into the political system of the German Reich, which would be beneficial to all involved: it would mean the SPD, alongside the Empire, would reach a degree of political 'maturity' he so cherished.[103]

98. Bernard Manin, *The Principles of Representative Government*, Cambridge, Cambridge University Press, 1997, p. 208.

99. Ibid., p. 233.

100. Mommsen, 'Robert Michels', p. 126.

101. Ibid., p. 130.

102. Michels, *Sociologie du parti*, pp. 539–540; Scaff, 'Weber and Michels', p. 1282

103. Mommsen, 'Weber and Michels', p. 107; Michels, *Political Parties*, p. 340.

At this point Weber of course was still looking for political parties and the parliamentary system to provide the type of leaders Germany needed. As such, that parties should be 'oligarchic' in the sense Michels described posed no real threat to him: leadership was a fact of life, and indeed Weber was quite concerned about ensuring the freedom to act of the political leaders he was looking for, so the least they were constrained by their party, the better.[104] But over time Weber became convinced that the domination bureaucracy exerted over politics was becoming too preponderant, and that the future choice was to be between a 'leadership democracy' and a 'leaderless democracy', leading him to advocate a 'plebiscitary democracy', in which a popularly elected charismatic leader should be given substantial presidential power to break out from the 'iron cage of modernity'.[105] That, in the end, started to look quite similar to Michels' endorsement of Mussolini: Michels thought bureaucracy made his Rousseauian direct form of democracy impossible, whilst Weber though bureaucracy jeopardised the type of leadership democracy he advocated. Both came to look for solutions outside the realm of bureaucracy to attain the ideal they were striving for.[106]

IV: Michels and Mussolini

There is no question that in his later life Michels rallied to Mussolini. In 1928, he accepted, upon a personal invitation of Mussolini, a professorship at the University of Perugia (he had been teaching at the University of Basle, where he had sat out the war, and where he had met Pareto, who was also teaching and living there),[107] one of the three universities set up by *Il Duce* to teach the new 'political science' of the regime. Michels would teach both there and finally at the University of Rome until his death in 1936.[108] The question is, rather, why.

A number of theories have been put forward: Wilfried Röhrich has argued that Michels should be seen within the broader revolt against reason typical of this period, and Arthur Mitzman sees Michels fall into fascism as part of the

---

104. Mommsen, 'Weber and Michels', pp. 110–1.

105. Ibid., pp. 112–5.

106. Scaff, 'Weber and Michels', pp. 1281–4.

107. Bonnell, *Robert Michels, Socialism, and Modernity*, pp. 22–23.

108. Cook, 'Michels's Political Parties', p. 778; David Beetham, 'From Socialism to Fascism: The Relation between Theory and Practice in the Work of Robert Michels. II. The Fascist Ideologue', *Political Studies*, vol. XXV, no. 2, 1977, p. 161.

'psychopathology of political idealism': disenchanted with the syndicalism of his youth, Michels was in search for a 'new faith' that he found in fascism.[109] H. Stuart Hughes also sees Michels' disillusioned turn as linked to the discovery of the same oligarchic tendencies in socialist parties as in their conservative opponents.[110] The role nationalism played in that conversion has been explored by Duncan Kelly and Corrado Malandrino: Michels certainly seems to have done his best to integrate into his adoptive homeland and be a good patriot, for which, due to his 'Latin' background, he felt much sympathy towards.[111] It is from this period that he latinised his first name to Roberto, as he has often been referred to since.[112] David Beetham, on the other hand, explains Michels' conversion to fascism as the natural consequence of the application of the new elitist political sociology he learnt from Mosca and Pareto to the Italian politics of his day, particularly in his 1936 book *Nuovi studi sulla classe politica*. There he identified three different elements of what he calls variously the 'political' or 'dominant' class, or, again, the 'directing strata'— namely economic, cultural and political elites[113]—explaining that if Bolshevism had made a clean sweep of all three, fascism had only replaced the political class, and thus it was seeking to assert control over the other two.[114]

There is truth to all these claims. Michels undoubtedly remained the *Gesinnungsethiker* he had been in his youth throughout his life, and always seemed to judge the political condition he found himself in through moral categories: Weber had already reproached him of 'too much preaching' in his review-letter to him.[115] Inspired by Pareto, who saw the basis of most human behaviour in

109. Wilfried Röhrich, *Robert Michels: Vom sozialistisch-syndikalistischen zum faschistischen Credo*, Berlin, Duncker & Humblot, 1972 and Arthur Mitzman, 'Robert Michels' in *Sociology and Estrangement: Three Sociologists of Imperial Germany*, New York, Knopf, 1973, pp. 267–338.

110. Hughes, *Consciousness and Society*, pp. 252–3.

111. Duncan Kelly, 'From Moralism to Modernism: Robert Michels on the History, Theory and Sociology of Patriotism', *History of European Ideas*, vol. 29, no. 3, 2003, pp. 339–363 and Corrado Malandrino, 'A Critique of the Democratic Party and Mythology of Patriotism in Robert Michels', *Revista europea de historia de las idea politicas y de las insituciones públicas*, vol. 6, 2013, pp. 187–200. See, further, Bonnell, *Robert Michels, Socialism, and Modernity*, p. 129.

112. See Beetham, 'From Socialism to Fascism I', p. 4; Beetham, 'From Socialism to Fascism II', p. 180.

113. See also Michels, *Lectures in Political Sociology*, pp. 106–7.

114. Beetham, 'From Socialism to Fascism II', p. 161, pp. 167–170.

115. Michels, *Sociologie du parti*, p. 538; Scaff, 'Weber and Michels', pp. 1271–6; Mommsen, 'Weber and Michels', pp. 103–9; and Beetham, 'From Socialism to Fascism I', p. 20.

'non-logical actions',[116] Michels can also be seen as part of the 'revolt against reason', and there is no doubting the influence Mosca and Pareto had on him: Mosca himself talks of Michels' 'conversion to the new school'.[117] Yet, *pace* Beetham, that influence was present long before Michels' rallying to Mussolini—it was present at least from his 1908 article for the *Archiv* '*Die oligarchischen Tendenzen des Gesellschaft*'—and Michels seems to have been aware of Mosca's 1903 Inaugural Address at the University of Turin.[118] As such, it doesn't best capture Michels' move from a disappointed syndicalist to a full-throated supporter of fascism, and separating out cleanly Michels the social scientist from Michels the political agitator is not so easy to do..

Instead, what has been somewhat overlooked is what Beetham hints at the end of his two-part essay on Michels, namely the role 'charisma' played in Michels' conversion to the cause.[119] Indeed, in the preface to the second 1925 Kröner edition of *Sociology of the Party*, Michels, whilst admitting that fascism is 'theoretically undemocratic' but yet full of 'profound contempt for the representative system'—a contempt he shared going all the way back to his youthful syndicalist years—praised the 'hero' Mussolini for fully assuming his role of leader, which he enacts 'under the high luminous sky of Rome and with the absolute and unlimited consciousness of his right', of a 'dominating party comprised of more than a million members: *Tempo Primo e Secondo*'.[120]

In the contemporary lecture series he was giving in Rome and published in 1927 as *Corso di Sociologia Politica*—translated into English in 1949 as *First Lectures in Political Sociology*—Michels elaborates on his theory of charismatic leadership, explicitly referencing Weber, who had already made his move to advocating a 'plebiscitary' form of democracy, one anchored in the legitimacy of charisma, for which Michels readily gives as the main example—alongside the Prophets—*Il Duce*.[121] Directly following this passage, Michels offers an explanation for the intrinsic link between the advent of a political 'duce' and

116. Vilfredo Pareto, *The Mind and Society*, trans. Andrew Bongiorno and Arthur Livingston, New York, Harcourt, Brace, 1935, Vol I #146–#154.

117. Beetham, 'From Socialism to Fascism I', p. 14.

118. Kelly, 'From Moralism to Modernism', p. 349

119. Beetham, 'From Socialism to Fascism II', pp. 175–8. See also Francesca Antonini, 'Between Weber and Mussolini: The Issue of Political Leadership in the Thought of the Late Michels', *Intellectual History Review*, published online 18 September 2023, pp. 1–18.

120. Michels, *Sociologie du parti*, pp. 32–3.

121. Michels, *Lectures in Political Sociology*, 1949, pp. 122–3; Mommsen, 'Robert Michels', p. 135; Scaff, 'Weber and Michels', p. 1283.

democracy itself: it is much easier to find the extraordinary man from a larger pool than from a more restricted 'oligarchic' one, such that 'the precondition for the emergence of leaders consists in democracy or in the free and unconditional process of the "circulation of the elites"'.[122]

In the same manner that Weber saw in charisma the last chance to break out of the 'iron cage' of modern bureaucracy, Michels also came to see charisma as the only means to overcome the 'iron law of oligarchy' he had theorised: it is only when the members identify directly with their leader, one who has arrogated to himself the unquestionable right to lead, over the heads of their officials and representatives, that the middle strata where oligarchy finds its home can be taken out of the equation. Nationalism plays a role too, as Kelly has pointed out, in that nationalism also plays on the plain of charisma, which helps explain Michels' move from international socialism to Italian nationalism.[123] Moreover, in his under-explored writings on patriotism and nationalism, Michels identifies Machiavelli's *The Prince* as the first call for Italian unity and nationalism, which fits in well with the broader Italian tradition of political thinking Mosca and Pareto were part of, even if Mosca himself was quite critical of the Florentine.[124]

V: Democracy's Two Palliatives

Yet the first edition of *Sociology of the Party*—or at least the revised 1915 English translation of it—ended on a cheerier note.[125] As LaVenia points out, at that point Michels still considered himself to be a 'committed democrat'.[126] There Michels wrote that although the ideal government would be an 'aristocracy of persons at once morally good and technically efficient', it is nonetheless true that 'as a form of social life we must choose democracy as the least of evils'.[127] Recognising this—that democracy, whatever its faults, is still

122. Michels, *Lectures in Political Sociology*, p. 123.

123. Bonnell, *Robert Michels, Socialism, and Modernity*, p. 227.

124. Kelly, 'From Moralism to Modernism', pp. 352, 360.

125. Bonnell, *Robert Michels, Socialism, and Modernity*, pp. 23, 143, is right to point out that Michels 'moved to more bourgeois liberal positions by 1914', or, again, 'centrist, even liberal-conservative, political positions'. Yet, just because his move from the far-left to the far-right did not occur in a 'straight line' (ibid., p. 128) does not mean we should not maintain Zeev Sternhell's thesis about him linking revolutionary syndicalism to fascism.

126. LaVenia, 'Rethinking Robert Michels', p. 127.

127. Michels, *Political Parties*, p. 370.

better than aristocracy—will help argue against a return to aristocracy once the scoria of aristocracy is recognised. That scoria is, of course, the iron law of oligarchy itself.

But here Michels goes one step further. He argues that democracy carries within itself two natural palliatives, prophylactics, or regulative principles, against the iron law. These are:

1. The *ideological* tendency of democracy towards criticism and control;
2. The *effective* counter-tendency of democracy towards the creation of parties ever more complex and ever more differentiated—parties, that is to say, which are increasingly based on the competence of the few.[128]

Thus democracy, *selon* Michels, on the one hand involves an increase in education of the masses, which leads to an increase in their ability to criticise and control their leaders: remember, Michels thought the role of intellectuals was to educate and civilise the masses so they would be ready to assume political control. 'A wider education involves an increasing capacity for exercising control'.[129] The task of social education is therefore to 'raise the intellectual level of the masses, so that they may be enabled, within the limits of the possible, to counteract the oligarchic tendencies of the working-class movement'.[130] On the other hand, democracy will lead to the development of other, ever more complex and differentiated parties that will effectively cancel each other out. That is to say: different oligarchies will compete with one another.

It is important to note here that Michels not only believed that democracy will lead to the development of more parties, but that that development holds also within the different parties themselves: his account of the reigning oligarchy is not monolithic.[131] Writing on attempts towards decentralisation within national parties he explained: 'while they suffice to prevent the formation of a single gigantic oligarchy, [they] result merely in the creation of a number of smaller oligarchies, each of which is no less powerful within its own sphere',[132] and Michels readily admitted that there could be 'prolonged struggle for

128. Ibid.
129. Ibid.
130. Ibid., p. 369.
131. Beetham, 'Michels and His Critics', p. 90.
132. Michels, *Political Parties*, p. 202.

dominion between two factions' within the part.[133] So, competition exists between—and *within*—parties.[134]

Although these two claims, and particularly the second, appear to prefigure much post-war Schumpeterian conceptions of competitive democracy, they have been almost systematically overlooked.[135] Indeed, Michels seems to antedate his near-contemporary's theory of 'minimalist' democracy when he writes, 'the democratic system is reduced, in ultimate analysis, to the right of the masses, at stated intervals [elections], to choose masters to whom in the interim they owe unconditional obedience.'[136] If this does not sound like 'rule by politicians'—or, again, 'competition for political leadership', as we shall see in the next chapter—then it's not clear what does.

Part of the reason we might have lost sight of these palliatives is that Michels himself abandoned them in his 1925 reworking of the conclusion: whilst the discussion of the pedagogical effects of democracy are still present, the two palliatives as explicitly listed above have disappeared, and there remains no trace of the thought of different parties effectively counter-balancing themselves.[137] This seems to underline the passage of a Michels still sympathetic to democracy in 1915 to a leading *fascisant* thinker a decade later. Yet the standard English translation of *Sociology of the Party* remained the 1915 *Political Parties* edition, so there is no reason for Anglophone commentators like Robert Dahl, whom will we turn to in chapter 5, to have missed them, nor indeed to have seen that Michels would later drop them.

In 1915, Michels thought that democracy would naturally give rise to palliatives within the system itself—something he seemed to have abandoned in favour of Fascist charisma by 1925. And although in his earlier phase he also thought that political parties would be a natural breeding ground for democratic leaders, Weber would soon turn to plebiscitary democracy to save modern politics. There is, however, a difference between the 1915 Michels and the later Weber, which we might characterise as the difference between an *internal* and an *external* conception of political salvation: for Michels, democracy would find from *within* the means to regulate itself, whereas with Weber it

133. Ibid., p. 102.

134. Ibid., p. 339; Hands, 'Roberto Michels and the Study of Political Parties', p. 171; Linz, *Robert Michels*, p. 60; Beetham, 'Michels and His Critics', p. 94.

135. The notable exception is Femia, *Against the Masses*, p. 109.

136. Michels, *Political Parties*, p. 217.

137. See Michels, *Sociologie du parti*, pp. 522–8 for a reconstruction of what was cut and what wasn't for the final edition of 1925.

would be charismatic leaders who would break, from the *outside*, the iron cage of bureaucracy.[138] As Mommsen puts it: '"plebiscitarian democracy" . . . served as a counterweight to the bureaucratisation of the apparatuses of power'.[139] So, for Weber, it is exogenous factors that would push back against the tyranny of bureaucracy, whereas for Michels bureaucracy and oligarchy endogenously produced its own palliatives.

That the 'iron law' should admit certain palliatives within its bosom that militate against it suggests that the law is not as iron-clad and inflexible as we might have at first thought: Giovanni Sartori nicely suggests that the law should be renamed a 'bronze' law.[140] If Michels has tapped into a 'persistent and persisting trend', it remains that: a trend.[141] Indeed, Philip Cook has pointed out that 'the English version "who says organisation, says oligarchy," is a noticeably stronger formulation than the original German, which reads *"Wer Organization sagt, sagt Tendenz zur Oligarchie"'*, namely, that the law is more a tendency than an 'iron' law itself, and that the original 1908 article was titled '*Die oligarchischen Tendenzen des Gesellschaft*', in which the emphasis here is again on tendencies.[142]

Michels will posit the 'fundamental problem of politics as a science' at the end of *Sociology of the Party* not as whether 'ideal democracy is realisable', but rather as 'to what point and in what degree democracy is desirable, possible and realisable at a given moment'; that is to say: to what degree can democracy, understood as the two palliatives, push back against the iron law. Oligarchy as such is not static, but we should instead talk of different degrees of oligarchy: more or less; or, to put it another way, more or less democratic.[143] As Juan Linz has helpfully suggested, democracy and oligarchy should not be understood as pure dichotomies but rather 'polar tendencies on a continuum'.[144] Beetham seems to have captured it best when he concludes that *Sociology of the Party* works best when 'its iron laws are recast in the form of more pliable tendencies'.[145]

138. Thanks to Richard Tuck for this point.

139. Mommsen, 'Robert Michels', p. 132.

140. Sartori, *The Theory of Democracy Revisited*, p. 149; Linz, *Robert Michels*, p. 63.

141. Sartori, *The Theory of Democracy Revisited*, p. 149.

142. Cook, 'Michels's Political Parties', p. 787; Hands, 'Roberto Michels and the Study of Political Parties', p. 157.

143. Femia, *Against the Masses*, p. 101.

144. Linz, *Robert Michels*, p. 38.

145. Beetham, 'Michels and His Critics', p. 99.

VI: Dynamic Democracy

There are, as has often been pointed out, a number of conceptions of democracy in operation in Michels' work.[146] The first is 'Rousseauian' direct democracy, which Michels thinks can never be achieved. For the epigraph to his 'Final Considerations' of *Sociology of the Party*, Michels quotes from *The Social Contract*: 'to take the term in its fully rigorous meaning, there has never existed a true democracy and one will never exist. It is against the natural order of things that the great number governs and that the small number be governed'.[147] This is a claim he will repeat over the course of his subsequent writings.[148] The second concerns the question of representation, as brought up by Lipset, but we have seen how for Michels representatives are part of the problem: they are the oligarchy itself. Third, there are democracy's two 'palliatives', as we've just explored.[149] Finally, there is the notion of dynamic democracy, to which we now turn.

The question Michels asks is: if it is always the small number who rule, if there is an iron law of oligarchy, then what can democracy mean if popular sovereignty is only ever a myth, if the 'mass will never rule except *in abstracto*'?[150] To answer that question Michels will offer two metaphors at the close of *Sociology of the Party* that are meant to capture his new definition of democracy. The first is a reference to Aesop's fable of the old peasant on his death-bed telling his sons there is a buried treasure in the field:

> after the old man's death the sons dig everywhere in order to discover the treasure. They do not find it. But their indefatigable labour improves the soil and secures for them a comparative well-being. The treasure in the fable may well symbolise democracy. Democracy is a treasure that no one will ever discover by deliberate search. But in continuing our search, in labouring indefatigably to discover the undiscoverable, we shall perform a work which will have fertile results in the democratic sense.[151]

---

146. Hands, 'Roberto Michels and the Study of Political Parties', pp. 158–9; Angaut, 'Postface', p. 561.

147. Michels, *Political Parties*, pp. 73, 364.

148. Michels, *Lectures in Political Sociology*, pp. 89, 106, 141.

149. 'Demagogic' democracy also appears in Michels' writings, but it is not something he explicitly theorises, or endorses.

150. Michels, *Political Parties*, p. 366.

151. Ibid., p. 368.

True Rousseauian democracy will never be achieved, but in striving towards it certain democratic benefits will arise. This is the best we can hope for in the world of the iron law of oligarchy. Democracy for Michels can therefore only be the movement of successive waves breaking against the shoal:

> The democratic currents of history resemble successive waves. They break ever on the same shoal. They are ever renewed. This enduring spectacle is simultaneously encouraging and depressing. When democracies have gained a certain stage of development, they undergo a gradual transformation, adopting the aristocratic spirit, and in many cases also the aristocratic forms, against which at the outset they struggled so fiercely. Now new accusers arise to denounce the traitors; after an era of glorious combats and of inglorious power, they end by fusing with the old dominant class; whereupon once more they are in their turn attacked by fresh opponents who appeal to the name of democracy. It is probable that this cruel game will continue without end.[152]

A number of points are in order to make sense of what Michels is trying to articulate. The first is that much like his two palliatives, the first metaphor of the field is substantially reduced in the second 1925 Kröner edition of *Sociology of the Party*: thereby underlining the shift in Michels' thinking from seeing how democracy might internally resolve itself, to the demand for an outside leader to take control of it.[153] The second is that much like the two palliatives, these two metaphors have been little remarked upon in the secondary literature, and in the rare instances they have been, they have often been quoted without further elaboration.[154]

This chapter submits that what Michels is here trying to articulate is what might be called a *dynamic* theory of democracy. It is one that identifies the continual challenge to elite rule as the true location of democracy: that it is in the movement to challenge the oligarchy where democracy is in fact to be found. As LaVenia writes: 'while oligarchy might be impossible to cure, the

---

152. Ibid., p. 371.

153. Michels, *Sociologie du parti*, p. 526.

154. Femia, *Against the Masses*, pp. 108–9 regrets the 'strangely neglected coda to *Political Parties*'; Alfred de Grazia, 'Introduction' in Michels, *Lectures in Political Sociology*, p. 8; and Beetham, 'From Socialism to Fascism I', p. 19.

use of democratic movements against oligarchy was to wear down its worst aspects over time'.[155] Democracy's true location is thus not where it is usually thought to lie: it is neither to be found in institutions or principles, but to be located in the movement itself. This displacement means democracy is not an end-point, but a continuous movement: the never-ending challenge to elite rule which, even though it never fully achieves its aim, nevertheless through this challenge is able to offer certain democratic benefits. It is therefore not the by-product of this struggle, but the struggle itself: it is the democratic benefits that are the by-products. In many ways this is how one might read the German SPD that Michels studied: although it never succeeded in achieving its own ideology of democratic revolution, nevertheless in striving towards it, it achieved real welfare benefits for its members. This might be a pessimistic, elitist, or reformist theory of democracy, but it is a theory of democracy nonetheless.

Michels' near-contemporary was Schumpeter, theorist of 'minimalist' democracy.[156] Yet we have seen above that the notion of 'competition' is in fact a central—if overlooked—component of Michels' theory of democracy at least since the 1915 English edition of *Sociology of the Party*, subsequently further elaborated on in particular in his *Lectures on Political Sociology*, where he writes: 'in democracy . . . there can be perceived various elites, which in the form of political parties, all governed by a special staff, struggle for power'.[157] Although he worried about the stability of the system, Michels also saw how democracy, even if it appears to promote middle-class leaders instead of aristocratic ones, 'offers a certain guarantee to the members of the various elites of the repetition . . . of their turn at the helm of the state'. Earlier in the *Lectures*, he lauded democracy for having built its institutions in such a way that greatly expands the opportunities for the selection of members of the elite. Democracy thus facilitates exchange of personnel among the social classes. This advantage is a true one, logically indisputable.[158] No ruling class whose ranks have remained hermetically sealed have survived; only those who have allowed the injection of new blood have endured. Democracy is the system that best allows for that circulation.

155. LaVenia, 'Rethinking Robert Michels', p. 133.
156. Joseph Schumpeter, *Capitalism, Socialism and Democracy*, Abingdon, Routledge, 2010.
157. Michels, *Lectures in Political Sociology*, p. 119.
158. Ibid., p. 105.

Schumpeter, however, as we shall see in chapter 4, was influenced by Weber and Pareto,[159] and seems to have been unaware of Michels' work. But bringing Mosca and Pareto back into the fold can help shed light not solely on Michels but also on his theory of democracy. There is little doubt that the 'iron law of oligarchy' was influenced by Mosca's idea of 'the ruling class'. As he writes in *Sociology of the Party*: 'Mosca ... declares that no highly developed social order is possible without a "political class," that is to say, a politically dominant class, the class of a minority'.[160] Through Mosca, Michels interprets the struggle between the aristocracy and democracy as the struggle between an 'old minority, defending its actual predominance, and a new ambitious minority, intent upon the conquest of power, desiring either to fuse with the former or to dethrone and replace it'.[161]

Fusing or dethroning is the way Pareto thought the 'circulation of elites' worked: sometimes the new elite merges with the old, sometimes, in more revolutionary times, it overthrows it completely. But Michels thought that the former was more likely than the latter, and indeed in the *Lectures on Political Sociology* he spent a whole chapter explaining, by tracing the family names of those in power, how the old high nobility in fact endured over time.[162] In *Sociology of the Party*, Michels explained: 'Pareto's *théorie de la circulation des élites* must, however, be accepted with considerable reserve, for in most cases there is not a simple replacement of one group of *élites* by another, but a continuous process of intermixture, the old elements incessantly attracting, absorbing, and assimilating the new'. In an earlier passage, he instead proposed: a '*réunion des élites*, an amalgam, that is to say, of the two elements',[163] and the theme of 'perennial amalgamation', rather than 'absolute exchange', will again make an appearance in Michels' discussion of Pareto in the *Lectures*.[164]

Moreover, Michels integrated these 'elitists' theories into a Marxist conception of history:

159. David Beetham, *Max Weber and the Theory of Modern Politics*, Cambridge, Polity Press, 1985; Joel Isaac, *Working Knowledge: Making the Human Sciences from Parsons to Kuhn*, Cambridge (MA), Harvard University Press, 2012.

160. Michels, *Political Parties*, p. 342.

161. Ibid.

162. Michels, *Lectures in Political Sociology*, pp. 63–87.

163. Michels, *Political Parties*, pp. 343, 182.

164. Michels, *Lecture in Political Sociology*, p. 63.

There is no essential contradiction between the doctrine that history is the record of a continued series of class struggles and the doctrine that class struggles invariably culminate in the creation of new oligarchies which undergo fusion with the old. The existence of a political class does not conflict with the essential content of Marxism, considered not as an economic dogma but as a philosophy of history.[165]

Conclusion

Michels has often been dismissed simply as a 'synthesiser', as the least 'original' of the 'Machiavellians'.[166] In *Consciousness and Society*, Hughes writes: 'there is a quaint justice in the fact that it was the least original among the trio of neo-Machiavellians who found fascism the least troubling'.[167] Certainly Pareto tried to offer an all-encompassing psycho-scientific account of the world, whilst Mosca, with his notions of 'ruling class', 'political formula' and 'juridical defence', might have proposed a more comprehensive theory of politics. But even if it was left to Michels to apply Mosca's 'ruling class' or Pareto's 'circulation of elites'—and Michels was able to stay on good terms with both, a feat in itself[168]—to modern political parties,[169] he was amongst the first, alongside Moisei Ostrogorski and James Bryce, to fully capture that novel development, which neither Mosca nor Pareto did in its entirety. Moreover, and again perhaps not to the same depth and extent as Weber,[170] Michels did offer a theory of bureaucratisation, offering a strong thesis on the link between organisation and oligarchy. He also, as Bonnell has pointed out, had an interesting reflection on 'modernity', which he tended to see in positive, linear terms, in contrast to Mosca and Pareto, who saw it as more cyclical.[171]

So what do we learn from Michels? A number of points spring to mind. First, that any sort of direct democracy, in a modern setting, is practically, apart

165. Ibid., p. 354.

166. Hughes, *Consciousness and Society*, p. 251; Beetham, 'Michels and His Critics', p. 85; Mommsen, 'Robert Michels', p. 121.

167. Hughes, *Consciousness and Society*, p. 272.

168. Beetham, 'From Socialism to Fascism I', p. 13.

169. Ibid., p. 256.

170. On the 'Machiavellians' being somewhat 'less' than Weber, see ibid., pp. 250, 262–3.

171. Bonnell, *Robert Michels, Socialism, and Modernity*, pp. 254–257. Michels associated modernity with economic modernisation and women's emancipation.

from on a very small scale, impossible. Second, that any type of organisation will naturally produce a class of leaders—a 'political class' or 'ruling elite' will arise because of the 'iron law of oligarchy'—more or less independent from those they are responsible to. When we think about politics, this sounds about right: politicians are more or less independent from voters; they are never fully responsible to them. How much is an empirical question, and this isn't to deny that numerous factors, including the structure of organisation, that might serve to reduce that independence.[172] But we are here always talking of degree, never of a complete reduction.

Perhaps Cassinelli got it right when he wrote that by the 'law of oligarchy' was meant: 'the executive or leadership activities in an organisation are free from control by the other activities; or, putting it another way, the people who hold positions of authority within an organization are not checked by those who hold subsidiary positions within the organization', and yet that 'freedom from control does not mean that the leaders can completely ignore the actions and desires of the lower ranks in the organization'.[173] This seems to capture Michels' sentiment well when he writes in *Sociology of the Party*, 'the thesis of the unlimited power of the leaders in democratic parties requires, however, a certain limitation. . . . The old leader must therefore keep himself in permanent touch with the opinions and feelings of the masses to which he owes his position',[174] or in his *Lectures*: 'the elite is no longer able to maintain its power without the explicit or tacit consent of the masses upon which it in numerous ways depends'.[175]

But ultimately it still is, as the *Merriam-Webster* puts it, the 'few who rule'. Jeffrey Winters in his recent *Oligarchy* has criticised Michels for supposedly having obscured the fact that since its first theorisation with Aristotle oligarchy has meant the rule of the rich and not simply the rule of the few.[176] Pareto would agree, seeing wealth and capacity naturally flowing to the top of his pyramid, although, as we've seen, Mosca thought it was the middle-class who should rule. Even if Winters' point might not be entirely consonant with the dictionary definition, it does allow us to see that for Michels it is through

172. Linz, *Robert Michels*, p. 62; Hands, 'Roberto Michels and the Study of Political Parties', p. 169.

173. Cassinelli, 'The Law of Oligarchy', pp. 778–9.

174. Michels, *Political Parties*, p. 172.

175. Michels, *Lectures in Political Sociology*, p. 152.

176. Jeffrey Winters, *Oligarchy*, Cambridge, Cambridge University Press, 2001, p. 26.

bureaucratisation that riches can be acquired: that it is through the *institution* of the party that members can rise up to a petty bourgeois existence, and guarantee a better quality of life for their children. Extended to the rest of politics the implication of a 'political class' gaining riches are clear.[177]

Gerhardt Lenski has also highlighted the predictive power of Michels' 'iron law of oligarchy'. Distinguishing between analytical and normative elitism, he posits that analytical elitists have a '*theory with remarkable powers of prediction*'. He cites Michels' view that 'the problem of socialism is not merely a problem of economics . . . [but] also an administrative problem'[178] as anticipating the rise of the *nomenklatura* in Eastern Europe and Soviet Russia after the war.[179] Indeed, in the earlier literature it was quite common to compare Michels' *Sociology* to the Yugoslav former second-in-command to Tito Milovan Djilas, who theorised the rise of *The New Class* in state socialism.[180]

If *Sociology of the Party* strikes us as a little dated today, this is for two reasons. The first is that although Michels does offer considerable empirical data and engages in the type of statistical analysis that is recognisable as the beginnings of the type of work social scientists engage in today[181]—thereby rightly making him one of the founders of political sociology[182]—the book overall comes across as a little more impressionistic and journalistic. This might be because, as Linz points out, Michels, unlike Weber and Durkheim, did not collect his own data—perhaps due to lack of time, family pressure, or economic concerns—nor was he able to develop an original methodology akin to Durkheim's, or possess the synthesising and systematising abilities of Weber.[183] The second is because the questions he raised concerning party organisation and democracy are those social scientists (Lipset, Talcott Parsons, Maurice Duverger, C. Wright Mills) and democratic theorists (Schumpeter, Dahl, Norberto Bobbio, Sartori, Raymond Aron) have been arguing over ever since, which we will turn to in the second part of the book.[184]

---

177. Femia, *Against the Masses*, pp. 72–81.

178. Michels, *Political Parties*, p. 350.

179. Lenski, 'In Praise of Mosca and Michels', pp. 2–3, 8; Linz, *Robert Michels*, p. 26.

180. Lenski, 'In Praise of Mosca and Michels', p. 5; Lipset, 'Introduction', p. 20; Cook, 'Michels's Political Parties', p. 786.

181. Michels, *Political Parties*, pp. 88, 106, 257–8, 268–9, 310–11; Femia, *Against the Masses*, pp. 92, 101.

182. Linz, *Robert Michels*, p. 3.

183. Ibid., pp. 20–21.

184. Lipset, 'Introduction', pp. 20–39; Linz, *Robert Michels*, pp. 63–68.

Moreover Michels, with his theory of 'dynamic' democracy, offers us a means through which to conceptualise how to continually apply pleasure to make the iron law of oligarchy more pliable: democracy, in this conception, must be understood as a continuum between oligarchy on one side and democracy on the other. The question, therefore, is whether the 'iron law' is stronger or weaker: whether it is more or less oligarchic, more or less democratic. As such, he offers us not solely an empirical study of the possibility of democracy within political parties and political systems—and the analysis of the law is always a historically situated one—but also an aim—what both Mommsen and Sartori have called an ethical 'yardstick'[185]—that we may never reach, but from which, in our striving to reach it, democratic benefits will accrue. This combination of realism (awareness of the facts) and idealism (value pressure upon the facts) is precisely the account of democracy Sartori prescribes in his *Theory of Democracy Revisited*.[186] And although the peasant's sons will never find the non-existent buried treasure in the field, nonetheless their work is not in vain, as from having been tilled, the land will have been made richer, thereby making them richer too.

In his Inaugural Address at the University of Turin—a lecture Michels was aware of—Mosca had rejected the thesis of the 'futile labour of Sisyphus', explaining that if there is always a political class, the question remained open as to how good that political class could be, and that 'some minorities have the necessary attitudes to direct the social corpus beneficially'.[187] As such, Joseph Femia's view that Mosca, Pareto and Michels are the greatest exponents of the 'futility' thesis in his *Against the Masses*—that true democracy, where a majority rules over a minority, will never be achieved—must be accepted with some reserve: if it is the case that a minority will always rule, that does not mean things cannot change, and indeed for the better.[188]

Femia himself concedes the point when he mentions both Aesop's fable and Michels' 'palliatives'—he is one of the few to do so—requesting that these reflections be deepened. He concludes: 'pursuit of the unattainable is not always a waste of time; the futility thesis, correctly understood, need not be a

185. Mommsen, 'Max Weber and Roberto Michels', p. 109; Mommsen, 'Robert Michels', p. 128; Sartori, *The Theory of Democracy Revisited*, p. 159.

186. Sartori, *The Theory of Democracy Revisited*, pp. 159, 164.

187. Beetham, 'From Socialism to Fascism II', p. 162.

188. Femia, *Against the Masses*, pp. 9–10.

counsel of despair'.[189] Indeed, for Femia the futility thesis, when correctly understood—that if democracy is not *impossible* it is at least *imperilled*—has in fact made 'the most profound contribution to democratic theory'.[190] Seeing the challenges democracy faces forces us to rethink how to defend it. This may be a pessimistic view of democracy, yet it is one, to reprise a Nietzschean phrase, of strength: there remains the possibility for change, even perhaps a positive one.

Bringing Mosca and Pareto into the conversation can help deepen the 'dynamic' conception of democracy, as Michels on his own cannot carry the whole weight of the theory. Beetham, for instance, ridicules the parable of the sons digging for the treasure in the field as pertaining to the domain of 'gross self-deception'.[191] Do those who are challenging elite rule need to truly *believe* in democracy to be able to engage in their work? Already from Michels' second metaphor for democracy—of waves breaking against the shoal—we see this needn't be the case: a new elite will arise to denounce the aristocratic slide of the old elite, and that challenge will continue without end. Pareto had already suggested in his *Systèmes socialistes* that new elites will ally themselves with the people to challenge the old elites, and Mosca had systematically talked about the need for new blood.[192] It is in these moments that the cursor of the iron law gets pulled towards the democratic side. Of course, true democracy is never achieved, and the people, in Michels' account or Pareto's, are betrayed, but for the system to work all that is needed is for the appearance of a new elite that feels excluded enough from power to want to challenge the old guard for its place within the ruling class.

189. Ibid., p. 109.
190. Ibid., p. 15.
191. Beetham, 'From Socialism to Fascism I', p. 19.
192. Femia, *Against the Masses*, p. 88.

4

Schumpeter and Elite
Competition

JOSEPH SCHUMPETER's theory of 'minimalist democracy' remains one of the most influential theories of democracy today, whether it is in the academy or with the public at large. In academic circles, thinkers such as Adam Przeworski, Ian Shapiro and, to a lesser extent, Jeffrey Green have claimed the term as their own, both to defend and deepen it:[1] as John Medearis has pointed out, it remains the 'prototype' for much work in democratic theory.[2] Even those who explicitly reject Schumpeter's theory, to develop instead a 'participatory', 'agonistic' or indeed 'deliberative' model of democracy, have felt the need to engage with his thought.[3]

Robert Dahl, whose theory of 'polyarchy' is perhaps the biggest rival to minimalism's post-war pre-eminence, explained in a 2002 interview that he elaborated his own theory of democracy in direct response to Schumpeter's.[4]

---

1. Adam Przeworski, 'Minimalist Conception of Democracy: A Defense' in Ian Shapiro and Casiano Hacker-Cordon, eds., *Democracy's Value*, Cambridge, Cambridge University Press, 1999, pp. 23–55; Ian Shapiro, *The State of Democratic Theory*, Princeton, Princeton University Press, 2003; Ian Shapiro, *Politics Against Domination*, Cambridge (MA), Harvard University Press, 2016; Jeffrey Green, *The Eyes of the People: Democracy in an Age of Spectatorship*, Oxford, Oxford University Press, 2010.

2. John Medearis, *Joseph Schumpeter's Two Theories of Democracy*, Cambridge (MA), Harvard University Press, 2001, p. 2.

3. Carole Pateman, *Participation and Democratic Theory*, Cambridge, Cambridge University Press, 1970; William Connolly, *Identity/Difference: Democratic Negotiations of Political Paradox*, Minneapolis, University of Minnesota Press, 2002; Jurgen Habermas, *Between Facts and Norms: Contributions to a Discourse Theory of Law and Democracy*, Cambridge (MA), MIT Press, 1998.

4. 'Robert Dahl: Normative Theory, Empirical Research, and Democracy' in Gerardo Munch and Richard Snyder, eds., *Passion, Craft, and Method in Comparative Politics*, Baltimore, The Johns Hopkins University Press, 2007, pp. 113–149.

As Giovanni Sartori writes: 'Dahl takes on where Schumpeter leaves off; that is, Dahl seeks a pluralistic diffusion and reinforcement, throughout the society as a whole, of inter-elite competition'.[5] Dahl, as we shall see in the following chapter, wanted to increase participation in democracy. And although in the wider public Schumpeter may not be a household name, at least not when it comes to democratic theory, the view of democracy as being especially tied to elections holds firm: when power appears to change hands then some sort of democratic action—however minimal—is generally understood to have taken place.[6]

There are at least two reasons to be surprised by this. The first is that Schumpeter was not, first and foremost, a democratic theorist. Rather he was an economist, like Vilfredo Pareto. He is best known for having popularised the term 'creative destruction', borrowed from Werner Sombart. And it is as an economist that his reputation still lies: the introduction to the recent Routledge Classics edition to his 1942 masterpiece *Capitalism, Socialism and Democracy*—apparently the third most cited book in the social sciences published before 1950, behind Karl Marx's *Capital* and *The Wealth of Nations* by Adam Smith[7]—was written by Joseph Stiglitz, Nobel prize winner in economics. In 2009, *The Economist* launched a new column on business and management under his name, putting him on the same footing as Walter Bagehot (British politics) and Charlemagne (European affairs).[8] If having a column in *The Economist* named after you is not recognition, one wonders what is.

---

5. Giovanni Sartori, *The Theory of Democracy Revisited. Part One: The Contemporary Debate*, Chatham, Chatham House Publishers, 1987, p. 154.

6. Sartori (ibid., pp. 162, 165) sees the 'competitive-polyarchal' model of democracy as a 'state of facts', a 'descriptive theory that actually explains how democracies work and perform'. The challenge, then, is to give it a normative or 'prescriptive' basis (ibid., p. 163), which he thinks is possible through the qualities of good 'leadership'. Democracy should be a 'selective polyarchy' or a 'polyarchy of merit' (ibid., pp. 167, 169), meaning those of the best qualities should also be in positions of power.

7. Elliott Green, 'What Are the Most-Cited Publications in the Social Sciences (according to Google Scholar)?', *LSE Impact Blog*, 12 May 2016 (https://blogs.lse.ac.uk/impactofsocialsciences /2016/05/12/what-are-the-most-cited-publications-in-the-social-sciences-according-to-google -scholar/, accessed on 11 February 2021).

8. Joseph Stiglitz, 'Introduction' in Joseph Schumpeter, *Capitalism, Socialism and Democracy*, London, Routledge, 2010, pp. ix–xiv; 'Schumpeter: Taking Flight', *The Economist*, 17 September 2009 (https://www.economist.com/business/2009/09/17/taking-flight, accessed on 11 February 2021).

The second is that within the reams of writings and publication on economic theory, history, development, method, economists, sociologists, taxation, imperialism, social classes, business cycles, entrepreneurs and inflation, democratic theory occupies a rather small place in Schumpeter's work, buried in four short, sharp chapters, 20–23 (out of twenty-eight), that make up part IV, 'Socialism and Democracy', of *Capitalism, Socialism and Democracy*. The work's aim was to show that capitalism, in agreement with Marx but not for the same reasons, was in decline and was to be replaced by a certain form of socialist corporatism, something akin to what Robert Michels said about the role of intellectuals in socialist politics.[9]

So how is it that minimalist democracy, from such inauspicious beginnings, came to occupy the prominent position it does today? The thesis of this chapter is that Schumpeter was able to achieve two interrelated goals with this theory. On the one hand, he was able to domesticate—or democratise—elite theory.[10] That is to say, Schumpeter seized upon the work of those we now call the 'elite theorists of democracy', Gaetano Mosca, Pareto and Michels—and in this case Pareto in particular—and was able to democratise a school of thought by reducing what at first had a much larger range.[11] In short, by constraining competition between elites to solely within the political sphere, instead of postulating the wider societal circulation the earlier thinkers extolled, he made elitism safe for democracy. By his doing so, however, namely by his rigidifying the political structure around political competition, minimalist democracy lost out on much of the dynamism that characterised the earlier work, which was not as unsympathetic to democracy as might have first appeared.

On the other hand, and relatedly, he made democracy safe for capitalism: minimalist democracy was a way to stave off the stronger democratic transformations that socialism demanded, socialist demands that Schumpeter, as

9. For an overview of some of Schumpeter's work, see Joseph Schumpeter, *The Economics and Sociology of Capitalism*, Princeton, Princeton University Press, 1991.

10. Kyong-Min Son, *The Eclipse of the Demos: The Cold War and the Crisis of Democracy before Neoliberalism*, Lawrence, University of Kansas Press, 2020. For a review, see Hugo Drochon, 'Kyong-Min Son, The Eclipse of the Demos: The Cold War and the Crisis of Democracy before Neoliberalism', *Perspectives on Politics*, Vol. 19, No. 1, 2021, pp. 604–605. On democratic elitism, see, further, Peter Bachrach, *The Theory of Democratic Elitism: A Critique*, Lanham, University Press of America, 1980; Tom Bottomore, *Elites and Society*, London, Routledge, 1993; and Geraint Parry, *Political Elites*, Colchester, ECPR Press, 2005.

11. Medearis, *Joseph Schumpeter's Two Theories of Democracy*, p. 8

Medearis has so convincingly shown, had experienced first-hand.[12] Minimalist democracy was a way to save some aspects of the old order Schumpeter had done so well in from being completely overwhelmed by the new.[13] In this it should come as no surprise that he turned to thinkers such as Max Weber and Pareto: thinkers who explicitly engaged with Marx but who formulated alternative, and less revolutionary, views of what the future had in store. As Pareto puts it in the *Trattato*, social systems can be either static or dynamic.[14]

Schumpeter saw how dynamic democracy could be, and feared the changes that would come from it, restricting that dynamism to a more limited—'minimalist'—political field. If movement there still occurred, society at large would be preserved from the larger transformation. In short, he wanted the system as a whole to become more static, save for a small field of political competition. His solution was to combine elite circulation with institutional stability by limiting the former to a narrow field. As Medearis puts it: 'the transformative conception of democracy highlighted the radicalised, dynamic effects of movements that attempt to realise democratic values and act on democratic ideologies, while his better-known elite model depicted democracy in static terms and as institutionally stable'.[15]

First, this chapter offers an exposition of Schumpeter's 'minimalist' democracy, exploring, second, how his economic theory of innovation, entrepreneurship and monopoly influenced, third, his democratic one. It argues that although Schumpeter opened the door to what we now call 'economic' theories of democracy, most notably Anthony Downs' 1957 classic *An Economic Theory of Democracy*, Schumpeter's economic theory puts him at odds with many of these subsequent elaborations and interpretations, such as Shapiro's.[16] Fourth, this chapter pays attention to the numerous, and often overlooked, preconditions Schumpeter posited for his 'elite competitive' model to work. Indeed, 'minimalist democracy' was never a term Schumpeter used, but was rather coined by Przeworski to be used polemically against participatory and deliberative theories of democracy in particular, and normative theories that assign edifying components in terms of representativeness, equality, justice and redistribution to democracy—notions Schumpeter rejected out of hand—in

12. Ibid., pp. 19–77.

13. John Medearis, *Joseph A. Schumpeter*, London, Bloomsbury, 2013.

14. Vilfredo Pareto, *The Mind and Society*, New York, Harcourt, Brace, 1935, #2067.

15. Medearis, *Joseph Schumpeter's Two Theories of Democracy*, p. 4.

16. Anthony Downs, *An Economic Theory of Democracy*, New York, Harper & Row, 1957.

general.[17] As we shall see, Schumpeter's 'minimalist' theory was not minimal at all. Fifth, this chapter reconstructs the under-theorised influence Pareto, himself an economist-turned-democratic-theorist, had on Schumpeter, and therefore the impact 'elite theory' had on his thought. Even though 'elite', much like 'minimalism', was not a term Schumpeter himself used—'elite competition' is a post-facto reconstruction of his theory—nevertheless it seems impossible to apprehend his 'leadership' democracy, the term he did use, without it.

In conclusion, it will ask what has been lost in Schumpeter's distilling of the earlier 'elitists' into a static account of democracy centred on the institution or 'procedure' of elections, and whether a return to the thought of Mosca, Pareto and Michels offers us a fuller and more dynamic account of politics today. It will also explore the relationship dynamic democracy entertains with Medearis' 'transformative' or 'oppositional' democracy to show that although they share the same analytical premises in seeing democracy as beyond simply the political sphere, extending to social and economic fields, and both share an interest in political movements and their interaction with political institutions, nevertheless dynamic democracy remains more of a defence of liberal-parliamentarism than Medearis' more participatory approach.

I: Elite Competition

The democratic method is that institutional arrangement for arriving at political decisions in which individuals acquire the power to decide by means of a competitive struggle for the people's vote.[18]

This was Schumpeter's new definition of democracy. A few aspects stand out, most noticeably the emphasis on *method* and *institutions*, which has led the theory to be dubbed a 'procedural' account, as opposed to a more substantial one in which certain values—equality, liberty—are already baked in. In effect, what Schumpeter was saying is that democracy is a *means* to making decisions, and not an *end* in itself. In fact, Schumpeter argued, if we understand democracy as 'Rule by the People', namely giving the people want they want, then

17. Przeworski, 'Minimalist Conception of Democracy: A Defense'. Thanks to Nadia Urbinati for highlighting this point.

18. Schumpeter, *Capitalism, Socialism and Democracy*, p. 241.

democracy, or at least democratic institutions like elections—which is the key criterion here—are often ill-suited for that purpose.[19] To prove his point, Schumpeter gave the example of Napoleon's 1801 concordat with the Pope, which he claimed would have been impossible to achieve democratically, even if this was what the majority of French people wanted, because of the anti-church sentiment that was the legacy of the French Revolution. As such, Napoleon had to impose those decisions from above. 'If results that prove satisfactory to the people at large are made the test of government *for* the people', Schumpeter writes, 'then government *by* the people, as conceived by the classical doctrine of democracy, would often fail to meet it.'[20]

Schumpeter prided himself in having achieved a number of things. The first was offering a criterion—elections—as a way of delineating between different regimes. If democracy is giving people what they want, then democracy might be better served by an autocratic ruler like Napoleon. But if we focus on democracy as a *means* rather than an *end*, then it is easier to recognise regimes with elections as 'democratic' instead of others.[21] This view, it should be noted, has not come without criticism, with some wondering whether elections are sufficient to distinguish between a democratic and an aristocratic regime: a more limited franchise, such as the one that existed during the Renaissance Venetian Republic, might still qualify on this account as a 'democracy' even if it excluded the majority of the 'people'.[22] As Sartori puts it, in a slightly different setting: 'a political system can be polyarchal without being based on popular suffrage'.[23] Schumpeter left it up to the people to determine the extent of the franchise, in a relativist turn, meaning it could be very limited indeed:

19. Ibid., pp. 217–9.

20. Ibid. pp. 229–30. On the preconditions needed for democracy to overcome partisanship and gridlock, see William Selinger, 'Schumpeter on Democratic Survival', *The Tocqueville Review/La Revue Tocqueville*, Vol. 36, No. 2, 2015, pp.127–157.

21. Jan-Werner Müller has underlined how this element of 'uncertainty'—that the results of elections are uncertain, in contrast with Napoleon's decisions that are not—is a key element of our understanding of democracy (Jan-Werner Müller, *Democracy Rules: Liberty, Equality, Uncertainty*, New York, Farrar, Strauss and Giroux, 2021).

22. See Gerry Mackie, 'Schumpeter's Leadership Democracy', *Political Theory*, Vol. 37, No. 1, 2009, pp. 128–153. For a discussion, see Jeffrey Green, 'Three Theses on Schumpeter: Response to Mackie', *Political Theory*, Vol. 38, No. 2, 2010, pp. 268–275 and Gerry Mackie, 'Reply to Green', ibid., pp. 276–281.

23. Sartori, *The Theory of Democracy Revisited*, p. 155. See also Medearis, *Joseph Schumpeter's Two Theories of Democracy*, pp. 124–129 for a similar critique.

something worth keeping in mind when considering African-American disenfranchisement.[24]

In spite—or indeed in large parts thanks to this—Schumpeter congratulated himself in having integrated what he termed the 'vital fact of leadership' into his theory of democracy, his second point.[25] Following from his Napoleon example, Schumpeter saw politics as top-down; as, in essence, elite-led. Democracy is 'deciding who the leading man shall be'.[26] The section in which Schumpeter elaborated his 'alternative' theory of democracy is entitled 'Competition for political leadership', and this is very much how he understood democracy: it is a competition between political elites to capture the vote of the people, leading him to dub his theory 'rule by politicians'.[27] This, then, is a reversal of the usual understanding of democracy, that sees the people first decide what they want and second elect representatives to enact their will: 'the selection of representatives is made secondary'.[28] Schumpeter, instead, started with the representatives themselves, then looked to the electorate to see what they wanted.[29]

To help clarify this point it is worth returning to what Schumpeter labelled the 'Classical doctrine of democracy', which he defined as such:

> the democratic method is that institutional arrangement for arriving at political decisions which realises the common good by making the people itself decide issues through the election of individuals who are to assemble in order to carry out its will.[30]

24. Schumpeter, *Capitalism, Socialism and Democracy*, pp. 220, 415 n. 16.

25. Ibid., p. 242.

26. Ibid., p. 245.

27. Ibid., pp. 241, 253.

28. Ibid.

29. Sartori has an important gloss on Schumpeter's theory, explaining that '*democracy is the by-product of a competitive method of leadership recruitment . . . [and] competitive elections produce democracy*'. For him, Schumpeter's account of democracy is a '*competitive-feedback* theory of democracy'. This is because of Friedrich's rule of 'anticipated reactions' that combine inputs and outputs of democracy. Sartori explains: 'Elected officials seeking reelection (in a competitive setting) are conditioned, in their deciding, by the anticipation (expectation) of how electorates will react to what they decide. The rule of anticipated reactions thus provides the linkage between input and output, between the procedure (as stated by Schumpeter) and its consequences' (Sartori, *The Theory of Democracy Revisited*, p. 152. Italics in original).

30. Schumpeter, *Capitalism, Socialism and Democracy*, p. 225.

The important themes to pick out here are 'common good' and 'will', which combine elements of Rousseau's *volonté générale* and utilitarianism. As many have pointed out, these make for strange bedfellows, and Schumpeter's account of 'classical' democracy has often been decried as a 'myth' or a 'straw man', which fails to take into account the fact that a common will might be brought about through the democratic process itself, and need not pre-exist it (although this is closer to Rousseau's view, who thought the general will needed to be discovered).[31] But Schumpeter puts them together through John Stuart Mill's 'greatest happiness of the greatest number' principle, which supposedly ties Bentham to Rousseau's social contract.[32] The point is that for Schumpeter, democracy is conventionally understood as the people generating a common will they subsequently appoint representatives to execute. It is this bottom-up view of democracy Schumpeter wished to attack.

He did so in a section entitled 'Human Nature in Politics', section III of his chapter 21, 'The classical doctrine of democracy', where he developed seven lines of argument.[33] First, drawing from Gustave Le Bon's *psychologie des foules*, is that any group, however formal—whether a parliament, a committee or a council of war—will display, even in a reduced form, the features associated with the 'crowd' or 'rabble', namely 'a reduced sense of responsibility, a lower level of energy of thought and greater sensitiveness to non-logical influences',[34] in what sounds like a reprise of Plato's critique of democracy as 'mob-rule'. Second, the power of advertisement, according to Schumpeter, demonstrates that an a priori (democratic) will does not exist but is instead manufactured, thereby dismissing the existence of a genuine *volonté générale* that cannot in some way be manipulated (instead of discovered). Third, the modern bourgeois man is more interested in his own affairs than in politics, and whilst he might be a specialist in his own field, he becomes, fourth, an amateur again when it comes to politics, where his thinking becomes associative and affective, given to irrational prejudice and impulse. His distance from certain issues

---

31. Pateman, *Participation and Democracy Theory*, pp. 3–5; Josiah Ober, 'Joseph Schumpeter's Caesarist Democracy', *Critical Review*, Vol. 29, No. 4, 2017, pp. 473–491; Green, *The Eyes of the People*, pp. 172–7; Medearis, *Joseph Schumpeter's Two Theories of Democracy*, pp. 129–133.

32. Schumpeter, *Capitalism, Socialism and Democracy*, p. 223. For a defence, see Philip Pettit, 'Democracy before, in, and after Schumpeter', *Critical Review*, Vol. 29, No. 4, 2017, pp. 492–504.

33. See also Medearis, *Joseph Schumpeter's Two Theories of Democracy*, p. 16.

34. Ibid., p. 231. See, further, Medearis, *Joseph Schumpeter's Two Theories of Democracy*, p. 119 on Le Bon and Pareto.

will lead him, fifth, to act irresponsibly in those fields, and he will generally be
motivated by short-term rather than long-term gain, sixth, leading politics,
finally, because of this lack of knowledge and interest, to become dominated
by interest-groups.[35]

Schumpeter offered a number of interesting reflections as to why he
thought this 'classical doctrine' has persisted nonetheless (he liked lists),
including—perhaps influenced by Nietzsche, as we know Schumpeter's figure
of the 'entrepreneur' has *Übermenschlich* qualities[36]—the Protestant transmis-
sion of the voice of God to the voice of the people (i.e. Nietzsche's 'Shadows
of God');[37] the fact that it still fits certain places, like Switzerland, with a degree of approximation; that a majority of people still endorse this view of democracy, at least in everyday language; and the fact that politicians like to
flatter the masses precisely by using this type of phraseology, which they know
to be untrue, but that serves them to 'evade responsibility' and crush their
opponents 'in the name of the people'.[38] But for our purposes what is of most
interest is under who's intellectual tutelage Schumpeter placed his rejection of
the 'classical' doctrine. We have already identified two—Le Bon and economists' work on advertising—to which Théodule Ribot and Sigmund Freud
can be added. But Schumpeter also referred to Pareto's *Mind and Society*, the
title of the translation of Pareto's masterpiece *Trattato di sociologia generale*
(*Treatise on sociology*), which he praised for highlighting the 'importance of
the extra-rational and irrational element in our behaviour' that underpinned
his critique.[39]

35. See ibid., pp. 230–237.

36. Hugo Reinert and Erik Reinert, 'Creative Destruction in Economics: Nietzsche, Sombart, Schumpeter', in Jurgen Backhaus and Wolfgang Drechsler, eds., *Friedrich Nietzsche 1844–
2000: Economy and Society*, New York, Springer, 2006, pp. 55–85. For an alternative view, see
Natasha Piano, 'Neoliberalism, Leadership, and Democracy: Schumpeter on "Schumpeterian"
Theories of Entrepreneurship', *European Journal of Political Theory*, Vol. 21, No. 4, 2022, pp. 715–
737. See, further, Corey Robin, 'Nietzsche's Marginal Children: On Friedrich Hayek', *The Nation*,
7 May 2013 (https://www.thenation.com/article/archive/nietzsches-marginal-children
-friedrich-hayek/ accessed on 5 April 2024). Although Nietzsche's link to Schumpeter seems
averred, his link to Hayek appears more tenuous.

37. Hugo Drochon, *Nietzsche's Great Politics*, Princeton, Princeton University Press, 2016,
p. 103.

38. Ibid., pp. 237–40.

39. Ibid., p. 230. See, further, Michael Christensen, 'The Ssocial Facts of Democracy: Science
Meets Politics with Mosca, Pareto, Michels, and Schumpeter', *Journal of Classical Sociology*, Vol.
13, No. 4, 2013, pp. 460–486.

To save politics from becoming a 'stampede', Schumpeter defended his competitive theory of democracy, which he labelled 'realistic'.[40] Beyond the 'fact of leadership', it is more realistic because it integrates within its bosom the notion of the 'Manufactured Will', whilst giving the will of different groups their rightful due: 'such volitions do not as a rule assert themselves directly. Even if strong and definite they remain latent, often for decades, until they are called to life by some political leader who turns them into political factors'.[41] So there might indeed be something like a democratic 'will', but it only comes into existence when a political leader activates it. Thus proceeds Schumpeter's 'leadership' democracy. But Schumpeter underlined how if the role of the electorate is to produce a government by choosing this or that leader, its role is also to evict it. This does not necessarily make political leaders directly 'responsive' in some form or other to the electorate (feedback and responsiveness are not the same thing), as some subsequent political theory tried to make out—at least not for Schumpeter, and to understand that we will have to turn to how he understood the relation between economic and political competition—but it did allow him to take a definitive stand on a question of political theory: no Proportional Representation. The reason is that if democracy is competition between political elites, then PR muddies that competition and the electorate's yes/no vote becomes indeterminate. PR prevents democracies from producing 'efficient governments and thus proves a danger in times of stress', a point recently reiterated by Frances Rosenbluth and Ian Shapiro.[42]

II: Economic Competition

The figure who looms largest in *Capitalism, Socialism and Democracy* is Marx, and to understand Schumpeter's economy theory we must understand his relationship to Marx and Leon Walras, which we'll explore in turn.[43] Schumpeter actually agreed with Marx that capitalism would collapse and be replaced by socialism, something that might come as a surprise to contemporary readers used to seeing his name associated with *The Economist*. He wrote: 'Can

40. Ibid., pp. 251, 242.

41. Ibid., pp. 242–3.

42. Frances Rosenbluth and Ian Shapiro, *Responsible Parties: Saving Democracy from Itself*, New Haven, Yale University Press, 2018.

43. See Schumpeter, *Capitalism, Socialism and Democracy*, Part I.

capitalism survive? No. I do not think that it can'.[44] Of course, that is not the same as celebrating or even advocating its demise, which Schumpeter did not do. Nor indeed did it mean his prediction would be right: he was analysing trends.[45]

So what trends did he analyse? For Schumpeter, capitalism would collapse not because of a proletarian revolution that would overthrow the established order, as Marx had predicted—that might occur, according to Schumpeter, in the least developed capitalist societies (history here, with the Russian revolution, having proven him right); but in the more advanced ones, which Marx believed would be led by the revolutionary vanguard, Schumpeter instead believed that capitalism would collapse from within, to be replaced by a form of 'corporatism'.[46] Instead of the universal working class, Schumpeter thought the agent of change would be 'intellectuals', much like Michels, as we've seen in the previous chapter. Capitalism's division of labour would lead to a surplus that allows a growing number of the population access to higher education, which previously had been the privilege of the few. Equipped with higher cognitive faculties, this social class would grow resentful towards capitalism because of its inability to provide them with sufficiently intellectually fulfilling jobs, leading them to become increasingly critical of it.[47] Standing outside the classic worker-bourgeois class distinction, intellectuals would flock to social-democratic parties, bringing them electoral success, which would translate into the slow adoption of 'labourism', a form of industrial or workplace democracy, which Schumpeter associated with corporatism.[48]

What's wrong with corporatism? For Schumpeter it blocked what makes the economy—and indeed society more generally—progress, namely, entrepreneurship.[49] To understand that, we need to turn to Walras who, alongside his successor Pareto, belonged to the 'Lausanne school of economics', both part of the 'marginalist revolution' in economics, which we explored in chapter 2. As Stiglitz has underlined, what is important in this model is equilibrium, whose high-point is Pareto efficiency, the point where no one can be made

44. Ibid., p. 53.
45. John Medearis, 'Schumpeter, the New Deal, and Democracy', *The American Political Science Review*, Vo. 91, No .4, 1997, pp. 819–832.
46. See Schumpeter, *Capitalism, Socialism and Democracy*, Part II.
47. Ibid., pp. 130–8.
48. Ibid., pp. 139–46.
49. Ibid., pp. 116–9.

better off without making someone else worse off.[50] This, then, is the law of supply and demand, in which monopoly is a scourge.

Schumpeter rejected this view. For him the key mover of the economy is not equilibrium but innovation. 'Creative destruction', sometimes called 'Schumpeter's gale' or the 'gale of creative destruction', is the 'process of industrial mutation that continuously revolutionises the economic structure from within, incessantly destroying the old one, incessantly creating a new one'.[51] Innovation, that Dionysian force, is the gift of entrepreneurs.[52] The idea of 'creative destruction' is in part derived from Marx, through Sombart, both in the sense of capitalism overthrowing the older, medieval order and in the sense that the crises capitalism engenders within itself destroys wealth to make way for the creation of new wealth. In Schumpeter's account, innovation is principally a technological one: classic examples are how digital cameras have replaced Polaroid; MP3—and now online streaming services—have replaced cassettes and CDs; and how online advertisement has pushed many newspapers to go digital, if not bust altogether.

'Going bust' is a key element of the theory: when an innovation comes along, it makes an older one obsolete, and jobs in that sector will be lost. But in the long-run Schumpeter believed this will be good for the economy, and that in any case the gale is irresistible. He is also of the view that monopolies are the drivers of innovation, because they have the means to invest in technological innovation—a view not shared by Stiglitz:

> there is an important strand of research which argues that a large fraction of modern and key innovations originate in new and smaller firms. While some aspects of the innovation process can be routinised, real creativity can't be, and if large enterprises stifle opportunities for new entrants, innovation may suffer.[53]

Indeed, the question of barriers to entry is a key one for Schumpeter, because he still wanted to keep monopolies competitive. But what we can see here is that, for Schumpeter at least, the economy is not characterised by 'pure'

---

50. Stiglitz, 'Introduction', p. ix.

51. Schumpeter, *Capitalism, Socialism and Democracy*, pp. 73, 77–8.

52. Reinert and Reinert, 'Creative Destruction in Economics'.

53. Stiglitz, 'Introduction', p. xiii. On Schumpeter and monopolies, see Schumpeter, *Capitalism, Socialism and Democracy*, pp. 76–92.

competition as Walras and Pareto would have it, but rather by monopoly: if there is competition it is *for* the market, not *in* it.[54]

III: Economic Democracy

The parallels between Schumpeter's economic and political theories are clear: politicians are political 'entrepreneurs' who come up with an innovative manifesto they use to try to capture the market of votes, until another group of politicians comes up with a rival offer that renders their offer obsolete, the process of 'creative destruction' continuing unabated. Schumpeter drew the parallel between economic competition and democratic competition himself in his defence of his new theory of democracy—to return to the section organising our discussion—reiterating the point that competition is never 'perfect', and that in the democratic case, free competition was reserved to the sphere of the free vote.[55] Democratic politics, for Schumpeter, also had monopolistic tendencies—the competition was *for* the market of votes, another reason he rejected PR, which would have been a competition *in* the market—or in this case had the features of an oligopoly: we do well to remember that Schumpeter, like all good turn-of-the-century liberals, held the British political system in the highest esteem, and was obviously writing from the position of someone living in the US; hence the two-party structure.[56]

As in the economic sphere, the democratic arena has features that could be characterised as 'unfair' or 'fraudulent' restrictions on competition, especially in terms of barriers to new entrants. Schumpeter even went as far as granting that his theory was open to the charge that it might not be able to distinguish between democratic and autocratic regimes—'there is a continuous range of variation within which the democratic method of government shades off into the autocratic one by imperceptible steps'—thereby seemingly conceding to later criticism that because it overlooked questions such as civil rights, a free press and the rule of law, it fell victim to being unable of giving an account of

54. Stiglitz, 'Introduction', p. ix.

55. Schumpeter, *Capitalism, Socialism and Democracy*, p. 243.

56. Ibid., p. 246. Ober, 'Joseph Schumpeter's Caesarist Democracy', pp. 486–7. The one disagreement this chapter has with Medearis' analysis is that he sees Schumpeter's political theory as based on an unstable vision of equilibrium (see Medearis, *Joseph Scumpeter's Two Theories of Democracy*, pp. 9, 177–199). Yet the emphasis here on monopoly and capturing the market suggests that Schumpeter was not interested in equilibrium at all, which was the focus of the Lausanne School of Walras and Pareto he criticised.

democratic backsliding, which seems so evident in places like Hungary today.[57] It is precisely to underline these aspects that Dahl felt the need to elaborate a fuller theory of 'polyarchy'.[58]

In developing his economic theory of democracy, Anthony Downs famously stated: 'Schumpeter's profound analysis of democracy forms the inspiration and foundation of our whole thesis, and our debt and gratitude to him are great indeed'.[59] It is not clear, however, that Schumpeter understood his democratic theory as tracking the median voter as Downs did. As Green writes:

> Schumpeter thus refuted the very economic conception of democracy to which he is sometimes linked. Whereas the economic model sees citizens, and more generally the People, as consumers who choose candidates in order to maximize preexisting values, interests, opinions, and preferences, Schumpeter challenged this economic conception by arguing that it is incorrect to see the People as an exogenous source of legislative demands.[60]

The reason for that, as Green elegantly puts it, is that it is not that the 'People *chooses* leaders of their liking', but rather the competitive democratic process is one where, according to Schumpeter, 'the People functions as the prize to be won rather than the sovereign to be obeyed'.[61]

Green is therefore right to underline the 'plebiscitary' nature of democracy for Schumpeter: what is most important for him is that the electorate approve or reject the leaders, not that these somehow best represent the desires and interests of their constituents.[62] It is for the political entrepreneur—that *Übermenschlich* creator of new values—to come up with an innovative political position to try to capture the market of votes, not the professional manager to

57. Ibid. On democratic backsliding, see Steven Fish, 'Conclusion: Democracy and Russian Politics' in Zoltan Barany and Robert Moser, eds., *Russian Politics: Challenges of Democratisation*, Cambridge, Cambridge University Press, 2001, p. 219 and Larry Diamond, 'Elections without Democracy: Thinking about Hybrid Regimes', *Journal of Democracy*, Vol. 13, No .2, 2002, pp. 21–35.

58. Dahl, *Democracy and Its Critics*, pp. 121–31.

59. Downs, *An Economic Theory of Democracy*, p. 29, n. 11.

60. Green, *The Eyes of the People*, p. 176.

61. Ibid., p. 174.

62. See, further, Alfred Moore, 'Schumpeter's Not-So-Minimal Theory of Democracy', working paper.

successfully triangulate between the competing demands of the voters: this is, after all, a top-down model. So the monopoly of political power—or at least the oligopoly in this instance—remains key.

In his work on democratic theory, Shapiro, building on Schumpeter, has argued that competition in democracy should be increased, notably by extending antitrust legislation to make elections more competitive by involving judicial review in the process, and by extending competition beyond governmental institutions so as to serve 'consumer sovereignty'.[63] Whether or not this will benefit society is not for this chapter to judge, but these suggestions appear to go against Schumpeter's spirit: we have already seen the difficulties with the idea of the elector as a 'consumer' rather than as a 'judge' of leadership, and Schumpeter was clear he wanted competition to be limited to competition for votes.[64] For the rest, as discussed above, Schumpeter was quite happy with either 'unfair' or even 'fraudulent' restraints on competition. The reason for that was that he was afraid of democracy's transformative power.

IV: The Conditions of Minimalism

If Schumpeter's democratic theory is already buried within the four chapters that make up part IV of *Capitalism, Socialism and Democracy*, most readers will only concentrate on chapters 21, 'The Classical Doctrine of Democracy', and 22, 'Another Theory of Democracy'. But the final chapter of the part, chapter 23, 'The Inference', is often overlooked.[65] That is a shame, as it is highly interesting. There Schumpeter sets out the conditions for his democratic theory to work, which might immediately intrigue: why does a so-called 'minimalist' theory need pre-conditions for it to work? Of course, the point of it being 'minimalist' is that it focuses on one aspect *simpliciter*—elections—so as to offer a clear criterion to demark certain democratic regimes from others: it has all the advantages, as one critic put it, of 'simplicity, elegance, and parsimony'.[66] That is its strength. And in this Przeworski, beyond the polemical intent, is right. But why then the need for 'Conditions for the success of the democratic method',

63. Shapiro, *The State of Democratic Theory*, pp. 6, 50–77.
64. Schumpeter, *Capitalism, Socialism and Democracy*, p. 243.
65. Ober, 'Joseph Schumpeter's Caesarist Democracy' is an exception.
66. Fish, 'Conclusion: Democracy and Russian Politics', p. 219.

as Schumpeter titles his section.[67] If democracy is 'minimalist', then surely if there are elections then that is sufficient? What is noticeable too is the shift in tone: if in the previous two chapters the language was descriptive, to match the 'realistic' approach, here all of a sudden the language becomes one of 'ought': things 'should' be this way. Is 'empirical' democracy hiding its normative foundations?[68]

Schumpeter lists five conditions (again, he likes lists) for the success of his democratic method. First, he asks that politicians be of 'sufficiently high quality'.[69] There needs to be a 'social stratum, itself a product of a severely selective process, that takes politics as a matter of course', and again England, with its 'establishment', is offered as the only society to have fully fulfilled that criterion, which Weimar Germany so patently, according to Schumpeter, failed to do.[70] Second, the 'effective range of political decision should not be extended too far'.[71] This echoes the previous point about the competitive method being confined to the free vote, and not extended beyond that. 'Democracy does not require that every function of the state be subject to its political method', so that expertise can be called upon from the bureaucracy, and certain posts, such as those of judges or central bankers, should remain independent from outside political interference.[72] Following on from this, third, democratic governments should be able to call upon the services of a 'well-trained bureaucracy of good standing and tradition, endowed with a strong sense of duty and a no less strong *esprit de corps*', to ensure government doesn't descend into one of amateurs.[73] Fourth, there should be 'democratic self-control', both in the sense of 'loyal opposition' and in the sense that politicians should not lower themselves to demagogic behaviour that might destabilise the system.[74] Finally, there should be 'a large tolerance for difference of opinion'.

In all these things, however, Schumpeter warned that during troubled times democracy might be at a disadvantage, and that exceptional moments might

---

67. Schumpeter, *Capitalism, Socialism and Democracy*, p. 257.

68. Quentin Skinner, 'The Empirical Theorists of Democracy and Their Critics: A Plague on Both Their Houses', *Political Theory*, Vol. 1, No. 3, 1973, pp. 287–306.

69. Schumpeter, *Capitalism, Socialism and Democracy*, p. 257.

70. Ibid., p. 258.

71. Ibid., pp. 258–9.

72. Ibid., p. 260.

73. Ibid.

74. Ibid., p. 261.

require a temporary *dictator*, as in ancient Roman times.[75] This has led some scholars to wonder whether Schumpeter was in part responding to Carl Schmitt, and has led Josiah Ober to qualify Schumpeter's theory as 'Caesarist', especially when one considers that the 'social stratum' Schumpeter desires is a military one, and that one way of conceiving competition is through the metaphor of war.[76] There is undoubtedly something to this, but it is important to underline that the figure who is explicitly named—twice—in this section is Edmund Burke.[77] This appeal to Burke has lead Medearis to label Schumpeter a 'conservative', and that tag can be retained if it is associated with liberal, given at a minimum Schumpeter's economic position, making him a 'liberal-conservative'.[78]

Medearis argues that Schumpeter has not one but two theories of democracy: the 'elitist' and the 'transformative'. The former is what we have explored so far, but the second stresses 'the importance of democratic beliefs and ideology', highlighting the 'radicalising, dynamic effects of movements that attempt to realise democratic values and act on democratic ideologies', all elements the former downplays or denies.[79] If the 'transformative' conception recognises democracy as an ideology, a 'system of beliefs, practices, and values capable of motivating political action', the 'elite' model instead depicts 'democracy in static terms and as institutionally stable'.[80] In short, one is dynamic and the other is static. Medearis' point is that Schumpeter developed his 'elitist' conception of democracy in response to the 'transformative' one: he wanted to make democracy safe from the rising tide of democratic socialism he had experienced before coming to the US in 1932. His 'competitive' model was a way to theorise a form of society in which 'elites could restrain the pace and nature of democratic change'.[81]

Schumpeter was born into a wealthy textile manufacturing family in Triesch (now Třešť in the Czech Republic), then part of Austria-Hungary. He was Catholic, and considered himself part of the local German-speaking elite, not

75. Ibid., p. 263.

76. JanaLee Cherneski, 'An Unacknowledged Adversary: Carl Schmitt, Joseph Schumpeter, and the Classical Doctrine of Democracy', *Critical Review*, Vol. 29, No. 4, 2017, pp. 447–472 and Ober, 'Joseph Schumpeter's Caesarist Democracy'.

77. Schumpeter, *Capitalism, Socialism and Democracy*, pp. 259, 262.

78. Medearis, *Joseph A. Schumpeter*.

79. Medearis, *Joseph Schumpeter's Two Theories of Democracy*, p. 4.

80. Ibid., pp. 4, 8.

81. Ibid.

Czech. His father died when he was four and his mother brought him to Vienna, to integrate into the metropolitan elite. And Schumpeter succeeded, much to his mother's delight, becoming a university professor (Czernowitz, Graz, Bonn: a public profile that included involvement in policy debates), a (short-lived) Minister of Finance for the post-war Republic of German-Austria (he later proposed in *The Tax State* a capital levy to pay the war-debts),[82] and the president and board member of a number of banks (Biedermann, Kaufmann).[83] During his schooling at the Theresianum, Schumpeter is thought to have adopted the 'aristocratic attitude of ironic detachment', a pose he kept till his Harvard days—he emigrated to the US in 1932—where he was known for his 'mordant wit, the self-admitted and only slightly self-depreciating snob, the teller of tales, many exaggerated, others self-aggrandising'.[84] He is thought to have said in his youth that he had set himself three goals in life: to be the greatest economist in the world, to be the best horseman in all of Austria and the greatest lover in all of Vienna.[85] He said he had reached two of his goals, but never specified which two, but was once overheard saying that there were many fine horsemen in Austria. He was married three times.

Schumpeter, therefore, wanted to defend the society he had been successful in, one still dominated by the military aristocracy, but within which a provincial bourgeois like himself could arrive.[86] It is this model he idealised in the notion of English 'Tory' democracy.[87] This helps us make sense of *Capitalism, Socialism and Democracy*. If capitalism is to be replaced by a form of socialism, as the book made out, what of democracy? Would it be able to survive? To that question Schumpeter offered an ambiguous response: democracy, understood as the democratic method he defended, and socialism were not incompatible, but neither were they the same.[88] Non-democratic socialism is

82. Medearis, *Joseph A. Schumpeter*, p. 59.

83. Ibid., pp. 1–33.

84. Ibid., pp. 5, 24. On Schumpeter's irony and the impact on his political theory, see Natasha Piano, '"Schumpeterianism" Revised: The Critique of Elites in *Capitalism, Socialism and Democracy*', *Critical Review*, Vol. 29, No. 4, 2017, pp. 505–529; Peter Boettke, Solomom Stein and Virgil Storr, 'Schumpeter, Socialism, and Irony', *Critical Review*, Vol. 29, No. 4, 2017, pp. 415–446; Jerry Muller, 'Capitalism, Socialism, and Irony: Understanding Schumpeter in Context', *Critical Review*, Vol. 13, Nos. 3–4, 1999, pp. 239–267.

85. Ibid., p. 25.

86. Ibid., pp. 4–5, 13–4, 66.

87. Ibid., p. 9. Medearis, *Joseph Schumpeter's Two Theories of Democracy*, pp. 19ff.

88. Schumpeter, *Capitalism, Socialism and Democracy*, p. 252.

possible, but modern democracy is 'a product of the capitalist process'.[89] This meant both that capitalism and democracy could go together, but also that democracy might be saved from socialism, if socialism were limited to the economic sphere:

> this is no reason why they should have to disappear along with capitalism. General elections, parties, parliaments, cabinets and prime ministers may still prove to be the most convenient instruments for dealing with the agenda that the socialist order may reserve for political decision.[90]

The fear—and here Schumpeter's background as the son of a textile manufacturer reappeared—was that democracy be extended to the economic sphere. Even Karl Kautsky, according to Schumpeter, condemned the idea that 'managers of plants should be elected by the workmen of the same plants'.[91]

V: Pareto

The influence Weber had on Schumpeter's thought has been highlighted by a number of commentators, not least by David Beetham, David Held and Green.[92] Certainly it is uncomplicated to see Weber's imprint on Schumpeter's advocacy of bureaucracy or even a leadership-style democracy with a 'machine', but one might wonder whether an equally important figure is Pareto.[93] As we've seen, Schumpeter articulated his economic theory of 'creative destruction' in explicit contrast to Pareto and Walras' 'equilibrium' model, but that did not stop him from lauding Pareto as one of the ten great economists, much like Marx, whom he was also critical of.[94] More pointedly, we've also seen how Schumpeter relied on Pareto, whom he explicitly named, in the critique of the 'classical doctrine of democracy' he developed in his section on 'Human Nature in Politics'.

89. Ibid., pp. 264–5. See, further, George Thomas, 'Can Liberal Democracy Survive Capitalism?', *Critical Review*, Vol. 29, No. 4, 2017, pp. 530–544.

90. Ibid., p. 267.

91. Ibid.

92. David Beetham, *Max Weber and the Theory of Modern Politics*, Cambridge, Polity Press, 1985, p. 2; David Held, 'Competitive Elitism and the Technocratic Vision', *Models of Democracy*, Cambridge, Polity Press, 2006, pp. 125–157; Green, *The Eyes of the People*, p. 166.

93. Schumpeter, *Capitalism, Socialism and Democracy*, p. 251.

94. Schumpeter, 'Pareto'.

Joel Isaac has shown how Schumpeter was part of the seminal Harvard Pareto circle during the time of his writing of *Capitalism, Socialism and Democracy*; the circle was to play a key role in the development of the social sciences post-war.[95] Indeed, as Medearis has written, 'Weber's influence on Schumpeter is a somewhat difficult topic, because while Schumpeter explicitly referred to elite theory in the course of laying out his conception of democracy as method, he did not refer in these passages to Weber.'[96] The impact of Pareto, therefore, on Schumpeter's thought seems averred, but what this chapter wishes to claim is that Pareto is relevant not only for Schumpeter's economic thought or his critique of the 'classical' democratic model, but also for the development of his 'minimalist' alternative.

Putting Schumpeter in dialogue with the 'elitists' more generally, namely Mosca and Michels, already reveals a few of things. The first, most obviously, is that Schumpeter was not the first to claim that the majority do not rule: that honour belongs to Mosca, the first to pronounce this in a modern setting in his 1896 *The Ruling Class*. Nor can Schumpeter claim the paternity of the idea of 'having your friends elect you'—namely that a political class should decide which candidates should run and try to get them elected in a rather top-down way[97]—which again goes to Mosca, and Michels said something along these lines too, as we have seen. The idea that 'the people never actually rule but they can always be made to do so by definition' is already announced in Michels' damning conclusion of the possibility of democracy overcoming the 'iron law of oligarchy' in his 1911 *Political Parties*.[98] To be fair to Schumpeter, he did not seem directly aware of either Mosca's or Michels' work. The same, however, cannot be said of Pareto's work.

What did Pareto bring to Schumpeter? Beyond the principles of 'Pareto efficiency' discussed above, there is also the 'Pareto principle'—the 80/20 rule— that established that 80% of wealth will always belong to 20% of the population. Brought into the realm of politics, the elitist implications are clear. And of course Pareto was the first to give us the term *élite*, from the French, as we use it today. He first did so in his 1902 book *Les systèmes socialistes*, in which he tried to determine what a new socialist elite would look like, and what consequences

95. Joel Isaac, *Working Knowledge: Making the Human Sciences from Parsons to Kuhn*, Cambridge (MA), Harvard University Press, 2012, pp. 63–91.

96. Medearis, *Joseph Schumpeter's Two Theories of Democracy*, p. 113.

97. Schumpeter, *Capitalism, Socialism and Democracy*, p. 251.

98. Ibid., p. 222.

it would have for politics and the economy. Put beside *Capitalism, Socialism and Democracy*, we can see the kindred spirit that animated both books, and it should come as no surprise that Schumpeter was drawn to thinkers who, like him, engaged with Marx without wanting to come to the same conclusions.

It is noticeable, however, that although the 'elite' epithet is ascribed to his theory, much as it has been done throughout this chapter, Schumpeter did not use the word. Instead, he wrote of 'leadership', which brings him closer to Weber.[99] Using 'leadership' was a way to frame 'elite' theories in a more democratic way, a move Dahl would explicitly make, as we shall see in the following chapter. Yet in his section on the 'conditions' of success of his democratic method, Schumpeter stipulated the need for the 'human material' in politics to be of 'sufficiently high quality', often code for an elite.[100] He continued by explaining that what has guaranteed so far that requisite 'high quality' has been 'the existence of a social stratum, itself a product of a severely selective process, that takes to politics as a matter of course'.[101] It is here that we reconnect with Pareto, who identified two strata in society:

(1) a lower stratum, the *non-élite*, with whose possible influence on government we are not just here concerned; then (2) a higher stratum, *the élite*, which is divided into two: (*a*) a governing *élite*; (*b*) a non-governing *élite*.[102]

Both Pareto and Schumpeter were interested in the governing elite. But what is important to see is that by making a 'social stratum' a key pre-requisite for his 'minimalist democracy', Schumpeter integrated elites into his theory of democracy. Much as he had made democracy safe for capitalism, he made 'elite theory' safe for democracy.

Conclusion: Dynamic, Transformative and Oppositional Democracy

With his 'minimalist' democracy, Schumpeter achieved two aims. First, he was able to formulate a theory of democracy that was resistant to the (socialist) transformative claims associated with it at the time: namely that all aspects of the state should be run along the lines of the 'will of the people'. Against this,

---

99. Medearis, *Joseph Schumpeter's Two Theories of Democracy*, pp. 7, 113–114.
100. Schumpeter, *Capitalism, Socialism and Democracy*, p. 257.
101. Ibid., p. 258; Ober, 'Joseph Schumpeter's Caesarist Democracy', pp. 486–7.
102. Pareto, *The Mind and Society*, Vol. III, #2234.

second, he offered a definition of democracy in which the people's participation would be limited to choosing their leaders—and would not extend beyond it. The rest of 'politics'—the bureaucracy, banking, military, the political class itself—would remain the realm of the higher social stratum, or, in other words, the elite. In this way Schumpeter was able to save parts of the old world—the Austro-Hungarian Empire he had done so well in—for the new, namely, the coming socialist wave.

Given the dominance of Schumpeter's ideas in both the academy and in the public, where elections still serve as the benchmark for judging whether a regime is democratic or not, he may well have achieved what he set out to do: when we think of democracy today, we think about it how Schumpeter would have wanted us, as elite competition, and not as ideological transformation. But how much has been lost along the way? The elitist underpinning of Schumpeter's theory is clear to see, and his concession that his theory would struggle with theorising autocratic regimes, when we see many authoritarian figures claiming 90% support at the ballot box, may have returned to bite. Perhaps the biggest loss, however, is that in his attempt to rigidify and reduce elite theory to his minimalist conception, much of the richness and subtlety of the theory has disappeared. To talk only of Pareto, the idea of 'foxes' and 'lions' already offers us a useful conceptual tool to make sense of what type of rulers we are dealing with. All three theorists—Mosca, Pareto and Michels— had a much fuller and more dynamic account of how political change might occur: one Schumpeter explicitly wanted to stop.

Schumpeter wanted to slow down the democratic dynamic, to constrain it within a limited political sphere. Although his theory has movement at its core—elite competition, i.e. the circulation of political elites competing for votes—his desire was for the overall system to be static. Movement would be restricted to a very limited field, namely elections, where it could be kept in check, whilst the rest of society would be preserved from its more transformative claims: claims Mosca, Pareto and Michels were much more open to, and often encouraged (Mosca the middle class, Pareto the circulation of elites, Michels syndicalism). Schumpeter opposed these transformations *en connaissance de cause*: he had experienced first-hand socialist revolutions in his native Austria, and feared them. This was his warning to his American friends: *Capitalism, Socialism and Democracy* was published during Schumpeter's time at Harvard.[103] This knowledge is what makes Schumpeter such a fascinating

103. Medearis, 'Schumpeter, the New Deal, and Democracy', pp. 819–832.

transitional figure between the early elitists (Mosca, Pareto and Michels) and the latter (Dahl, Mills, Aron), whom we shall now turn to. He knew both worlds; he is the link between them. He set the tone in restricting the theories of Mosca, Pareto and Michels to a rather narrower, static, base. But denying change is not the same as stopping it. It may be time to look beyond Schumpeter to see what we might learn anew for democracy.[104]

Medearis' aim with *Joseph Schumpeter's Two Theories of Democracy* was to rehabilitate the 'transformative' vision of democracy against Schumpeter's 'minimalist' one. Building on the velvet revolutions of 1989, with their notions of 'antipolitics' and 'civil society', in his conclusion to the book Medearis defended transformative democracy as a means to increase the 'participatory and developmental arguments for democracy'.[105]

There are interesting overlaps between Medearis' 'transformative' democracy and the type of dynamic democracy defended in this book. First, both posit a distinction between dynamic (transformative) and static (elite theory, in Schumpeter's version) theories of democracy. Second, transformative democracy integrates social and economic structures into the theory: 'a transformative conception emphasises that democratic beliefs and practices could be applied to social and economic structures as well as political ones.'[106] This isn't without recalling, for instance, Mosca's notion of 'social forces'. Third, there is a focus on social movements and the impact they can have on institutions and social structures—'a transformative conception further emphasises the importance of social movements and groups who articulate their interests and formulate their programmes of action in democratic terms'[107]—and in the introduction we have

104. Graeme Duncan and Steven Lukes, 'The New Democracy', *Political Studies*, Vol. 9, No. 2, 1963, pp. 156–177.

105. Medearis, *Joseph Schumpeter's Two Theories of Democracy*, p. 210. Medearis offers a nice story about how Eastern European movements wanted to achieve 'authentic workers' self-government', but that the anti-communist context meant that those ideas were discredited, not helped by the neo-liberal 'Washington consensus', such that Eastern Europeans found themselves with classic—Schumpeterian—liberal-democracies (ibid., pp. 203–207).

106. Medearis, *Joseph Schumpeter's Two Theories of Democracy*, p. 201. See also ibid., p. 210: 'a transformative conception of democracy embraces the economic and social implications of democratic ideologies and values—indeed, it embraces the potential application of democratic principles to the full range of social, economic, and political institutions'.

107. Ibid., p. 201. See also ibid., p. 209: 'a transformative conception of democracy focuses squarely on reshaping institutions and changing enduring social structures. . . . One of the most important aspects of democratic ideologies has been their connection to movements for social reconstruction'.

explored how dynamic democracy focuses on the interaction of social movements and political parties, and how political change can occur when one part
of the established elite rallies to the cause of the movement. Yet there are differences too. Medearis sees transformative democracy as a critique of liberal-
democracy—'one of the key reasons for reclaiming a transformative conception
of democracy is to deploy it critically against liberal capitalist institutions and
models'[108]—whereas dynamic democracy uses elite theories precisely to *defend*
liberal-democracy (e.g. Mosca's 'juridical defence').

In his subsequent book *Why Democracy Is Oppositional*, Medearis developed a truly novel theory of 'oppositional' democracy.[109] Building on his work
on Schumpeter, Medearis anchored his theory of 'oppositional' democracy in
a theory of alienation grounded in Marx and John Dewey, drawing from the
latter the theory that we are often the agents of our own oppression—we are
the ones who unconsciously build the hierarchical structures in the world that
oppress us—to study the different resistance movements to structures of oppression, from the post-war 'workers' councils', the Civil Rights movements
and Occupy Wall Street.[110]

Like 'transformative' democracy before it, 'oppositional' democracy shares
a focus on social movements. This comes as a critique of much contemporary
political theory, which it sees as blind to social movements, seeing them as
either 'tainted activities' or simply a 'means to an end' in a non-ideal world.[111]
Instead, oppositional democracy sees movements as a core feature of democracy, and indeed democracy as a never-ending struggle to combat the oppressive structures we invertedly build.[112] Democracy is therefore not understood
to be some ideal-type 'regime', but as a form of 'action' in a pre-existing world:
it is an 'intervention' in a structure already in place.[113] There are no 'legislative'
foundings, as theories of constituent power might propose.[114] This also means
that power, coercion and violence are explicitly theorised in the framework.[115]
Indeed, much like 'oppositional democracy' desires to collapse the distinction

108. Ibid., p. 207.

109. John Medearis, *Why Democracy Is Oppositional*, Cambridge (MA), Harvard University
Press, 2015.

110. Ibid., pp. 3–7.

111. Ibid., pp. 17, 51.

112. Ibid., pp. 1–2, 5, 49, 132, 146–147.

113. Ibid., pp. 17, 132, 138, 150.

114. Ibid., p. 133.

115. Ibid., p. 147.

between ideal and non-ideal theory, between 'realism' and an 'ideal'—
movements are the reality of politics, but are also the vehicle through which
certain ideals of participation can be, if not achieved, better approximated—it
also collapses the distinction between democracy and democratisation, between having 'achieved' the state of democracy or continually striving towards
it: in the struggle for democracy itself (democratisation), certain ideals of
equality and participation can be realised.[116] Finally, as part of this construction, oppositional democracy sees much of contemporary political theory,
especially in its 'deliberative' or 'elite' strands, as fundamentally static, building
walls to isolate itself from the tumult of real politics: 'elite' theorist quarantin-
ing itself from the people, in its Schumpeterian version, or, again, 'deliberative'
democracy finding a 'refuge' from the reality of politics to come to pure, equal
decisions, even if it finds certain affinities with participatory, agonistic or fugitive theories of democracy.[117]

Dynamic democracy happily shares many features with 'oppositional democracy', and teasing out those affinities, alongside the differences between
the two, allows us to more clearly identify the contours of dynamic democracy.
The first is that both see democracy as a never-ending struggle. Medearis puts
it nicely that it is an 'ongoing struggle . . . without any expectation of transcen-
dent victory',[118] or indeed that democracy, in a rather Nietzschean turn of
phrase, is something that is always in a 'continual, active process of
becoming'.[119] There is a shared view of democracy not as an end-point but
rather an ongoing process, collapsing the democratic/democratisation divide,
with certain 'actions', or, in the language of dynamic democracy, the application of force to the 'iron law of oligarchy' to make it more pliable. Democracy
is therefore not a regime but a place on a continuum between more democratic or more oligarchic, in the sense of how loose or firm the control by the
elite is. Nor is it some abstract ideal to be achieved.

Instead, democracy is an 'intervention' in a specific historical, structural
context, and needs to be understood and analysed in that way: the time and
historical dimensions to dynamic politics are key, not some ahistorical artifact.
Both, moreover, share a focus on the state:[120] changing politics is about the

116. Ibid., pp. 13, 34, 51.
117. Ibid., pp. 9, 17, 22, 24, 31, 40, 49, 149.
118. Ibid., p. 2.
119. Ibid., p. 3.
120. Ibid., pp. 135, 145, 147.

type of pressure or force social movements can exert on those—elites—who control the institutional levers of power. There is no 'legislative' founding, which in the dynamic account can only be something like Mosca's 'political formula' or Pareto's 'derivation', a post-facto justification for established elite rule. And linked to that, fundamentally, is an interest in the role movements play in democratic politics. Finally, there is the reproduction of a dynamic/static divide, with 'oppositional' democracy opposing the wall-building of both Schumpeterian and deliberative theories of democracy. Looking for 'publicly giving reasons' for decisions can only be, again, in a dynamic context, a post-facto derivation of an interest or decisions already made.[121]

There are, however, differences. The most important is that whilst dynamic democracy shares with Medearis' oppositional theory the view that Schumpeter tried to slow down the dynamism of democracy—to make it more static—dynamic democracy finds its inspiration from the earlier elitists, Mosca, Pareto and Michels, whom Schumpeter himself engaged with, instead of Marx and Dewey. The point is that dynamism is already in existence with the earlier 'elitists': there is no need to throw out the dynamic baby with the Schumpeterian bathwater.

The second concerns movements. Medearis writes:

> My argument about alienation does not purport to show that democracy is reducible to movements, that distinctive movement activities are somehow the true core of democracy, or that other, more widely recognised democratic practices that are not associated with movements are somehow diminished by that fact.[122]

Of course, in this context Medearis is talking about social movements per se, whereas dynamic democracy is focused on the movement, often brought about by movements themselves, of challenges to established elite rule. So there is a conceptual difference here: Medearis is interested in the role of movements *within* democracy and democratic theory, whereas dynamic democracy thinks democracy *is* the movement of challenge to elites. Medearis is quick to point out that 'not all movements are democratic',[123] and this is something dynamic democracy acknowledges too, that certain challenges to

---

121. Ibid., p. 21.

122. Ibid., p. 147. See also ibid., p. 18: 'movements do not somehow *define* democracy (as some would say voting or deliberation do [*sic*])'.

123. Ibid.

established elite rule might reinforce, rather than loosen, oligarchic power. Yet within this, oppositional democracy also offers a further reasoning as to why these challenges will continually appear. Medearis writes: 'the recurrence of the conditions that make movements necessary entails the continuation or return of certain kinds of power relations'.[124] In short: the exclusionary nature of power means that there will always be disgruntled forces that will arise to challenge the inequal distribution of power. That is in the nature of power itself. In the language of dynamic democracy: a new elite will always rise to challenge the established elite.

Third, dynamic democracy remains sceptical that the people can actually rule. In this it remains fundamentally elitist—it 'deprecates the agency of ordinary people'[125]—in the sense that it does not believe the people on their own are able to rise up, but are in essential need of leadership. It does not deny, therefore, that new leaders can arise from the people—a point oppositional democracy might agree with—to challenge and perhaps replace the old ones, but it remains committed to the view that elites always rule, and the people in themselves never will; in Pareto's A-B-C formulation: the new leaders will become the new elite (B), having challenged to old elite (A) with the help of the people (C), but C remains out of power. Certainly, in their challenge to the old elite, new elites might increase participation and indeed maintain that in their rule—that is the hope of 'democratising' the iron law of oligarchy—but the realisation of some form of Port Hudson participatory democracy remains forlorn in this conception.[126] This is why dynamic democracy remains a theory of liberal-democracy.

As with oppositional democracy, this distinction also allows us to differentiate dynamic democracy from other forms of democratic theory, not least agonistic and fugitive democracy. In his account of agonism, Medearis focuses on the construction of identity through conflict and Chantal Mouffe's theory of agonistic democracy and its inability to construe race in its mapping out of political oppositions.[127] What dynamic democracy can say to that is that identities can indeed come out in the struggle for power, but are broadly constrained to two: lions or foxes. More to the point: what dynamic democracy wishes to reveal is the fundamentally elitist basis for an agonistic democracy, whose

124. Ibid., p. 50.
125. Ibid., p. 17
126. Ibid., p. 157.
127. Ibid., pp. 159–162.

emphasis on struggle it necessarily shares: the type of time, energy and work demanded by agonistic democracy can only realistically be undertaken by a very select group of people.[128] So the claim here is that agonistic democracy can be welcomed into the bosom of dynamic democracy: it is one element that can help articulate the creation of a new elite, but it cannot offer a theory of political change more broadly. The other—fugitive—theory of democracy appears to share a desire for movement, but this is a desire for a momentary escape from the constraints of modern power structures, not an engagement with them.[129]

Indeed, if there is a final difference between oppositional democracy and dynamic democracy, it is that the former, as its name suggests, is quite defensive, trying to counter the weight of oppressive regimes. Dynamic democracy has a more positive or active conception of politics, even if it is one of 'pessimism of strength'. Whilst it acknowledges the perennialism of power, it sees politics as a continual process of change, not one always fighting the same oppressive, economic, bureaucratic and political forces. With dynamism things do change, even if we need to always keep fighting for it. Here at least there is a final agreement between dynamic and transformative democracy: 'each generation must provide that for itself'.[130]

128. See Hugo Drochon, 'Nietzsche and Politics', *Nietzsche-Studien*, Vol. 39, 2010, pp. 663–677.

129. Medearis, *Why Democracy Is Oppositional*, p. 164.

130. Medearis, *Joseph Schumpeter's Two Theories of Democracy*, p. 212.

5

Dahl and Mills, Polyarchy or Power Elite?

1956 SAW the start of a debate in America that had a fundamental impact on the development of the social sciences in general and democratic thinking in particular. On the one hand the motorbike-riding, pipe-smoking maverick 'New Left' sociologist and public intellectual C. Wright Mills (1916–1962) published *The Power Elite*,[1] which argued that in the US a 'power elite'—a combination of political, commercial and military elites—now ruled the country behind the façade of democratic politics.[2] On the other, Robert Dahl (1915–2014) published his *A Preface to Democratic Theory*,[3] which put forward what has come to be viewed as the opposing 'pluralist' case: that power in American is in reality much more diffuse.[4] Instead of a 'power elite' controlling everything, Dahl argued that different groups and parties all compete for influence

1. C. Wright Mills, *The Power Elite*, Oxford, Oxford University Press, 2000.

2. Irving Horowitz, *C. Wright Mills: An American Utopian*, New York, The Free Press, 1984; Tom Hayden, *Radical Nomad: C. Wright Mills and His Times*, Abingdon, Routledge, 2016; Stanley Aronowitz, *Taking It Big: C. Wright Mills and the Making of Public Intellectuals*, New York, Columbia University Press, 2012; Daniel Geary, *Radical Ambition: C. Wright Mills, the Left, and American Social Thought*, Berkeley, University of California Press, 2009; Jim Miller, 'Democracy and the Intellectual: C. Wright Mills Reconsidered', *Salmagundi*, Vol. 70/71, 1986, pp. 82–101; Richard Gillam, 'C. Wright Mills and the Politics of Truth: The Power Elite Revisited', *American Quarterly*, Vol. 27, No. 4, 1975, pp. 461–479.

3. Robert Dahl, *A Preface to Democratic Theory*, Chicago, University of Chicago Press, 2006.

4. Note that Dahl claimed he never developed a theory of [legal] pluralism, but rather a 'theory of *democracy* in which organisational pluralism plays a part' ('Robert A. Dahl: Normative Theory, Empirical Research, and Democracy' in Gerardo Munck and Richard Snyder, eds., *Passion, Craft, and Method in Comparative Politics*, Baltimore, Johns Hopkins University Press, 2007, p. 118).

over the political process, none of them able to establish a permanent position of control. It is from this competition that political liberty is to be found.

Mills' writings, especially his subsequent *The Sociological Imagination* (1959),[5] had a major influence on the growth of American sociology, and *The Power Elite* has been in continuous print since its first publication: a new edition was published in 2000, with Alan Wolfe concluding in his afterword that '*The Power Elite* is rivalled by only very few books of its period in terms of longevity'.[6] Even Fidel Castro, whom Mills interviewed in Cuba during the 1960s, claimed to have read it.[7] Five years after its first publication President Eisenhower, in his 1961 Farewell Address, famously denounced the 'military-industrial complex': he may even have wanted to say (the claim is disputed) the 'military-industrial-*congressional* complex', but the congressional part was struck out from the early drafts of the speech as being too *risqué*.[8] The irony of course is that Eisenhower, a former military man who served as president of Columbia University where Mills taught, personified exactly the 'power elite' type Mills decried. Dahl, who died in 2014, has often been described as the 'doyen' of American political science,[9] and his theory of polyarchy remains central to our thinking about democracy today.[10]

At stake within this debate was American democracy itself. Had it become a 'power elite' oligarchy, as Mills decried, or was it still democracy's best modern approximation, as Dahl's theory of 'polyarchy' prescribed? The debate also politically positioned its two main participants: Mills as the radical talking 'truth' to power, Dahl as the conservative defender of the American status quo.

Both, however, shared a number of assumptions. They shared, for instance, a residual fear of the masses: Dahl, as Kyong-Min Son has shown, because he

---

5. C. Wright Mills, *The Sociological Imagination*, Oxford, Oxford University Press, 1959.

6. Alan Wolfe, 'Afterword' in Mills, *The Power Elite*, p. 378.

7. Kathryn Mills and Pamela Mills, eds., *C. Wright Mills: Letters and Autobiographical Writings*, Berkeley, University of California Press, 2000, p. 312.

8. Geoffrey Perret, *Eisenhower*, New York, Random House, 1999; Aronowitz, *Taking It Big*, pp. 175–8; Geary, *Radical Ambition*, pp. 156, 166–7.

9. Joseph Femia, *Against the Masses: Varieties of Anti-Democratic Thought since the French Revolution*, Oxford, Oxford University Press, 2001, p. 4.

10. David Baldwin and Mark Haugaard, 'Robert A. Dahl: An Unended Quest', *Journal of Political Power*, Vol. 8, No. 2, 2015, pp. 159–166.

worried that mass participation might destabilise the democratic regime;[11] Mills, although he advocated Deweyian 'educated publics'—never entirely mass-based to begin with—always thought they should be led by intellectuals like him. Yet both also demanded greater participation in the political sphere: Mills' ideas led to the development of 'participatory democracy',[12] whilst Dahl maintained throughout his life an interest in economic democracy, and belatedly came to demand the better inclusion of African-Americans in the political process.[13] What is most striking, however, is that neither party to the dispute contested the existence of elites within the democratic system: Mills' 'power elite', naturally, but Dahl's polyarchy was also characterised by '*minorities rule*'.[14] In doing so, both harked back to the debate at the turn of the twentieth century between those we now call, following S. M. Lipset, the 'elite theorists of democracy': Gaetano Mosca, Vilfredo Pareto and Robert Michels.[15]

The goal of this chapter is twofold. First, it aims to reconstruct the debate between Mills and Dahl from the vantage point of the earlier elite theorists of democracy, Mosca, Pareto and Michels. It will argue that both Mills and— perhaps more surprisingly—Dahl were in reality much closer to the concerns of these earlier elitists, and Michels in particular, than is usually supposed. This also means that their positions were closer to one another than is commonly

11. Kyong-Min Son, *The Eclipse of the Demos: The Cold War and the Crisis of Democracy before Neoliberalism*, Lawrence, University of Kansas Press, 2020. For a review, see Hugo Drochon, 'Kyong-Min Son, The Eclipse of the Demos: The Cold War and the Crisis of Democracy before Neoliberalism', *Perspectives on Politics*, Vol. 19, No. 1, 2021, pp. 604–605.

12. Hayden, *Radical Nomad*, pp. 163–192; Miller, 'Democracy and the Intellectual', p. 96; Aronowitz, *Taking It Big*, p. 167.

13. See Tom Hoffman, 'The Quiet Desperation of Robert Dahl's (Quiet) Radicalism', *Critical Review*, Vol. 15, No. 1–2, 2003, pp. 87–122; Richard Krouse, 'Polyarchy & Participation: The Changing Democratic Theory of Robert Dahl', *Polity*, Vol. 14, No. 3, 1982, pp. 441–463; Robert Mayer, 'Robert Dahl and the Right to Workplace Democracy', *The Review of Politics*, Vol. 63, No. 2, 2001, pp. 221–247; Robert Dahl, 'A Right to Workplace Democracy? Response to Robert Mayer', *The Review of Politics*, Vol. 63, No. 2, 2001, pp. 249–253; Robert Mayer, 'A Rejoinder to Robert Dahl', *The Review of Politics*, Vol. 63, No. 2, 2001, pp. 255–257.

14. Dahl, *Preface*, pp. 131–133.

15. S. M. Lipset, 'Introduction' to Robert Michels, *Political Parties: A Sociological Study of the Oligarchic Tendencies of Modern Democracy*, trans. Eden and Cedar Paul, New York, The Free Press, 1962, p. 33. Giovanni Sartori, *The Theory of Democracy Revisited. Part One: The Contemporary Debate*, Chatham, Chatham House Publishers, 1987, p. 157, writes: 'the Schumpeter-Dahl line of authors are made to appear as a continuation of the Mosca-Pareto tradition of thought'.

understood. The reason is that both Mills and Dahl reproduced the intellectual framework of the earlier theorists in starting with the existence of elites within the system and then thinking about ways in which they can be controlled. As such the usual depiction of the 'elite' Mills versus the 'pluralist'—and therefore in some sense more 'democratic'—Dahl is misconstrued: the real point of divergence between them is whether elites are more likely to coordinate (Mills) or compete (Dahl). This does not mean that they did not differ in their evaluation of the elites they identified—Mills rejected the power elite whereas Dahl approved of polyarchy—but against this backdrop of the early elite theorists of democracy, Mills and Dahl in fact appear to be two sides of the same (elite) coin.

Second, in reconstructing the debate between Mills and Dahl, this chapter seeks to contribute to our understanding of the growth of the social sciences in America post-World War II. It means not to offer an alternative account to many that have been offered before—the attempted mapping of the 'hard sciences' onto social phenomena, often developed within certain interdisciplinary university seminars, and the role rational-choice theories, alongside the Americanisation of European liberalism, played in it[16]—but instead to build on these accounts by highlighting first how much that growth was articulated through these early figures (i.e. Mosca, Pareto and Michels) and second the language they employed to describe their societies, not least the word 'elite' itself. Indeed, it is precisely in the Harvard Pareto Seminar, started in 1932 by the biochemist Lawrence Joseph Henderson, that many of the future leading lights of American social science—Joseph Schumpeter, Pitirim Sorokin, Thomas North Whitehead, Henry Murray, Crane Brinton, Talcott Parsons—first developed their thoughts through reading Pareto's *Trattato*.[17] If the impact of these early elite theorists of democracy is averred, then one conclusion one might draw from this study is that the growth of the social sciences that drew from this tradition was in fact grounded in a fundamentally elitist view of the world.

---

16. Bernard Crick, *The American Science of Politics: Its Origins and Conditions*, London, Routledge and Kegan Paul, 1959; Joel Isaac, *Working Knowledge: Making the Human Sciences from Parsons to Kuhn*, Cambridge [MA], Harvard University Press, 2012; S. M. Amadae, *Rationalizing Capitalist Democracy: The Cold War Origins of Rational Choice Liberalism*, Chicago, Chicago University Press, 2003; Robert Adcock, *Liberalism and the Emergence of American Political Science: A Transatlantic Tale*, Oxford, Oxford University Press, 2014.

17. Isaac, *Working Knowledge*, pp. 63–91.

The first part of the chapter offers an historical reconstruction of the dispute between Mills and Dahl, starting in 1956 with the publication of Mills' *The Power Elite*, followed by, second, Dahl's *Preface*. After exploring, third, the criticism of Mill's book as a conspiracy theory, it moves to, fourth, Dahl's classic 1961 study of New Haven, *Who Governs?*,[18] and the publication Dahl himself considered to be his 'most complete formulation'[19] of democratic theory, *Democracy and its Critics* (1989).[20] That book, in many ways, represents his final engagement with that debate and offers a natural closing point to this study: the *bon vivant* and self-styled Don Juan Mills, who married four times (twice the same woman), and who was aware of his heart condition, which made him live a 'hurried' life, met his untimely death from his fourth heart attack in 1962 at the age of 45 (Dahl, in contrast, lived over twice that age, to 98).[21] It will highlight both the crucial role played by the early elitists in the debate and their impact on the elaboration of Mills' and Dahl's theories, thereby underlining the parallels between the two accounts of democracy.

By 1989 Dahl had moved away from his position of the mid-1950s to the 1960s to a more pessimistic view of American society, often overlooked in the literature, best articulated in his new 1976 preface to *Politics, Economics, and Welfare* with Charles Lindblom, which echoed Mills' view on the 'imperial' presidency, inequality and managers.[22] But one of the claims of this chapter, fifth, is that many of the ideas Dahl defended from the 1970s onwards, notably Yugoslav social-democracy or workplace democracy, were in fact already present during his time as a PhD student. In the end, Jeffrey Isaac might be right to see the 1950s and the 1960s as a period of exception rather than the rule in Dahl's political thought: a move rightwards towards the Cold War 'vital centre', in tension with his earlier—and indeed later—more left-wing inclinations.[23]

18. Robert Dahl, *Who Governs? Democracy and Power in an American City*, New Haven, Yale University Press, 2005.

19. Robert Dahl, 'Reflections on *A Preface to Democratic Theory*', in Dahl, *Preface*, pp. xii, xvi and xix.

20. Robert Dahl, *Democracy and Its Critics*, New Haven, Yale University Press, 1989.

21. Horowitz, *C. Wright Mills*, pp. 5–6. See Miller, 'Democracy and the Intellectual', p. 84 for a description of Mill's sexual exploits: 'old hands at Texas still tell the story about Mills and the coed he seduced after call one night—on a desk, with lights blazing, in front of a window, in full view of another class meeting in a building directly opposite'.

22. Robert Dahl and Charles Lindblom, *Politics, Economics, and Welfare*, New Brunswick, Transaction Publishers, 2020.

23. Jeffrey Isaac, *Power and Marxist Theory: A Realist View*, Ithaca, Cornell University Press, 1987. See also Jeffrey Isaac, 'Robert Dahl as Mentor', *The Washington Post*, 11 February 2014.

The penultimate section will argue that Mills and Dahl, because of their interest in the development of elites *within* (albeit different) institutions—parties, social clubs, the government, the military, companies—ties them closer to Michels than either Mosca or Pareto, because Michels was fundamentally concerned with the oligarchic nature of *political institutions*, whereas Mosca and Pareto sought to develop an *historical* or a *sociological* account of society in which institutions as such played a more minor role. Indeed, the focus on political institutions maps itself well onto accounts of the continuing role the state played in the development of American sciences after the war, as Ira Katznelson has pointed out.[24] We should therefore be wary of the temptation—very much present in Dahl[25]—to lump Mosca, Pareto and Michels together. Moreover, this proximity to Michels reinforces the proximity between Mills and Dahl themselves. Finally, if Mills and Dahl had had a fuller engagement with Michels, they would have realised that what they were both advocating, namely, increased competition and better responsiveness within the democratic system, in reality echoed how Michels thought the 'iron law of oligarchy' ought to be tackled in his original 1911 *Political Parties*.

The conclusion will reflect upon the renewed interest in Mosca, Pareto and Michels in recent work on democracy.[26] If Michels' emphasis on *institutional* domination seemed to be the fulcrum around which thinking surrounding democracy in the mid-twentieth century revolved, today's concern with the nefarious influence of *wealth* on democratic institutions suggests that Pareto's theory of 'demagogic plutocracy', with its emphasis on how the wealthy few manage to divert wealth to themselves, might serve as the more promising guide to thinking about our current political predicament.[27]

Retrieved 2 December 2014. https://www.washingtonpost.com/news/monkey-cage/wp/2014/02/11/robert-dahl-as-mentor/.

24. Ira Katznelson, 'A Seminar on the State' in *Desolation and Enlightenment: Political Knowledge after Total War, Totalitarianism, and the Holocaust*, New York, Columbia University Press, 2003, pp. 107–151.

25. Dahl, *Democracy and Its Critics*, pp. 268–77.

26. Jeffrey Green, *The Eyes of the People: Democracy in the Age of Spectatorship*, Oxford, Oxford University Press, 2011; Nadia Urbinati, *Democracy Disfigured: Opinion, Truth, and the People*, Cambridge [MA], Harvard University Press, 2014.

27. Thomas Piketty, *Capital in the Twenty-First Century*, Cambridge (MA), Harvard University Press, 2014; Martin Gilens, *Affluence and Influence: Economic Inequality and Political Power in America*, Princeton, Princeton University Press, 2014; Martin Gilens and Benjamin Page, 'Testing Theories of American Politics: Elites, Interest Groups, and Average Citizens', *Perspectives on Politics* Vol. 12, No. 3, 2014, pp. 564–581; Jeffrey Green, *The Shadow of Unfairness: A Plebeian Theory of Liberal Democracy*, Oxford, Oxford University Press, 2016; John McCormick,

I: The Power Elite

Both Mills and Dahl explicitly refer to the elite theorists of democracy in their writings. In *The Power Elite*, Mills based his interpretation of the elite directly on Pareto's theory: 'the statistical idea of choosing some value and calling those who have the most of it an elite derives, in modern times, from the Italian economist, Pareto'.[28] But he ultimately discarded Pareto's scheme, explaining that 'those who follow this approach end up not with one elite, but with a number corresponding to the number of values they select'.[29] For Pareto, every field of activity, whether the law, commerce or, indeed, thievery, has its own elite, whereas Mills wanted to argue that the political, commercial and military elites now consisted in *one* power elite. This power elite was composed of those who control the 'command posts' of the three major hierarchies: the 'Very Rich', 'Chief Executives' and the 'Corporate Rich' (i.e. the major landowners and those who control the largest corporations) control the economy; the 'Warlords' and the 'Military Ascendency' (senior military officers and the Joint Chiefs of Staff) control the military; and the 'Political Directorate' (the 'fifty-odd' men who control the executive branch of the US government, alongside senior politicians and civil servants) control politics.[30]

In preparation for *The Power Elite*, Mills had sketched some 'Notes on Mosca', which he subsequently published as an appendix to *The Sociological Imagination*.[31] There he explained that Mosca helped him finesse 'in a neat and meaningful way the Paretian distinction of governing and non-governing elites, in a way less formal than Pareto['s]', namely by portraying the three elements of the power elite as a type of ruling class separated from other,

---

Machiavellian Democracy, Cambridge, Cambridge University Press, 2011; John McCormick, *Reading Machiavelli: Scandalous Books, Suspect Engagements, and the Virtue of Populist Politics*, Princeton, Princeton University Press, 2018.

28. Mills, *The Power Elite*, p. 384 n. 3. The influence of Mosca, Pareto and Michels on Mills has been noted by Geary, *Radical Ambition*, p. 152; Bell, 'The Power Elite-Reconsidered', pp. 239, 245–6; Horowitz, *C. Wright Mills*, pp. 257, 263; and Gillam, 'C. Wright Mills and the Politics of Truth', p. 470.

29. Ibid.

30. Mills, *The Power Elite*, pp. 9–15; Geary, *Radical Ambition*, pp. 152–6; Horowitz, *C. Wright Mills*, p. 264.

31. C. Wright Mills, *The Sociological Imagination*, Oxford, Oxford University Press, 1959, pp. 203–4.

non-ruling, elites.[32] But in *The Power Elite* he rejected Mosca's trans-historical thesis as being tautological:

> It is not my thesis that for all epochs of human history and in all nations, a creative minority, a ruling class, an omnipotent elite, shape all historical events. Such statements, upon careful examination, usually turn out to be mere tautologies, and even when they are not, they are so entirely general as to be useless in the attempt to understand the history of the present.[33]

Mills' argument was that *at that specific moment and time*, i.e. 1950s' America, there existed something close to an omnipotent elite, but that had not always been the case and, hopefully, on Mills' account, wouldn't be in the future either.[34] What Mills was challenging was less the fact that minorities always rule than the inertia and fatality such a viewpoint engenders: he wanted majorities to organise to help counterbalance the power of the power elite.[35]

Building on his 1948 study of how labour leaders had been captured by 'bread and butter' economic politics in his *The New Men of Power: America's Labour Leaders,* and his 1951 account of how bureaucracies had 'politically emasculated and culturally stultified' middle-class workers in *White Collar: The American Middle Classes,* Mills' aim with *The Power Elite* was to shake the American public at large, and particularly what he took to be its maligned intelligentsia, out of its political slumber, so as to tackle the power elite and change the course of American history.[36] Indeed, Mills considered the three books a trilogy, in which he would uncover, in turn, the bottom, middle and top of the American social order.[37] The intellectuals he had in mind were his Cold War 'end of ideology' liberal colleagues at Columbia or farther up the street at the Union Theological Seminary: Daniel Bell, Arthur Schlesinger, S. M. Lipset, Richard Hofstadter and Reinhold Niebuhr.[38] Richard Gillam

---

32. Ibid., p. 204.

33. Mills, *The Power Elite,* p. 20, p. 386, n. 7; Horowitz, *C. Wright Mills,* p. 263.

34. Ibid., pp. 16–20. See Geary, *Radical Ambition,* p. 263.

35. C. Wright Mills, 'The Power Elite: Comment on Criticism', in John Summers, ed., *The Politics of Truth: Selected Writings of C. Wright Mills,* Oxford, Oxford University Press, 2008, p. 149.

36. Aronowitz, *Taking It Big,* p. 186.

37. Geary, *Radical Ambition,* p. 151; Aronowitz, *Taking It Big,* p. 172; Miller, 'Democracy and the Intellectual', pp. 90–1.

38. C. Wright Mills, 'Letter to the New Left', *New Left Review,* Vol. 1, No. 5, 1960; Geary, *Radical Ambition,* pp. 144–6, 165–6; Horowitz, *C. Wright Mills,* p. 271; Gillam, 'C. Wright Mills

puts it nicely when he writes: 'always something of a headhunter, Mills liked nothing better than to take his trophies from the bodies of opponents he had stalked personally on Morningside Heights—preferably in the familiar corridors of Fayerweather or Hamilton Halls'.[39] An insight into Mills' mind-set can be captured by his attitude towards the slogan of the French Revolution: liberty—yes, equality—yes, fraternity—no.

This explains why much of the debate surrounding Mosca takes place within a broader discussion of the theory of history and the role different agents have in shaping that history: 'we must not confuse the conception of the elite . . . with one theory about their role: that they are the history-makers of our time'.[40] Frustrated with what he took to be the unfulfilled promise of political equality, Mills developed a 'new radicalism' that, drawing on the tradition of John Dewey, called for active 'educated publics' led by intellectuals like himself—in this he remained an elitist[41]—to challenge the power elite who had irresponsibly subverted democracy to pursue their own ends.[42] Although the term wasn't yet used at the time, what Mills appeared to be advocating was a form of 'participatory democracy', and that is certainly how some of the 'New Left' radicals like Tom Hayden, who drafted the Students for a Democratic Society's Port Huron Statement, understood it.[43]

Michels is not directly referred to in *The Power Elite*, but his most famous maxim—the 'iron law of oligarchy'—makes an appearance in the chapter on 'The Mass Society'. The passage in question reads:

> The gap between speaker and listener, between power and public, leads less to any iron law of oligarchy than to the law of spokesmanship: as the pressure group expands, its leaders come to organise the opinions they 'represent'. So elections, as we have seen, become contests between two giant and unwieldy parties, neither of which the individual can truly feel that he influences, and neither of which is capable of winning psychologically

and the Politics of Truth', p. 462; Richard Gillam, 'Richard Hofstadter, C. Wright Mills, and the "Critical Ideal"', *The American Scholar*, Vol. 4, No. 1, 1978, pp. 69–85.

39. Gillam, 'C. Wright Mills and the Politics of Truth', p. 464.

40. Mills, *The Power Elite*, p. 20.

41. Gillam, 'Richard Hofstadter', C. Wright Mills, p. 78.

42. Geary, *Radical Ambition*, pp. 143–5, 160, 168; Aronowitz, *Taking It Big*, pp. 184–5; Gillam, 'C. Wright Mills and the Politics of Truth', p. 462; Horowitz, *C. Wright Mills*, p. 259; Miller, 'Democracy and the Intellectual', pp. 84, 91–3.

43. Hayden, *Radical Nomad*; pp. 163–192; Miller, 'Democracy and the Intellectual', p. 96; Aronowitz, *Taking It Big*, p. 167.

impressive or politically decisive majorities. And, in all this, the parties are of the same general form as other mass associations.[44]

Mills thus seems to accept Michels' view that 'who says organisation, says oligarchy',[45] rebranding it as a law of 'spokesmanship'. But there should be no doubt as to the oligarchic nature of this spokesmanship. Indeed, the 'iron law of oligarchy' would, at first sight, seem to go very much in the direction in which Mills wanted it to go: the US was now run by a politico-military-commercial oligarchy. Mills essentially conceded the point in a reply to his critics published in the 1957 Winter issue of *Dissent*, entitled 'Comment on Criticism', where he explained: 'Pareto's theory of the circulation of the elite? I don't accept that. Michels' iron law of oligarchy? I think it's a fairly good description of what has in fact happened in most mass organisations'.[46]

As a student of Weber, it is not surprising that Mills was acquainted with Michels' work, who was himself a student, and friend, of Weber's, and Mills explicitly recognised the filiation in the introduction to the edited collection of Weber's writings *From Max Weber*, which he compiled with Hans Gerth in 1946.[47] Moreover, the same year *The Power Elite* was published, Mills' colleague at Columbia Lipset published his study of trade-union democracy under the title *Union Democracy: The Internal Politics of the International Typographical Union* (1956), which took at its starting point Michels' law.[48] Indeed, Lipset would continue to engage with Michels throughout his writings, from editing and introducing Michels' *Political Parties* (1962) up to and including

---

44. Mills, *The Power Elite*, p. 308.

45. Michels, *Political Parties*, p. 365.

46. Mills, 'Comment on Criticism', p. 152.

47. Hans Gerth and C. Wright Mills, eds., *From Max Weber: Essays in Sociology*, Abingdon, Routledge, 2009, pp. LXXI, 19–21. As Mills' recent biographer Daniel Geary has noted (Geary, *Radical Ambition*, p. 153), in *Character and Social Structure*, Mills and Gerth identified five social orders that were drawn directly from Weber: 'by locating power in the political, economic, and military realms (three of the five social orders identified by Mills and Gerth in *Character and Social Structure*), Mills denied significant autonomous power to institutions of religion and kinship'. See, further, Gillam, 'C. Wright Mills and the Politics of Truth', p. 470. Franz Neumann's *Behemoth* divides power into four blocks (army, industry, state, bureaucracy), which also influenced Mills (see ibid.). Thanks to Andrew McKenzie-McHarg for this insight.

48. See Patrick McGovern, 'The Young Lipset on the Iron Law of Oligarchy: A Taste of Things to Come', *The British Journal of Sociology*, Vol. 61, No. 1, 2010, pp. 29–42.

his own *Political Man* (1964), thereby underlining the role Michels, and these theorists in general, played in the development of American political science.[49]

II: Minorities Rule

Another seminal book published in 1956 was Dahl's first great study of democracy, *A Preface to Democratic Theory*. There Mosca plays a key role. The book can be read as a long answer to Madison's fear of 'populist democracy', namely a form of tyranny of the majority.[50] But to that fear Mosca offers a critical objection—what Dahl labels the second 'empirical problem'—which is that 'every society develops a ruling class. Widespread popular control (certainly rule by a majority) is impossible.[51] As such, Madisonian fears about majority rule are unfounded, as a majority will never rule. Yet this does not mean we should endorse Mosca's view that a minority always rules: Dahl posits, instead, '*minorities* rule.[52] 'Minorities', instead of a single minority, rule because of

> continuous political competition among individuals, parties, or both. Elections and political competition do not make for government by majorities in any very significant way, but they vastly increase the size, number, and variety of minorities whose preferences must be taken into account by leaders in making policy choices.[53]

This is what the 'American hybrid' of democracy really is—minorities rule—and Dahl notes in conclusion to the *Preface* that his theory of democracy is in one sense a direct response to Mosca's challenge.[54]

In a series of interviews in the early 2000s—one in 2007 with Richard Snyder and another in 2009 with Margaret Levi—Dahl registered his debt to Italian 'elite theorists' Mosca and Pareto, who provided the 'classic formulation of

49. S. M. Lipset, *Political Man*, London, Mercury Books, 1964, pp. 28–30.

50. Thanks to Ian Shapiro for this insight.

51. Dahl, *Preface*, p. 54. See Cristóbal Rovira Kaltwasser, 'The Responses of Populism to Dahl's Democratic Dilemmas', *Political Studies*, Vol. 62, No. 3, 2014, pp. 470–487.

52. Ibid., pp. 54–55, 131–133.

53. Ibid., p. 132.

54. See ibid., p. 55, n. 15, as an indication of this. Note also how this competition between minorities—what Dahl subsequently terms 'polyarchy'—parallels Madison's view in the *Federalist* No. 10 that the best way to counter factions is through other factions.

ruling elite theory'.[55] In his 2007 interview, Dahl explained that the 'elite theorists' had an early influence on him around the same time he was—tellingly—moving away from Karl Marx. But he was also heavily influenced by a more contemporary elite theorist: Joseph Schumpeter. He explained: 'Schumpeter was another major thinker with whom I disagreed early on, especially his reduction of the democratic process to a competition between elites'. Although he agreed with Schumpeter's view that competition between elites could help tame power, he felt that view was incomplete because it did not sufficiently take into account the 'institutional requirements and the elements of popular participation on which the elite depends', which he tried to articulate through his more inclusive concept of polyarchy.[56]

Dahl first taught Schumpeter's *Capitalism, Socialism, and Democracy* (1942) in a graduate seminar he ran with Lindblom at Yale, which gave rise to their *Politics, Economics and Welfare* (1953). It is interesting to note that the discussion of Schumpeter there took place within a discussion of Michels' 'iron law of oligarchy', where they wrote: 'political parties, as Michels observed, tend to be oligarchical—or as we would say hierarchical. But two or more political parties competing with one another for the votes of citizens can make a polyarchy'.[57] This claim—that just because political parties are oligarchic does not mean the political system itself need be oligarchic—is precisely a claim Dahl would reiterate 36 years later in *Democracy and Its Critics*.[58] Moreover, Dahl and Lindblom would write there that leaders are subject to two conditions: competition between themselves and the need to keep their supporters on their side. 'The presence of these two conditions', they write, 'forces a balance between the "iron law" of oligarchy and the counteracting "law" of reciprocity'.[59] In a democratic context this meant competition and elections.

It is in *Politics, Economics, and Welfare* that Dahl first started using the term 'polyarchy' as 'a process of control over leaders'. Dahl was always open about the fact that true democracy could never be fulfilled in the modern context,

55. Munck and Snyder, 'Robert A. Dahl', p. 117; Robert Dahl and Margaret Levi, 'A Conversation with Robert Dahl', *Annual Review of Political Science*, Vol. 12, 2009, pp. 1–9.

56. Munck and Snyder, 'Robert A. Dahl', p. 117.

57. Robert Dahl and Charles Lindblom, *Politics, Economics, and Welfare: Planning and Politico-Economic Systems Resolved into Basic Social Processes*. New York, Harper & Row, 1953, p. 283.

58. Dahl, *Democracy and Its Critics*, p. 276.

59. Dahl and Lindblom, *Politics, Economics and Welfare*, p. 283.

polyarchy representing its best modern approximation.[60] As he explained in the foreword to the 2006 expanded edition of the *Preface*:

> During the writing of *Politics, Economics, and Welfare* (1953), Lindblom and I sketched out a theory about modern democracy as a process of control over leaders (as distinguished from hierarchy, or control by leaders, and bargaining, or control among leaders). After consulting the *OED* and a colleague or two in the Classics Department we settled on the word *polyarchy* as an appropriate term for modern approximations to democracy.[61]

Returning to the *Preface*, the image of 'minorities rule' that Dahl gives us is of different elites competing for influence over the decision-making process whilst never achieving a permanent position of dominance: it should be clear that these minorities are themselves elite-led, both in their internal structuring but also because the members of these 'minorities' will be taken from the political elite itself. Dominance is prevented both because of the competition between different elites as described above, but also through elections—it is here that Dahl differs from Schumpeter—which Dahl does not see as a mechanism through which the 'will' of the people will ever be revealed, but rather as a means of controlling leaders. As such, there are always 'leaders', but what demarks polyarchy from dictatorships, as Dahl starkly puts it within the context of the Cold War, are these two 'methods of social control'—competition, elections—over these leaders. Dictatorships, like Soviet Russia, may still have competition between different leaders but not elections in any meaningful sense.[62]

He concludes:

> I defined the 'normal' American political process as one in which there is a high probability that an active and legitimate group in the population can make itself heard effectively at some crucial stage in the process of decision. To be 'heard' covers a wide range of activities, and I do not intend to define the word rigorously. Clearly, it does not mean that every group has equal control over the outcome.[63]

---

60. Levi, 'A Conversation with Robert Dahl', p. 5.

61. Dahl, *Preface*, p. xviii. For an alternative account of polyarchy as 'a term that I think had been developed in the eighteenth century, as you know from the Greek meaning "many rulers" (poly; archon)', see Levi, 'A Conversation with Robert Dahl', p. 5. See also Giancarlo Bosetti, ed., *Robert A. Dahl: Intervista Sul Pluralismo*, Bari, Laterza, 2002, where he attributes the term to Althusius' *Politica Methodice Digesta*. Thanks to David Ragazzoni for this reference.

62. Dahl, *Preface*, p. 132.

63. Ibid., p. 145.

This 'pluralist'—or 'theory of balance'—view of competing parties Mills relegated to the 'middle ground' of politics, most visibly Congress, where politicians serve as brokers for the competing interests and maintain equilibrium in the system, which he viewed as being in 'stalemate'.[64] Much as the 'middle-class' had been disempowered by the growth of national corporations, so the 'middle levels' of power have been excluded from the 'big decisions' of foreign and military policy, which have been concentrated in the hands of a few top leaders in the powerful and often secretive national security state.[65] So it is not that Mills fundamentally disagreed with the pluralist claim about competing interest groups at the legislative level; he just no longer thought that was where true power was located. Rather, it was behind the scenes, at the 'higher levels' of the corporate, military and political worlds, that the real decisions were being made. 'The old lobby, visible or invisible', Mills writes, 'is now the visible government'.[66]

Beyond the important structural similarities between Dahl and Mills in terms of their positing the existence of elites within the political system, we can nevertheless discern three differences between their respective accounts. First, whilst Dahl sees a number of different elites competing for power, in Mills' view these have been reduced to three: the military, the political and the business elites. Second, Mills sees these elites as more prone to cooperation than to conflict, which is more in line with Dahl's view. Finally, if for Dahl elections still serve a function of control over elites, in Mills' view elections are part of the formal but ineffectual 'middle levels' of power above which the real decisions are made.

III: Conspiracy Theories

Numerous critics were quick to point out that Mills' theory of the power elite could easily slip into a conspiracy theory.[67] In his 1958 review, Bell wrote: 'although Mills contends that he does not believe in a conspiracy theory, his loose account of the centralisation of power among the elite comes

64. Mills, *The Power Elite*, pp. 16, 28, 256; Mills, 'Comment on Criticism', p. 150; Gillam, 'C. Wright Mills and the Politics of Truth', p. 470.

65. Aronowitz, *Taking It Big*, pp. 170–1; Geary, *Radical Ambition*, pp. 152, 158, 164; Miller, 'Democracy and the Intellectual', p. 93; Horowitz, *C. Wright Mills*, p. 273.

66. Mills, *The Power Elite*, pp. 28, 267.

67. Horowitz, *C. Wright Mills*, pp. 263–4; Gillam, 'C. Wright Mills and the Politics of Truth', pp. 469, 473.

suspiciously close to it'.[68] For Bell the question was not solely 'who constitutes the power elite', but also 'how cohesive they are'.[69] In his review of the same year, Dahl made similar points. Showing himself to have good psychological insights into those who espouse elite theories, Dahl identified those 'with a strong strain of frustrated idealism' being drawn to them, and also having a utopian desire for political equality, which maps itself back well onto Mills himself.[70]

Although he did not explicitly use the term, Dahl also presented elite theory in his 1958 review 'A Critique of the Ruling Elite Model' as 'cast in a form that makes it virtually impossible to disprove', a key component of a conspiracy theory.[71] For him the 'ruling elite model' is a type of 'quasi-metaphysical theory made up of what might be called an infinite regress of explanations'. As he explained: 'if the overt leaders of a community do not appear to constitute a ruling elite, then the theory can be saved by arguing that behind the overt leaders there is a set of covert leaders who do'.[72] And so on and so forth.

Explicitly referring to Mills, Dahl writes that 'potential for control is not . . . equivalent to actual control', namely that if Mills had shown the existence of various elites, he had yet to show that these elites constituted an actual *ruling* elite.[73] As Giovanni Sartori puts it, Dahls' two demands were 'that a ruling class (if assumed to be such) be concretely identified, and that power imputations be verifiable'.[74] This harked back to the work Dahl had done with Lindblom in *Politics, Economics, and Welfare* to show that ownership of companies did not equate to *control* over companies: managers might do that. For Mills to have shown control by the power elite—and not just their existence, which he didn't deny—he would have had to offer, according to Dahl, an array of case studies beyond the two main ones he had proposed: Hiroshima and Dien Bien Phu.[75]

68. Bell, 'The Power Elite-Reconsidered', p. 241.

69. Ibid.

70. Robert Dahl, 'A Critique of the Ruling Elite Model', *The American Political Science Review*, Vol. 52, No. 2, 1958, pp. 463–5.

71. Ibid., p. 463.

72. Ibid.

73. Ibid., p. 465; Geary, *Radical Ambition*, p. 164.

74. Sartori, *The Theory of Democracy Revisited*, p. 147.

75. Dahl, 'A Critique of the Ruling Elite Model', p. 466. See Mills, *The Power Elite*, p. 24: 'it was no "historical necessity", but a man named Truman who, with a few other men, decided to drop the bomb on Hiroshima. It was no historical necessity, but an argument within a small

Bell seized on this point as well, adding that it was no surprise that only a 'few men' were involved in these decisions, given that the US constitution invested foreign affairs precisely in the office of the president.[76] And both questioned his understanding of power: Dahl referred back to his article on the 'Concept of Power' he had penned the year before, whilst Bell criticised Mills for following too closely Weber's association of dominance with violence.[77]

It is worth remembering in this context that Dahl was an advocate of behaviouralism, which, modelling itself on the natural sciences, wanted to formulate a *quantifiable* and *demonstrable* approach to predicting human behaviour: simply theorising it or showing it historically was insufficient in this account.[78] Moreover, Dahl, referring back to his earlier article on the 'Concept of Power', in which he had lamented the difficulty in formerly defining it, criticised Mills' understanding of power as being too top-down and linked to violence.[79]

We know that, behind the brash bravura, Mills was quite hurt by these criticisms. And although 'Comment on Criticism' was published before Dahl's two reviews above, it dealt with similar themes.[80] There Mills defended himself from the accusation of having peddled a 'conspiracy theory', claiming that instead he had offered an 'interpretation of well-known historical events, not a notion of a secret cabal making decisions'.[81] In doing so he did not question the fact that he had only concentrated on key events—Hiroshima, Dien Bien Phu—but it is interesting to note that in his preparatory 'Notes on Mosca' he had jotted down: 'project: select three of four key decisions of the

circle of men that defeated Admiral Radford's proposal to bomb troops before Dien Bien Phu'. Aronowitz, *Taking It Big*, p. 173.

76. Bell, 'The Power Elite-Reconsidered', pp. 240, 243; Geary, *Radical Ambition*, p. 164; Horowitz, *C. Wright Mills*, p. 273.

77. Dahl, 'A Critique of the Ruling Elite Model', p. 463 (the reference of the article on power is to Robert Dahl, 'The Concept of Power', *Behavioral Science*, Vol. 2, No. 3, 1957, pp. 201–215); Bell, 'The Power Elite-Reconsidered', pp. 240, 243. See, further, Steven Lukes, 'Robert Dahl on Power', *Journal of Political Power*, Vol. 8, No. 2, 2015, pp. 261–271; David Baldwin, 'Misinterpreting Dahl on Power', *Journal of Political Power*, Vol. 8, No. 2, 2015, pp. 209–227.

78. Isaac, *Power and Marxist Theory*, 1988.

79. Dahl, 'A Critique of the Ruling Elite Model', p. 463; Dahl, 'The Concept of Power'; Steven Lukes, 'Robert Dahl on Power', *Journal of Political Power*, Vol. 8, No. 2, 2015, pp. 261–271; David Baldwin, 'Misinterpreting Dahl on Power', *Journal of Political Power*, Vol. 8, No. 2, 2015, pp. 209–227.

80. Mills, 'Comment on Criticism', p. 139.

81. Ibid., pp. 146–7.

last decade—to drop the atom, to cut or raise steel production, the GM strike of 45', suggesting that he had thought of more domestic examples too.[82] Indeed, already in *The Power Elite* Mills had been careful to distance himself from the 'conspiracy theory of history', yet without falling into the liberal view of history as 'drift'.[83] The way for him to square the circle was to rely on Hofstadter's view—who would go on to famously dissect the conspiratorial worldview in *The Paranoid Style* (1964)—that '"there is a great difference . . . between locating conspiracies *in* history and saying history *is*, in effect, a conspiracy"'.[84]

Whilst Mills accepted in his reply that by power he did, ultimately, mean force, there are two reasons to believe that the theory of the power elite is not, in fact, a conspiracy theory.[85] The first is that, as we saw previously, Mills wasn't claiming that there had always been a power elite, but rather that it had come about at a certain moment in time, namely Cold War America: it would not 'last forever'.[86] There was a '"coincidence" of several structural trends'— Mills, after all, was a sociologist—one of them being the present size of American corporations.[87] If in the eighteenth and nineteenth centuries democratic citizenship was rooted in small free independent proprietors—a context within which the Jeffersonian 'theory of balance' could still hold[88]—this system in the twentieth century had, according to Mills, come to pass. Henceforth industry, because of the forces of centralisation and bureaucratisation, had become concentrated in the hands of giant national corporations, and the new movers and shakers of the business world were the senior managers and CEOs of these companies, to the detriment of the old independent middle-class.[89]

Such a situation made it difficult to distinguish between the interests of certain large American companies and the interests of the nation as a whole, making economics and national politics, which itself had become increasingly centralised at the expense of domestic politics, with power increasingly concentrated in the executive, rather than the legislative, branch, necessarily

82. Mills, 'Comment on Criticism', p. 148; Mills, 'Notes on Mosca', p. 204.
83. Mills, *The Power Elite*, p. 27.
84. Ibid., p. 293.
85. Mills, 'Comment on Criticism', p. 150.
86. Ibid., p. 152.
87. Ibid., p. 147.
88. Aronowitz, *Taking it Big*, p. 185.
89. Mills, *The Power Elite*, p. 7.

intertwined: 'what is good for General Motors', as the saying goes, 'is good for America'.[90] One need only add the Cold War to the mix, with its international dimension, nuclear deterrence and the rise of a professional army that replaced the former traditional state militias—all of which reinforced the executive power—to see how the economic-political-military nexus had come into being.[91]

Mills, therefore, was not saying that the power elite forms some sort of unity, nor indeed that the power elite is the realisation of some sort of plan.[92] Rather, it was a 'conjunction of historical circumstances', including bureaucratisation, centralisation and the Cold War, that led elites to realise that they might best achieve their goals by working together.[93] And just because, second, this power elite was increasingly 'interchangeable'—that there was a 'revolving door' between one high position and another, whether political, economic or military—and seemed to be drawn from similar milieus and institutions, notably Ivy League universities, such that we might even talk of a 'social class identity', this did not mean either that the power elite was a 'homogenous circle of a specified number of men whose solidified will continuously prevails against all obstacles'.[94] Indeed, Mills completely conceded that there were competing interests or factions within the power elite itself, but when push comes to shove, especially in times of international crises, then the power elite will coordinate: 'the power elite is composed of political, economic, and military men, but this instituted elite is frequently in some tension: it comes together only on certain coinciding points and only on certain occasions of "crisis"'.[95]

IV: Muncie or New Haven?

The view that 'beneath the façade of democratic politics a social and economic elite will usually be found actually running things' is the view Dahl set out to challenge in his subsequent book, *Who Governs? Democracy and*

90. Geary, *Radical Ambition*, p. 156.

91. Mills, *The Power Elite*, p. 7; Aronowitz, *Taking It Big*, pp. 172, 179; Geary, *Radical Ambition*, pp. 153, 166.

92. Mills, 'Comment on Criticism', p. 147; Mills, *The Power Elite*, pp. 18–20.

93. Mills, *The Power Elite*, pp. 20, 28.

94. Mills, 'Comment on Criticism', p. 148; Mills, *The Power Elite*, pp. 10–12, 18; Geary, *Radical Ambition*, pp. 156–7; Horowitz, *C. Wright Mills*, p. 265.

95. Mills, *The Power Elite*, p. 276.

Power in an American City, published in 1961.[96] Whilst Mills is not explicitly referred to in the work, the structure of the argument he is attacking is clear. Mills had focused on the national level, whereas Dahl directed his attention to the local level, targeting in the process Robert and Helen Lynd, who, along with Floyd Hunter, had written books on 'Middletown' (Muncie, Indiana) and Atlanta in 1929 and 1953, respectively.[97] Both books argued that local elites dominated the nominal workings of democracy in the towns they studied.[98] These works, along with Mills' *The Power Elite*, had proved to be very popular and had started a trend Dahl and his colleagues were keen to repel (Dahl's study in turn triggered a debate about pluralism in American political science).[99]

To do so, Dahl turned to study the town most easily accessible to a Yale professor: New Haven. Indeed, already in his 1958 review of Mills he had used New Haven a couple of times to illustrate his points.[100] And although Dahl focused on the local level in his refutation of Lynd and Hunter, he was quite clear that New Haven offered 'analogies with national politics',[101] thereby linking *Who Governs?* back to his critique of Mills. Dahl concluded from his work that 'within a century a political system dominated by one cohesive set of leaders', whom he called 'The Patricians', 'had given way to a system dominated by many different sets of leaders'—the 'New Men'—'each having access to a different combination of political resources. It was, in short, a pluralist system'.[102] New Haven had moved from an oligarchy to pluralism.[103]

Whilst he had countenanced the idea that 'the more recent politicians, who seem to lack some of the most important resources of the patricians and the entrepreneurs, may be political handmaidens of the well-to-do' in his chapter on the social and economic notables, which he titled 'Shadow and Substance',

96. Robert Dahl, *Who Governs? Democracy and Power in an American City*, New Haven, Yale University Press, 2005, p. 6.

97. G. William Domhoff, 'C. Wright Mills, Power Structure Research, and the Failures of Mainstream Political Science', *New Political Science*, Vol. 29, 2007, pp. 97–114.

98. Dahl, *Who Governs?*, p. 6.

99. Douglas Rae, 'Foreword' to Dahl, *Who Governs?*, p. vii; Nelson Polsby, *Community Power and Political Theory*, New Haven, Yale University Press, 1980.

100. Dahl, 'A Critique of the Ruling Elite Model', p. 465.

101. Dahl, *Who Governs?*, p. xiii.

102. Ibid., p. 86.

103. Ibid., p. 12. For a critique, see G. William Domhoff, *Who Rules America? The Triumph of the Corporate Rich*, New York, McGraw-Hill, 2014.

Dahl again concluded that the economic elite had in fact minimal influence on the political workings of the city.[104] Dahl was not so naïve to believe that this meant New Haven had become some sort of utopian democracy, but the main point was that resources had become dispersed, which allow for the development of the competitive model of democracy he advocated: 'in the political system of today, inequalities in political resources remain, but they tend to be *noncumulative*. The political system of New Haven, then, is one of *dispersed inequalities*'.[105]

Dahl's 'Patricians' were prototypical WASPs, which included religious leaders who often doubled as university administrators, and it was they whom Mills had specifically targeted in his critique of the power elite.[106] But the story Dahl wanted to tell was that the ruling class was challenged over time by two new rising immigrant groups: the Irish and the Italians, both, of course, Catholic. Thus, the initial ruling class, bound together through a certain Protestantism, was broken up into separate political, economic and social elites, within which various religions now competed for political, economic, social and spiritual power.

Mills never responded to Dahl's charges: he met his untimely death in 1962. But we might imagine he would have said, all well and good, Dahl has shown us how power is distributed at the local levels of power, but the power elite exists precisely at the *national* level, to which the local is completely divorced.[107] In reality, the only explicit comment we have from Mills on Dahl is from when he reviewed his and Lindblom's *Politics, Economics, and Welfare* for the *American Sociological Review* in 1954. There Mills praised it as a 'major work', calling it an 'insurgent's book'—probably one of the highest compliments Mills could ever make—and lauded it for attempting to marry socialism with liberalism.[108] The feeling was mutual: in his 2009 interview Dahl declared he had 'great respect for C. Wright Mills', although he couldn't say the same for Floyd Hunter's work.[109]

That admiration continued through to what Dahl considered to be his 'most complete formulation' of democratic theory, *Democracy and Its Critics*,

104. Ibid., pp. 61–84.

105. Ibid., p. 85.

106. Geary, *Radical Ambition*, p. 154; Horowitz, *C. Wright Mills*, p. 267.

107. Mills, *The Power Elite*, p. 6; Aronowitz, *Taking It Big*, p. 168.

108. C. Wright Mills, 'Politics, Economics, and Welfare. By Robert A. Dahl and Charles E. Lindblom', *American Sociological Review*, Vol. 19, No. 4, 1954, pp. 495–6.

109. Levi, 'A Conversation with Robert Dahl', p. 6.

published in 1989. There, in the chapter 'Minority Domination', he lauded Mills as one of the most convincing of the elite theorists of democracy, and returned to one of the criticisms he had rejected as an 'improper' test of the existence of the ruling elite in his 1958 article, namely one of control: 'potential for control is not . . . equivalent to actual control'.[110] In his footnote on Mills, echoing a sentiment expressed about the definition of power above, Dahl writes:

> What these studies characteristically fail to do, however, is to provide much evidence on the chain of control from these elites to the outcomes—e.g. beliefs, agendas, or government decisions—over which they presumably dominate. The disproportion between evidence on backgrounds and evidence bearing on the chain of control is striking.[111]

V: Radical or Conservative?

Mills was an outsider.[112] He was, to use Orwell's phrase, 'outside the whale'.[113] Born part-Irish Catholic on his mother's side in Bible Belt Waco, where he served as a local choir boy, Mills' father was an insurance salesman who moved around a lot for work, bringing his young family with him. He would come to teach at Columbia on a motorcycle, wearing boots and carrying his papers in an army surplus bag: quite in contrast to the tweed look his Jewish 'New York Intellectuals' colleagues affected.[114]

It is not clear when he lost his faith, and although his funeral took place in the non-denominational Columbia University Chapel, a couple of years after the publication of *The Power Elite*, Mills declared himself a pagan in his 'A Pagan Sermon to the Christian Clergy', delivered in Toronto on 27 February 1958 to the annual meeting of the Board of Evangelical and Social Service, United Church of Canada.[115] There, in a rousing speech, Mills accused

110. Dahl, 'Critique', p. 465.

111. Dahl, *Democracy and Its Critics*, p. 367, n. 15; Isaac, *Power and Marxist Theory*.

112. Bell, 'The Power Elite-Reconsidered', p. 239; Miller, 'Democracy and the Intellectual', p. 100.

113. Miller, 'Democracy and the Intellectual', p. 83.

114. Ibid., pp. 83–7; Horowitz, *C. Wright Mills*, p. 6: Gillam, 'Richard Hofstader, C. Wright Mills', p. 75.

115. Horowitz, *C. Wright Mills*, p. 6; C. Wright Mills, 'A Pagan Sermon to the Christian Clergy' in Summers, *The Politics of Truth*, p. 171.

Christians of having lost their moral fibre, becoming solely a satrap to the military powers that be, which may explain why he excluded religion from the five social orders he had originally identified with Gerth.[116] He harangued his audience, asking them whether it was acceptable, within the context of the Cold War, for Christians to kill other Christians, and indeed with the nearing onset of World War III, whether Christians could stand by and watch the world be destroyed so that there would be no humans left to even be Christian at all.[117]

It was only in the 1940s during World War II that Mills became politicised, but after that, and unlike his contemporaries Bell, Hofstadter, Schlesinger and others who moved to the right and the 'vital centre', Mills became more radicalised and moved to the left.[118] His politics were the 'politics of truth', of speaking truth to power, debunking official definitions of reality in the belief that ideas move people to act.[119] This explains the somewhat schizophrenic nature of *The Power Elite*, which often reads like two books welded together: a core ground-breaking sociological study of elites bookended with a highly florid and moralising call to arms (it is in the introduction and concluding chapters that his most famous phrases, 'crackpot realism' and 'the higher ignorance', appear).[120] Moreover, in his 'Comment on Criticism', Mills responded directly to those who accused 'elite theory' as having a 'latent (conservative) political bias' against radicalism, arguing instead that the theory allowed him to formulate a critique of the power structures of his day.[121]

As Horowitz has argued, this combination makes Mills a sort of utopian too. Not the type like Plato who fashion a precise image of future social and political structures, but rather one 'less concerned with locating the secular garden of Eden than with ridding mankind of the scourges of oppression associated with civilisation'.[122] As someone more interested in 'process' than in 'outcomes', Mills was content simply to point out the existence of a power elite instead of having to demonstrate the nitty-gritty of how those structures in reality play out. As he put it in opening to *The Power Elite*: 'whether they do or

---

116. Ibid., p. 176. The other—kinship—might have been lost to Mills' attitude towards the French Revolution.

117. Ibid., pp. 166–8.

118. Gillam, 'C. Wright Mills and the Politics of Truth', p. 465.

119. Geary, *Radical Ambition*, pp. 143–5; Miller, 'Democracy and the Intellectual', p. 89.

120. Wolfe, 'Afterword', pp. 377–8; Horowitz, *C. Wright Mills*, p. 256.

121. Mills, 'Comment on Criticism', pp. 152–153.

122. Horowitz, *C. Wright Mills*, p. 6.

do not make such decisions is less important than the fact they do occupy such pivotal positions'.[123]

An important interlocutor for Mills was Ortega y Gasset, who had argued in *The Revolt of the Masses* (1930) that the modern democratic 'masses' would swamp the Nietzschean cultural elite.[124] Mills, rather, turning Ortega on his head, claimed instead that the active and contestatory American public he so cherished was being transformed into an inarticulate, manipulated and powerless mass, unable to challenge the power elite.[125] His aim, ultimately, was for the radical intelligentsia to unite an informed and participatory public to wrest democratic power back from the power elite:

> The top of the American system of power is much more unified and much more powerful, the bottom is much more fragmented, and in truth, impotent, than is generally supposed by those who are distracted by the middling units of power which neither express such will as exists at the bottom nor determine the decisions at the top.[126]

By 1989 and *Democracy and Its Critics*, Dahl had become more pessimistic about American democracy. This was most clearly articulated in his new 1976 preface to *Politics, Economics, and Welfare* with Lindblom. There Dahl and Lindblom worried about the unchecked power of the 'imperial' presidency, the impact of inequality on political participation, and the outsized role of the 'businessman' in the political system: all themes resonant of Mills' original

---

123. Mills, *The Power Elite*, p. 4.

124. José Ortega y Gasset, *The Revolt of the Masses*, New York, W. W. Norton, 1993. The main theme of Ortega's book was the conflict between the 'mass-man' and 'elite-man': the 'mass-man' is 'empty' inside, looking suspiciously close to Nietzsche's 'last man', who thinks he is the end of history, whilst the 'elite-man' is, conversely, something close to Nietzsche's *Übermensch*, someone who has 'something inside' and is driven by a project he has given himself, in contrast to the 'mass-man', who just goes with the flow. 'Elite' and 'mass' were not meant to distinguish between rulers and the ruled; rather the whole point of *Revolt* was that the 'mass-man' had taken over at the same time that the 'elite-man' had abdicated. So, Ortega was not denouncing elites as such, but positing rather that the ruling class had been taken over by bourgeois complacent philistines. On Ortega, see, further, Brendon Westler, *The Revolting Masses: José Ortega y Gasset's Liberalism against Populism*, Philadelphia, University of Pennsylvania Press, 2024.

125. Mills, *The Power Elite*, pp. 28, 301, 309, 324, 385 n. 5; Mills, 'Pagan Sermon', p. 170; Aronowitz, *Taking It Big*, p. 185; Geary, *Radical Ambition*, pp. 161, 167; Gillam, 'C. Wright Mills and the Politics of Truth', p. 469; Miller, 'Democracy and the Intellectual', pp. 92–4; Horowitz, *C. Wright Mills*, p. 261.

126. Mills, *The Power Elite*, p. 29.

critique.[127] Indeed, Dahl and Lindblom developed an historical account of US history from the nineteenth to the twentieth century that had strong echoes of Mills' own, especially in how the 'manager' had replaced the independent farmer, and the consequences of that for American democracy.[128]

Yet it would be a mistake to think that Dahl simply became more radical as he got older: that radicalism was there from the start. Dahl was born in a small town in Iowa with a population of less than a thousand, and moved to the town of Skagway in Alaska at the age of ten, a thriving metropolis of about 500 souls. As he recounted in his 2007 interview, it was only when he moved to Washington DC in 1937, at the height of the New Deal, to work in the National Labour Relations Board that he encountered diversity in the form of radical socialist Jews. These encounters had a 'very powerful impact' on him, leading him to join the Socialist Party, and, upon his return to Yale, to undertake a PhD on socialism and democratic politics.[129] Although this is impossible to quantify in any meaningful sense, we might ponder what this first encounter with ethno-religious diversity had on someone who was to become the leading advocate of 'pluralism'.

As such, interest in Yugoslavian 'democratic socialism', which he returned to in the 1970s,[130] was in reality already there from his time as a PhD student. The same might be said of the—linked—theme of 'workplace democracy', which Dahl started publishing on in earnest in the 1980s, notably with his *A Preface to Economic Democracy*:[131] as a young man Dahl declared himself to be a Norman Thomas socialist, and spent his summers unionising dock workers in Alaska.[132] It is true that Dahl would belatedly call for a greater integration of African-Americans, starting with the 1973 preface to *Politics, Economics, and Welfare*: Mills was also guilty of overlooking race in *The Power Elite*.[133]

127. Dahl and Lindblom, *Politics, Economics, and Welfare*, pp. xxv–xlv.

128. Ibid., pp. xxxii–xxxiii.

129. Munck and Snyder, 'Robert A. Dahl', p. 115.

130. Robert Dahl, 'Pluralism Revisited', *Comparative Politics*, Vol. 10, No. 2, 1978, pp. 191–203.

131. Robert Dahl, *A Preface to Economic Democracy*, Berkeley, University of California Press, 1986. See, further, Cyrus Ernesto Zirakzadeh, 'Theorising about Workplace Democracy: Robert Dahl and the Cooperative of Mondragon', *Journal of Theoretical Politics*, Vol. 2, No. 1, 1990, pp. 109–126.

132. Levi, 'A Conversation with Robert Dahl', p. 2.

133. G. William Domhoff, 'Mills's "The Power Elite" 50 Years Later', *Contemporary Sociology*, Vol. 35, No. 6, 2006, pp. 547–550.

If Dahl became increasingly disillusioned with the prospects for American democracy near the end of his life,[134] Isaac is surely right to see a right-wing turn in Dahl towards the liberal Cold War centre during the 1950s and the 1960s.[135] This led to his clash with Mills, yet was at odds with his more left-leaning earlier and later views. The pluralist and defender of the status quo Dahl that we know best is therefore a strong creation of this particular—Cold War—moment in time, and we can now recover the more radical underlayer of his thought. We would do well also to remember that the economic and polyarchic strand in Dahl's thought were not in tension, but in fact analogical: if elections are defendable in the political realm, they should be in the economic realm too. Dahl wanted to reproduce polyarchy in an economic setting, confirming that the two projects were always meant to work in tandem.

VI: Mosca, Pareto or Michels?

The influence Mosca, Pareto and Michels had on the thinking of Mills and Dahl is patent. Mills developed his notion of the power elite by seizing on Pareto's theory, but used Mosca's 'ruling class' to put the emphasis on the 'governing' elite. Dahl, on the other hand, developed his concept of 'minorities rule' through an explicit dialogue with Mosca, and the 'Pareto, Mosca and Michels' triumvirate is in full force come Dahl's self-declared masterpiece *Democracy and Its Critics*, with Michels being an interlocutor as early as during his work with Lindblom, *Politics, Economics and Welfare*.

What can Mosca, Pareto and Michels be brought to say to Dahl and Mills? Mills' power elite can very much be described as Mosca's 'ruling class', although Mills rejected the permanence of such a class as 'tautological'. And although Mills does talk about the 'revolving door' between the three elements of his power elite, this isn't quite comparable to Pareto's 'circulation of elites' because in the former it is the same elites that circulate whereas in the latter it is a struggle between two competing elites, the 'lions' and the 'foxes',

---

134. Hoffman, 'The Quiet Desperation of Robert Dahl's (Quiet) Radicalism'; Richard Krouse, 'Polyarchy & Participation: The Changing Democratic Theory of Robert Dahl', *Polity*, Vol. 14, No. 3, 1982, pp. 441–463. For a debate on workplace democracy, see Robert Mayer, 'Robert Dahl and the Right to Workplace Democracy', *The Review of Politics*, Vol. 63, No. 2, 2001, pp. 221–247; Robert Dahl, 'A Right to Workplace Democracy? Response to Robert Mayer', *The Review of Politics*, Vol. 63, No. 2, 2001, pp. 249–253; and Robert Mayer, 'A Rejoinder to Robert Dahl', *The Review of Politics*, Vol. 63, No. 2, 2001, pp. 255–257.

135. Jeffrey Isaac, 'Robert Dahl as Mentor'.

although with their emphasis on unity, centralisation and force, perhaps the 'power elite' can be described as the arrival of the 'lions' to power.

What about Dahl? There no longer is a unified 'ruling class' in New Haven as Mosca might have had it; instead there are different political, financial, social elites, none of them ruling in a direct sense, politics being rather the jockeying for position between all these competing groups no longer able to achieve a permanent position of power which the patricians enjoyed. Again, although he doesn't use that language, this move might be captured through Pareto's 'circulation of elite', that sees, in contrast to Mills, a move from the 'lions' to 'foxes'.

But ultimately it is Michels both are closest to. Mills, as we have seen, entirely conceded the point in his reply to his critics, explaining that Michels' 'iron law of oligarchy' is a 'fairly good description of what has in fact happened in most mass organisations'.[136] This separation of wealth and social standing from political power also leads Dahl back to Michels' position, as the focus of his study of New Haven was political parties, where he thought power was located, and he was quite happy to grant that these were oligarchic in nature. Dahl had engaged with Michels from as early as his seminal book with Lindblom, where they wrote that although political parties themselves are oligarchic, the political system itself need not be—it could be polyarchic—and it is precisely in this competition and elections that polyarchy found its source. What is striking is that, 36 years later, in the key passage on the 'theorists of minority domination' in *Democracy and Its Critics*, Dahl repeated exactly the same claim: 'even if we grant that political parties are oligarchical, *it does not follow that competing political parties necessarily produce an oligarchical political system*'.[137]

The reason Mills and Dahl are closer to Michels is that all three were interested in oligarchic elites that arise out of bureaucracies—the modern corporation and the political party—and less in developing a trans-historical ('tautological' in Mills' view) and psychological account (Dahl was interested in *behaviour*) of minority rule, as were Mosca and Pareto. As such not only were Mills and Dahl closer to one another than they portray themselves to be, but their specific intellectual link back to the early elite theorists of democracy is also through Michels. This makes Michels not only closer to mid-century concerns, but also further from Mosca and Pareto than he is usually presented (as in Dahl's account) as being.

136. Mills, 'Comment on Criticism', p. 152.
137. Dahl, *Democracy and Its Critics*, p. 276.

Indeed, in an oft-overlooked passage in the conclusion to *Political Parties*, as we've explored in chapter 3, Michels explained that democracy will give rise to two natural palliatives against the iron law of oligarchy:

3. The *ideological* tendency of democracy towards criticism and control;
4. The *effective* counter-tendency of democracy towards the creation of parties ever more complex and ever more differentiated—parties, that is to say, which are increasingly based on the competence of the few.[138]

In essence, what Michels is saying is that democracy will lead to higher education levels that will allow citizens to keep a better intellectual check on their leaders, and that this will give rise to competing oligarchies that will balance each other out.

There is remarkable similarity between the two 'social means of control' Dahl posited—elections and competition between parties—and Michels' two palliatives: both Michels and Dahl saw the salvation of the democratic system in the development of numerous competing elites, and in keeping them in check through criticism (education) and control (elections), another term for 'reciprocity' as Dahl had theorised all the way back in his and Lindblom's 1953 *Politics, Economics, and Welfare*. This led not to believing that the 'people' as such really do rule, but to conceiving of the system as more a process of control over elites: exactly the meaning of polyarchy. And although they diverged in emphasising either control/elections (Dahl) or criticism/greater social education (Michels) as the other means of control, both had the same objective in mind.

Indeed, one might add that Michels and Dahl both understood democracy as being fundamentally Rousseauian, in that the people need to, somehow, directly rule (failing, *en passant*, to see that Rousseau laid the groundwork for a theory of legitimate sovereignty rather than democracy, which he thought only fit for 'Gods'). This explains why Dahl's polyarchy will always be second best, as true—Rousseauian—democracy can never be achieved. In *After the Revolution?* (1970), Dahl proposed to correct elitism by introducing sortition, an idea brought into the realm of deliberate democracy by Dahl's pupil James Fishkin.[139] Indeed, the notion of 'lottocracy', with assemblies chosen by lot,

138. Michels, *Political Parties*, p. 370.

139. Robert Dahl, *After the Revolution? Authority in a Good Society*, New Haven, Yale University Press, 1990; James Fishkin, *When the People Speak: Deliberative Democracy and Public Consultation*, Oxford, Oxford University Press, 2009.

whether through citizens' assemblies as seen in Ireland or other methods, has gained recent traction.[140] But it is unclear whether this idea escapes the charge of elitism either, often bringing into politics those already heavily invested in it whilst simultaneously disenfranchising those who do not have the time for it.[141] As Oscar Wilde said of socialism: the trouble is that it takes up too many evenings.

Like Michels and Dahl, Mill's objective with *The Power Elite* was to call for intellectuals to challenge the contemporary power-nexus by allying with 'educated publics', which also maps itself particularly well onto Michels' idea that democracy's role was the 'social education' of the masses so that they could intellectually challenge their leaders, in tandem with competing elites. Mills, Dahl and Michels all also shared a vision of politics as mediated through voice: Mills, playing on Michels' 'iron law of oligarchy', put forward the concept of the 'iron law of spokesmanship', whilst Dahl's polyarchic system is premised on different groups making themselves 'heard'. Michels, for his part, saw control of the means of communication as key to the dominance of the leaders over members of the party.

Conclusion

In a rather tetchy exchange for someone who can only be considered an American gent,[142] Dahl directly responded to the charge he was an 'elite theorist of democracy' in a 1966 article, 'Further Reflections on "The Elitist Theory of Democracy"'.[143] Perhaps it had struck a nerve. There he completely acceded to

140. David Van Reybrouck, *Against Elections: The Case for Democracy*, London, Bodley Head, 2016; Hélène Landemore, *Open Democracy: Reinventing Popular Rule for the Twenty-First Century*, Princeton, Princeton University Press, 2020; Yves Sintomer, Yves, *The Government of Chance: Sortition and Democracy from Athens to the Present*, Cambridge, Cambridge University Press, 2023; Alexander Guerrero, *Lottocracy: Democracy without Elections*, Oxford, Oxford University Press, 2024; Samuel Bagg, 'Sortition as Anti-Corruption: Popular Oversight against Elite Capture', *American Journal of Political Science*, Vol. 68, No. 1, 2024, pp. 93–105. For a critique, see Hugo Drochon, 'Paradoxes of Liberalism', *History of European Ideas*, Vol. 45, No. 5, 2019, pp. 754–760.

141. Thanks to Nadia Urbinati for highlighting the points raised in this paragraph.

142. Isaac, 'Robert Dahl as Mentor'.

143. Robert Dahl, 'Further Reflections on "The Elitist Theory of Democracy"', *The American Political Science Review*, Vol. 60, No. 2, 1966, pp. 296–305. This was a response to Jack Walker, 'A Critique of the Elitist Theory of Democracy', ibid., pp. 285–295. See, further, Jack Walker, 'A Reply to "Further Reflections on 'The Elitist Theory of Democracy'"', ibid., pp. 391–2.

the empirical existence of elites, although he preferred the term 'leadership' because of the pejorative connotation the term had taken on, no doubt thanks to Mills who is again referred to in the text. But he defended himself from normatively advocating elitism.[144] Indeed, he opened the discussion distinguishing between elite theorists who are 'sympathetic to popular rule' from those who are not, the 'anti-democratic' writers, siding firmly with the former.[145] Whilst Dahl is right in stating there is no such thing as *one* theory of elite rule, by his own admission he still is an elite thinker, admittedly a pro-democratic one. After all, as Floyd Hunter pointed out in his review of *Who Governs?*, if elites in New Haven compete with one another, we are still only talking about less than 1% of the population.[146]

Geary has noted that 'Mills's most basic challenge to the pluralists rested not on his different empirical description of American politics but on his competing value judgements', and there is something to that.[147] In the end, both might be considered what Peter Bachrach termed 'democratic elitists': Mills and Dahl both analysed the existence of elites within the democratic system, and affirmed them too, either as 'intellectual' elites who were to lead the 'educated publics', or within polyarchy itself.[148] And both wanted greater participation in the political system: Mills' ideas subsequently gave rise to the notion of 'participatory democracy', whilst Dahl called for the greater integration of African-Americans in the political sphere and wanted democracy extended to the economic sphere.[149] They both worried about the obstacles in place to achieve that vision. Where they differed, at least in the 1950s and the 1960s, was whether elites were more likely to cooperate or compete, although Dahl would later move closer to Mills' view.

144. Ibid., pp. 297–8; Geary, *Radical Ambition*, p. 157; Nannerl Keohane, 'Dahl's Concept of Leadership: Notes towards a Theory of Leadership in a Democracy', *Journal of Political Power*, Vol. 8 No. 2, 2015, pp. 229–247.

145. Ibid., p. 296.

146. Floyd Hunter, 'Who Governs: Democracy and Power in an American City. By Robert A. Dahl', *Administrative Science Quarterly*, Vol. 6, No. 4, 1962, pp. 517–8.

147. Geary, *Radical Ambition*, p. 159.

148. Peter Bachrach, *The Theory of Democratic Elitism: A Critique*, Lanham, University Press of America, 1980. See, further, Graeme Duncan and Steven Lukes, 'The New Democracy', *Political Studies*, Vol. 11, No. 2, 1962, pp. 156–177.

149. Hayden, *Radical Nomad*, pp. 163–192. For a critique of 'more participation', see Sartori, *The Theory of Democracy Revisited*, p. 151.

We are now entering into a third moment of elite discussion, with the theme, and indeed Mosca, Pareto and Michels, all featuring prominently in recent work by John McCormick, Green, Urbinati, Jeffrey Winters and Pierre Rosanvallon, amongst others.[150] One distinctive feature of today's debate about elites is its focus on wealth. This marks a departure from the mid-century debate between Mills and Dahl, who were more concerned with the oligarchic nature of modern institutions: in *Who Governs?*, Dahl clearly separated wealth from political influence, whilst Mills in *The Power Elite* wrote that 'wealth also is acquired and held in and through institutions',[151] and not the other way round (wealth leads to control over institutions). In contrast, today's theorists see wealth—the recent *Zeitgeist* best captured by the unexpected success of Thomas Piketty's *Capital in the Twenty-First Century*—as the main force behind the influence of policy-making.

As such, Michels, with his focus on institutions, might not serve as the best touchstone for these debates. Pareto, with his theory of 'demagogic plutocracy', where the rich rule behind the façade of democracy, might be more helpful. It is Pareto, after all, who first coined the 80/20 rule: that 80% of the wealth of the country always belongs to 20% of the population. There is a strong—if intensified—echo of that notion in the slogan of the 99% v. 1%.

150. McCormick, *Machiavellian Democracy*; McCormick, *Reading Machiavelli*; Green, *The Eyes of the People*; Green, *The Shadow of Unfairness*; Urbinati, *Democracy Disfigured*; Jeffrey Winters, *Oligarchy*, Cambridge, Cambridge University Press, 2011; Pierre Rosanvallon, *The Society of Equals*, Cambridge [MA], Harvard University Press, 2016; Luke Mayville, *John Adams and the Fear of American Oligarchy*, Princeton, Princeton University Press, 2016; Gordon Arlen, 'Aristotle and the Problem of Oligarchic Harm Insights for Democracy', *European Journal of Political Theory*, Vol. 18, No. 3, 2019, pp. 393–414.

151. Mills, *The Power Elite*, p. 9.

6

Aron and Divided Elites

RECENT INTEREST in Raymond Aron (1905–1983) in Anglophone scholarship has centred on his 'Cold War Liberalism'.[1] There, Aron, often paired with Isaiah Berlin and Karl Popper, is presented as an anti-Marxist and anti-Communist thinker who defended a 'negative' or 'minimum' version of liberalism, one sometimes associated with what Judith Shklar identified as the 'liberalism of fear': what needed to be avoided first and foremost was cruelty.[2] As such, rather than propose a positive or indeed coherent political theory, Aron instead defended certain values (pluralism, tolerance), drawn, like all good liberals, from an idealised vision of England, and advocated an attitude or sensibility (prudence, moderation) in the face of the perils Cold War politics.[3]

1. See Stuart Campbell, 'Raymond Aron: The Making of a Cold Warrior', *Historian*, Vol. 51, No. 4, 1989, pp. 551–573; Brian Anderson, ed., *Raymond Aron: The Recovery of the Political*, New Brunswick, Transaction Publishers, 1997, pp. 1–18; Jan-Werner Müller, 'Fear and Freedom: On "Cold War Liberalism"', *European Journal of Political Theory*, Vol. 7, No. 1, 2008, pp. 45–64; Aurelian Craiutu, 'The Lucidity of Moderation: Raymond Aron as a "Committed Observer"' in *Faces of Moderation: The Art of Balance in an Age of Extremes*, Philadelphia, University of Pennsylvania Press, 2017, p. 60; and Or Rosenboim, *The Emergence of Globalism: Visions of World Order in Britain and the United States, 1939–1950*, Princeton, Princeton University Press, 2017, p. 27.

2. Judith Shklar, 'The Liberalism of Fear' in Nancy Rosenblum, ed., *Liberalism and the Moral Life*, Cambridge (MA), Harvard University Press, 1989, pp. 21–38. On Shklar, see Katrina Forrester, 'Judith Shklar, Bernard Williams and Political Realism', *European Journal of Political Theory*, Vol. 11, No. 3, 2012, pp. 247–272.

3. Müller, 'Fear and Freedom'; Joshua Cherniss, *Liberalism in Dark Times: The Liberal Ethos in the Twentieth Century*, Princeton, Princeton University Press, 2021, pp. 102–136. This Aron is obviously linked to the Aron theorist of international relations, who had the ear of Henry Kissinger. See Stanley Hoffmann, 'Raymond Aron and the Theory of International Relations', *International Studies Quarterly*, Vol. 29, No. 1, 1985, pp. 13–27. See, further, Paul Mazgaj, 'Raymond

Whilst this characterisation of Aron undeniably rings true, it leaves open a rather large field within which to place him. Is he, as he has often been depicted, a Tocquevillian 'liberal'?[4] Or is he a 'neo-liberal', when we know of his participation in the infamous *Colloque Walter Lippmann* in Paris 1938, where the term was first coined?[5] This latter we might exclude immediately. Aron was no doubt a 'new' type of liberal for the twentieth century,[6] much like Tocqueville had been for the nineteenth, willing to think politics in the *'gros temps'* of the Cold War, but the epithet 'neo', in particular in terms of what it has come to mean, does not seem to capture him well at all.

For one, many of the participants in the *Colloque*—Ludwig von Mises, Friedrich von Hayek, Wilhelm Röpke, Aron himself—rejected the term or did not use it.[7] What we now identify as neoliberalism developed later, in the 1970s, and is associated with the rising influence of Milton Friedman, Gary Becker's Chicago School, and the Virginia School of Public Choice theorists James Buchanan and Gordon Tullock.[8] But that type of neoliberalism, which

Aron, the United States, and the Early Cold War, 1945–1953', *The International History Review*, Vol. 43, No. 4, 2021, pp. 796–814.

4. On Aron's liberalism and its legacies, see Daniel Mahoney, *The Liberal Political Science of Raymond Aron*, Lanham, Rowman and Littlefield, 1992; Jeremy Jennings, 'Raymond Aron and the Fate of French Liberalism', *European Journal of Political Theory*, Vol. 2, No. 4, 2003, pp. 365–371; Michael Behrent, 'Liberal Dispositions: Recent Scholarship on French Liberalism', *Modern Intellectual History*, Vol. 13, No. 2, 2016, pp. 447–477; and Emile Chabal, 'In the Shadow of Raymond Aron: The "Liberal Revival" of the 1980s' in *A Divided Republic: Nation, State and Citizenship in Contemporary France*, Cambridge, Cambridge University Press, 2015, pp. 135–157.

5. Nicholas Gane, 'In and Out of Neoliberalism: Reconsidering the Sociology of Raymond Aron', *Journal of Classical Sociology*, Vol. 16, No. 3, 2016, pp. 261–279. See also Perry Anderson, '*Dégringolade*: The Fall of France', *London Review of Books*, 2 September 2004 and Perry Anderson, '*Union Sucrée*: The Normalizing of France', *London Review of Books*, 23 September 2004.

6. H. S. Jones and Iain Stewart, 'Positive Political Science and the Uses of Political Theory in Post-War France: Raymond Aron in Context', *History of European Ideas*, Vol. 39, No. 1, 2013, pp. 35–50.

7. See Serge Audier, 'The French Reception of American Neoliberalism in the Late 1970s' in Stephen Sawyer and Iain Stewart, eds., *In Search of the Liberal Moment: Democracy, Antitotalitarianism, and Intellectual Politics in France since 1950*, Basingstoke, Palgrave Macmillan, 2016, pp. 167–8.

8. On the development of neoliberalism, see Daniel Stedman Jones, *Masters of the Universe: Hayek, Friedman, and the Birth of Neoliberal Politics*, Princeton, Princeton University Press, 2014; Angus Burgin, *The Great Persuasion: Reinventing Free Markets since the Depression*, Cambridge [MA], Harvard University Press, 2015; Quinn Slobodian, *Globalists: The End of Empire and the Birth of Neoliberalism*, Cambridge (MA), Harvard University Press, 2018; Serge Audier,

wished, in particular in its Becker Chicago School incarnation, to extend *economic* logic to all aspects of life, is far removed from the type of *political* liberalism Aron defended, which formally drew from a group of Francophone liberal thinkers (Montesquieu, Alexis de Tocqueville, Benjamin Constant, François Guizot) utterly foreign to the economic thinking of the Chicago School. That *political* liberalism is premised on a clear separation between economic and political spheres, precisely the separation neo-liberals want to void by bringing everything under the aegis of economics.

Nor can Aron's thought be subsumed under the banner of Hayek's libertarianism. As Jan-Werner Mueller succinctly puts it: 'Aron explicitly criticised Hayek's notion of liberty for being one-dimensional and ahistorical, and argued that the advanced industrial societies of the West had managed to find a *synthèse démocratico-libérale* which had absorbed the socialist critique of a purely negative understanding of liberty.'[9] Moreover, Aron was willing to entertain a degree of economic planning and welfare redistribution, something anathema to Hayek, and which led, on the latter's account, onto *The Road to Serfdom* (1944).[10] For Aron it was democracy, that is to say *politics*, that came first, with the market a tool to help foster political liberties, whereas for Hayek it was the market that needed to be defended from the encroachments of democratic politics.[11] As Micheal Behrent has written in another context: if Aron was 'in' the neoliberal moment, he was not 'of' it.[12]

This openness on Aron's part to entertain market planning and social redistribution—whether for conservative reasons or not, or indeed whether within different historical circumstances he would have defended the same ideas—has led Serge Audier to argue that Aron is best understood as a

---

Néo-libéralisme(s): Une archéologie intellectuelle, Paris, Grasset, 2012; and Serge Audier, *Le colloque Lippmann: Aux origines du 'néo-libéralisme'*, Lormont, Le Bord de l'eau, 2012.

9. Müller, 'Fear and Freedom', p. 56. See, in particular, Aron's critique of Hayek, 'La définition libérale de la liberté', in Raymond Aron, *Études Politiques*, Paris, Gallimard, 1972, pp. 195–215; his *Essai sur les libertés*, Paris, Pluriel, 2014; and his final course at the Collège de France, *Liberté et égalité*, Paris, Editions de l'EHESS, 2013, recently translated into English by Samuel Zeitlin as Raymond Aron, *Liberty and Equality*, Princeton, Princeton University Press, 2023.

10. See Craiutu, *Faces of Moderation*, pp. 62–5.

11. For more on Aron and Hayek, see Gwendal Châton, 'Libéralisme ou démocratie? Raymond Aron lecteur de Friedrich Hayek', *Revue de philosophie économique*, Vol. 17, No. 1, 2016, p. 103–134. See, further, Gwendal Châton, *Introduction à Raymond Aron*, Paris, La Découverte, 2023.

12. Michael Behrent, 'Foucault and France's Liberal Moment' in Sawyer and Stewart, *In Search of the Liberal Moment*, p. 156.

'social-liberal', one willing to try to reconcile socialism (Aron identified his own intellectual roots as coming from the left) with liberalism.[13] This places Aron in a lineage stretching back to Emile Durkheim, whom he wrote about throughout his career.[14] It also, of course, through attempting to combine liberty and equality, links him back to Tocqueville, and that association has been the longest and strongest.[15] This seems to have been publicly avowed in Aron's introduction to his classic sociological study *Les étapes de la pensée sociologique* (1967), where he declared his admiration for the '*limpide et triste*' (clear and sad) prose of Tocqueville's *Democracy in America*, leading to the sobriquet of labelling Aron himself a '*liberal triste*'.[16]

Whilst Aron's long reflections on modern democracy throughout his productive career naturally tie him to Tocqueville, that is not the full story. In fact, in the introduction to *Les étapes* in question, Aron placed his general reflections under the banner of the 'opposition Tocqueville-Marx'. He confessed that whilst he had been reading Marx for the past thirty-five years, he had only recently turned to Tocqueville, in the last ten years, as a way of criticising Marx. Ultimately, however, he would never hesitate between *Capital*, whose 'mysteries' never ceased to intrigue him, and *Democracy in America*: if his conclusions belonged to the 'English School' of Tocqueville, then his 'training' was in the 'German School' of Marx.[17]

13. Serge Audier, *Raymond Aron: La démocratie conflictuelle*, Paris, Michalon, 2004, pp. 61–88. On Audier and social-liberalism, see Daniel Steinmetz-Jenkins and Kevin Brookes, 'The Many Liberalisms of Serge Audier', *Journal of the History of Ideas*, Vol. 79, No. 1, 2018, pp. 45–63.

14. See, in particular, his chapter on Durkheim in Raymond Aron, *Les étapes de la pensée sociologique*, Paris, Gallimard, 1967, pp. 315–405. This was translated as *Main Currents of Sociological Thought*, New Brunswick, Transaction Publishers, 1998. The French editions are here cited and the translations are original.

15. See Stuart Campbell, 'The Tocquevillian Liberalism and Political Sociology of Raymond Aron', *The Historian*, Vol. 53, No. 2, 1991, pp. 303–316 and Stanley Hoffman's classic 'Aron et Tocqueville', *Commentaire*, Vol. 8, No. 28–29, 1985, pp. 200–212.

16. Aron, *Les étapes*, p. 21. See Giulio De Ligio, *La Tristezza del pensatore politico: Raymond Aron e il primato des politico*, Bologna, Bononia University Press, 2007.

17. Ibid. For the German *formation* of Aron's thought, see Iain Stewart, *Raymond Aron and Liberal Thought in the Twentieth Century*, Cambridge, Cambridge University Press, 2019, pp. 49–76. For a great review see Gianna Englert, 'Raymond Aron and Liberal Thought in the Twentieth Century. By Iain Stewart', *Perspectives on Politics*, Vol. 18, No. 3, 2020, pp. 932–933.

I: Machiavellians

Bringing Marx—and, in particular, critics of Marx—back into the fold (Aron was to continue to write on Marx long after *Les étapes*)[18] links the anti-Marxist and anti-Communist 'Cold War Liberal' Aron to the Tocquevillian Aron thinker of modern democracy. This chapter will argue that what ties the two— the anti-Communist and Tocquevevillian Aron—are the early twentieth century elite theorists of democracy whom Aron, following James Burnham, dubbed the 'Machiavellians': Gaetano Mosca, Vilfredo Pareto and Robert Michels.[19] It is through his engagement with these thinkers that Aron was able to articulate, on the one hand, his anti-Marxist critique of totalitarianism during World War II and the Cold War, and, on the other, develop his theory of democracy, which took as its basis the anti-Marxist 'fact of oligarchy', which these authors had, on Aron's account, first demonstrated.

The importance Mosca, Michels and, in particular, Pareto played in the development of Aron's thinking has been highlighted before, not least by Stuart Campbell's study of 'The Four Paretos of Raymond Aron', and Audier's more recent *Raymond Aron: La démocratie conflictuelle*.[20] The latter even develops what he calls a 'Tocquevillian-Machiavellian' paradigm to interpret Aron's democratic theory. Recognising the role the Machiavellians play in identifying the hierarchical nature of modern society in Aron's thought, Audier adds a Tocquevillian dimension to underline how Tocqueville had identified a specific egalitarian dynamic to modern life. Whilst Audier is undoubtedly correct in underlining this Tocquevillian dynamic, he is mistaken to think that the Machiavellians did not see the disappearance of old aristocracies: quite the opposite, their whole point was to show that even in modern egalitarian democracies that had overthrown their aristocratic class, elites stilled ruled, through their theories of the 'ruling class' (Mosca), 'circulation of elites' (Pareto), or the 'iron law of oligarchy' (Michels).[21] Moreover, these theories were developed in explicit contradistinction to the Marxist notion

---

18. See Raymond Aron, *D'une sainte famille à l'autre. Essai sur le marxisme imaginaire*, Paris, Gallimard, 1969 and *Le Marxisme de Marx*, Paris, Éditions de Fallois, 2002. For Aron's critique of Marx, see Daniel Mahoney, 'Aron, Marx, and Marxism', *European Journal of Political Theory*, Vol. 2, No. 4, 2003, pp. 415–427.

19. James Burnham, *The Machiavellians: Defenders of Freedom*, New York, John Day, 1943.

20. Stuart Campbell, 'The Four Paretos of Raymond Aron', *Journal of the History of Ideas*, Vol. 47, No. 2, 1986, pp. 287–298 and Audier, *La démocratie conflictuelle*.

21. Audier, *La démocratie conflictuelle*, pp. 53–5.

that once the proletarian revolution completed, all hierarchies would melt away—that the 'government of people', as Engels, borrowing from Saint-Simon, put it, would give way to the 'administration of things'—which is why Aron, in his desire to criticise Marxism, was so taken by them.

Placing the Machiavellians back into the heart of Aron's thinking allows us to see that Aron's liberalism was not simply a negative or minimalist one. Rather, in articulating a theory of democracy based on the 'fact of oligarchy', Aron, notably in his seminal *Démocratie et totalitarisme* (1965), was able to elaborate a positive theory of democracy (a 'Constitutional-Pluralist' regime), one which he actively defended against totalitarianism (a 'Party Monopolistic' regime).[22] The Machiavellian basis of his thought also provides a coherence to his political theory,[23] from elaborating his critique of totalitarianism on the international sphere to developing his sociological theory of hierarchical modern democratic society on the domestic one. Moreover, beyond political theory, international relations and sociology, there is reason to believe that these elitist notions underpinned his work in the philosophy of history too:[24] in *Dimensions de la conscience historique* (1961), Aron explained that history is the interplay between two central notions, *drama* and *process*. If *process* attempts to account for the necessary transformation of society, notably in this case the development of industrial society, *drama* captures the contingent action of men within this longer history. So if process is concerned with structural factors, drama is the fact of a small number of individuals; or, in other words, of an elite.[25]

Building on Campbell's and Audier's work, this chapter will at first deepen Aron's engagement with the Machiavellians, by tracing his intellectual dialogue with Pareto and how that gave him the intellectual tools to critique totalitarian regimes on the one hand and develop a positive theory of democracy on the other. It will be particularly attentive, second, to the shift in Aron's appreciation of Pareto, from seeing him in his early days as an apologist of fascism to a fellow-in-arms critic of totalitarianism and defender of democracy.

22. Alan Scott, 'Raymond Aron's Political Sociology of Regime and Party', *Journal of Classical Sociology*, Vol. 11, No. 2, 2011, pp. 155–171.

23. On Aron developing a 'distinctively French style of liberal political theory', see Steven Smith, 'Raymond Aron: Philosopher of Liberties', *Society*, Vol. 60, 2023, pp. 944–953.

24. Iain Stewart, 'Existentialist Manifesto or Conservative Political Science? Problems in Interpreting Raymond Aron's *Introduction à la philosophie de l'histoire*', *European Review of History: Revue européenne d'histoire*, Vol. 16, No. 2, 2009, pp. 217–233.

25. Raymond Aron, *Dimensions de la conscience historique*, Paris, Les Belles Lettres, 2011, p. 238.

The role the ex-Trotskyist Burnham's now forgotten book, *The Machiavellians: Defenders of Freedom* (1943), played in this change of heart will be key. Third, it will turn its attention to Aron's often overlooked sociological writings of the 1950s and 1960s, where he developed, through his engagement with the Machiavellian thinkers, his concept of a 'divided' (*divisée*) and 'unified' (*unifiée*) elite, which was to serve as the basis for distinguishing liberal-democratic from non-democratic regimes. How Aron articulated the passage from political sociology to political philosophy, notably in *Les étapes* and *Démocratie et totalitarisme*, will be of particular interest.

The final part will *comfort* and *extend* Audier's thesis of a French 'Machiavellian moment' in post-war French political philosophy.[26] *Comfort* in underlining how Aron partook in the two types of reflections John Pocock attributes to his original 'Machiavellians' (Machiavelli, Savonarola, Guicciardini, Giannotti) in his reference *The Machiavellian Moment*: a concern about providing a secular conception of the sequence of time, and an anxiety surrounding the stability of regimes and their temporal finitude.[27] Aron, through his engagement with Max Weber in particular, sustained a continuous interest in political rationality—indeed, Aron is possibly best remembered today for his political judgement—and, alongside his work in the philosophy of history, both these aspects involved a serious reflection upon the sequence of time and how it might be understood and anticipated;[28] precisely what Machiavelli was attempting to address through his notions of 'virtue' and 'fortune'.

Moreover, Aron's writings during the war on the totalitarian threat to liberal democracies, and his post-war theorisation of the internal causes of corruption of 'Constitutional-Pluralist' regimes—a subject he returned to throughout *Démocratie et totalitarisme*[29]—echoed the worry Pocock's 'Machiavellians' had

---

26. Serge Audier, *Machiavel, conflit et liberté*, Paris, Vrin, 2005. Thanks to Iain Stewart for pushing on this point.

27. John Pocock, *The Machiavellian Moment: Florentine Political Thought and the Atlantic Republican Tradition*, Princeton, Princeton University Press, 2016, pp. xxi–xxiv.

28. On Aron's philosophy of history and its relation to political 'action', see Sophie Marcotte Chénard, *Devant l'histoire en crise: Raymond Aron et Leo Strauss*, Montréal, Les Presses de l'Université de Montréal, 2022 and Sophie Marcotte-Chenard, 'What Can We Learn from Political History? Leo Strauss and Raymond Aron, Readers of Thucydides', *The Review of Politics*, Vol. 80, 2018, pp. 57–86.

29. See chapters 9–11 and 18–19 in Raymond Aron, *Démocratie et totalitarisme*, Paris, Gallimard, 1965, pp. 166–219, 337–70 (translated as *Democracy and Totalitarianism*, New York, Praeger, 1969).

concerning their respective Republics. Aron, after all, lived through the transition from the Fourth to the Fifth French Republic, of which he attempted to give an account of in the introduction to *Démocratie*.[30] *Extend* in the sense that these reflections should not be solely limited to Aron, Maurice Merlau-Ponty and Claude Lefort, as (correctly) with Audier, but should also encompass some of Lefort's colleagues at the Centre Raymond Aron, notably Pierre Manent, Bernard Manin and Pierre Rosanvallon, for whom the themes of conflict, balanced government, and the stability of the regime, mediated through Aron, are central.[31]

The conclusion will offer some thoughts on how Aron's use of the Machiavellians differs from recent 'Neo-Republican' understandings offered by Pocock, Quentin Skinner and Philip Pettit—or the more recent 'populist' interpretation of John McCormick—to emphasise a liberal reading where it is the struggle between the *plebs* and the *patricians*, read through Mosca's theory of the ruling class, that guarantees liberty.[32] As Audier has argued, Aron's 'Machiavellianism' centres on a 'conflictual pluralism'[33] that sees liberty as emerging from within the space opened up by competing parties, interests, and groups. That conception of liberty, this chapters submits, emerged through his engagement with his own 'Machiavellians'—Mosca, Pareto, and Michels—instead of Machiavelli as such.

The theme of 'conflictual pluralism' did not die with Aron: it is present not solely in Lefort's work, but also in the work of Manent, Manin and Rosanvallon. Indeed, Rosanvallon's dialogue with Michels and Moisie Ostrogorski—a figure almost entirely forgotten today—dates back at least to his time as a young *auto-gestionnaire*. The final part of this chapter will thus explore the legacy of Aron's Machiavellianism and how its figures were used to address new questions, notably regarding representation, and in close the chapter will

---

30. Ibid., pp. 9–19.

31. On the Centre Raymond Aron, see Kevin Duong, '"Does Democracy End in Terror?" Transformations of Antitotalitarianism in Postwar France', *Modern Intellectual History*, Vol. 14, No. 2, 2017, pp. 537–563.

32. Pocock, *The Machiavellian Moment*; Quentin Skinner, *Liberty before Liberalism*, Cambridge, Cambridge University Press, 1998; Philip Pettit, *Republicanism: A Theory of Freedom and Government*, Oxford, Clarendon Press, 1997; John McCormick, *Machiavellian Democracy*, Cambridge, Cambridge University Press, 2011; John McCormick, *Reading Machiavelli: Scandalous Books, Suspect Engagements, and the Virtue of Populist Politics*, Princeton, Princeton University Press, 2018.

33. Audier, *Machiavel, conflit et liberté*, p. 28.

ask whether, with our political system awash with money, Aron's critique of the 'plutocratic' nature of modern democracies, drawn from Pareto, still captures something essential about the world we live in today.

II: Pareto and Burnham

Aron engaged with Pareto from very early on, and that engagement was to continue through his productive career. His first published piece came in 1937, whilst he was still finishing his PhD. It was entitled 'La sociologie de Pareto' ('Pareto's Sociology'), and it was published in Max Horkheimer's *Zeitschrift für Sozialforschung*.[34] In it Aron was highly critical of Pareto, presenting him as a proto-Fascist thinker: by rejecting the Marxist idea of a forthcoming proletarian revolution that would do away with class inequality by affirming the historical, social and political persistence of elites, Aron saw in Pareto's sociology a theory that reactionary bourgeois could seize upon to fight a rear-guard action against revolutionary forces. Yet Aron also drew three key insights from his study of Pareto, which he retained throughout his life. First, that the sphere of politics was autonomous from the economic and social spheres: a highly significant move in a French context dominated by Marxist accounts of the primacy of economics, or Durkheimian views on the pre-eminence of the social.[35] Aron's view that it was politics that came first is crucial to understanding the fact that whilst the modern world is characterised by being an industrial society, the type of political regime that goes with it—democratic or not[36]—is ultimately a political question, and it is that question that will mark the trilogy of lectures Aron will give at the Sorbonne in the 1950s and 1960s: *Dix-huit leçons sur la société industrielle* (1963), *La Lutte des classes* (1964), and *Démocratie et totalitarisme* (1965).[37]

---

34. Raymond Aron, 'La sociologie de Pareto' in *Zeitschrift für Sozialforschung*, Vol. 6, No. 3, 1937, pp. 489–521.

35. On the primacy of the political, see Giulio De Ligio, 'The Question of Political Regime and the Problems of Democracy: Aron and the Alternative of Tocqueville' in José Colen and Elisabeth Dutartre-Michaut, eds., *The Companion to Raymond Aron*, New York, Palgrave Macmillan, 2015, pp. 119–135; and Daniel Mahoney 'Introduction: Raymond Aron and the Persistence of the Political', *Perspectives on Political Science*, Vol. 35, No. 2, 2006, pp. 73–74.

36. Roy Pierce, 'Liberalism and Democracy in the Thought of Raymond Aron', *The Journal of Politics*, Vol. 25, No. 1, 1963, pp. 14–35.

37. This suggests that whilst Aron thought that Eastern and Western societies shared certain characteristics, he was not a straight proponent of 'convergence theory'. On convergence theory,

Second, Aron drew from Pareto's sociology a theory of fascist leadership, which he explained as a hypocritical demagogue, willing to use any type of myth to excite the crowds, but who defended the interests of the elites, whom he ultimately ruled in favour of.[38] This more analytical Pareto was the one Aron was to grow closer to over the next decades. Indeed, Pareto the analyst of fascism, rather than its spokesman, was to become the dominant interpretation of Pareto that Aron would develop over time, most notably in his later *Les étapes*. Aron imparted blame of the rise of the fascist leader to the liberal bourgeoisie, who, losing their nerve in face of communist agitation, were willing to throw in their lot with a violent elite.[39] This seems not solely quite perceptive in terms of both the rise of Mussolini and Hitler, who relied at first on traditional conservative elites to cement their power, before disposing of them, but also offered Aron his third insight derived from Pareto: that liberalism had to be defended, sometimes even with force.

When the article was reprinted some forty years later in 1978 in the *Revue européenne des sciences sociales*, Aron explicitly distanced himself from his early piece, explaining in a brief preamble that the views expressed there no longer represented his current views.[40] What had changed? In a seminal article published in 1986, based on an interview conducted with Aron in 1982, one year before his death, Campbell analysed the 'four Paretos' Aron claimed to have been in existence in his work.[41] These four Paretos, which Aron himself identified in his 1973 text 'Lectures de Pareto', were: the fascist Pareto, the authoritarian Machiavellian Pareto, the liberal Machiavellian Pareto, and the Pareto the cynic.[42] There is much to be said about reading Aron's Paretos in this way. We have already explored the fascist Pareto, and it is true that during his wartime journalist writings Aron started to use the more analytical Pareto as a way of making sense of rising totalitarianism in Europe, whether Fascist, National-Socialist, or Communist: what Campbell identifies as the 'authoritarian

see Daniel Mahoney, 'The Totalitarian Negation of Man: Raymond Aron on Ideology and Totalitarianism' in Colen and Dutartre-Michaut, eds., *The Companion to Raymond Aron*, pp. 137–148.

38. Aron, 'La sociologie', pp. 516–9.

39. Ibid., pp. 518–9.

40. Raymond Aron, 'La sociologie de Pareto' in *Revue européenne des science sociales*, Vol. 16, No. 43, 1978, pp. 5–33.

41. Campbell, 'Four Paretos', p. 287.

42. Raymond Aron, 'Lectures de Pareto' in *Machiavel et les tyrannies modernes*, Paris, Editions de Fallois, 1993, pp. 263–7.

Machiavellian Pareto'. Indeed, the first piece he would write for *La France libre*, which he was editing from London as part of the wartime effort under Charles de Gaulle, with whom he had an oftentimes fractious relationship, was entitled 'Le machiavélianisme, doctrine des tyrannies modernes' (1940).[43] Inspired by his mentor Elie Halevy's *L'Ère des tyrannies* (1938),[44] Aron set out to analyse the rise of both fascism and communism through the lenses of 'Machiavellianism'.[45] Fascism on this account, as we saw above, adopted a Machiavellian/Paretean philosophy, whilst Communism adopted Machiavellian tactics.[46]

Whilst these four Paretos are undeniably in existence in Aron's work, and offer helpful prisms through which to understand it, it would be a mistake, however, to think of these Paretos as temporal and sequential Paretos for Aron, which would somehow map themselves back onto Aron's own development. We have already explored the evolution of the 'Fascist Pareto', from apologist of fascism in the pre-war writings to analyst of fascism post-war. Pareto the cynic, which we haven't much discussed, is present throughout Aron's writing on Pareto, from his early 1937 piece on 'La Sociologie' to his later 1967 *Les étapes*, and through to his 'Lectures de Pareto' of 1974: although that Aron himself would become more cynical at the end of his life is a point well taken.[47] Finally, it seems difficult to disentangle the so-called 'authoritarian' from the 'liberal' Machiavellian Pareto of the 1940s/50s to 1960s, the Pareto used both to critique totalitarianism and to develop a theory of democracy, an inseparable task in the context of the Cold War. Rather than these four different moments, what seems of most importance is the shift from Aron's early view of Pareto as a proto-Fascist to his having a more positive view of Pareto—a Pareto who ultimately served the cause of freedom—as Aron himself

43. Raymond Aron, 'Le machiavélisme, doctrine des tyrannies modernes' in Raymond Aron, *Penser la liberté, penser la démocratie*, Gallimard, Paris, 2005, pp. 115–124. See also the wartime texts collected as 'L'Homme contre les tyrants' in ibid., pp. 107–384 and in Aron, *Machiavel et les tyrannies modernes*. On this period, see Cherniss, *Liberalism in Dark Times*, pp. 110–115, and on Aron and his time at *La France libre*, see Elias Forneris, 'Raymond Aron's War: A "History of the Present" (1940–1944)', *The Tocqueville Review/La Revue Tocqueville*, Vol. 43, no. 2, 2022, pp. 7–38.

44. Iain Stewart, *Raymond Aron and the History of Liberal Thought in France*, pp. 79–84.

45. Nicolas Guilhot, *After the Enlightenment: Political Realism and International Relations in the Mid-Twentieth Century*, Cambridge, Cambridge University Press, 2017.

46. Campbell, 'Four Paretos', p. 289.

47. See, variously, Aron, 'La sociologie', pp. 519–520; Aron, *Les étapes*, p. 20; Aron, 'Lectures', p. 263. On Aron's cynicism, see Campbell, pp. 297–8.

acknowledged in the 1982 interview.[48] And that shift came about as a result of his discovery of Burnham in the 1940s.

Burnham, a disappointed Trotskyist turned reactionary critic of bureaucracy, is best remembered for his 1941 book *The Managerial Revolution*.[49] That book, in the era of Donald Trump, is going through a mini-renaissance,[50] but his 1943 follow-up *The Machiavellians: Defenders of Freedom* is now almost completely forgotten, and no longer in print. Aron, who met Burnham, however, was very taken by it, and personally arranged for it to be published in the 'Liberté de l'esprit' series he was directing at Calmann-Lévy in 1949.[51] In a 1949 article, 'Histoire et politique', Aron registered his debt to Burnham, explaining that his reading of Pareto and the other Machiavellians, who proposed a more 'realistic' or 'pessimistic' account of power, in which power was needed to check power, served as a critique of the millenarianism of Communism: that societies that aim for the highest level of perfection concerning their regimes are in fact the ones most likely to use oppressive and totalitarian means to achieve it.[52] What was needed instead was a 'divided' elite that aimed not for a perfect society, but made best do with the imperfect societies in which they lived.

This critique of millenarianism Marxism, married to a more positive formulation of what a society that wishes to uphold liberty should look like, means that the Machiavellian authoritarian and the Machiavellian liberal Pareto go hand in hand. It also underlines how central Burnham's reading of Pareto and his Machiavellian colleagues was to Aron's understanding of them, and particularly in his more positive, post-war, reappraisal of them. Indeed, by emphasising how power needs to be checked and not given unlimited reign— that it is counter-powers that are the best guarantors of freedom—Pareto and the Machiavellians, on Aron's account, fundamentally furthered the cause of modern freedom, as the subtitle to Burnham's book had intimated. As he would come to fully theorise in both his sociological and political writings of the 1950s and 1960s, liberty was to be found, for Aron, from the fact that

48. Campbell, 'Four Paretos', p. 287.

49. James Burnham, *The Managerial Revolution*, Harmondsworth, Pelican Books, 1945.

50. See Julius Krein, 'James Burnham's Managerial Elite', *American Affairs*, Vol. I, No. 1, 2017, pp. 126–51. *American Affairs*, with Julius Krein as its editor, was launched in 2017 to 'help explain Trumpism'. See, further, Alan Wald, 'From Trotsky to Buckley', *Jacobin*, 15/09/2017.

51. James Burnham, *Les Machiavéliens: Défenseurs de la liberté*, Paris, Calmann-Lévy, 1949.

52. Raymond Aron, 'Histoire et politique' in Aron, *Penser la liberté, penser la démocratie*, p. 533.

different political, social and economic elites all compete for power. It is within the space opened up between these opposing forces that liberty can flourish.

III: Divided and Unified Elites

In the second chapter of *Démocratie et totalitarisme*, entitled 'From philosophy to political sociology', Aron questioned the relation political philosophy, which he defined as the exercise of judging political regimes, entertained with sociology, which comprised a factual study of different regimes. He started with Aristotle, whose *Politics* combined both political sociology, in its classification of regimes into monarchies, aristocracies and polities—alongside their corrupted versions tyranny, oligarchy and democracy—and political philosophy, in that it judged these regimes according to a human telos.[53] In a contemporary sociological text, one we'll have occasion to return to, Aron pointed out that when Aristotle came to the detailed description of the ancient Greek cities, he left aside his abstract classification and posited instead a perennial conflict between oligarchy and democracy, between the rich and the poor, between the rulers and the ruled.[54]

Nevertheless, what follows in *Démocratie* is a slightly potted history of ideas, where Aron discusses the relation between sociology and politics in figures such as Montesquieu, Hobbes, Marx and Popper. Montesquieu's new classification of regimes into republic, monarchy and despotism will in fact serve as the opening for the later *Les étapes*, where Aron examined the passage from political theory to sociology by exploring how Montesquieu, after elaborating his new conceptual schema, turned to studying the political sociology of these regimes, by analysing both their *material* (climate, geography) and *social* (religion, commerce) causes.[55]

But the notion of the conflict between ruler and ruled remained. Aron located the birth of *modern* political sociology in the nineteenth century, notably with the work of Comte and Marx. This modern sociology taught us two things: that all regimes are essentially defined by the struggle for power, and

---

53. Aron, *Démocratie et totalitarisme*, pp. 38–41. On Aron and Aristotle see Alexis Carré, 'Raymond Aron and the Moral and Cultural Conditions of Liberal Democracy during War Time', *History of European Ideas*, Vol. 49, No. 4, 2023, pp. 722–736.

54. Raymond Aron, 'Catégories dirigeantes ou classe dirigeante?' in Raymond Aron, *Études Sociologiques*, Paris, PUF, 1988, p. 88.

55. Aron, *Les étapes*, pp. 27–52.

the fact that it is always the few who rule.[56] These two new '*savoirs*' Aron attributed to the Machiavellians, and to Pareto in particular: whilst Marx was right to identify the conflictual nature of politics, he was mistaken to think that the class struggle would come to an end after the proletarian revolution, and that the 'rule of the (few) men' could be replaced with the 'administration of things', to use Engel's—borrowed from Saint-Simon—formulation. Pareto's answer to Marx was that the conflict would continue in the future, and the question of politics continued to be 'who rules?'.[57]

This 'Machiavellian' critique of democracy—that all regimes are in fact oligarchic, that it is always the few who rule—Aron had already developed in his 1950s lectures *Introduction à la philosophie politique* at l'*École nationale d'administration* (ENA), set up by de Gaulle after the war to train the future high civil service in charge of reconstructing the country, and which in reality continues to furnish France with a large portion of its political class even today.[58] There he explicitly cited Pareto, Mosca and Burnham as being the originators of this theory, but he did not leave it at that, arguing that once the oligarchic nature of democracy had been stated, then the question of how that oligarchy is constituted and what its relation to the masses is become the key political questions.[59] In *Démocratie*, Aron went further still, criticising the 'Machiavellian' conception as being too 'cynical'—a throwback to our discussion of Pareto above—as it concentrates solely on the struggle for power, but overlooks the fact that one can still judge between regimes to see which one is best.[60]

The type of political sociology, then, that Aron wished to practice is one that does not simply affirm the Machiavellian struggle for power, nor indeed grounds itself on an Aristotelian telos of human nature. Instead, basing itself on the 'fact of oligarchy', which modern sociology has brought to light, it desires to evaluate the different regimes in existence to see which one is more legitimate, which one can be considered the best.[61] This is precisely what Aron

56. Aron, *Démocratie*, p. 51.

57. Ibid., pp. 49–50.

58. See Hugo Drochon, 'De Gaulle's Long Shadow: The Making and Unmaking of France's Fifth Republic', *The Nation*, 18 February 2020.

59. Raymond Aron, *Introduction à la philosophie politiques: Démocratie et révolution*, Paris, Éditions du Fallois, 1997, pp. 55–8.

60. Aron, *Démocratie*, pp. 51–3.

61. Ibid.

did in the rest of *Démocratie*, comparing the Western European and American 'Constitutional-Pluralist' regimes to the Eastern 'Party Monopolistic' regime of the USSR, coming down heavily in favour of the former. But to get a better sense of the make-up of these regimes, we must return to Aron's sociological writings of the 1950s and 1960s, where he developed his theory of the 'divided' and 'unified' elite.

IV: Political Sociology

In three fundamental sociological texts of the 1950s and 1960s—'Structure sociale et structure de l'élite' (1950), 'Classe sociale, classe politique, classe dirigeante' (1960) and 'Catégoies dirigeantes ou classe dirigeante?' (1965)— Aron fleshed out his theory of elite rule. Building explicitly on Pareto, Mosca and Michels, read again through Burnham,[62] Aron presented what he termed a 'synthesis' between Marx and Pareto.[63] It is in the 1960 text, 'Classe sociale, classe politique, classe dirigeante', that the notion of the 'fact of oligarchy'— alongside Michels, its originator—first appears,[64] although Aron had already theorised the idea that if one can talk of democracy as government 'for' the people, it would be a mistake, because of the fact that it is always the few who rule, to talk of government 'by' the people.[65] The theme of Paretian 'cynicism' returns here too, with Aron admitting that one could read—as he had done in the past—these Machiavellian thinkers as being, in their rejection of socialism, proto-Fascists.[66]

The main notion Aron developed over the course of these writings is the view that societies are determined by the relation between what he calls either the *classes* or *catégories dirigeantes*—what in English we might term the *ruling*

---

62. See, variously, Raymond Aron, 'Structure sociale et structure de l'élite', 'Classe sociale, classe politique, classe dirigeante' and 'Catégorie dirigeantes ou classe dirigeante?' in Aron, *Études Sociologiques*, pp. 111, 123, 141, 143, 188, 191.

63. Raymond Aron, 'Structure sociale et structure de l'élite', pp. 111, 142. This paper was first given at the LSE in 1949, and published in English as 'Social Structure and the Ruling Class', *British Journal of Sociology*, Vol. 1, No. 1, 1950, pp. 1–16 and No. 2, pp. 126–143. Tocqueville, and indeed Comte, are present here too (Aron, 'Classe sociale, classe politique, classe dirigeante', pp. 147, 153; 'Catégories dirigeantes ou classe dirigeante?', p. 194).

64. Aron, 'Classe sociale, classe politique, classe dirigeante', pp. 149, 155.

65. Aron, 'Structure sociale et structure de l'élite', pp. 121–2.

66. Aron, 'Classe sociale, classe politique, classe dirigeante', pp. 149, 161.

classes (the plural is key)[67]—and the *classe* or *personnel politique*, namely the more directly political class or politicians.[68] This is an anti-Marxist point: what Aron is saying is that it is not the relation between social classes (capitalists v. the proletariat) that determines society, as Marx would have it, but, rather, the relation the different social, economic, bureaucratic elites—the 'ruling classes'—entertain with politicians that defines the regime.[69] By 'ruling classes' Aron gives trade union leaders, captains of industry, the high civil service, the judiciary and the military as examples, namely leaders of the different spheres that make up society (masses, money, bureaucracy, military).[70]

In elaborating this theory of elite rule, Aron built on each of the earlier Machiavellian thinkers. From Michels he borrowed the 'iron law of oligarchy', but transformed it into a 'fact' that itself needs to be evaluated, and from which other sociological questions—how is this oligarchy formed? who is it in and how are they recruited?—emanate. From Pareto he took the notion of 'elite', namely those who are the leaders in their respective fields, and used Mosca's term of the 'ruling class' to designate them. But on the basis that there is not *one* ruling class, but in fact as many as there are spheres without which governing would not be possible—the economy, workforce, military[71]—he turned Mosca's term into a plural—ruling *classes*—and came up with a new term, the political *personnel*, to designate politicians in the strict sense of the word.

Aron articulated the relation the ruling classes entertain with the political personnel through the notion of a 'divided' or 'unified' elite, namely whether political, economic, social, military or legal elites find themselves within the same institution, for example, a unified political party, or whether they are divided within themselves, that is, they have their own, independent, institutions that are in competition with one another.[72] The question for Aron is whether all the political, economic, social, etc. decisions will be taken by the

67. Remember that the paper 'Structure sociale et structure de l'élite', first given in English, had the title 'Social Structure and the Ruling Class'. *The Ruling Class* is the English title given to Mosca's main work.

68. Aron, 'Classe sociale, classe politique, classe dirigeante', pp. 151, 154, 157; 'Catégories dirigeantes ou classe dirigeante? ', p. 187, 193.

69. Aron, 'Classe sociale, classe politique, classe dirigeante', p. 157.

70. Aron, 'Catégoies dirigeantes ou classe dirigeante', pp. 193–4. These different categories are what Comte, according to Aron, named the 'temporal power'.

71. Aron, 'Classe sociale, classe politique, classe dirigeante', p. 151,

72. Aron, 'Structure sociale et structure de l'élite', p. 123.

same people, at the same time, and within the same institutions, or whether these decisions will be taken by different people, at different—and often conflicting—times and going in conflicting directions, in different settings.

That is, for Aron, the difference between a divided and unified elite, and the regime will be determined by how *constitutionally* the relation between the different elites is organised. Aron, however, did not believe that a unified elite would mean conflict would disappear. Quite the contrary: conflict is inescapable; it is part of the genetic make-up of our societies. And because all the interests are centralised in a common institution, it will manifest itself through extra-institutional and extra-constitutional ways, most probably through violence—already we see here how Aron will favour a divided over a unified elite.[73]

Aron engaged in these writings in a fruitful debate with C. Wright Mills' recently published *The Power Elite* (1956), which posited the existence of a *united* elite, one that takes all its decisions in common and for its own benefit, in cooperation and not in competition with itself, which was the opposing theory Robert Dahl developed in his answer to Mills in *Who Governs?* (1961), as we have seen in the previous chapter.[74] Based on his view that conflict will always manifest itself, Aron rejected Mills' thesis as conspiracy theorising: he explained that he is not convinced the examples Mills provides are clearly of collusion.[75] Instead, he argued that reality is to be found somewhere between the two extremes—Mills' power elite and Dahl's polyarchy—between pure collusion and pure competition.[76] A ruling class will never be purely unified or purely divided—those are Kantian/Weberian, two thinkers would strongly influenced Aron,[77] 'ideal-types'—but elites will be more or less divided.

Whilst Aron could see how a unified elite might be more efficient in its rule,[78] his own preference is division. He explained that when a unified elite concentrates within its grasp all political, economic and social power, then the

73. Ibid., p. 139.

74. For Aron's engagement with the debate between Mills and Dahl, see Aron's famous 1964 text 'Macht, Power, Puissance: prose démocratique ou poésie démonique?' in Aron, *Études Politique*, pp. 171–194.

75. Aron, 'Classe sociale, classe politique, classe dirigeante', pp. 151, 156, 162; 'Catégorie dirigeantes ou classe dirigeante?', p. 191, 200.

76. Aron, 'Catégories dirigeantes ou classe dirigeante?', p. 201.

77. Reed Davis, 'The Phenomenology of Raymond Aron', *European Journal of Political Theory*, Vol. 2, No. 4, 2003, pp. 401–413.

78. Aron, 'Classe sociale, classe politique, classe dirigeante', p. 165.

masses find themselves defenceless against them.[79] He expressed a preference
for dialogue between the rulers and the ruled that is constitutionally organised: as with conflict, dialogue between the two always happens, but when
formally organised, bloodshed can be avoided.[80] In the end, checks and bal-
ances are still for Aron the best guarantor of liberty,[81] and, like all good liberals,
he offered a romanticised version of the English 'Establishment' as his ideal
ruling class: one situated between the two extremes of unity and division,
which, although it has a ruling class, is one open to talent and is willing to as-
similate within it the leaders of those who oppose it.[82]

In *Démocratie et totalitarisme*, Aron used his notions of a 'unified' and 'divided' elite to analyse the political systems of the East and the West,[83] classifying the former as a 'Party Monopolistic' regime, one where the totality of the
ruling classes is concentrated in the Party, and the latter as a 'Constitutional-
Pluralist' regime, which allows for structured competition between different
political parties, and where the ruling classes are divided: the emphasis on
political party here comes from Michels, who concentrated his 'iron law of
oligarchy' in his study of modern, highly centralised and hierarchical, political
parties. The Machiavellians—Pareto, Mosca, Michels, Burnham—are again at
the centre of his reflections; indeed one of his chapters on the Western
'Constitutional-Pluralist' regime is entitled 'The oligarchic character of the
Constitutional-Pluralist regimes'.[84] And the themes developed in his
sociological studies provide the bedrock upon which Aron constructed his
own democratic theory: Mosca's political personnel, the 'fact' of oligarchy and
the further political questions its raises, government *for* rather than *by* the
people, even ruling class conspiracies surrounding Jesuits, Freemasons and
petrol companies make an appearance.[85]

His conclusions are the same too: he attributes directly to Mosca the
thought that a divided 'Constitutional-Pluralist' regime provides the 'best

79. Aron, 'Structure social et structure de l'élite', pp. 124–5.

80. Aron, 'Classe sociale, classe politique, classe dirigeante', p. 162.

81. Aron, 'Structure social et structure de l'élite', p. 142.

82. Aron, 'Classe sociale, classe politique, classe dirigeante', p. 155.

83. The notion of 'divided' and 'unified' elite also appears in *La lutte des classes*, the second
of the Sorbonne 'trilogy' (Raymond Aron, *La lutte des classes* in Aron, *Penser la liberté, penser la
démocratie*, pp. 1088–1098).

84. Aron, *Démocratie*, pp. 128–132.

85. Ibid., pp. 128–132, 149. Interestingly, Aron himself Jewish, does not mention antisemitic
conspiracy theories.

guaranties for the governed'.[86] As he had explained in his *Introduction à la philosophie politique* lectures, if human nature, as the Machiavellians had pointed out, should be understood pessimistically, then democracy is the least worst regime because it legally regulates competition between groups, leading to what Audier terms the 'conflictual balance of social forces'.[87] Yet keeping to his idea that extremes are to be avoided, if Aron had expressed fears about a too-unified elite, he also in *Démocratie* expressed concerns about a too-divided elite, one which would be too dispersed, unstable and inefficient to be able to rule in an effective manner.[88] Democracies have to find the right balance and not fall into demagogy.[89]

V: The Centre Raymond Aron

This emphasis on corruption and the imperfection of the political regime—topics that appear as chapter titles in the Conclusion of *Démocratie*[90]—places Aron squarely within the themes of the 'Machiavellian Moment' Pocock had first theorised in 1975. For Pocock, that moment—which he would subsequently extend to seventeenth-century England and the work of James Harrington, and to eighteenth-century American debates over virtue and commerce—was marked by a dual reflection entertained by the (original) 'Machiavellians' (Machiavelli, Savonarola, Guicciardini, Giannotti): the problem of elaborating a non-transcendental account of the passage of time, married to confronting the temporal finitude of the republic.[91]

With his wartime writings on the 'Machiavellian' threat of totalitarianism to Western liberal-democratic regimes, and studies of the inevitable corruption of the 'Constitutional-Pluralist' regime, Aron, who also lived through de Gaulle's forceful passage from the Fourth to the Fifth Republic, which he attempted to account for in the introduction to *Démocratie*, perfectly mirrored

86. Ibid., pp. 134–5.

87. Aron, *Introduction à la philosophie politique*, pp. 135–6; Audier, *La démocratie conflictuelle*, p. 46.

88. Aron, *Démocratie*, p. 149. For the view that a stable liberal-democracy needs a 'consensual united elite', and that either 'disunited' or 'ideologically united' elites leads to either authoritarian or totalitarian regimes, respectively, see John Highley and Michael Burton, *Elite Foundations of Liberal Democracy*, Lanham, Rowman & Littlefield, 2006.

89. Aron, *Introduction à la philosophie politique*, p. 56.

90. Aron, *Démocratie*, pp. 337–54.

91. Pocock, *The Machiavellian Moment*, p. xxiv.

the republican concerns of his 'Machiavellian' predecessors. Moreover, in large part due to his lifelong engagement with Weber's work on political rationality,[92] Aron thought long and hard about how to formulate a secular account of time, notably through his work on the philosophy of history that had been the subject of his PhD, and Aron is perhaps still best remembered today as he who exercised the best political judgement during these turbulent years.[93]

This has led Audier to posit a post-war *'moment machiavélien francais'*, encompassing Aron, the phenomenologist Maurice Merleau-Ponty and the political philosopher Claude Lefort.[94] Indeed, Lefort wrote his PhD on Machiavelli under Aron's supervision during the 1960s, and is known to have attended Aron's lectures at the Sorbonne that were to become *Démocratie et totalitarisme*. That PhD, completed in 1971, was published one year later as *Le travail de l'oeuvre Machiavel*. As Iain Stewart has argued, however, Lefort, whilst acknowledging Aron's input, would ultimately reject Aron's more institutional and sociological understanding of democracy in favour of a Merleau-Ponty influenced symbolic conception.[95] Nevertheless, his theory of democracy as a *lieu vide*—an 'empty space'—which he developed in his seminal text, 'La question de la démocratie', did posit a fundamental (Machiavellian) division at the root of society.[96] Moreover, as Keving Duong has recently reminded us, Lefort's early work, alongside Cornelius Castoriadis' in their jointly founded journal *Socialisme ou Barbarie*, was a critique of socialist bureaucracy, a theme reminiscent of Michels, although there does not seem to have been any direct references to his work.[97]

Audier is undeniably right in identifying a French 'Machiavellian moment' in the works of Aron, Merleau-Ponty and Lefort, but a strong contender for

---

92. See Raymond Aron, 'La rationalité politique', *Commentaire*, No. 156, 2016, pp. 725–42, with an introduction by Sophie Marcotte Chénard.

93. His PhD, entitled *Introduction à la philosophie de l'histoire. Essai sur les limites de l'objectivité historique*, was published the same year it was defended, in 1938, by Gallimard.

94. Audier, *Machiavel, conflit et liberté*.

95. Iain Stewart, *Raymond Aron and the History of Liberal Thought in France*, p. 213. See, further, Samuel Moyn, 'Claude Lefort, Political Anthropology, and Symbolic Division', *Constellations: An International Journal of Critical and Democratic Theory*, Vol. 19, No. 1, 2012, pp. 37–50.

96. Claude Lefort, 'La question de la démocratie' in *Essais sur le politique, XIX-XX siècles*, Paris, Editions du Seuil, 1986, pp. 17–32.

97. Duong, '"Does Democracy End in Terror?"', pp. 541–550; Gerasimos Karavitis, 'Castoriadis versus Michels: A Reflection on the Iron Law of Oligarchy', *Thesis Eleven*, Vol. 146, No. 2, 2018, pp. 24–41.

the continuation of that moment must be the Centre Raymond Aron itself. Originally launched as an informal *groupe de reflexion* in 1977 by François Furet, the famous historian of the French Revolution, the seminar in political philosophy at the École des Hautes Études en Sciences Sociales formally morphed into the Institut Raymond Aron in 1984, before becoming the Centre de recherches politiques Raymond Aron in 1992, and transforming itself yet again in 2009 into its present incarnation, the CESPRA (Centre d'Etudes Sociologiques et Politiques Raymond Aron).

At its peak the Centre brought together many of the leading lights of French political thinking: Aron, Furet and Lefort, of course, but also Pierre Manent, Marcel Gauchet, Pierre Rosanvallon and Bernard Manin. The Centre is known for having renewed the study of democratic theory by moving away from the dominant Marxist paradigm of the time, and having been at the forefront of the rediscovery of the French liberal tradition, notably through studies of Condorcet, Constant, Guizot and Tocqueville, and the reintroduction of classical philosophy in contemporary political studies. It would be a mistake, however, to lump all the thinkers brought together within its bosom as 'liberals': Manent is a Catholic conservative, Gauchet's and Rosanvallon's backgrounds are in the French anti-authoritarian 'second left', Lefort himself was an anti-totalitarian thinker, whilst Manin is known for his study of representative government. What characterised the Centre, according to Rosanvallon, was pluralism, an ethos of discussion, and a desire to rehabilitate the classics.[98]

The Machiavellian themes of conflict, balanced government and the stability of the republic regime—mediated through Aron's own Machiavellian reflections drawing from Mosca, Pareto and Michels—are central to many of the Centre's members' work. Manent for instance, considered by some as one of Aron's inheritors,[99] placed his general reflections in his *Cours familier de*

98. On whether the Centre, and indeed Aron himself, should be considered left or right, see Hugo Drochon, 'Democracy, Anti-Totalitarianism and Liberalism', *Politics, Religion and Ideology*, Vol. 18, No. 3, 2017, pp. 333–336.

99. Daniel Steinmetz-Jenkins, 'Why Did Raymond Aron Write that Carl Schmitt Was Not a Nazi? An Alternative Genealogy of French Liberalism', *Modern Intellectual History*, Vol. 11, No. 4, 2014, p. 572. Note that one of Aron's student, Julien Freund, who wrote a PhD on Carl Schmitt—one of the first such studies in France—under Aron's supervision in 1965 (Julien Freund, *L'Essence du politics*, Paris, Daloz, 2003), also, alongside his numerous works on Weber, wrote a book on Pareto (Julien Freund, *Pareto: la théorie de l'équilibre*, Paris, Seghers, 1974). Freund is a controversial figure who started out as a resistance fighter in his native Moselle but was also later associated with the far-right group GRECE.

philosophie politique (2001) under the aegis of Machiavelli's 'effective truth', much as his mentor had done.[100] Moreover, he completely acceded to the fact that political sociology has demonstrated the undeniable oligarchic nature of modern democracies, within which political parties play an important role: all rather reminiscent of Michels.[101] And the definition Manent gave of democracy is the '*organisation of separations*', that modern politics is organised around two separations: between represented/representatives, whose relationship is centred on the dichotomy command/obedience, one where the represented *authorise* their representatives to decide on their behalf; and the more classic 'separation of powers', namely a divided elite.[102] It is these two divisions, between the elite and the masses, and within the elites themselves, that modern liberty is to be found, which had been Burnham's point all along.[103]

What Manent was trying to elaborate, in short, was a theory of balanced government rooted in a social and political separation of powers. That notion of balanced government is also the key concern of Manin's classic *Principes du gouvernement représentatif* (1995). Manin accepts the 'oligarchic' or 'elitist' nature of elections, which he readily attributes to Pareto.[104] He also affirms Michels' critique of the oligarchic nature of modern mass parties, which brought about new elites cut off from the general party membership.[105] Manin's argument, of course, was in part intended as a refutation of the elite theorists of democracy, and in particular Schumpeter:[106] whilst modern democracy contains within it patently aristocratic elements, notably elections, it also contains democratic elements—it is a 'mixed' regime—in the sense that elections are open to all.[107] If Michels was right to point out the gap between members and their leaders within the party, Manin still held that those two groups were closer than rulers and the ruled at large because parties served an important function of representation.[108] Thus Manin's ultimate normative

100. Pierre Manent, *Cours familier de philosophie politique*, Paris, Gallimard, 2001, p. 11.

101. Ibid., pp. 24–5.

102. Ibid., pp. 29–31. See Aron, *Démocratie et totalitarisme*, p. 348 for 'l'organisation de la compétition'.

103. Ibid., p. 28.

104. Bernard Manin, *Principes du gouvernement représentatif*, Paris, Flammarion, 2012, pp. 189–190.

105. Ibid., pp. 265–7.

106. Ibid., pp. 207–8.

107. Ibid., pp. 306–8.

108. Ibid., p. 300.

claim is that for the regime to be stable—another key Machiavellian theme—it needs to maintain a balance between the aristocratic and democratic features of the modern mixed regime.

The quest for stability in the face of a 'crisis of representation' has been a guiding thread in Rosanvallon's—another prominent member of the Centre Aron, and now professor at the Collège de France—work.[109] And this crisis has been the by-product of the decline of the political party, which at its apex at the turn of the twentieth century offered a synthesis between the *anciens corps intermédiaires* and modern forms of individualism and singularity.[110] Embedded within a pluralistic institutional framework, the political party, allied to the rise of syndicalism, provided the stability to the Third Republic within which Rosanvallon thought he had found the synthesis of Lefort's understanding of democracy as conflict and Furet's quest to end the French Revolution.[111] As the new intermediary body, the political party had momentarily resolved, at the end of the nineteenth century, the contradictory legacy of the French Revolution—*liberté* et *égalité*—thus ensuring the stability of the regime.

That the political party should be so central to Rosanvallon's thinking means that Michels and Ostrogorski—the latter almost entirely forgotten today, but whose legacy includes all the political terminology surrounding 'party machine', 'party boss', 'omnibus party' and 'Single-Issue' parties, and whose emphasis, much like Michels, was on the modern centralised, hierarchical and highly bureaucratised political party—feature strongly and consistently throughout Rosanvallon's work. Indeed, whilst he was still an *auto-gestionnaire* syndicalist in the late 1970s, he was writing of the dangers of centralisation facing trade unionism that Michels and Ostrogorski had identified. In a series of texts—'Avancer avec Michels' (1977), 'Trois textes pour un débat' (1978) and 'Connaissez-vous Ostrogorski?' (1979)—in the syndicalist journal *Faire* he was editing, Rosanvallon affirmed the existence of an 'iron law of oligarchy',

109. Gregory Conti and William Selinger, 'The Other Side of Representation: The History and Theory of Representative Government in Pierre Rosanvallon', *Constellations: An International Journal of Critical and Democratic Theory*, Vol. 23, No. 4, 2016, pp. 548–562 and Andrew Jainchill and Samuel Moyn, 'French Democracy between Totalitarianism and Solidarity: Pierre Rosanvallon and Revisionist Historiography', *The Journal of Modern History*, Vol. 76, No. 1, 2004, pp. 107–154.

110. Conti and Selinger, 'The Other Side of Representation', pp. 153–4; Jainchill and Moyn, 'French Democracy between Totalitarianism and Solidarity', pp. 142–3.

111. Conti and Selinger, 'The Other Side of Representation', p. 522.

but argued that this was a present *political* problem that needed to be resolved, presumably through his decentralised and self-organising *auto-gestionnaire* movement, rather than a past *historical* preoccupation.[112]

His engagement with Michels and Ostrogorski would not simply survive his transition into academia—and this transition was mediated, as Rosanvallon recognised in an interview with the *Journal of the History of Ideas*, through his encounter with Lefort, whose *Machiavel* resonated with the 'realist' sociologists Michels and Ostrogorski he was interested in[113]—but offered a bedrock upon which much of his subsequent reflection was built: he would write an introduction to an abridged edition of Ostrogorski's *La démocratie et les partis politiques* in 1979, whose sections he would pick out himself; he would preface Paolo Pombeni's translation into French of his *Introduction à l'histoire des partis politiques* (1992); Michels, Ostrogorski and indeed Pareto would play a key role in his historical trilogy *Le sacre du citoyen* (1992), *Le peuple introuvable* (1998) and *La démocratie inachevée* (2000), whilst he was also writing the entry on political parties for Raynaud and Rials' *Dictionnaire de philosophie politique* (1996); and the 'public pessimists', Michels and Ostrogorski, would be singled out as 'enormously helpful teachers of lucidity' in his inaugural lecture to the *Collège de France* in 2002.[114]

In fact, one can read his latest project, *Le Parlement des invisibles* (2014), as again premised on Michels and Ostrogorski. Rosanvallon's project *Raconter la vie* was to offer the opportunity to those who were '*mal-représentés*' to explain their existence, and this lack of representation, especially for the new working class—the 'invisibles'—comes from the professionalisation of political parties

112. Pierre Rosanvallon, 'Avancer avec Michels', *Faire*, Vol. 17, 1977, pp. 31–34; 'Trois textes pour un débat' (which introduced criticism from Michels, Ostrogorski, and Max Weber of professional politicians), *Faire*, Vol. 35, 1978, pp. 55–57; and 'Connaissez-vous Ostrogorski?', *Faire*, Vol. 50, 1979, pp. 23–26.

113. Javier Fernández Sebastián and Pierre Rosanvallon, 'Intellectual History and Democracy: An Interview with Pierre Rosanvallon', *Journal of the History of Ideas*, Vol. 68, No. 4, 2007, pp. 703–715.

114. See Moisie Ostrogorski, *La démocratie et les partis politiques*, Paris, Seuil, 1979, pp. 7–21; Paolo Pombeni, *Introduction à l'histoire des parties politiques*, Paris, PUF, 1992, pp. ix–xvi; Pierre Rosanvallon, *Le sacre du citoyen*, Paris, Gallimard, 1992, p. 497; Pierre Rosanvallon, *Le peuple introuvable*, Paris, Gallimard, 1998, pp. 247, 290; Pierre Rosanvallon, *La démocratie inachevée*, Paris, Gallimard, 2000, pp. 30, 263–4, 293, 401; Pierre Rosanvallon, 'Partis' in Philippe Raynaud and Stéphane Rials, *Dictionnaire de philosophie politique*, Paris, PUF, 1996, pp. 525–9; Pierre Rosanvallon, 'Inaugural Lecture, Collège de France' in Samuel Moyn ed, *Pierre Rosanvallon: Democracy Past and Future*, New York, Columbia University Press, 2006, pp. 41–2.

and the 'iron law of oligarchy' that eats away at political life.[115] As Gregory Conti and Willaim Selinger have pointed out, Rosanvallon has difficulty articulating how the 'crisis of representation' he has so adroitly documented might be addressed, notably because he has refused to undertake the type of political sociology Michels and Ostrogorski—and Aron in their wake—practised, which gave them a basis upon which to ground their proposals.[116] It is true that in its previous incarnation *Raconter la vie* took more the form of a literary 'representation-narrative' than an in-depth sociological study,[117] but in 2016 the Confédération Française Démocratique du Travail (CFDT), Rosanvallon's old trade union, conducted a detailed sociological study of 200,000 of its members, and that project, entitled *Parlons Travail*, has now been merged with Rosanvallon's original *Raconter la vie* to create *Raconter le travail*, which might bring some much needed sociology to Rosanvallon's historical and political work.

Conclusion

With its emphasis on conflict, balanced government and the stability of the republic, the French Machiavellian moment seems very much in existence within the Centre Raymond Aron. Much as Pocock's original Machiavellian moment got infused with the themes of commerce and credit once it crossed over to the New World in the eighteenth century, the French moment incorporated much of the elitist sociology of Mosca, Pareto and Michels, often mediated through Aron, which gives it its particular flavour and colouring.

As such, Aron's and the Aronians' reading of Machiavelli and the Machiavellians, one based on the constitutional organisation of conflict, is quite apart from the more recent 'Neo-Republican' readings of Machiavelli, present in the work of Pocock, Skinner and Pettit, which focus instead on the notion of non-domination, or, again, McCormick's recent 'populist' interpretation, which sees Machiavelli definitively taking the side of the plebs. As Daniel Steinmetz-Jenkins and Kevin Brookes have recently pointed out, 'unlike the British variant—which was primarily focused on neo-republicanism—the French interest in Machiavelli is directed at formulating an alternative to the Marxist

---

115. Pierre Rosanvallon, *Le parlement des invisibles*, Paris, Seuil, 2014, p. 14.

116. Conti and Selinger, 'The Other Side of Representation', pp. 556–8.

117. Rosanvallon, *Le parlement des invisibles*, p. 23.

version of class division'.[118] That alternative is the mass/elite distinction the French Machiavellians gleaned from the elite thinkers.

The guiding light for Aron's Machiavelli in particular is to be found in the *Discorsi I, 4*, when Machiavelli explains that there are two parties in every republic, that of the *grandi* and of the *popolo*, and that it is from the conflict between the two that all laws conducive to liberty take root: that it is within the space where different parties, interests, groups compete that liberty can be found. As Audier has pointed out, this ties Aron's conception of liberty closely to Mosca's theory of 'legal defence', namely the constitutional structure set up to organise institutionally and channel productively the antagonism between different social forces: what Audier dubs 'conflictual pluralism'.[119] That theme is perpetuated through the Centre Raymond Aron itself: not solely Merleau-Ponty and Lefort, but also Manent, Manin and Rosanvallon, as we have just seen: the French 'Machiavellian moment' extends to today. And this 'Machiavellian' understanding of liberty underlines how Aron did in fact propose a coherent political theory. As opposed to solely a 'minimum' or 'negative' defence of liberalism, Aron advocated a full Machiavellian theory of democracy: as he put it in his *Introduction à la philosophie politique*, if one is looking for a 'realistic' regime, then democracy, being the best of the worst regimes, is actually the best regime possible.[120]

In his conclusion to *Démocratie et totalitarisme*, much as he would do a couple of years later in *Les étapes*, Aron placed his reflection under the aegis of Tocqueville and Marx.[121] This chapter has argued that if we are to comprehend the relationship between Aron's understanding of society and his democratic theory, this must be done through grasping Aron's interpretation of the 'Machiavellians'—Mosca, Pareto and Michels—who provide the bridge between those two aspects of his thought. Moreover, in his *Mémoires* Aron explained that when he was writing his *magnum opus* in the 1950s and 1960s—the trilogy of books that would end with *Démocratie et totalitarisme*—what he was working towards was a 'synthesis Marx-Pareto'.[122]

---

118. Steinmetz-Jenkins and Brookes, 'The Many Liberalisms of Serge Audier', p. 55.

119. Serge Audier, 'A Machiavellian Conception of Democracy? Democracy and Conflict' in Colen and Dutartre-Michaut, eds., *The Companion to Raymond Aron*, p. 155.

120. Aron, *Introduction à la philosophie politique*, p. 135.

121. Aron, *Démocratie et totalitarisme*, p. 363.

122. Raymond Aron, *Mémoires: 50 ans de réflexion politique*, Paris, Julliard, 1983, pp. 345, 392–8.

Consciously relaying Pocock, and directly quoting Aron, the historian Patrick Boucheron, Rosanvallon's new colleague at the *Collège de France*, decided to spend the summer of 2016 rereading Machiavelli with his radio audience, and that programme was subsequently published in short-book form *Un été avec Machiavel*.[123] The current invocations of Machiavelli, he warned, were a sign that we were entering a new '*gros temps*' of political instability for modern democracies. So can Aron's own 'Machiavellian moment' be the bearer of any lights for us today?

Drawing directly from Pareto's critique of 1930s Italy, Aron described modern democracies as plutocracies: that behind the façade of democratic politics, where rhetoricians dominate, lurk the rich financiers, because much money is needed to win elections and to govern.[124] It is thus the rich, the financiers, the industrialists, businessmen and entrepreneurs who truly control modern democracies. Aron was writing in the 1960s, but, with the political system awash with money, there is no reason to think that things have drastically changed since. Indeed, with the Occupy movement and their rallying cry of the 1%, the election of Trump and Brexit, the relationships elites entertain with democracy has forcefully been brought back onto the political agenda. Are these elites divided or unified? What are the constitutional structures within which they operate? How do they recruit their members? What is their relation to the non-elite? These are all the questions Aron asked, and they are as urgent now as they were then.

123. Patrick Boucheron, *Un été avec Machiavel*, Paris, Editions des Equateurs, 2016. For both the Machiavellian moment and Aron, see p. 127. On Pocock, and, indeed, Lefort and Merlau-Ponty, see p. 145. We can note that Boucheron uses Machiavelli's quote on the 'effective truth', much as Aron and Manent before him, in the dust-jacket to the book.

124. Aron, *Introduction à la philosophie politique*, p. 56; Aron, *Démocratie et totalitarisme*, p. 130.

Conclusion

DYNAMIC DEMOCRACY

IF ELITES always rule, then democracy must mean the perpetual challenge of rising elites to established elites. This is dynamic democracy. Dynamic democracy is *interpretative, normative* and *analytical*. It is interpretative in that it offers an interpretation of Gaetano Mosca, Vilfredo Pareto and Robert Michels' political thought as laying the foundation for a *dynamic* theory of democracy: Mosca's ever-developing 'social forces' that come together in his parliamentary regime of 'juridical defence'; Pareto's 'circulation of elites'; and Michels' metaphor of democracy as waves continually crashing against the shoal. Joseph Schumpeter tried to slow down that dynamic aspect, limiting it to competition between politicians, and although many who came after him—C. Wright Mills, Robert Dahl, Raymond Aron—contributed to our understanding of democracy, much of that earlier conception has been lost. The aim of this book has been to recover it.

It is normative in that it identifies where political change—in the intersection between political movements and institutions—can and *should* happen. If we want our politics to change, then rising elites must convince a section of the established elites to come over to their side, otherwise the only option is revolt or revolution.[1] As work by Martin Gilens, Benjamin Page and Jeffrey

---

1. Think of the relation the Civil Rights Movement had with the Democratic Party, or, again, the Tea Party movement with the Republicans, in contrast with Black Lives Matter or, indeed, the Yellow Vests in France, who were unable to bring established elites over to their cause. On this topic, see, further, Daniel Schlozman, *When Movements Anchor Parties: Electoral Alignments in American History*, Princeton, Princeton University Press, 2015. Today, in America, it seems the only option is for the Democrats to unite, in league with the nascent 'Hands Off' protest movement, and bring dissenting Republicans over to their side, to stop the folly of Donald Trump.

Winters has shown, this is no easy feat, with success only guaranteed at best half the time.[2] But from the perspective of a Niezschean pessimism of strength, this looks like a glass half-full and not half-empty.

Finally, dynamic democracy is *analytical*, in that it offers a lens through which to understand political events. This is one view of the role of political theory: to offer a 'theory' of politics.[3] It is in the spirit of Mosca's 'political doctrine', or, again, Schumpeter's 'minimalist democracy', in that, by focusing on the interaction between elites and movement, it simplifies yet captures something essential about the subject at hand, and offers insights that might otherwise have been missed.

Populism, as discussed in the introduction, has been the main framework through which recent events have been interpreted. Yet this overlooks that populists are themselves often elites. Donald Trump is a member of the financial 1%—remember, it is Pareto who gave us the 80/20 rule, the precursor of the 99% v 1%—and a media personality through *The Apprentice*. Boris Johnson is as 'establishment' as they come, from Eton to Oxford. Marine Le Pen is the daughter of Jean-Marie Le Pen.

Here, Mosca's theory of the ruling class helps. PPE, Oxford's Philosophy, Politics and Economics course, has produced Prime Ministers from Harold Wilson, Edward Heath and David Cameron to Liz Truss (tellingly, Johnson read Classics). It permeates the UK's political, social and economic life to such an extent that *The Guardian* has labelled it the 'degree that runs Britain'.[4] In France, *énarques*, graduates from the *École nationale d'administration*, run the show, from politics (Valéry Giscard d'Estaing, Jacques Chirac, François Hollande, Emmanuel Macron) to national and international administration and business.[5] As Aron explained, the key relation to analyse is between the *personnel politique*—the politicians or political class—and the *catégories dirigeantes*—those who run the economic and social life of the country.

2. Martin Gilens and Benjamin Page, 'Testing Theories of American Politics: Elites, Interest Groups, and Average Citizens', *Perspectives on Politics*, Vol. 12, No. 3, 2014, pp. 564–581; Jeffrey Winters, *Oligarchy*, Cambridge, Cambridge University Press, 2011.

3. John Dunn, *Western Political Theory in the Face of the Future*, Cambridge, Cambridge University Press, 1993.

4. Andy Beckett, 'PPE: The Oxford Degree that Runs Britain', *The Guardian*, 23 February 2017 (https://www.theguardian.com/education/2017/feb/23/ppe-oxford-university-degree-that-rules-britain consulted on 23 March 2024).

5. Hugo Drochon, 'The Fall of the French Ruling Class?', *Project Syndicate*, 5 May 2017 (https://www.project-syndicate.org/onpoint/the-fall-of-the-french-ruling-class-by-hugo-drochon-2017-05).

Dynamic democracy allows us to see how the ruling class stretches across the usual left/right divide, but Mosca's biggest concern was to harmonise competing social forces within a civilisational whole. Aron, for his part, worried that a 'united elite' would arise from the fact that the political, social and economic elites all belonged to the same institution, to which he opposed a 'divided elite', spread across different institutions, better equipped, because competing amongst themselves, to maintain the liberty of the whole (Mills also worried about the creation of a 'power elite', formed of the political, business and military elites). Can a country that is dominated by one institution maintain a balance between its competing forces, or will that institution become oppressive—and potentially elicit a violent backlash—as Mosca, Aron and Mills had warned?

The original contest for the 2024 US presidency between Trump and Joe Biden was decried as gerontocratic, with the circulation of elites—of a rising new generation of politicians—having been slowed, if not halted altogether. Society in this instance had become 'crystallised', Mosca and Pareto's greatest fear. And as Pareto—who clearly saw that questions of identity, not solely economic reasons, could lead to revolution—had warned, if the sentiments of the people differ so starkly from that of their rulers, revolt becomes a possibility.[6]

Pareto's circulation of elites also cuts across the left/right divide. In the UK, Cameron's premiership of the Conservative Party could be labelled fox-like in its liberalism, but Theresa May's and Johnson's were much more lion-like in their centralisation and authoritarianism. Keir Starmer, with his focus on security, is probably in this vein too.[7] By all accounts, Truss' premiership of the United Kingdom was a disaster. She was dumped by her party after only forty-nine days in office—a record—following a calamitous mini-budget that led to a run on the pound and the intervention of the Bank of England to stabilise the markets.[8] This wouldn't have surprised Michels: Truss came to power with the backing of party

6. Evan Osnos, 'Ruling-Class Rules', *The New Yorker*, 29 January 2024.

7. The other famous animal pair is, of course, the fox and the hedgehog. The former knows many things and is content, whereas the latter wants to know 'one big thing' and is frustrated (Isaiah Berlin, *The Hedgehog and the Fox: An Essay on Tolstoy's View of History*, Princeton, Princeton University Press, 2013). Nietzsche, on this account, is a hedgehog. Berlin's point was that Tolstoy was *both* a fox and a hedgehog, or, more precisely, he was a fox who wanted to be a hedgehog. The same might be said of dynamic democracy: the theory is fox-like in that it knows democracy, as rule of the people, will never be achieved, but it is hedgehog-like in nevertheless perpetually striving towards it.

8. David Runciman, '"She Still Carries an Aura of Spectacular Failure": Why Hasn't Liz Truss Gone Away?', *The Guardian*, 30 March 2024. (https://www.theguardian.com/politics/2024/mar/30/she-still-carries-an-aura-of-spectacular-failure-why-hasnt-liz-truss-gone-away-accessed on 31 March 2024).

members, but without the support of the parliamentary party itself. She was the first to do so: Johnson, May and Cameron all had the support of both. At the first opportunity Tory MPs deposed her and installed their favourite, Rishi Sunak. This is the iron law of oligarchy.[9]

Worldwide, with Trump (following the fox Barack Obama), Xi Jinping, Vladimir Putin, Narendra Modi and Recep Erdogan, the lions are back in power. Trump used a new technology, Twitter/X (Mosca's social force), to fuel his ascent. Although a New York economic elite, he was not (originally) part of the established, Washington, DC political elite: a non-governing elite in Pareto's terminology. Indeed, the past ten years in American politics can be described as the struggle between the established elite—comprised of Democrats such as Obama and Joe Biden and 'Never-Trump' Republicans such as Mitt Romney and Liz Cheney—and a rising elite, formerly non-governing, around Trump. One of the big differences between Trump 2016 and Trump 2024, beyond the degree of preparation, is that in 2024 Trump had the 'tech-bros' Elon Musk, Jeff Bezos and Mark Zuckerberg et al. on his side: both the political class (the Republican Party) and a section of the ruling classes (the economic elite), in Aron's classification.

Trump's elite has completely replaced the old elite. One of Trump's slogans was, after all, 'drain the swamp': i.e. completely replace those in charge in DC (which is not, actually, built on a swamp, but on a riverbank). He has now done so, in what might best be described as a form of regime change, placing all power in the president's grasp, which is over and above not simply Congress, but the Supreme Court too.[10] Of course, new voters were brought into politics via the MAGA (Make America Great Again) movement, including the alt-right, conspiracy theorists and White supremacists, replacing the GOP (Grand Old Party) country-club Republicans (here the 2016 Republican primaries are the most instructive). So far, however, Trump's policies seem to favour tech oligarchs, instead of helping the American worker.[11] This is Pareto's A-B-C in action: Trump and the tech bros (B), have joined with the people (C), to overthrow the established elite (A). But C will never rule. Indeed, they are more likely, with tariff-induced inflation, to be worse off.

9. Hugo Drochon, 'Iron Law', *TLS*, 5 January 2024.

10. Patrick Deneen, *Regime Change: Towards a Postliberal Future*, Forum, London, 2023.

11. On the two warring factions within MAGA, see Matthew McManus, 'Will the Deep Fracture between Tech Oligarchs and White Working Class Nativists Split MAGA?', *The Un-Populist*, 3 April 2025.

Pareto denounced his contemporary Italy as a 'demagogic plutocracy', and Aron repeated that critique of his own France: that behind the façade of democratic politics, where rhetoricians dominate, lurk the rich financiers, because much money is needed to win elections and to govern. Pareto was on the side of the 'producers'—those who build things (and the theme of 'getting things done' has returned to politics in the face of rising populism)[12]—instead of the speculators, those solely interested in siphoning off wealth for their own personal gain. In fact, Pareto rejected the protective tariffs of his day as a form of elite 'spoliation'. He distinguished between utility *of* the community and utility *for* the community: the former benefiting certains individuals, whilst the latter benefiting the community as a whole. In reimposing tariffs, in his attempt to tear up the rules-based, liberal international world order, Trump and his acolytes seem intent on returning to this spoliation, for their own benefit (utility *of* the community) and not for America as a whole (utlity *for* the community).

The critique of the excess of money in the democratic system is not new—Aron, after all, was writing in the 1960s—and Pareto thought there was an intrinsic link between democracy and plutocracy, which he associated with the rule of the foxes. So far, Trump has the Silicon Valley 'speculators' on his side: speculators are usually associated with the foxes, whereas rentiers are associated with the lions. But Pareto's concern was whether 'demagogic plutocracy' would swing to a form of authoritarian 'military plutocracy', dominated by the lions.

Trump is a lion, and the question, in Mosca's terms, is whether the 'social forces' of social media and AI (Artificial Intelligence) that helped bring him to power will come to dominate all other forces and become tyrannical. Certainly, with Trump controlling both houses of Congress—the House of Representatives and the Senate—Musk using DOGE (Department of Government Efficiency) to gut the federal bureaucracy (note that Pareto's critique of demagogic plutocracy occurred under the heading, 'The Crumbling of Central Authority'), the Supreme Court having a conservative majority, three judges having been appointed by Trump himself, the media, including the Bezos-owned *The Washington Post*, turning in his favour, and institutions such as Columbia University, accused of antisemitism, bending their knee to the administration's demands, those social forces appear increasingly omnipotent.

---

12. Ezra Klein and Derek Thompson, *Abundance: How We Build a Better Future*, Profile Books, London, 2025; Marc Dunkelman, *Why Nothing Works: Who Killed Progress—and How to Bring It Back*, New York, Hachette, 2025.

We would do well to remember that for Pareto violence, at the heart of Trump's project, from the January 6 US Capitol attack to the recent deportations, is a weapon of the weak. One way to interpret Trump's rise is to see it as part of the concomitant decline of the American empire, leading the US to lash out at its former NATO allies. The European Union (EU), with its compromise and combination, is, after all, the quintessential fox-like project. It is no surprise it has been the target of the lion's ire, on both sides of the Atlantic.

Yascha Mounk has recently pointed out that the WASPs—the White Anglo-Saxon Protestants who once ruled America—are gone.[13] With them certain political norms have gone too. Back in 1961, in *Who Governs?*, Dahl had also wondered about the decline of the WASPs in his study of New Haven.

But perhaps the best place to return to see what might be lost with a dying elite is Mosca's Sicily. Or, more precisely, Guiseppe di Lampedusa's *The Leopard*, which can be read as a meditation on political education. Don Fabrizio's mistake, in marrying his favourite nephew Tancredi to Angelica, the upstart's daughter, instead of to his own daughter Concetta, is failing to pass on the noble manner of his rule to the new elite. Yes, Sedàra, Angelica's father, is ruthless, a quality the Salinas have lost—Fabrizio is based on Lampedusa's own great-grandfather—transformed from the eponymous wild leopard or serval to a domesticated great dane. But Sedàra lacks the finesse to secure the allegiance of his new subjects. He has 'force' without 'consent': the Sicilians are never made into Italians, the Mezzogiorno endures.

Trump and his cohort are ruthless, but will America be made great again? The interpretative, normative and analytical dimensions of dynamic democracy do not address the *practical* side. But political theory must know its limits: it can provide tools to understand politics, the application of which remains discretionary, and even point to where change may occur. But it cannot take action itself. Theory becomes practice when language, as Brian Friel puts it in Michael's final Nietzschean soliloquy in *Dancing at Lughnasa*,[14] has 'surrendered to movement'.[15]

13. Yascha Mounk, 'The WASPs Are Gone', *Persuasion*, 13 March 2025.

14. Friedrich Nietzsche, *Thus Spoke Zarathustra*, Cambridge, Cambridge University Press, 2006, p. 9: 'one must still have chaos in oneself in order to give birth to a dancing star'.

15. Brian Friel, *Dancing at Lughnasa*, London, Faber and Faber, 2023, p. 97.

BIBLIOGRAPHY

Adcock, Robert, *Liberalism and the Emergence of American Political Science: A Transatlantic Tale,* Oxford, Oxford University Press, 2014.

Adorno, Theodor, '"Static" and "Dynamic" as Sociological Categories', *Diogenes,* Vol. 9, No. 33, 1961, pp. 28–49.

Adorno, Theodor, and Max Horkheimer, *Dialectic of Enlightenment,* London, Verso, 1997.

Adorno, Theodor, *Introduction to Sociology,* Stanford, Stanford University Press, 2000.

Albertoni, Ettore, ed., *Studies on the Political Thought of Gaetano Mosca,* Milan, Giuffrè editore, 1982.

Albertoni, Ettore, ed., *Études sur la pensée politique de Gaetano Mosca: Classe politique et gouverne-ment,* Milan, Giuffrè Editore, 1984.

Albertoni, Ettore, *Mosca and the Theory of Elitism,* Oxford, Basil Blackwell, 1987.

Amadae, S. M., *Rationalizing Capitalist Democracy: The Cold War Origins of Rational Choice Liberalism,* Chicago, Chicago University Press, 2003.

Amenta, Edwin, Neal Caren, Elizabeth Chiarello, and Yang Su, 'The Political Consequences of Social Movements', *Annual Review of Sociology,* Vol. 36, 2010, pp. 287–307.

Anderson, Brian, ed., *Raymond Aron: The Recovery of the Political,* New Brunswick, Transaction Publishers, 1997.

Anderson, Perry, '*Dégringolade*: The Fall of France', *London Review of Books,* 2 September 2004.

Anderson, Perry, '*Union Sucrée*: The Normalizing of France', *London Review of Books,* 23 September 2004.

Antonini, Francesca, 'Between Weber and Mussolini: The Issue of Political Leadership in the Thought of the Late Michels', *Intellectual History Review,* Vol. 34, No. 4, 2024, pp. 773–790.

Aristotle, *The Politics and The Constitution of Athens,* Cambridge, Cambridge University Press, 1996.

Arlen, Gordon, 'Aristotle and the Problem of Oligarchic Harm: Insights for Democracy', *European Journal of Political Theory,* Vol. 18, No. 3, 2019, pp. 393–414.

Aron, Raymond, 'La sociologie de Pareto' in *Zeitschrift für Sozialforschung,* Vol. 6, No. 3, 1937, pp. 489–521.

Aron, Raymond, 'Social Structure and the Ruling Class', *British Journal of Sociology,* Vol. 1, No. 1, 1950, pp. 1–16 and No. 2, pp. 126–143.

Aron, Raymond, *Démocratie et totalitarisme,* Paris, Gallimard, 1965.

Aron, Raymond, *Les étapes de la pensée sociologique,* Paris, Gallimard, 1967.

Aron, Raymond, *Democracy and Totalitarianism,* New York, Praeger, 1969.

Aron, Raymond, *D'une sainte famille à l'autre. Essai sur le marxisme imaginaire*, Paris, Gallimard, 1969.

Aron, Raymond, *Études Politiques*, Paris, Gallimard, 1972.

Aron, Raymond, 'La sociologie de Pareto' in *Revue européenne des sciences sociales*, Vol. 16, No. 43, 1978, pp. 5–33.

Aron, Raymond, *Mémoires: 50 ans de réflexion politique*, Paris, Julliard, 1983.

Aron, Raymond, *Études Sociologiques*, Paris, PUF, 1988.

Aron, Raymond, *Machiavel et les tyrannies modernes*, Paris, Editions de Fallois, 1993.

Aron, Raymond, *Introduction à la philosophie politique: Démocratie et révolution*, Paris, Éditions du Fallois, 1997.

Aron, Raymond, *Main Currents of Sociological Thought*, New Brunswick, Transaction Publishers, 1998.

Aron, Raymond, *Le Marxisme de Marx*, Paris, Éditions de Fallois, 2002.

Aron, Raymond, *Penser la liberté, penser la démocratie*, Gallimard, Paris, 2005.

Aron, Raymond, *Dimensions de la conscience historique*, Paris, Les Belles Lettres, 2011.

Aron, Raymond, *Liberté et égalité*, Paris, Editions de l'EHESS, 2013.

Aron, Raymond, *Essai sur les libertés*, Paris, Pluriel, 2014.

Aron, Raymond, 'La rationalité politique', *Commentaire*, No. 156, 2016, pp. 725–42.

Aron, Raymond, *Liberty and Equality*, Princeton, Princeton University Press, 2023.

Aronowitz, Stanley, *Taking It Big: C. Wright Mills and the Making of Public Intellectuals*, New York, Columbia University Press, 2012.

Audier, Serge, *Raymond Aron: La démocratie conflictuelle*, Paris, Michalon, 2004.

Audier, Serge, *Machiavel, conflit et liberté*, Paris, Vrin, 2005.

Audier, Serge, *Le colloque Lippmann: Aux origines du 'néo-libéralisme'*, Lormont, Le Bord de l'eau, 2012.

Audier, Serge, *Néo-libéralisme(s): Une archéologie intellectuelle*, Paris, Grasset, 2012.

Bachrach, Peter, *The Theory of Democratic Elitism: A Critique*, Lanham, University Press of America, 1980.

Bagg, Samuel, *The Dispersion of Power: A Critical Realist Theory of Democracy*, Oxford, Oxford University Press, 2024.

Bagg, Samuel, 'Sortition as Anti-Corruption: Popular Oversight against Elite Capture', *American Journal of Political Science*, Vol. 68, No. 1, 2024, pp. 93–105.

Baldwin, David, 'Misinterpreting Dahl on Power', *Journal of Political Power*, Vol. 8, No. 2, 2015, pp. 209–227.

Baldwin, David, and Mark Haugaard, 'Robert A. Dahl: An Unended Quest', *Journal of Political Power*, Vol. 8, No. 2, 2015, pp. 159–166.

BBC, 'Study: US Is an Oligarchy, Not a Democracy', 17 April 2014 (https://www.bbc.co.uk/news/blogs-echochambers-27074746 consulted on 30 December 2023).

Beckett, Andy, 'PPE: The Oxford Degree that Runs Britain', *The Guardian*, 23 February 2017 (https://www.theguardian.com/education/2017/feb/23/ppe-oxford-university-degree-that-rules-britain consulted on 23 March 2024).

Beetham, David, 'From Socialism to Fascism: The Relation between Theory and Practice in the World of Robert Michels. I. From Marxist Revolutionary to Political Sociologist', *Political Studies*, Vol. 25, No. 1, 1977, pp. 3–24.

Beetham, David, 'From Socialism to Fascism: The Relation between Theory and Practice in the Work of Robert Michels. II. The Fascist Ideologue', *Political Studies*, Vol. 25, No. 2, 1977, pp. 161–181.

Beetham, David, 'Michels and His Critics', *European Journal of Sociology*, vol. 22, no. 1, 1981, pp. 80–99.

Beetham, David, *Max Weber and the Theory of Modern Politics*, Cambridge, Polity Press, 1985.

Behrent, Michael, 'Liberal Dispositions: Recent Scholarship on French Liberalism', *Modern Intellectual History*, Vol. 13, No. 2, 2016, pp. 447–477.

Bellamy, Richard, *Modern Italian Social Theory*, Cambridge, Polity Press, 1988.

Berlin, Isaiah, *The Hedgehog and the Fox: An Essay on Tolstoy's View of History*, Princeton, Princeton University Press, 2013.

Bobbio, Norberto, 'Introduction to Pareto's Sociology' in *On Mosca and Pareto*, Geneva, Droz, 1972, pp. 68–69.

Bobbio, Norberto, *On Mosca and Pareto*, Genève, Librarie Droz, 1972.

Bobbio, Norberto, *The Future of Democracy: A Defence of the Rules of the Game*, Cambridge, Polity, 1987.

Bobbio, Norberto, *Saggi sulla scienza politica in Italia*, Bari, Laterza, 2005.

Boettke, Peter, Solomon Stein, and Virgil Storr, 'Schumpeter, Socialism, and Irony', *Critical Review*, Vol. 29, No. 4, 2017, pp. 415–446.

Bonnell, Andrew, 'Oligarchy in Miniature? Robert Michels and the Marburg Branch of the German Social Democratic Party', *German History*, vol. 29, no. 1, 2011, pp. 23–35.

Bonnell, Andrew, *Robert Michels, Socialism and Modernity*, Oxford, Oxford University Press, 2023.

Bosetti Giancarlo, ed., *Robert A. Dahl: Intervista Sul Pluralismo*, Bari, Laterza, 2002.

Bottomore, Tom, *Elites and society*, London, Routledge, 1993.

Boucheron, Patrick, *Un été avec Machiavel*, Paris, Editions des Equateurs, 2016.

Bousquet, George-Henri, 'A propos de Marie Metenier, mère de V. Pareto: Faits et réflexions', *Cahiers Vilfredo Pareto*, Vol. 6, No. 15, 1968, pp. 223–229.

Burdeau, Georges, 'La dialectique de l'ordre et du mouvement', *Revue français de science politique*, Vol. 18, No. 1, 1968, pp. 5–19.

Burgin, Angus, *The Great Persuasion: Reinventing Free Markets since the Depression*, Cambridge (MA), Harvard University Press, 2015.

Burnham, James, *The Machiavellians, Defenders of Freedom*, New York, John Day, 1943.

Burnham, James, *The Managerial Revolution*, Harmondsworth, Pelican Books, 1945.

Burnham, James, *Les Machiavéliens: Défenseurs de la liberté*, Paris, Calmann-Lévy, 1949.

Burton, Michael, *Elite Foundations of Liberal Democracy*, Lanham, Rowman & Littlefield, 2006.

Campbell, Stuart, 'The Four Paretos of Raymond Aron', *Journal of the History of Ideas*, Vol. 47, No. 2, 1986, pp. 287–298.

Campbell, Stuart, 'Raymond Aron: The Making of a Cold Warrior', *Historian*, Vol. 51, No. 4, 1989, pp. 551–573.

Campbell, Stuart, 'The Tocquevillian Liberalism and Political Sociology of Raymond Aron', *The Historian*, Vol. 53, No. 2, 1991, pp. 303–316.

Carré, Alexis, 'Raymond Aron and the Moral and Cultural Conditions of Liberal Democracy during War Time', *History of European Ideas*, Vol. 49, No. 4, 2023, pp. 722–736.

Cassinelli, C. W., 'The Law of Oligarchy', *The American Political Science Review*, vol. 47, no. 3, 1953, pp. 773–784.

Chabal, Emile, *A Divided Republic: Nation, State and Citizenship in Contemporary France*, Cambridge, Cambridge University Press, 2015.

Châton, Gwendal, 'Libéralisme ou démocratie? Raymond Aron lecteur de Friedrich Hayek', *Revue de philosophie économique*, Vo. 17, No. 1, 2016, pp. 103–134.

Châton, Gwendal, *Introduction à Raymond Aron*, Paris, La Découverte, 2023.

Chénard, Sophie Marcotte, 'What Can We Learn from Political History? Leo Strauss and Raymond Aron, Readers of Thucydides', *The Review of Politics*, Vol. 80, 2018, pp. 57–86.

Chénard, Sophie Marcotte, *Devant l'histoire en crise: Raymond Aron et Leo Strauss*, Montréal, Les Presses de l'Université de Montréal, 2022.

Chenoweth, Erica, and Maria Stephan, *Why Civil Resistance Works: The Strategic Logic of Nonviolent Conflict*, New York, Columbia University Press, 2011.

Cherneski, JanaLee, 'An Unacknowledged Adversary: Carl Schmitt, Joseph Schumpeter, and the Classical Doctrine of Democracy', *Critical Review*, Vol. 29, No. 4, 2017, pp. 447–472.

Cherniss, Joshua, *Liberalism in Dark Times: The Liberal Ethos in the Twentieth Century*, Princeton, Princeton University Press, 2021.

Chomsky, Noam, *Syntactic Structures*, Berlin, De Gruyter, 2020.

Christensen, Michael, 'The Social Facts of Democracy: Science Meets Politics with Mosca, Pareto, Michels, and Schumpeter', *Journal of Classical Sociology*, Vol. 13, No. 4, 2013, pp. 460–486.

Cirillo, Renato, 'Was Vilfredo Pareto Really a "Precursor" of Fascism', *American Journal of Economics and Sociology*, Vol. 42, No. 2, 1983, pp. 235–245.

Clark, Christopher, *Revolutionary Spring: Fighting for a New World 1848–1849*, London, Penguin, 2023.

Colen, José, and Elisabeth Dutartre-Michaut, eds., *The Companion to Raymond Aron*, New York, Palgrave Macmillan, 2015.

Connolly, William, *Identity/Difference: Democratic Negotiations of Political Paradox*, Minneapolis, University of Minnesota Press, 2002.

Conti, Gregory, and William Selinger, 'The Other Side of Representation: The History and Theory of Representative Government in Pierre Rosanvallon', *Constellations: An International Journal of Critical and Democratic Theory*, Vol. 23, No. 4, 2016, pp. 548–562.

Conway, Martin, *Western Europe's Democratic Age 1945–1968*, Princeton, Princeton University Press, 2020.

Cook, Philip, 'Robert Michels's Political Parties in Perspective', *The Journal of Politics*, vol. 33, 1971, pp. 773–796.

Cook, Thomas, 'Gaetano Mosca's "The Ruling Class"', *Political Science Quarterly*, Vol. 54, No. 3, 1939, pp. 442–447.

Craiutu, Aurelian, *A Virtue for Courageous Minds: Moderation in French Political Thought, 1748–1830*, Princeton, Princeton University Press, 2012.

Craiutu, Aurelian, *Faces of Moderation: The Art of Balance in an Age of Extremes*, Philadelphia, University of Pennsylvania Press, 2017.

Crick, Bernard, *The American Science of Politics: Its Origins and Conditions*, London, Routledge and Kegan Paul, 1959.

Dahl, Robert, 'The Concept of Power', *Behavioral Science*, Vol. 2, No. 3, 1957, pp. 201–215.

Dahl, Robert, 'A Critique of the Ruling Elite Model', *The American Political Science Review*, Vol. 52, No. 2, 1958, pp. 463–5.

Dahl, Robert, 'Further Reflections on "The Elitist Theory of Democracy"', *The American Political Science Review*, Vol. 60, No. 2, 1966, pp. 296–305.

Dahl, Robert, 'Pluralism Revisited', *Comparative Politics*, Vol. 10, No. 2, 1978, pp. 191–203.

Dahl, Robert, *A Preface to Economic Democracy*, Berkeley, University of California Press, 1986.

Dahl, Robert, *Democracy and Its Critics*, New Haven, Yale University Press, 1989.

Dahl, Robert, *After the Revolution? Authority in a Good Society*, New Haven, Yale University Press, 1990.

Dahl, Robert, 'A Right to Workplace Democracy? Response to Robert Mayer', *The Review of Politics*, Vol. 63, No. 2, 2001, pp. 249–253.

Dahl, Robert, *Who Governs? Democracy and Power in an American City*, New Haven, Yale University Press, 2005.

Dahl, Robert, *A Preface to Democratic Theory*, Chicago, University of Chicago Press, 2006.

Dahl, Robert, and Margaret Levi, 'A Conversation with Robert Dahl', *Annual Review of Political Science*, Vol. 12, 2009, pp. 1–9.

Dahl, Robert, and Charles Lindblom, *Politics, Economics, and Welfare: Planning and Politico-Economic Systems Resolved into Basic Social Processes*, New York, Harper & Row, 1953.

Dahl, Robert, and Charles Lindblom, *Politics, Economics, and Welfare*, New Brunswick, Transaction Publishers, 2020.

Davis, Reed, 'The Phenomenology of Raymond Aron', *European Journal of Political Theory*, Vol. 2, No. 4, 2003, pp. 401–413.

Day, John, 'Democracy, Organization, Michels', *The American Political Science Review*, vol. 59, no. 2, 1965, pp. 417–429.

De Ligio, Giulio, 'The Iron Law of Elites and the Standards of Political Judgment', *Perspectives on Political Science*, Vol. 50, No. 4, 2021, pp. 262–277.

De Ligio, Giulio, *La Tristezza del pensatore politico: Raymond Aron e il primato des politico*, Bologna, Bononia University Press, 2007.

De Roberto, Federico, *The Viceroys*, London, Verso, 2015.

de Ste. Croix, G. E. M., *The Class Struggle in the Ancient Greek World*, London, Duckworth, 1981.

delle Piane, Mario, *Gaetano Mosca: Classe Politica e Liberalismo*, Naples, Edizioni Scientifiche Italiane, 1952.

Deneen, Patrick, *Regime Change: Towards a Postliberal Future*, London, Forum, 2023.

di Lampedusa, Giuseppe Tomasi, *The Leopard*, London, Vintage, 2007.

Diamond, Larry, 'Elections without Democracy: Thinking about Hybrid Regimes', *Journal of Democracy*, Vol. 13, No. 2, 2002, pp. 21–35.

Dienstag, Joshua, *Pessimism: Philosophy, Ethic, Spirit*, Princeton, Princeton University Press, 2006.

Domhoff, G. William, 'Mills's "The Power Elite" 50 Years Later', *Contemporary Sociology*, Vol. 35, No. 6, 2006, pp. 547–550.

Domhoff, G. William, 'C. Wright Mills, Power Structure Research, and the Failures of Mainstream Political Science', *New Political Science*, Vol. 29, 2007, pp. 97–114.

Domhoff, G. William, *Who Rules America? The Triumph of the Corporate Rich*, New York, McGraw-Hill, 2014.

Downs, Anthony, *An Economic Theory of Democracy*, New York, Harper & Row, 1957.

Drochon, Hugo, 'Nietzsche and Politics', *Nietzsche-Studien*, Vol. 39, 2010, pp. 663–677.

Drochon, Hugo, *Nietzsche's Great Politics*, Princeton, Princeton University Press, 2016.

Drochon, Hugo, 'Democracy, Anti-Totalitarianism and Liberalism', *Politics, Religion and Ideology*, Vol. 18, No. 3, 2017, pp. 333–336.

Drochon, Hugo, 'Between the Lions and the Foxes', *New Statesman*, 13 January 2017.

Drochon, Hugo, 'The Fall of the French Ruling Class?', *Project Syndicate*, 5 May 2017.

Drochon, Hugo, 'Aurelian Craiutu, *A Virtue for Courageous Minds* and *Faces of Moderation*', *Journal of Modern History*, Vol. 90, No. 4, 2018, pp. 918–921.

Drochon, Hugo, 'Paradoxes of Liberalism', *History of European Ideas*, Vol. 45, No. 5, 2019, pp. 754–760.

Drochon, Hugo, 'De Gaulle's Long Shadow: The Making and Unmaking of France's Fifth Republic', *The Nation*, 18 February 2020.

Drochon, Hugo, 'The Conspiratorial Style in Pandemic Politics', *Project Syndicate*, 1 May 2020.

Drochon, Hugo, 'Kyong-Min Son, The Eclipse of the Demos: The Cold War and the Crisis of Democracy before Neoliberalism', *Perspectives on Politics*, Vol. 19, No. 1, 2021, pp. 604–605.

Drochon, Hugo, 'From Dusk till Dawn: Bobbio on the Left/Right Dichotomy', *Journal of Political Ideologies*, Vol. 27, No. 3, 2022, pp. 330–346.

Drochon, Hugo, 'Iron Law', *TLS*, 5 January 2024.

Duncan, Graeme, and Steven Lukes, 'The New Democracy', *Political Studies*, Vol. 11, No. 2, 1963, pp. 156–177.

Dunkelman, Marc, *Why Nothing Works: Who Killed Progress—and How to Bring It Back*, New York, Hachette, 2025.

Dunn, John, *Western Political Theory in the Face of the Future*, Cambridge, Cambridge University Press, 1993.

Duong, Kevin, '"Does Democracy End in Terror?" Transformations of Antitotalitarianism in Postwar France', *Modern Intellectual History*, Vol. 14, No. 2, 2017, pp. 537–563.

Englert, Gianna, 'Raymond Aron and Liberal Thought in the Twentieth Century. By Iain Stewart', *Perspectives on Politics*, Vol. 18, No. 3, 2020, pp. 932–933.

Erbentraut, Philipp, 'Moisei Ostrogorski, Political Parties, and the Dawn of Realist Theories of Political Elites', presented at the Mancept Workshop 2019, University of Manchester, 9–11 September 2019.

Fear, Christopher, 'Collingwood's New Leviathan and Classical Elite Theory', *History of European Ideas*, Vol. 45, No. 7, 2019, pp. 1029–1044.

Femia, Joseph, *The Machiavellian Legacy: Essays in Italian Political Thought*, Basingstoke, Macmillan, 1998.

Femia, Joseph, *Against the Masses: Varieties of Anti-Democratic Thought since the French Revolution*, Oxford, Oxford University Press, 2001.

Femia, Joseph, *Pareto and Political Theory*, London, Routledge, 2011.

Finchelstein, Federico, *From Fascism to Populism in History*, Berkeley, University of California Press, 2017.

Finley, Moses, *Democracy Ancient and Modern*, New Brunswick, Rutgers University Press, 1985.

Finocchiaro, Maurice, *Beyond Right and Left: Democratic Elitism in Mosca and Gramsci*, New Haven, Yale University Press, 1999.

Fish, Steven, 'Conclusion: Democracy and Russian Politics', in Zoltan Barany and Robert Moser (eds)., *Russian Politics: Challenges of Democratisation*, Cambridge, Cambridge University Press, 2001.

Fishkin, James, *When the People Speak: Deliberative Democracy and Public Consultation*, Oxford, Oxford University Press, 2009.

Forneris, Elias, 'Raymond Aron's War: A "History of the Present" (1940–1944)', *The Tocqueville Review/La Revue Tocqueville*, Vol. 43, no. 2, 2022, pp. 7–38.

Forrester, Katrina, 'Judith Shklar, Bernard Williams and Political Realism', *European Journal of Political Theory*, Vol. 11, No. 3, 2012, pp. 247–272.

Freeman, Samuel, *Liberalism and Distributive Justice*, Oxford, Oxford University Press, 2018.

Freund, Julien, *Pareto: la théorie de l'équilibre*, Paris, Seghers, 1974.

Freund, Julien, *L'Essence du politique*, Paris, Daloz, 2003.

Friel, Brian, *Dancing at Lughnasa*, London, Faber and Faber, 2023.

Gane, Nicholas, 'In and Out of Neoliberalism: Reconsidering the Sociology of Raymond Aron', *Journal of Classical Sociology*, Vol. 16, No. 3, 2016, pp. 261–279.

Geary, Daniel, *Radical Ambition: C. Wright Mills, the Left, and American Social Thought*, Berkeley, University of California Press, 2009.

Gerth, Hans, and C. Wright Mills, eds., *From Max Weber: Essays in Sociology*, Abingdon, Routledge, 2009.

Giddens, Anthony, *Beyond Left and Right: The Future of Radical Politics*, Cambridge, Polity, 1994.

Giddens, Anthony, *The Third Way: The Renewal of Social Democracy*, Cambridge, Polity, 1998.

Gilens, Martin, *Affluence and Influence: Economic Inequality and Political Power in America*, Princeton, Princeton University Press, 2014.

Gilens, Martin, and Benjamin Page, 'Testing Theories of American Politics: Elites, Interest Groups, and Average Citizens', *Perspectives on Politics*, Vol. 12, No. 3, 2014, pp. 564–581.

Gillam, Richard, 'C. Wright Mills and the Politics of Truth: The Power Elite Revisited', *American Quarterly*, Vol. 27, No. 4, 1975, pp. 461–479.

Gillam, Richard, 'Richard Hofstadter, C. Wright Mills, and the "Critical Ideal"', *The American Scholar*, Vol. 4, No. 1, 1978, pp. 69–85.

Ginzburg, Carlo, 'Lire entre les lignes: Notule sur *Le Guépard*', in *Néanmois: Machiavel, Pascal, Lagrasse, Verdier*, 2018, pp. 257–266.

Goguel, François, *La politique des partis sous la III République*, Paris, Seuil, 1958.

Green, Elliott, 'What Are the Most-Cited Publications in the Social Sciences (according to Google Scholar)?', *LSE Impact Blog*, 12 May 2016 (https://blogs.lse.ac.uk/impactofsocialsciences/2016/05/12/what-are-the-most-cited-publications-in-the-social-sciences-according-to-google-scholar/).

Green, Jeffrey, *The Eyes of the People: Democracy in an Age of Spectatorship*, Oxford, Oxford University Press, 2010.

Green, Jeffrey, 'Three Theses on Schumpeter: Response to Mackie', *Political Theory*, Vol. 38, No. 2, 2010, pp. 268–275.

Green, Jeffrey, *The Shadow of Unfairness: A Plebeian Theory of Liberal Democracy*, Oxford, Oxford University Press, 2016.

Guerrero, Alexander, *Lottocracy: Democracy without Elections*, Oxford, Oxford University Press, 2024.

Guilhot, Nicolas, *After the Enlightenment: Political Realism and International Relations in the Mid-Twentieth Century*, Cambridge, Cambridge University Press, 2017.

Habermas, Jurgen, *The Theory of Communicative Action: Reason and Rationalisation of Society*, Cambridge, Polity, 1986.

Habermas, Jurgen, *Between Facts and Norms: Contributions to a Discourse Theory of Law and Democracy*, Cambridge (MA), MIT Press, 1998.

Hands, Gordon, 'Roberto Michels and the Study of Political Parties', *British Journal of Political Science*, vol. 1, no. 2, 1971, pp. 155–172.

Hayden, Tom, *Radical Nomad: C. Wright Mills and His Times*, Abingdon, Routledge, 2016.

Held, David, *Models of Democracy*, Cambridge, Polity Press, 2006.

Hirschman, Albert, *The Rhetoric of Reaction: Perversity, Futility, Jeopardy*, Cambridge (MA), Harvard University Press, 1991.

Hoffman, Stanley, 'Aron et Tocqueville', *Commentaire*, Vol. 8, No. 28–29, 1985, pp. 200–212.

Hoffmann, Stanley, 'Raymond Aron and the Theory of International Relations', *International Studies Quarterly*, Vol. 29, No. 1, 1985, pp. 13–27.

Hoffman, Tom, 'The Quiet Desperation of Robert Dahl's (Quiet) Radicalism', *Critical Review*, Vol. 15, No. 1–2, 2003, pp. 87–122.

Honig, Bonnie, *Political Theory and the Displacement of Politics*, Ithaca, Cornell University Press, 1993.

Hont, Istvan, *Jealousy of Trade: International Competition and the Nation-State in Historical Perspective*, Cambridge (MA), Harvard University Press, 2005.

Horowitz, Irving, *C. Wright Mills: An American Utopian*, New York, The Free Press, 1984.

Hughes, H. Stuart, *Consciousness and Society: The Reorientation of European Social Thought 1890–1930*, New York, Vintage, 1961.

Hughes, H. Stuart, *The Sea Change: The Migration of Social Thought, 1930–1965*, New York, Harper & Row, 1975.

Hunter, Floyd, 'Who Governs: Democracy and Power in an American City. By Robert A. Dahl', *Administrative Science Quarterly*, Vol. 6, No. 4, 1962, pp. 517–518.

Irving, Sean, 'Power, Plutocracy and Public Finance: James M. Buchanan and the "Italian Tradition"', *Global Intellectual History*, Vol. 6, No. 6, 2021, pp. 956–976.

Isaac, Jeffrey, *Power and Marxist Theory: A Realist View*, Ithaca, Cornell University Press, 1987.

Isaac, Jeffrey, 'Robert Dahl as Mentor', *The Washington Post*, 11 February 2014. (https://www.washingtonpost.com/news/monkey-cage/wp/2014/02/11/robert-dahl-as-mentor/ accessed on 2 December 2014).

Isaac, Joel, *Working Knowledge: Making the Human Sciences from Parsons to Kuhn*, Cambridge (MA), Harvard University Press, 2012.

Jainchill, Andrew and Samuel Moyn, 'French Democracy between Totalitarianism and Solidarity: Pierre Rosanvallon and Revisionist Historiography', *The Journal of Modern History*, Vol. 76, No. 1, 2004, pp. 107–154.

Jennings, Jeremy, 'Raymond Aron and the Fate of French Liberalism', *European Journal of Political Theory*, Vol. 2, No. 4, 2003, pp. 365–371.

Jones, H. S., and Iain Stewart, 'Positive Political Science and the Uses of Political Theory in Post-War France: Raymond Aron in Context', *History of European Ideas*, Vol. 39, No. 1, 2013, pp. 35–50.

Kahan, Alan, *Aristocratic Liberalism: The Social and Political Thought of Jacob Burckhardt, John Stuart Mill, and Alexis De Tocqueville*, London, Routledge, 2017.

Karavitis, Gerasimos, 'Castoriadis versus Michels: A Reflection on the Iron Law of Oligarchy', *Thesis Eleven*, Vol. 146, No. 2, 2018, pp. 24–41.

Katznelson, Ira, *Desolation and Enlightenment: Political Knowledge after Total War, Totalitarianism, and the Holocaust*, New York, Columbia University Press, 2003.

Keller, Suzanne, *Beyond the Ruling Class: Strategic Elites in Modern Society*, New Brunswick, Transaction Publishers, 2014.

Kelly, Duncan, 'From Moralism to Modernism: Robert Michels on the History, Theory and Sociology of Patriotism', *History of European Ideas*, Vol. 29, No. 3, 2003, pp. 339–363.

Keohane, Nannerl, 'Dahl's Concept of Leadership: Notes towards a Theory of Leadership in a Democracy', *Journal of Political Power*, Vol. 8, No. 2, 2015, pp. 229–247.

Klein, Ezra, and Derek Thompson, *Abundance: How We Build a Better Future*, London, Profile Books, 2025.

Klein, Steven, and Cheol-Sung Lee, 'Towards a Dynamic Theory of Civil Society: The Politics of Forward and Backward Infiltration', *Sociological Theory*, Vol. 37, No. 1, 2019, pp. 62–88.

Krein, Julius, 'James Burnham's Managerial Elite', *American Affairs*, Vol. I, No. 1, 2017, pp. 126–151.

Krouse, Richard, 'Polyarchy & Participation: The Changing Democratic Theory of Robert Dahl', *Polity*, Vol. 14, No. 3, 1982, pp. 441–463.

Laclau, Ernesto, *On Populist Reason*, London, Verso, 2005.

Landemore, Hélène, *Open Democracy: Reinventing Popular Rule for the Twenty-First Century*, Princeton, Princeton University Press, 2020.

Lasch, Christopher, *The Revolt of the Elites and the Betrayal of Democracy*, New York, W. W. Norton, 1996.

LaVenia, Peter, 'Rethinking Robert Michels', *History of Political Thought*, Vol. 40, No. 1, 2019, pp. 111–137.

Leboyer, Olivia, *Élite et libéralisme*, Paris, CNRS Editions, 2012.

Lefort, Claude, 'La question de la démocratie' in *Essais sur le politique, XIX-XX siècles*, Paris, Editions du Seuil, 1986, pp. 17–32.

Lenski, Gerhard, 'In Praise of Mosca and Michels', *Mid-American Review of Sociology*, Vol. 5, No. 2, 1980, pp. 1–12.

Lindsay, Adam, '"Pretenders of a Vile and Unmanly Disposition": Thomas Hobbes on the Fiction of Constituent Power', *Political Theory*, Vol. 47, No. 4, 2019, pp. 475–499.

Linz, Juan, *Robert Michels, Political Sociology, and the Future of Democracy*, New Brunswick, Transaction Publishers, 2006.

Lippmann, Walter, *The Phantom Public*, New York, Harcourt, Brace, 1925.

Lipset, S. M., *Political Man*, London, Mercury Books, 1964.

Lukes, Steven, 'Robert Dahl on Power', *Journal of Political Power*, Vol. 8, No. 2, 2015, pp. 261–271.

Lyttelton, Adrian (ed.), *Liberal and Fascist Italy*, Oxford, Oxford University Press, 2002.

Machiavelli, *The Prince*, Cambridge, Cambridge University Press, 2019.

Mackie, Gerry, 'Schumpeter's Leadership Democracy', *Political Theory*, Vol. 37, No. 1, 2009, pp. 128–153.

Mackie, Gerry, 'Reply to Green', *Political Theory*, Vol. 38, No. 2, 2010, pp. 276–281.

McManus, Matthew, 'Will the Deep Fracture Between Tech Oligarchs and White Working Class Nativists Split MAGA?', *The UnPopulist*, 3 April 2025.

Mahoney, Daniel, *The Liberal Political Science of Raymond Aron*, Lanham, Rowman and Littlefield, 1992.

Mahoney, Daniel, 'Aron, Marx, and Marxism', *European Journal of Political Theory*, Vol. 2, No. 4, 2003, pp. 415–427.

Mahoney, Daniel, 'Introduction: Raymond Aron and the Persistence of the Political', *Perspectives on Political Science*, Vol. 35, No. 2, 2006.

Mair, Peter, *Ruling the Void: The Hollowing of Western Democracy*, London, Verso, 2013.

Malandrino, Corrado, 'A Critique of the Democratic Party and Mythology of Patriotism in Robert Michels', *Revista europea de historia de las idea politicas y de las insituciones públicas*, Vol. 6, 2013, pp. 187–200.

Mance, Henry, 'Britain Has Had Enough of Experts, Says Gove', *Financial Times*, 3 June 2016 (https://www.ft.com/content/3be49734-29cb-11e6-83e4-abc22d5d108c).

Manent, Pierre, *Cours familier de philosophie politique*, Paris, Gallimard, 2001.

Mangset, Marte, Fredrik Engelstad, Mari Teigen, and Trygve Gulbrandsen, 'The Populist Elite Paradox: Using Elite Theory to Elucidate the Shapes and Stakes of Populist Elite Critiques', *Comparative Social Research*, Vol. 34, 2019, pp. 203–222.

Manin, Bernard, *The Principles of Representative Government*, Cambridge, Cambridge University Press, 1997.

Manin, Bernard, *Principes du gouvernement représentatif*, Paris, Flammarion, 2012.

Martinelli, Claudio, 'Gaetano Mosca's Political Theories: A Key to Interpret the Dynamics of Power', *Italian Journal of Public Law*, Vol 1, 2009, pp. 10–11.

Marx, Fritz Morstein, 'The Bureaucratic State: Some Remarks on Mosca's Ruling Class', *The Review of Politics*, Vol. 1, No. 4, 1939, pp. 457–472.

Matthews, Kyle, 'Social Movements and the (Mis)use of Research: Extinction Rebellion and the 3.5% Rule', *Interface: A Journal for and about Social Movements*, Vol. 12, No. 1, 2020, pp. 591–615.

Mayer, Robert, 'A Rejoinder to Robert Dahl', *The Review of Politics*, Vol. 63, No. 2, 2001, pp. 255–257.

Mayer, Robert, 'Robert Dahl and the Right to Workplace Democracy', *The Review of Politics*, Vol. 63, No. 2, 2001, pp. 221–247.

Mayville, Luke, *John Adams and the Fear of American Oligarchy*, Princeton, Princeton University Press, 2016.

Mazgaj, Paul, 'Raymond Aron, the United States, and the Early Cold War, 1945–1953', *The International History Review*, Vol. 43, No. 4, 2021, pp. 796–814.

McCormick, John, *Machiavellian Democracy*, Cambridge, Cambridge University Press, 2011.

McCormick, John, *Reading Machiavelli: Scandalous Books, Suspect Engagements, and the Virtue of Populist Politics*, Princeton, Princeton University Press, 2018.

McGovern, Patrick, 'The Young Lipset on the Iron Law of Oligarchy: A Taste of Things to Come', *The British Journal of Sociology*, Vol. 61, No. 1, 2010, pp. 29–42.

Medearis, John, 'Schumpeter, the New Deal, and Democracy', *The American Political Science Review*, Vol. 91, No. 4, 1997, pp. 819–832.

Medearis, John, *Joseph Schumpeter's Two Theories of Democracy*, Cambridge (MA), Harvard University Press, 2001.

Medearis, John, *Joseph A. Schumpeter*, London, Bloomsbury, 2013.

Medearis, John, *Why Democracy Is Oppositional*, Cambridge (MA), Harvard University Press, 2015.

Meisel, James *The Myth of the Ruling Class: Gaetano Mosca and the Elite*, Ann Arbor, University of Michigan Press, 1962.

Michels, Robert, *Political Parties: A Sociological Study of the Oligarchic Tendencies of Modern Democracy*, trans. Eden and Cedar Paul, New York, The Free Press, 1962.

Michels, Robert, *Critique de socialisme: Contribution aux débats du début de XX siècle*, Paris, Editions Kimé, 1992.

Michels, Robert, *Sexual Ethics: A Study of Borderland Questions*, New Brunswick, Transaction Publishers, 2002.

Michels, Robert, *Sociologie du parti dans la démocratie moderne*, trans. Jean-Christophe Angaut, Paris, Gallimard, 2015.

Michels, Roberto, 'Some Reflections on the Sociological Character of Political Parties', *American Political Science Review*, vol. 21, no. 4, 1927, pp. 753–772.

Michels, Roberto, *First Lectures in Political Sociology*, trans. Alfred de Grazia, Minneapolis, University of Minnesota Press, 1949.

Miller, Jim, 'Democracy and the Intellectual: C. Wright Mills Reconsidered', *Salmagundi*, Vol. 70/71, 1986, pp. 82–101.

Mills, C. Wright, 'Politics, Economics, and Welfare. By Robert A. Dahl and Charles E. Lindblom', *American Sociological Review*, Vol. 19, No. 4, 1954, pp. 495–496.

Mills, C. Wright, *The Sociological Imagination*, Oxford, Oxford University Press, 1959.

Mills, C. Wright, 'Letter to the New Left', *New Left Review*, Vol. 1, No. 5, 1960.

Mills, C. Wright, *The Power Elite*, Oxford, Oxford University Press, 2000.

Mills, C. Wright, 'The Power Elite: Comment on Criticism', in John Summers, ed., *The Politics of Truth: Selected Writings of C. Wright Mills*, Oxford, Oxford University Press, 2008.

Mills, Kathryn, and Pamela Mills, eds., *C. Wright Mills: Letters and Autobiographical Writings*, Berkeley, University of California Press, 2000.

Mitzman, Arthur, *Sociology and Estrangement: Three Sociologists of Imperial Germany*, New York, Knopf, 1973.

Mommsen, Wolfgang, 'Max Weber and Roberto Michels: An Asymmetrical Partnership', *European Journal of Sociology*, vol. 22, no. 1, 1981, pp. 100–116.

Mommsen, Wolfgang, 'Robert Michels and Max Weber: Moral Conviction versus the Politics of Responsibility' in Wolfgang Mommsen and Jürgen Osterhammel, eds., *Max Weber and His Contemporaries*, London, Allen and Unwin, 1987, pp. 121–138.

Moore, Alfred, 'Schumpeter's Not-So-Minimal Theory of Democracy', working paper.

Mornati, Fiorenzo, *Vilfredo Pareto: An Intellectual Biography, Volume 1: From Science to Liberty (1848–1871)*, London, Palgrave Macmillan, 2018.

Mosca, Gaetano, *The Ruling Class: Elementi di Scienza Politica*, ed. Arthur Livingston, trans. Hannah Kahn, New York, McGraw-Hill, 1939.

Mosca, Gaetano, *Partiti e Sindacati nella crisi del regime parlamentare*, Bari, Laterza, 1949.

Mosca, Gaetano, *What Is Mafia*, trans. Marco Lazzarotti with a preface by David O'Kane, M&J Publishing House, 2014.

Mosca, Gaetano, and Gaston Bouthoul, *Histoire des doctrine politiques*, Paris, Payot, 1965.

Mouffe, Chantal, *On the Political*, Abingdon, Routledge, 2005.

Mounk, Yascha, 'The WASPs Are Gone', *Persuasion*, 13 March 2025.

Moyn, Samuel, 'Claude Lefort, Political Anthropology, and Symbolic Division', *Constellations: An International Journal of Critical and Democratic Theory*, Vol. 19, No. 1, 2012, pp. 37–50.

Mudde, Cas, and Cristóbal Rovira Kaltwasser, *Populism: A Very Short Introduction*, Oxford, Oxford University Press, 2017.

Müller, Jan-Werner, 'Fear and Freedom: On "Cold War Liberalism"', *European Journal of Political Theory*, Vol. 7, No. 1, 2008, pp. 45–64.

Müller, Jan-Werner, *Contesting Democracy: Political Ideas in Twentieth-Century Europe*, New Haven, Yale University Press, 2011.

Müller, Jan-Werner, *What Is Populism?*, Philadelphia, University of Pennsylvania Press, 2016.

Müller, Jan-Werner, *Democracy Rules: Liberty, Equality, Uncertainty*, New York, Farrar, Strauss and Giroux, 2021.

Muller, Jerry, 'Capitalism, Socialism, and Irony: Understanding Schumpeter in Context', *Critical Review*, Vol. 13, Nos. 3–4, 1999, pp. 239–267.

Nietzsche, Friedrich, *Thus Spoke Zarathustra*, Cambridge, Cambridge University Press, 2006.

Oakeshott, Michael, 'On Being Conservative', in *Rationalism in Politics and Other Essays*, London, Methuen, 1962, pp. 168–96.

Ober, Josiah, *Mass and Elite in Democratic Athens: Rhetoric, Ideology, and the Power of the People*, Princeton, Princeton University Press, 1989.

Ober, Josiah, 'Joseph Schumpeter's Caesarist Democracy', *Critical Review*, Vol. 29, No. 4, 2017, pp. 473–491.

Ortega y Gasset, José, *The Revolt of the Masses*, New York, W. W. Norton, 1993.

Osnos, Evan, 'Ruling-Class Rules', *The New Yorker*, 29 January 2024.

Ostrogorski, Moisei, *La democratic et les partis politiques*, Paris, Seuil, 1979.

Pareto, Vilfredo, *The Mind and Society*, trans. Andrew Bongiorno and Arthur Livingston, New York, Harcourt, Brace, 1935.

Pareto, Vilfredo, *Sociological Writings*, London, Pall Mall Press, 1966.

Pareto, Vilfredo, *Les systèmes socialistes*, Genève, Droz, 1978.

Pareto, Vilfredo, *The Rise and Fall of Elites: An Application of Theoretical Sociology*, New Brunswick, Transaction Publishers, 1991.

Pareto, Vilfredo, *The Transformation of Democracy*, New Brunswick, Transaction Publishers, 2009.

Pareto, Vilfredo, *Trasformazione della democrazia*, Rome, Lit, 2016.

Parry, Geraint, *Political Elites*, Colchester, ECPR Press, 2005.

Parsons, Talcott, *The Social System*, London, Routledge, 1991.

Pateman, Carole, *Participation and Democratic Theory*, Cambridge, Cambridge University Press, 1970.

Perret, Geoffrey, *Eisenhower*, New York, Random House, 1999.

Pettit, Philip, *Republicanism: A Theory of Freedom and Government*, Oxford, Clarendon Press, 1997.

Pettit, Philip, 'Democracy before, in, and after Schumpeter', *Critical Review*, Vol. 29, No. 4, 2017, pp. 492–504.

Pettit, Philip, *The State*, Princeton, Princeton University Press, 2023.

Piano, Natasha, '"Schumpeterianism" Revised: The Critique of Elites in *Capitalism, Socialism and Democracy*', *Critical Review*, Vol. 29, No. 4, 2017, pp. 505–529.

Piano, Natasha, 'Neoliberalism, Leadership, and Democracy: Schumpeter on "Schumpeterian" Theories of Entrepreneurship', *European Journal of Political Theory*, Vol. 21, No. 4, 2022, pp. 715–737.

Piano, Natasha, *Democratic Elitism: The Founding Myth of American Political Science*, Cambridge (MA), Harvard University Press, 2025.

Pierce, Roy, 'Liberalism and Democracy in the Thought of Raymond Aron', *The Journal of Politics*, Vol. 25, No. 1, 1963, pp. 14–35.

Piketty, Thomas, *Capital in the Twenty-First Century*, Cambridge (MA), Harvard University Press, 2014.

Pocock, John, *The Machiavellian Moment: Florentine Political Thought and the Atlantic Republican Tradition*, Princeton, Princeton University Press, 2016.

Polsby, Nelson, *Community Power and Political Theory*, New Haven, Yale University Press, 1980.

Pombeni, Paolo, *Introduction à l'histoire des parties politiques*, Paris, PUF, 1992.

Przeworski, Adam, 'Minimalist Conception of Democracy: A Defense', in Ian Shapiro and Casiano Hacker-Cordon, eds., *Democracy's Value*, Cambridge, Cambridge University Press, 1999, pp. 23–55.

Puppo, Alberto, 'Gaetano Mosca et la théorie de la classe politique: une pensée antidémocratique au service de la liberté', *Revue Française d'Histoire des Idées Politiques*, Vol. 2, No. 22, 2005, pp. 17–31.

Purdy, Jedediah, 'Normcore', *Dissent*, Vol. 65, 2018, pp. 120–128.

Ragazzoni David, and Nadia Urbinati, 'Theories of Representative Government and Parliamentarism in Italy from the 1840s to the 1920s', in Pasi Ihalainen, Cornelia Ilie, and Kari Palonen, eds., *Parliament and Parliamentarism: A Comparative History of a European Concept*, New York, Berghahn, 2016.

Rahman, K. Sabeel, *Democracy against Domination*, Oxford, Oxford University Press, 2016.

Rawls, John, *A Theory of Justice*, Cambridge (MA), Harvard University Press, 1999.

Rawls, John, *Justice as Fairness: A Restatement*, Cambridge (MA), Harvard University Press, 2001.

Reinert, Hugo, and Erik Reinert, 'Creative Destruction in Economics: Nietzsche, Sombart, Schumpeter', in Jurgen Backhaus and Wolfgang Drechsler, eds., *Friedrich Nietzsche 1844–2000: Economy and Society*, New York, Springer 2006, pp. 55–85.

'Robert Dahl: Normative Theory, Empirical Research, and Democracy', in Gerardo Munch and Richard Snyder, eds., *Passion, Craft, and Method in Comparative Politics*, Baltimore, The Johns Hopkins University Press, 2007, pp. 113–149.

Robin, Corey, 'Nietzsche's Marginal Children: On Friedrich Hayek', *The Nation*, 7 May 2013 (https://www.thenation.com/article/archive/nietzsches-marginal-children-friedrich -hayek/).

Röhrich, Wilfried, *Robert Michels: Vom sozialistisch-syndikalistischen zum faschistischen Credo*, Berlin, Duncker & Humblot, 1972.

Rosanvallon, Pierre, 'Avancer avec Michels', *Faire*, Vol. 17, 1977, pp. 31–34.

Rosanvallon, Pierre, 'Trois textes pour un débat', *Faire*, Vol. 35, 1978, pp. 55–57.

Rosanvallon, Pierre, 'Connaissez-vous Ostrogorski?', *Faire*, Vol. 50, 1979, pp. 23–26.

Rosanvallon, Pierre, *Le moment Guizot*, Paris, Gallimard, 1985.

Rosanvallon, Pierre, *Le sacre du citoyen*, Paris, Gallimard, 1992.

Rosanvallon, Pierre, 'Partis' in Philippe Raynaud and Stéphane Rials, *Dictionnaire de philosophie politique*, Paris, PUF, 1996, pp. 525–529.

Rosanvallon, Pierre, *Le peuple introuvable*, Paris, Gallimard, 1998.

Rosanvallon, Pierre, *La démocratie inachevée*, Paris, Gallimard, 2000.

Rosanvallon, Pierre, 'Inaugural Lecture, Collège de France' in Samuel Moyn, ed., *Pierre Rosanvallon: Democracy Past and Future*, New York, Columbia University Press, 2006, pp. 41–2.

Rosanvallon, Pierre, *Le parlement des invisibles*, Paris, Seuil, 2014.

Rosanvallon, Pierre, *The Society of Equals*, Cambridge (MA), Harvard University Press, 2016.

Rosenbluth, Frances, and Ian Shapiro, *Responsible Parties: Saving Democracy from Itself*, New Haven, Yale University Press, 2018.

Rosenboim, Or, *The Emergence of Globalism: Visions of World Order in Britain and the United States, 1939–1950*, Princeton, Princeton University Press, 2017.

Rousseau, Jean-Jacques, *The Social Contract and Other Later Political Writings*, Cambridge, Cambridge University Press, 2019.

Rovira Kaltwasser, Cristóbal, 'The Responses of Populism to Dahl's Democratic Dilemmas', *Political Studies*, Vol. 62, No. 3, 2014, pp. 470–487.

Rubinelli, Lucia, *Constituent Power: A History*, Cambridge, Cambridge University Press, 2020.

Runciman, David, '"She Still Carries an Aura of Spectacular Failure": Why Hasn't Liz Truss Gone Away?', *The Guardian*, 30 March 2024 (https://www.theguardian.com/politics/2024/mar/30/she-still-carries-an-aura-of-spectacular-failure-why-hasnt-liz-truss-gone-away accessed).

Sartori, Giovanni, *The Theory of Democracy Revisited. Part One: The Contemporary Debate*, Chatham, Chatham House Publishers, 1987.

Sartori, Giovanni, *Parties and Party Systems: A Framework for Analysis*, Colchester, ECPR Press, 2005.

Sauer, Pjotr, and Andrew Roth, 'Vladimir Putin Claims Landslide Russian Election Victory', *The Guardian*, 18 March 2024 (https://www.theguardian.com/world/2024/mar/17/kremlin-vladimir-putin-claim-landslide-russian-election-victory).

Sawyer, Stephen, and Iain Stewart, eds., *In Search of the Liberal Moment: Democracy, Antitotalitarianism, and Intellectual Politics in France since 1950*, Basingstoke, Palgrave Macmillan, 2016.

Scaff, Lawrence, 'Max Weber and Robert Michels', *The American Journal of Sociology*, Vol. 86, No. 6, 1981, pp. 1269–1286.

Schattschneider, E. E., *The Semisovereign People: A Realist's View of Democracy in America*, Boston, Wadsworth, 1975.

Schlozman, Daniel, *When Movements Anchor Parties: Electoral Alignments in American History*, Princeton, Princeton University Press, 2015.

Schumpeter, Joseph, *The Economics and Sociology of Capitalism*, Princeton, Princeton University Press, 1991.

Schumpeter, Joseph, *Capitalism, Socialism and Democracy*, Abingdon, Routledge, 2010.

Sciascia, Leonardo, *The Day of the Owl*, London, Granta, 2013.

Scott, Alan, 'Raymond Aron's Political Sociology of Regime and Party', *Journal of Classical Sociology*, Vol. 11, No. 2, 2011, pp. 155–171.

Sebastián, Javier Fernández, and Pierre Rosanvallon, 'Intellectual History and Democracy: An Interview with Pierre Rosanvallon', *Journal of the History of Ideas*, Vol. 68, No. 4, 2007, pp. 703–715.

Segre, Sandro, 'Notes and Queries: On Weber's Reception of Michels', *Max Weber Studies*, Vol. 2, No. 1, 2001, pp. 103–113.

Selinger, William, 'Schumpeter on Democratic Survival', *The Tocqueville Review/La Revue Tocqueville*, Vol. 36, No. 2, 2015, pp. 127–157.

Sereno, Renzo, 'The Anti-Aristotelianism of Gaetano Mosca and Its Fate', *Ethics*, Vol. 48, No. 4, 1938, pp. 509–518.

Sereno, Renzo, *The Rulers*, New York, Praeger, 1962.

Shapiro, Ian, *The State of Democratic Theory*, Princeton, Princeton University Press, 2003.

Shapiro, Ian, *Politics Against Domination*, Cambridge (MA), Harvard University Press, 2016.

Shklar, Judith, 'The Liberalism of Fear', in Nancy Rosenblum, ed., *Liberalism and the Moral Life*, Cambridge (MA), Harvard University Press, 1989, pp. 21–38.

Silverman, Lawrence, 'The Ideological Mediation of Party-Political Responses to Social Change', *European Journal of Political Research*, Vol. 13, No. 1, 1985, pp. 69–93.

Simmel, George, *Nietzsche and Schopenhauer*, Champaign, University of Illinois Press, 1991.

Simonton, Matthew, *Classical Greek Oligarchy: A Political History*, Princeton, Princeton University Press, 2017.

Sintomer, Yves, *The Government of Chance: Sortition and Democracy from Athens to the Present*, Cambridge, Cambridge University Press, 2023.

Skinner, Quentin, 'The Empirical Theorists of Democracy and Their Critics: A Plague on Both Their Houses', *Political Theory*, Vol. 1, No. 3, 1973, pp. 287–306.

Skinner, Quentin, *Liberty before Liberalism*, Cambridge, Cambridge University Press, 1998.

Skinner, Quentin, 'Meaning and Understanding in the History of Ideas', in *Visions of Politics, Volume I: Regarding Method*, Cambridge, Cambridge University Press, 2002, pp. 57–89.

Slobodian, Quinn, *Globalists: The End of Empire and the Birth of Neoliberalism*, Cambridge (MA), Harvard University Press, 2018.

Smith, Dwight, *The Mafia Mystique*, New York, Basic Books, 1975.

Smith, Steven, 'The Political Teaching of Lampedusa's *The Leopard*', in *Modernity and Its Discontents: Making and Unmaking the Bourgeois from Machiavelli to Bellow*, New Haven, Yale University Press, 2016, pp. 313–329.

Smith, Steven, 'Raymond Aron: Philosopher of Liberties', *Society*, Vol. 60, 2023, pp. 944–953.

Son, Kyong-Min, *The Eclipse of the Demos: The Cold War and the Crisis of Democracy before Neoliberalism*, Lawrence, University of Kansas Press, 2020.

Stedman Jones, Daniel, *Masters of the Universe: Hayek, Friedman, and the Birth of Neoliberal Politics*, Princeton, Princeton University Press, 2014.

Steinmetz-Jenkins, Daniel, 'Why Did Raymond Aron Write that Carl Schmitt Was Not a Nazi? An Alternative Genealogy of French Liberalism', *Modern Intellectual History*, Vol. 11, No. 3, 2014, pp. 549–574.

Steinmetz-Jenkins, Daniel, and Kevin Brookes, 'The Many Liberalisms of Serge Audier', *Journal of the History of Ideas*, Vol. 79, No. 1, 2018, pp. 45–63.

Sternhell, Zeev, *Neither Right nor Left: Fascist Ideology in France*, Berkeley, University of California Press, 1986.

Stewart, Iain, 'Existentialist Manifesto or Conservative Political Science? Problems in Interpreting Raymond Aron's *Introduction à la philosophie de l'histoire*', *European Review of History: Revue européenne d'histoire*, Vol. 16, No. 2, 2009, pp. 217–233.

Stewart, Iain, *Raymond Aron and Liberal Thought in the Twentieth Century*, Cambridge, Cambridge University Press, 2019.

Tashjean, John, 'Mosca Revisited: Exegesis of an Elitist Argument', *Revue européenne des sciences sociales*, Vol. 10, No. 217, 1972, pp. 123–126.

The Economist, 'Schumpeter: Taking Flight', 17 September 2009 (https://www.economist.com/business/2009/09/17/taking-flight).

The New York Times, 'James H. Meisel, 90, Political Scientist, Dies', Obituaries, 12 March 1999 (https://www.nytimes.com/1991/03/12/obituaries/james-h-meisel-90-political-scientist-dies.html).

Thomas, George, 'Can Liberal Democracy Survive Capitalism?', *Critical Review*, Vol. 29, No. 4, 2017, pp. 530–544.

Thompson, Paul, Frederick Harry Pitts, Jo Ingold, 'A Strategic Left? Starmerism, Pluralism and the Soft Left', *The Political Quarterly*, Vol. 92, No. 1, 2021, pp. 32–39.

Tomasi, John, *Free Market Fairness*, Princeton, Princeton University Press, 2012.

Urbinati, Nadia, *Democracy Disfigured: Opinion, Truth, and the People*, Cambridge (MA), Harvard University Press, 2014.

Van Reybrouck, David, *Against Elections: The Case for Democracy*, London, Bodley Head, 2016.

Vergara, Camila, 'Republican Constitutional Thought: Elitist and Plebian Interpretations of the Mixed Constitution', *History of Political Thought*, Vol. 43, No. 5, 2022, pp. 28–55.

Volpe, Giorgio, *Italian Elitism and the Reshaping of Democracy in the United States*, Abingdon, Routledge, 2021.

Wald, Alan, 'From Trotsky to Buckley', *Jacobin*, 15/09/2017.

Walker, Jack, 'A Critique of the Elitist Theory of Democracy', *The American Political Science Review*, Vol. 60, No. 2, 1966, pp. 285–295.

Walker, Jack, 'A Reply to "Further Reflections on 'The Elitist Theory of Democracy'"', *The American Political Science Review*, Vol. 60, No. 2, 1966, pp. 391–392.

Weber, Max, 'Politics as Vocation', in *Political Writings*, Cambridge, Cambridge University Press, 1994.

Westler, Brendon, *The Revolting Masses: José Ortega y Gasset's Liberalism against Populism*, Philadelphia, University of Pennsylvania Press, 2024.

Winters, Jeffrey, *Oligarchy*, Cambridge, Cambridge University Press, 2011.

Winters, Jeffrey, *Domination through Democracy: Why Oligarchs Win*, Penguin Random House, forthcoming.

Wolin, Sheldon, *Democracy Incorporated: Managed Democracy and the Specter of Inverted Totalitarianism*, Princeton, Princeton University Press, 2008.

Wolin, Sheldon, *Fugitive Democracy and Other Essays*, Princeton, Princeton University Press, 2016.

Zanden, James Vander, 'Pareto and Fascism Reconsidered', in *American Journal of Economics and Sociology*, Vol. 19, No. 4, 1960, pp. 399–411.

Zeringue, Marshal, 'Hugo Drochon's "Nietzsche's Great Politics"', the Page 99 Test', 23 July 2016 (https://page99test.blogspot.com/2016/c7/hugo-drochons-nietzsches-great-politics .html).

Zirakzadeh, Cyrus Ernesto, 'Theorising about Workplace Democracy: Robert Dahl and the Cooperative of Mondragon', *Journal of Theoretical Politics*, Vol. 2, No. 1, 1990, pp. 109–126.

INDEX

academic freedom, Weber on, 127

Adorno, Theodor: *Dialectic of Enlighten-*
ment, 21; 'dynamic' conception of
society, 19

Aesop's fable, dynamic democracy, 12,
145, 152

AFD (*Alternative für Deutschland*), 1

After the Revolution? (Dahl), 208

Against the Masses (Femia), 30, 152

agonistic democracy, Mouffe's theory,
180–81

AI (Artificial Intelligence), 243

American Sociological Review (journal), 201

Ancien régime, 87; Taine's, 82n5; Taine's
study of, 69

anti-semitism, Columbia University, 243

Application of Theoretical Sociology, An
(Pareto), 87, 97, 98–101, 106–7

Apprentice, The (television show), 2, 240

aristocracies, 25, 82, 98, 99, 105; term, 87

aristocrats, label, 105

Aristotle, 77; on oligarchy, 150; *Politics*, 224;
tripartite of political regimes, 25, 69

Aron, Raymond, 151; Burnham and, 220,
223–24; *catégories dirigeantes*, 121; 'Cold
War Liberalism' of, 212, 216; Cold War
theory of democracy, 8; divided and
unified elites, 224–26; on drama and
process, 217; Machiavellianism, 219;
Machiavellians, 216–20; 'new' type of
liberal, 213; Pareto and, 220–23; on Pareto
as 'Machiavellian' defender of liberty, 20;
political sociology, 226–30; reading of

Machiavelli, 7; understanding democracy, 239

Athenian democracy, degree of, 27

Audier, Serge, on Aron, 214–15, 231, 237

Austro-Hungarian Empire, 175

auto-gestionnaire, 219, 234–35

Bachrach, Peter, 'democratic elitists'
term, 210

Bagehot, Walter, 155

Bagg, Samuel, on democracy as resisting
state capture, 24

Bakunina, Alessandrina 'Dina': Pareto's
divorce of, 119; Pareto's marriage to, 90

Bank of England, 241

Bank of Sicily, 47

Battle of Adwa, 49

Bebel, August, Michels and, 126

Becker, Gary, neoliberalism influence, 213

Becker Chicago School, 213–14

Beetham, David: influence of Weber on
Schumpeter, 172; on iron law, 144; on
Michels' turn, 139

Behrent, Michael, on Aron, 214

Bell, Daniel: Mills' colleague, 189, 203; on
Mills' theory of power elite, 195–97

Bellamy, Richard: challenge of ruling class,
59; on compulsory education, 90–91; on
descent into clientelism, 52–53; on ideal
mixture of tendencies and principles, 77;
on Italian parliament, 40–41; on
Machiavellian issues, 54; *Modern Italian*
Social Theory, 51; on Mosca's belief on

A NOTE ON THE TYPE

This book has been composed in Arno, an Old-style serif typeface in the classic Venetian tradition, designed by Robert Slimbach at Adobe.